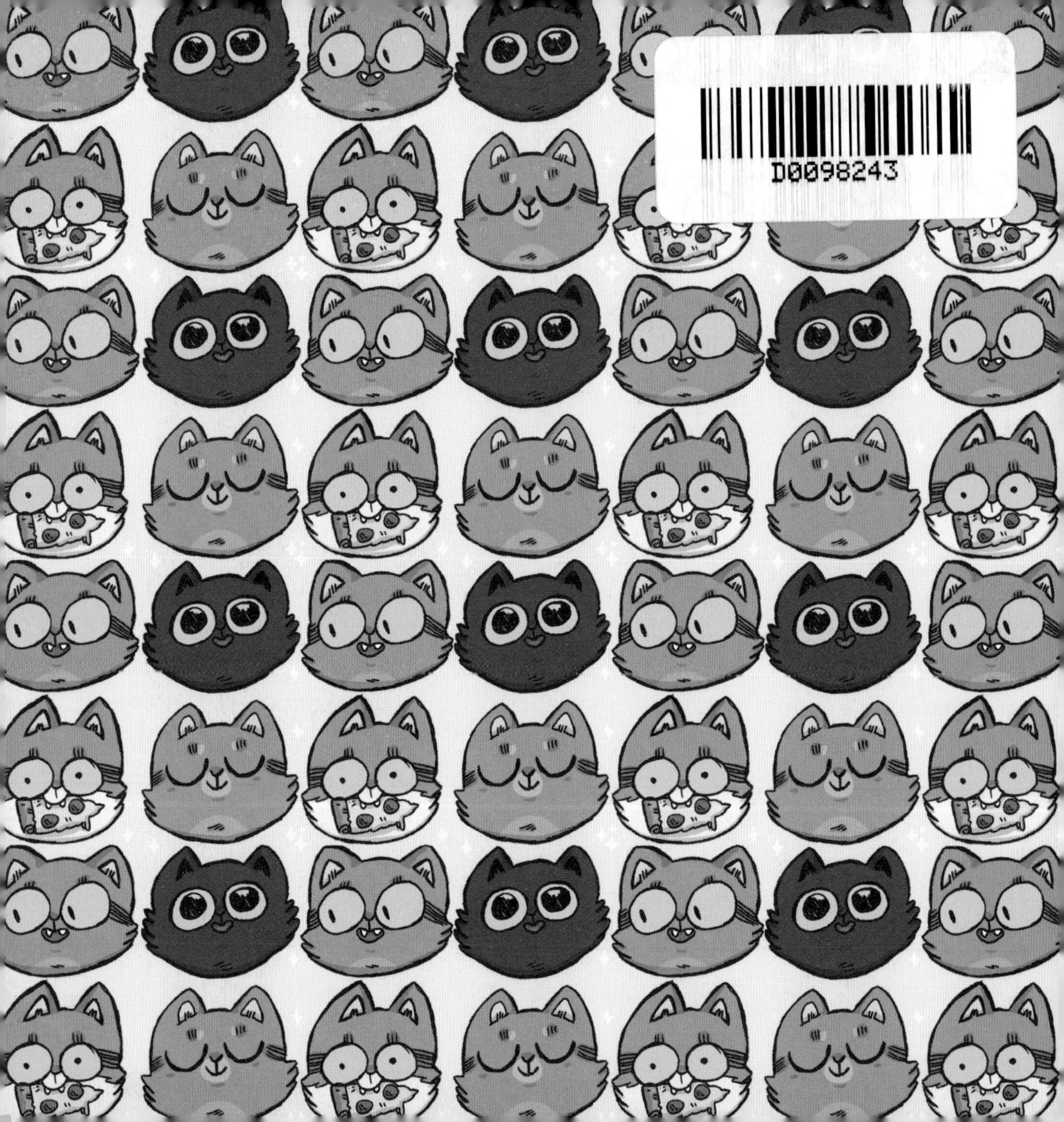

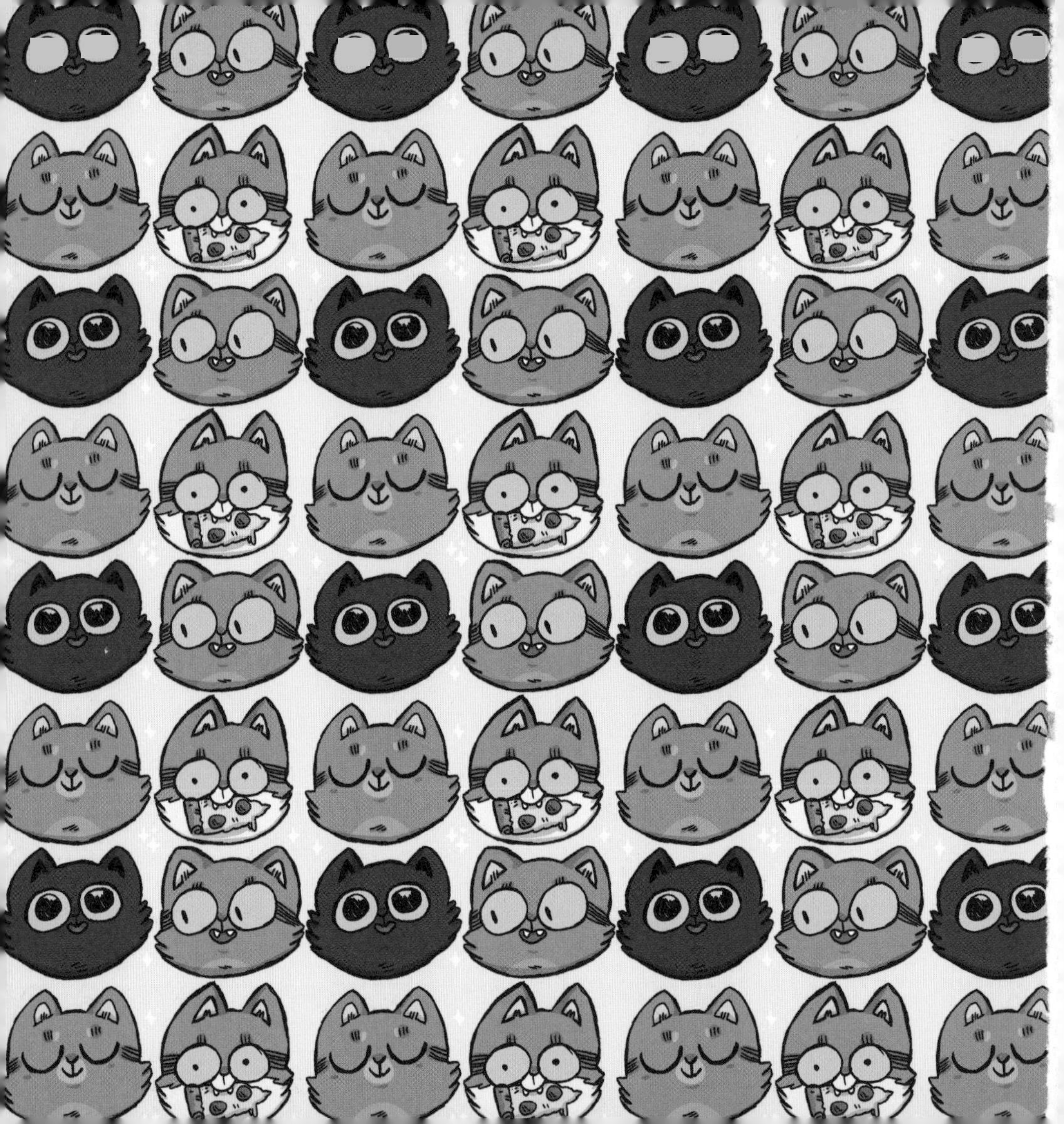

OUR SUPER ADVENTURE
PRESS START TO BEGIN
SARAH GRALEY

AN ONI PRESS
PUBLICATION

EDITED BY *ARI YARWOOD*
BOOK DESIGN BY *SARAH GRALEY* & *STEF PURENINS*

PUBLISHED BY *ONI PRESS, INC.*
JOE NOZEMACK, FOUNDER & CHIEF FINANCIAL OFFICER × *JAMES LUCAS JONES*, PUBLISHER
CHARLIE CHU, V.P. OF CREATIVE & BUSINESS DEVELOPMENT × *BRAD ROOKS*, DIRECTOR OF OPERATIONS
MELISSA MESZAROS, PUBLICITY MANAGER × *MARGOT WOOD*, DIRECTOR OF SALES × *SANDY TANAKA,* MARKETING DESIGN MANAGER
AMBER O'NEILL, SPECIAL PROJECTS MANAGER × *TROY LOOK*, DIRECTOR OF DESIGN & PRODUCTION
KATE Z. STONE, SENIOR GRAPHIC DESIGNER × *SONJA SYNAK,* GRAPHIC DESIGNER × *ANGIE KNOWLES*, DIGITAL PREPRESS LEAD
ARI YARWOOD, EXECUTIVE EDITOR × *SARAH GAYDOS,* EDITORIAL DIRECTOR OF LICENSED PUBLISHING
ROBIN HERRERA, SENIOR EDITOR × *DESIREE WILSON*, ASSOCIATE EDITOR × *MICHELLE NGUYEN*, EXECUTIVE ASSISTANT
JUNG LEE, LOGISTICS COORDINATOR × *SCOTT SHARKEY,* WAREHOUSE ASSISTANT

ORIGINALLY SELF-PUBLISHED UNDER THE TITLE "OUR SUPER ADVENTURE."

1319 SE MARTIN LUTHER KING, JR. BLVD.
SUITE 240
PORTLAND, OR 97214

ONIPRESS.COM
FACEBOOK.COM/ONIPRESS
TWITTER.COM/ONIPRESS
ONIPRESS.TUMBLR.COM
INSTAGRAM.COM/ONIPRESS

OURSUPERADVENTURE.COM
SARAHGRALEY.COM
@SARAHGRALEYART

FIRST EDITION: MARCH 2019
RETAIL EDITION ISBN: 978-1-62010-582-5   *ARTIST EDITION ISBN:* 978-1-62010-583-2

PRINTED IN CHINA.

LIBRARY OF CONGRESS CONTROL NUMBER: 2018950889
10 9 8 7 6 5 4 3 2 1

FOR STEF.

INTRODUCTION

WELCOME TO *PRESS START TO BEGIN* - A COLLECTION OF 200 DIARY COMICS ORIGINALLY DRAWN BETWEEN 2012 AND 2015, ALL ABOUT ME, MY PARTNER, STEF, OUR FOUR WONDERFUL CATS, AND THE LIFE THAT WE SHARE TOGETHER!

OUR SUPER ADVENTURE STARTED AS A BLACK-AND-WHITE ZINE THAT I GAVE AWAY FOR FREE AT THOUGHT BUBBLE IN LEEDS IN 2012. OVER THE NEXT FEW YEARS, I THEN GOT THREE DIFFERENT SMALLER VOLUMES OF COMICS PRINTED (ONLY ABOUT 200 OF EACH OF THESE EXIST!).

IN 2015, I RAN A KICKSTARTER TO FUND THE ORIGINAL PRINT RUN OF THIS BOOK. THE KICKSTARTER WAS MORE SUCCESSFUL THAN I'D EVER IMAGINED IT WOULD BE - WE OVERSHOT THE ORIGINAL GOAL BY 400%! IT MEANT WE GOT TO INCLUDE MORE STUFF IN THE BOOK, AND ALSO MAKE THE BOOK A BIT NICER TOO! IT MEANT A LOT TO HAVE THAT SUPPORT BACK THEN, AND IT STILL MEANS A LOT NOW.

WE GET SO MANY GREAT COMMENTS ONLINE - WHETHER WE'RE READING COMMENTS ON WEBTOON, OR INSTAGRAM, OR TUMBLR, OR FACEBOOK, IT IS SO NICE AND SURREAL TO SEE THAT SO MANY PEOPLE RELATE TO THESE COMICS! WE'VE HAD HUNDREDS OF REAL LIFE CONVERSATIONS WITH PEOPLE AT CONVENTIONS OVER THE LAST COUPLE OF YEARS WHO HAVE LITERALLY VALIDATED SO MANY WEIRD THINGS THAT WE DO! I THINK WE HAVE THIS REALLY NICE SHARED SILLINESS WITH SO MANY PEOPLE OUT THERE AND IT'S KINDA COOL.

WE HOPE YOU ENJOY THIS COLLECTION OF COMICS!

- SARAH AND STEF

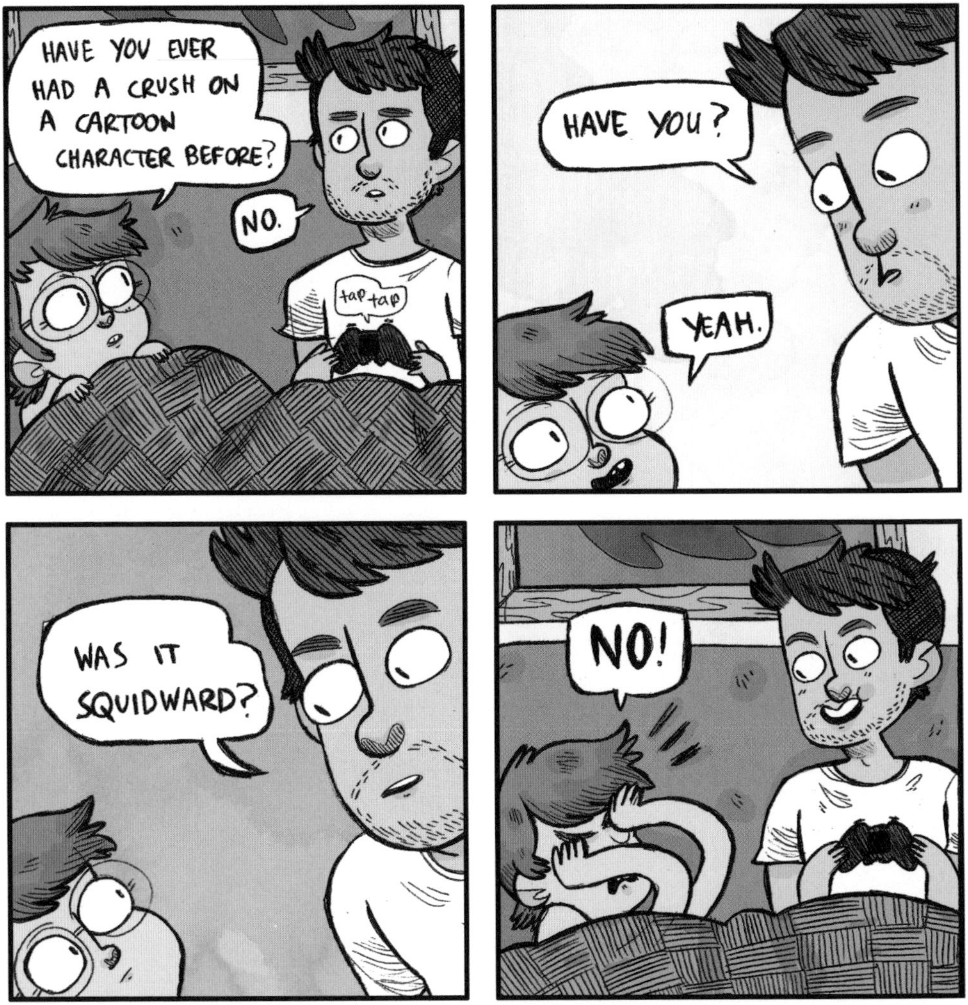
HAVE YOU EVER HAD A CRUSH ON A CARTOON CHARACTER BEFORE?
NO.
tap tap
HAVE YOU?
YEAH.
WAS IT SQUIDWARD?
NO!

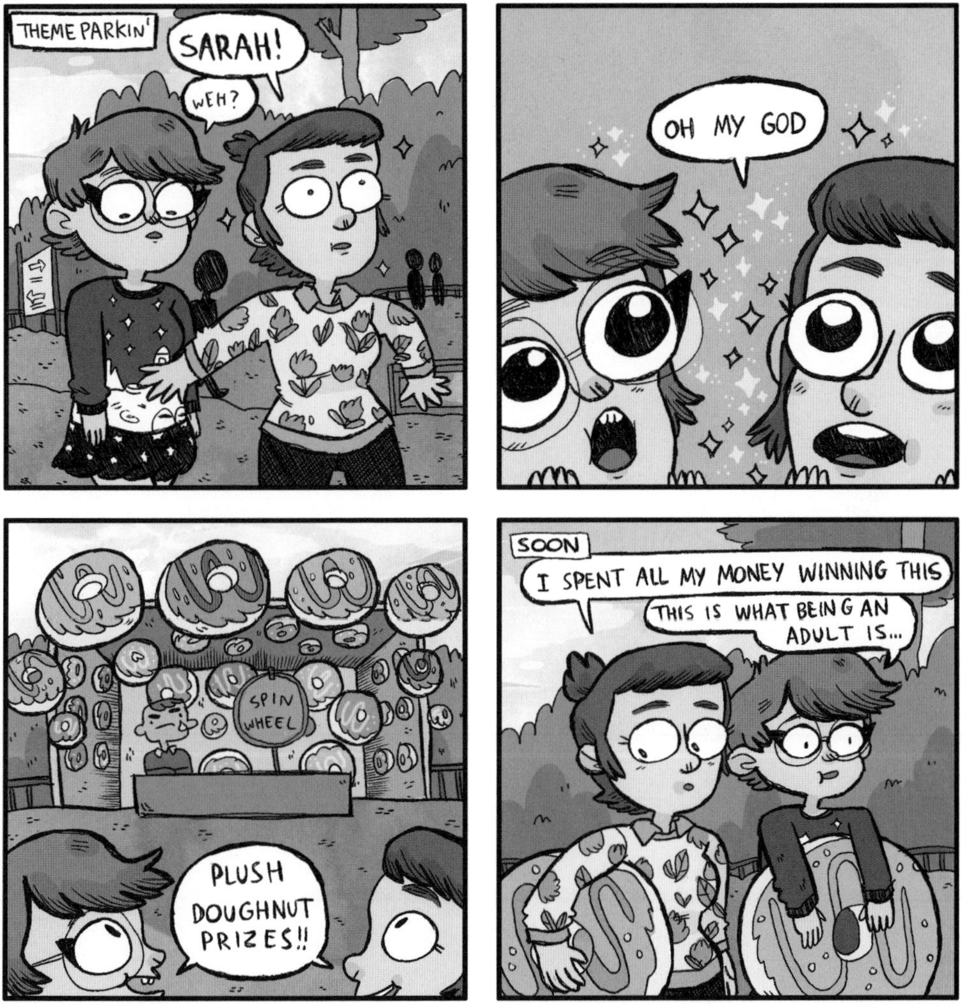
THEME PARKIN'
SARAH!
WEH?
OH MY GOD
SPIN WHEEL
PLUSH DOUGHNUT PRIZES!!
SOON
I SPENT ALL MY MONEY WINNING THIS
THIS IS WHAT BEING AN ADULT IS...

YOU SHOULDN'T LIE ON YOUR FRONT!! IT HAS YOUR FACE AND BOOBS WHICH ARE GREAT!!
BUT YOUR BACK HAS YOUR BUTT SO...!

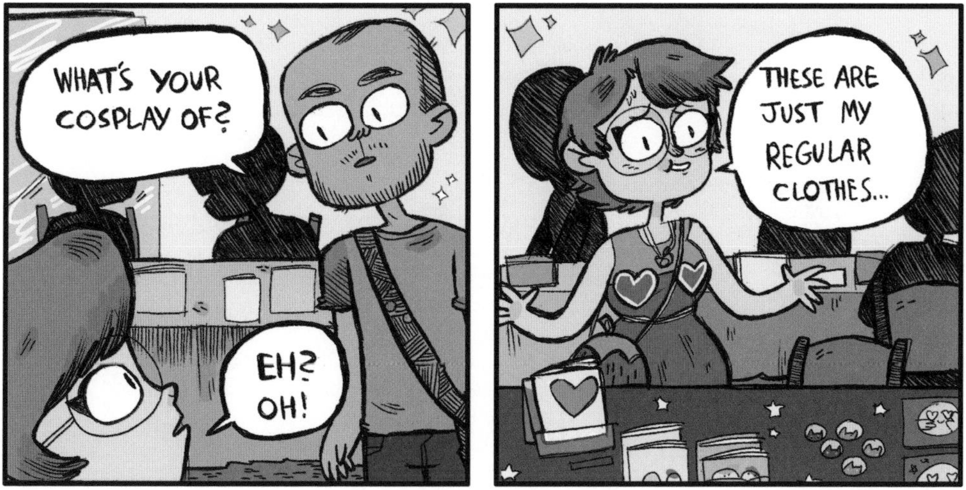
WHAT'S YOUR COSPLAY OF?
EH? OH!
THESE ARE JUST MY REGULAR CLOTHES...

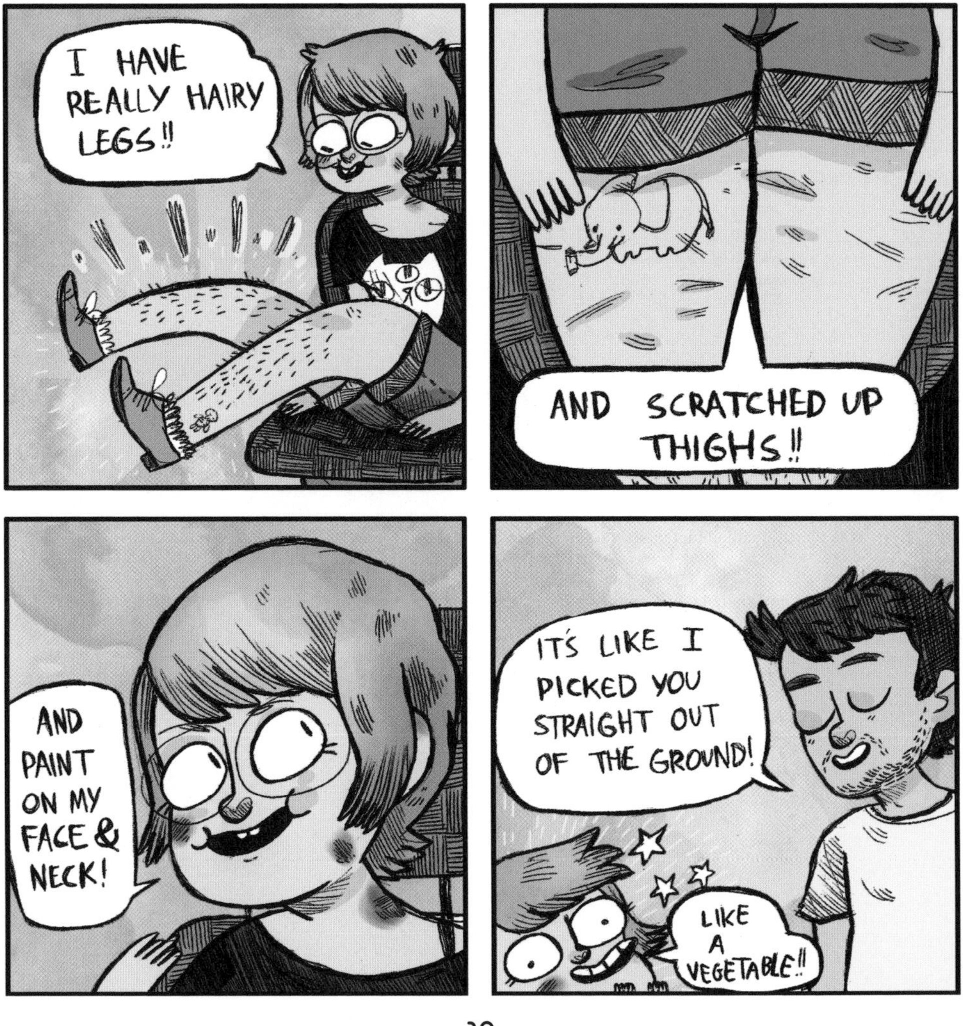
I HAVE REALLY HAIRY LEGS!!
AND SCRATCHED UP THIGHS!!
AND PAINT ON MY FACE & NECK!
IT'S LIKE I PICKED YOU STRAIGHT OUT OF THE GROUND!
LIKE A VEGETABLE!!

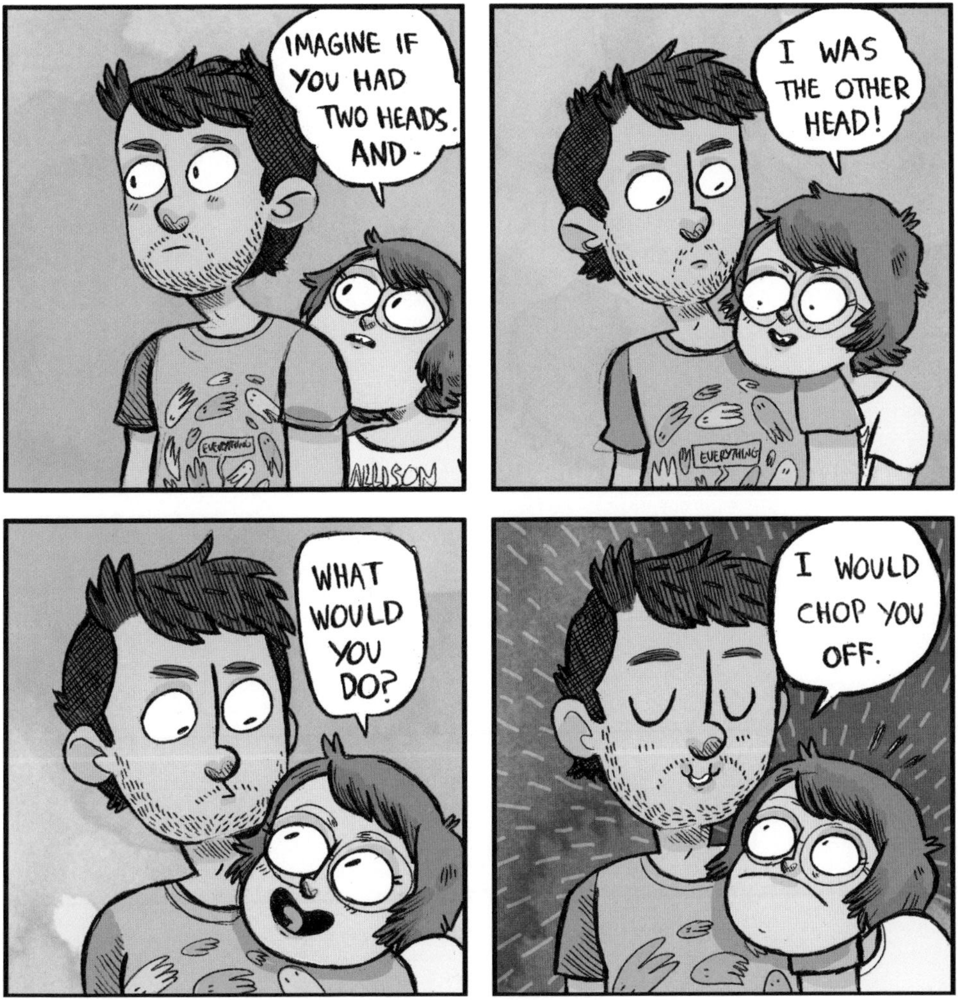
IMAGINE IF YOU HAD TWO HEADS. AND-
EVERYTHING
ALLISON
I WAS THE OTHER HEAD!
EVERYTHING
WHAT WOULD YOU DO?
I WOULD CHOP YOU OFF.

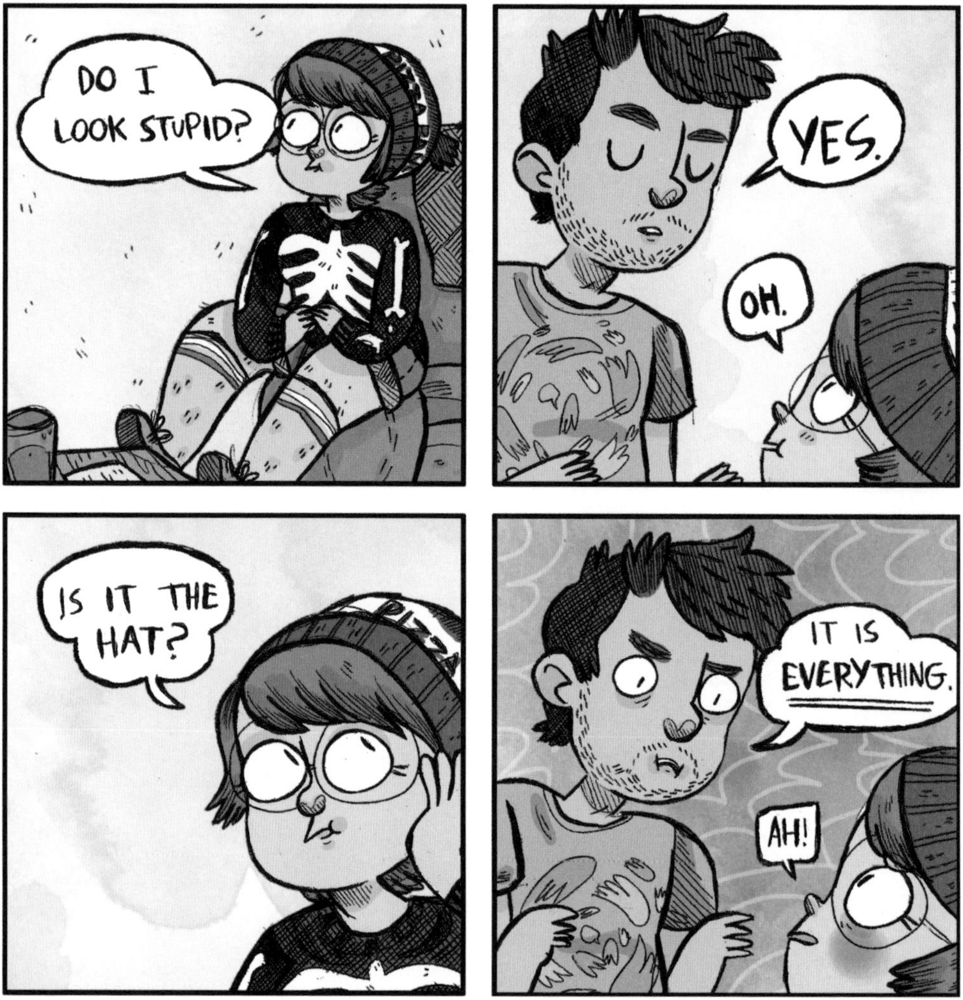
DO I LOOK STUPID?
YES.
OH.
IS IT THE HAT?
PIZZA
IT IS EVERYTHING.
AH!

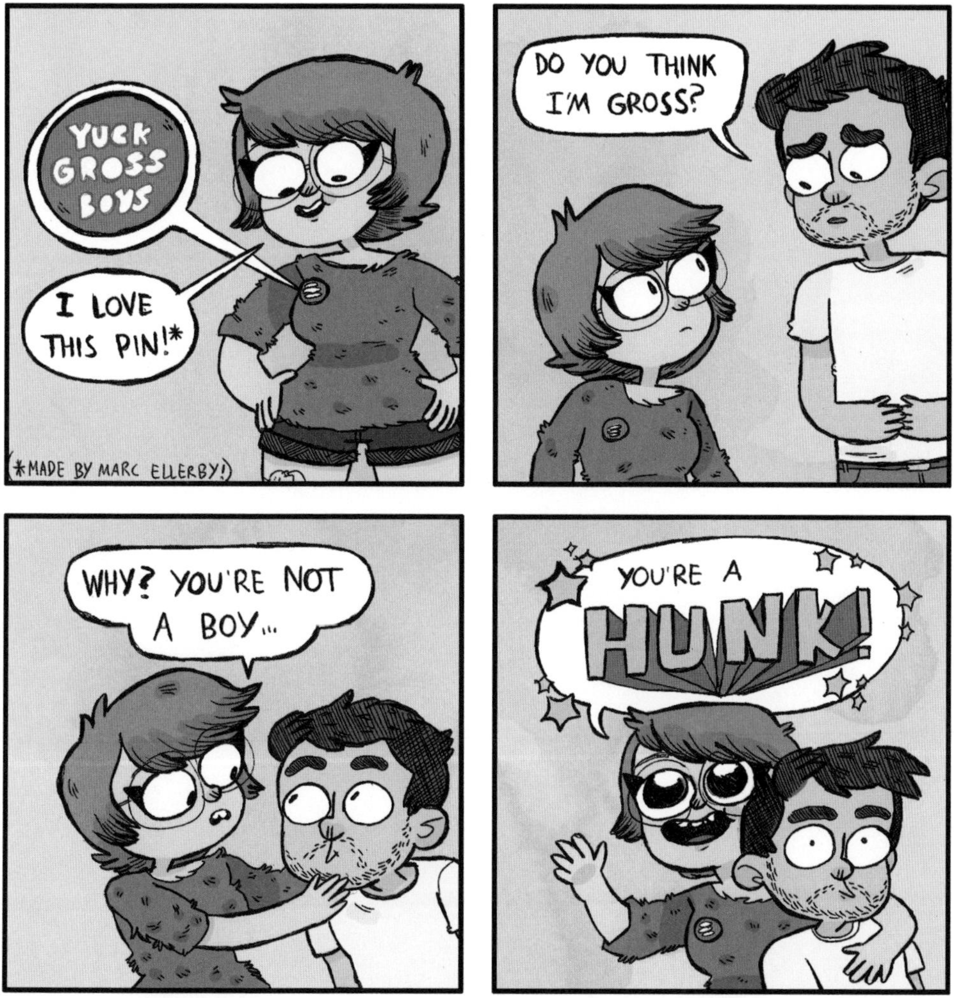
YUCK GROSS BOYS
I LOVE THIS PIN!*
(*MADE BY MARC ELLERBY!)
DO YOU THINK I'M GROSS?
WHY? YOU'RE NOT A BOY...
YOU'RE A HUNK!

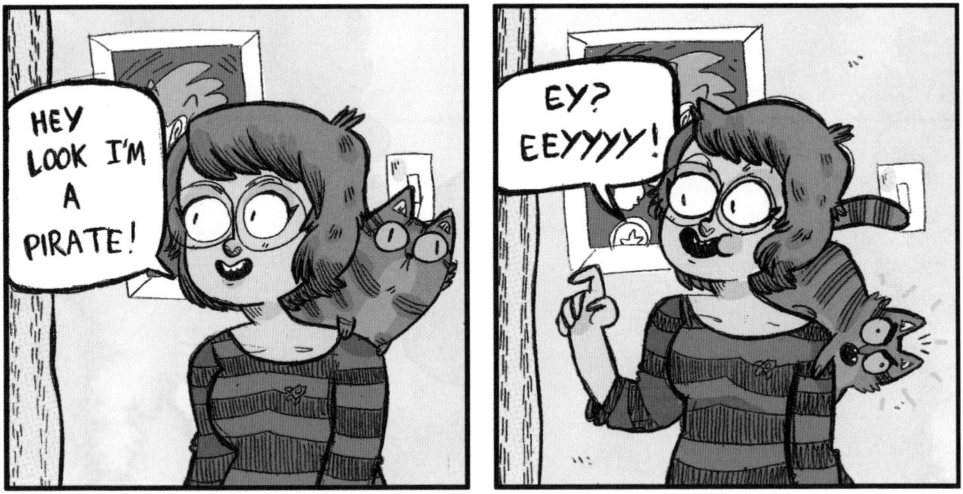
HEY LOOK I'M A PIRATE!
EY? EEYYYY!

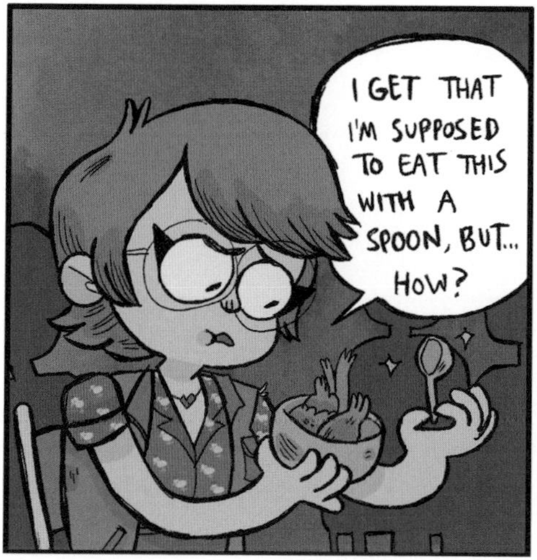
I GET THAT I'M SUPPOSED TO EAT THIS WITH A SPOON, BUT... HOW?

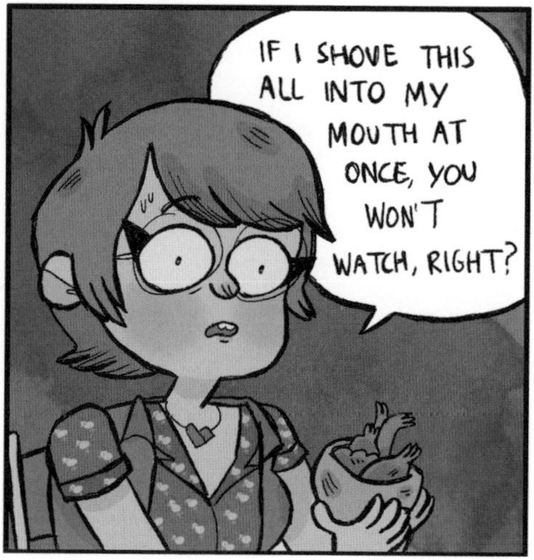
IF I SHOVE THIS ALL INTO MY MOUTH AT ONCE, YOU WON'T WATCH, RIGHT?

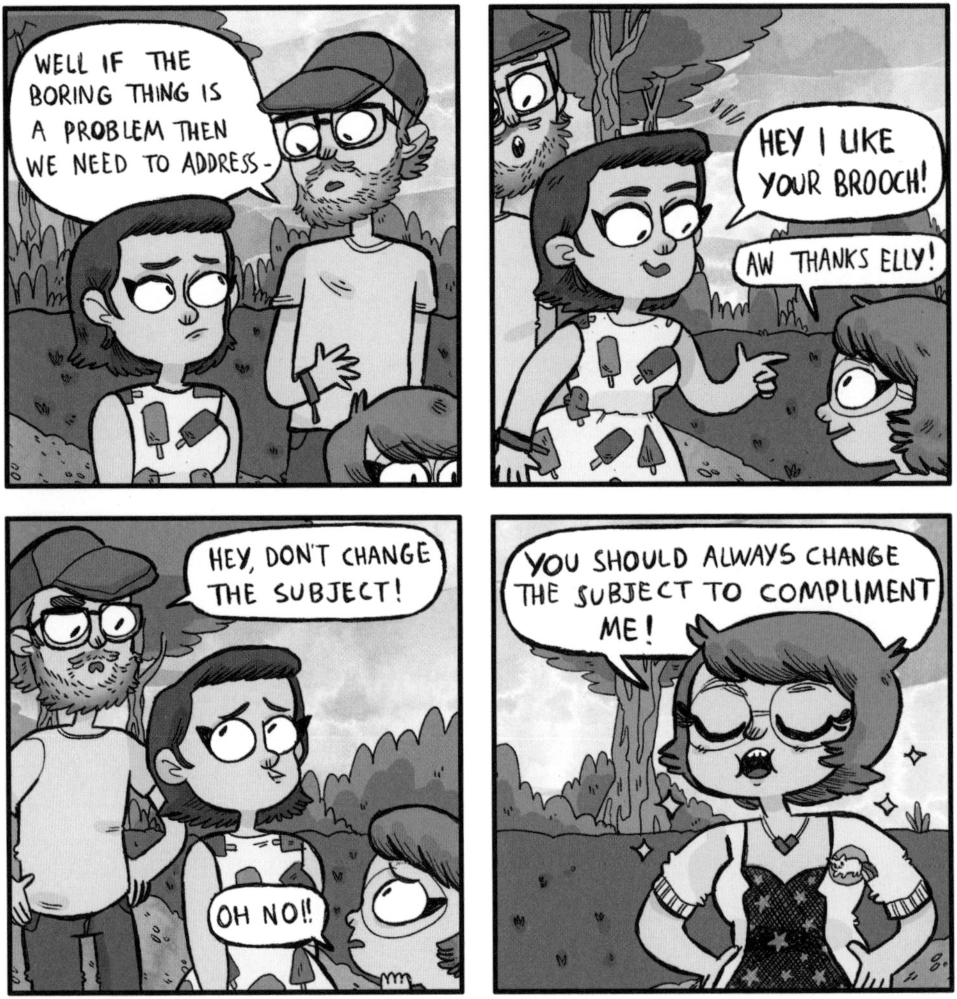
WELL IF THE BORING THING IS A PROBLEM THEN WE NEED TO ADDRESS-
HEY I LIKE YOUR BROOCH!
AW THANKS ELLY!
HEY, DON'T CHANGE THE SUBJECT!
OH NO!!
YOU SHOULD ALWAYS CHANGE THE SUBJECT TO COMPLIMENT ME!

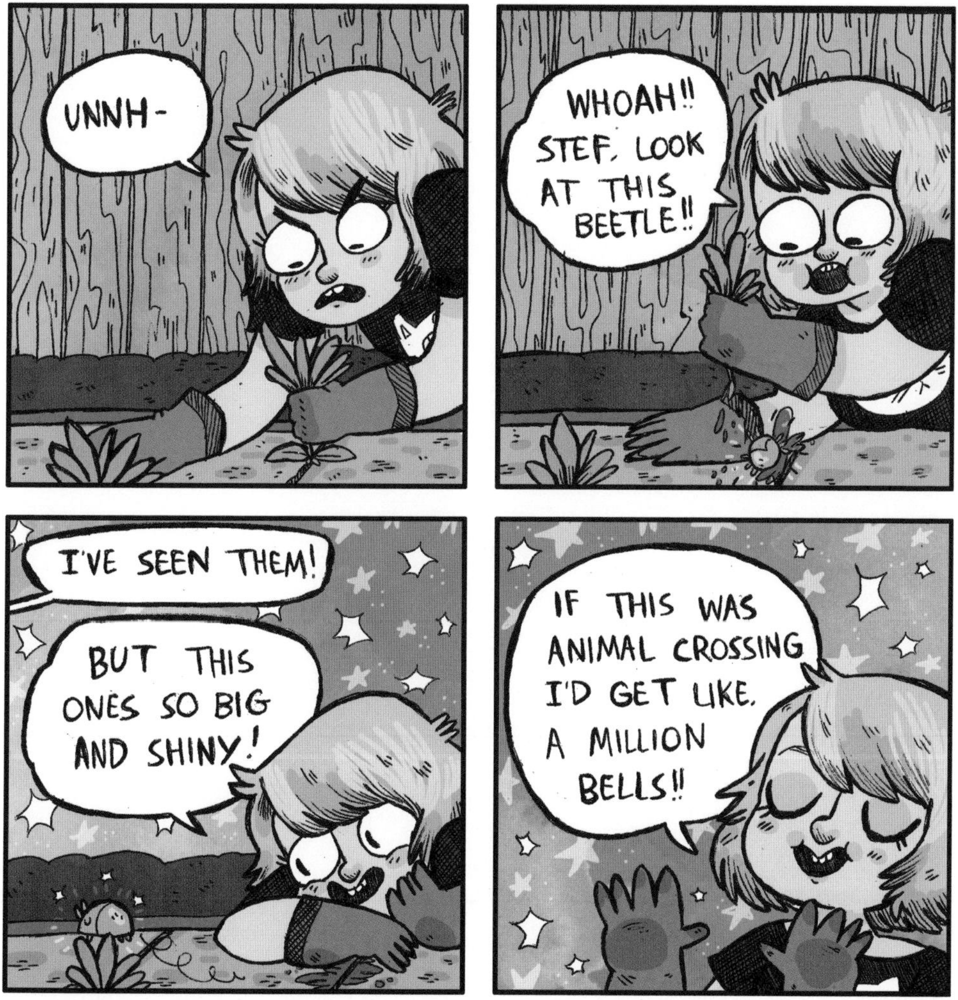
UNNH-
WHOAH!! STEF, LOOK AT THIS BEETLE!!
I'VE SEEN THEM!
BUT THIS ONES SO BIG AND SHINY!
IF THIS WAS ANIMAL CROSSING I'D GET LIKE, A MILLION BELLS!!

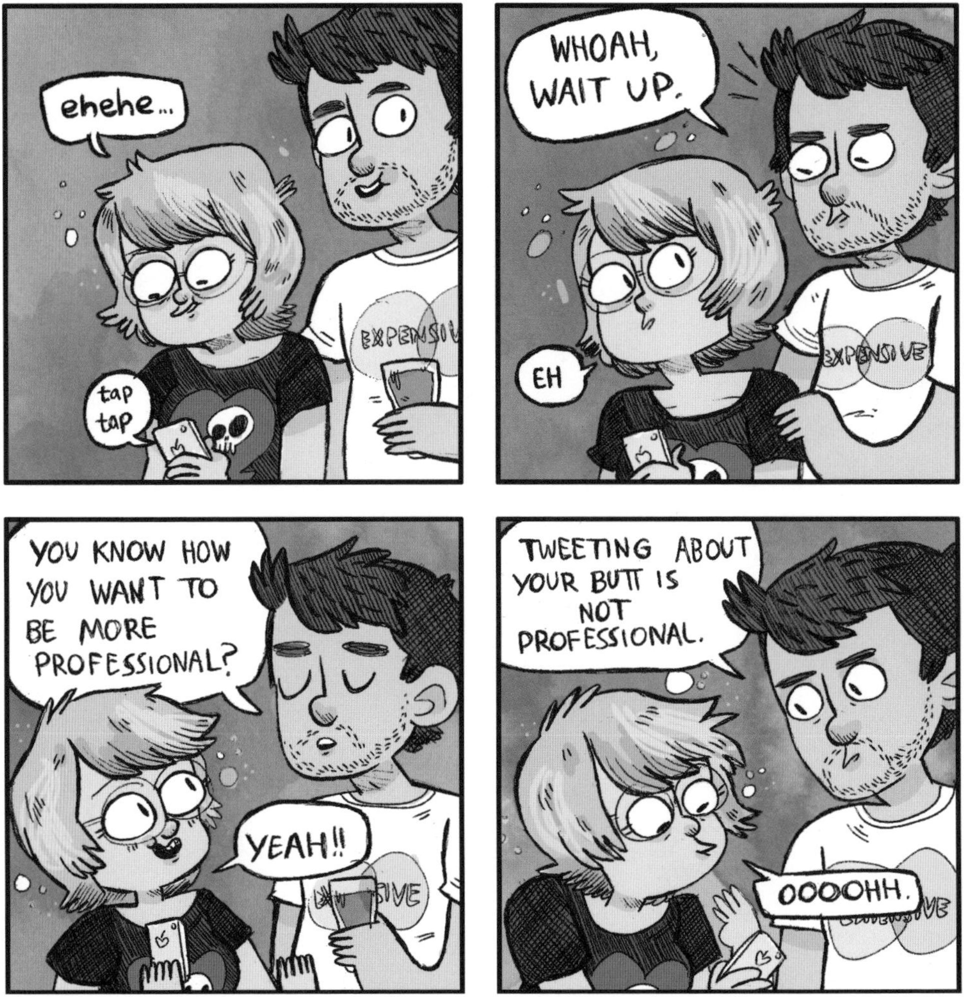
ehehe...
tap tap
WHOAH, WAIT UP.
EH
YOU KNOW HOW YOU WANT TO BE MORE PROFESSIONAL?
YEAH!!
TWEETING ABOUT YOUR BUTT IS NOT PROFESSIONAL.
OOOOHH.

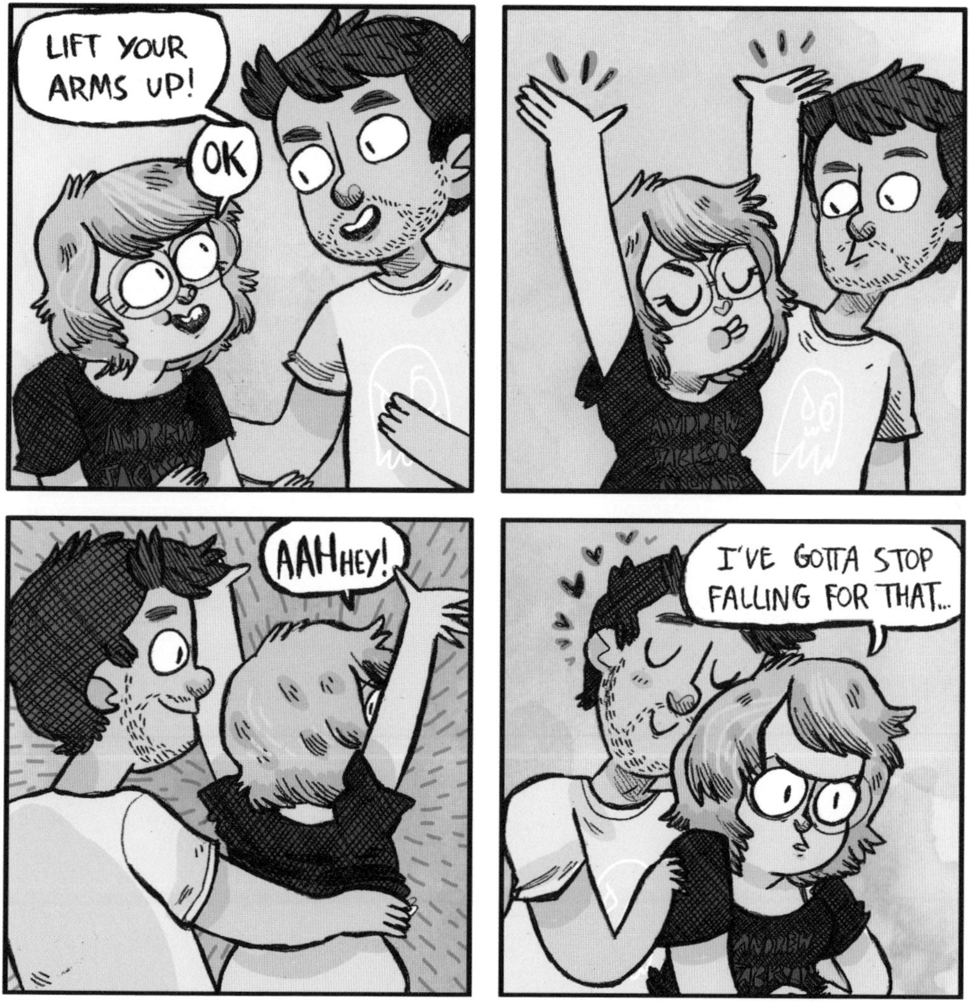
LIFT YOUR ARMS UP!
OK
AAHHEY!
I'VE GOTTA STOP FALLING FOR THAT...

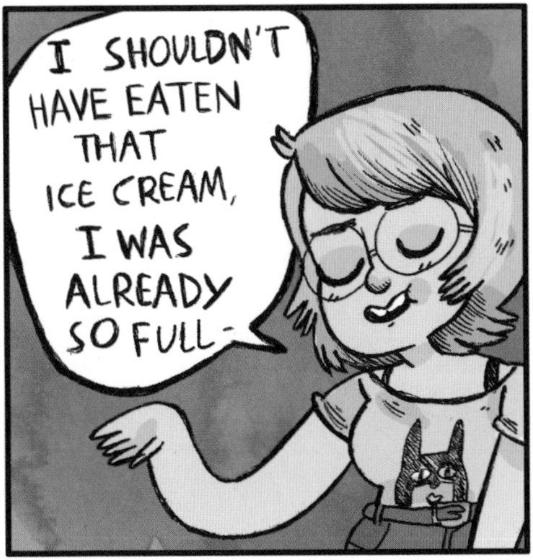
I SHOULDN'T HAVE EATEN THAT ICE CREAM, I WAS ALREADY SO FULL-

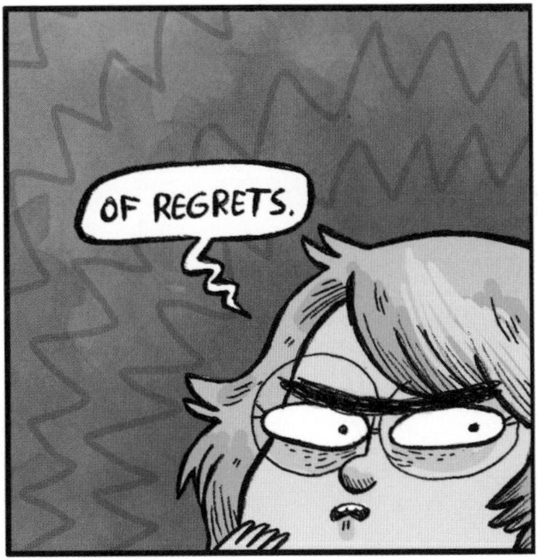
OF REGRETS.

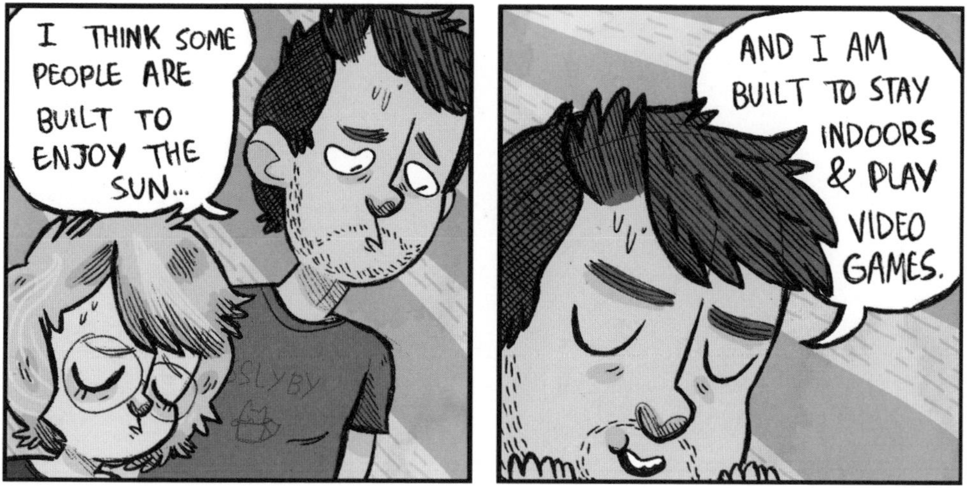
I THINK SOME PEOPLE ARE BUILT TO ENJOY THE SUN...
AND I AM BUILT TO STAY INDOORS & PLAY VIDEO GAMES.

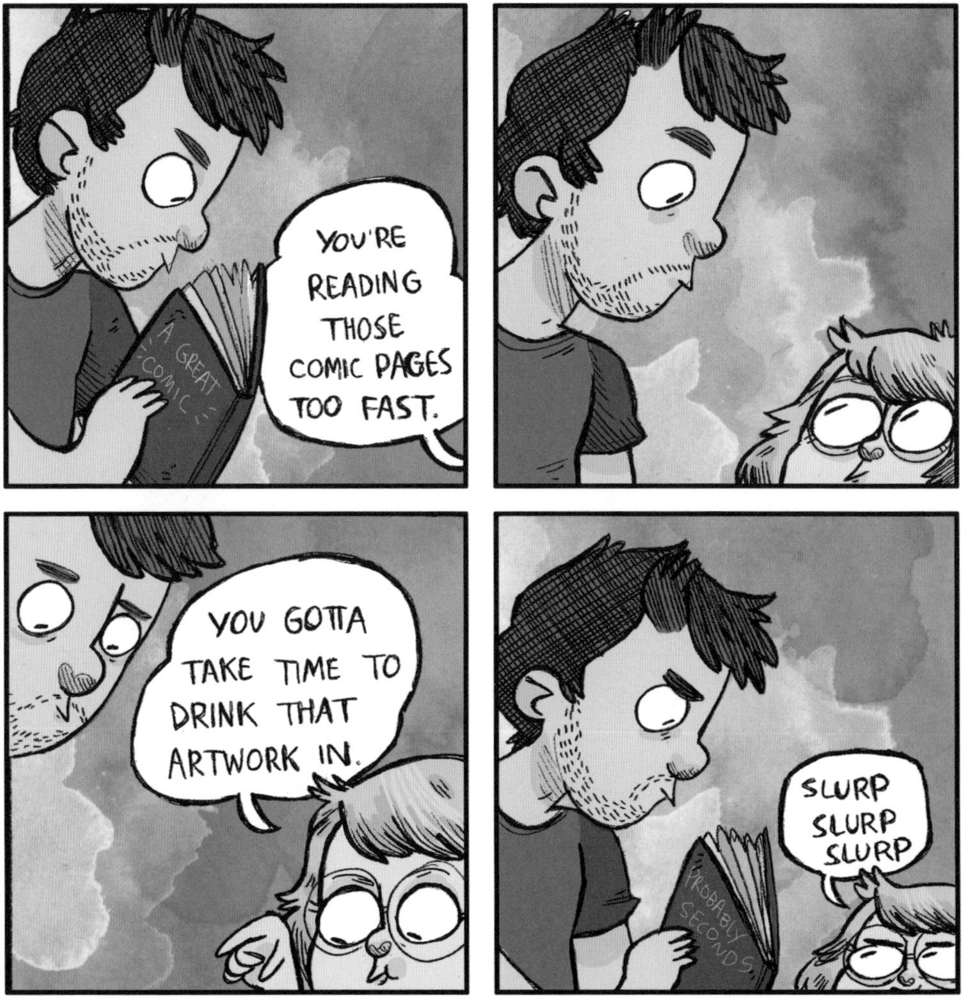
YOU'RE READING THOSE COMIC PAGES TOO FAST.
A GREAT COMIC
YOU GOTTA TAKE TIME TO DRINK THAT ARTWORK IN.
SLURP SLURP SLURP
PROBABLY SECONDS

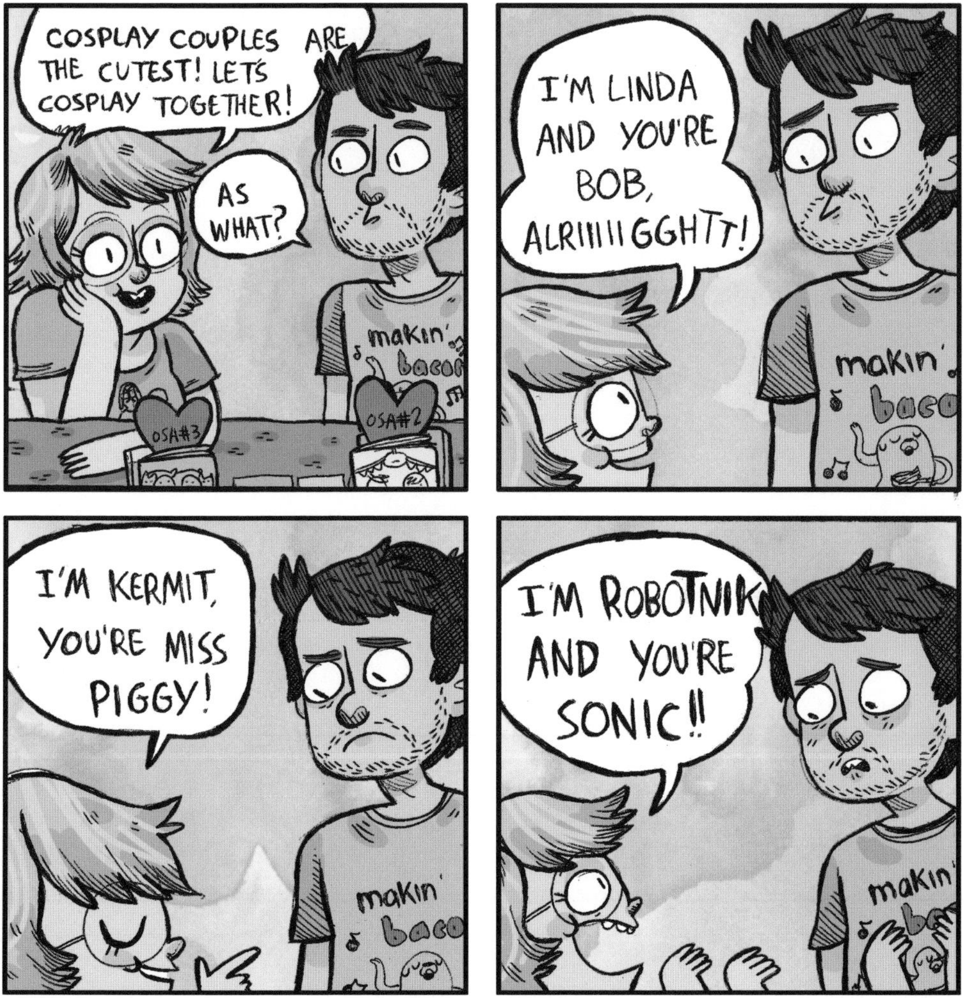
COSPLAY COUPLES ARE THE CUTEST! LET'S COSPLAY TOGETHER!
AS WHAT?
OSA#3
OSA#2
I'M LINDA AND YOU'RE BOB, ALRIIIIIGGHTT!
I'M KERMIT, YOU'RE MISS PIGGY!
I'M ROBOTNIK AND YOU'RE SONIC!!

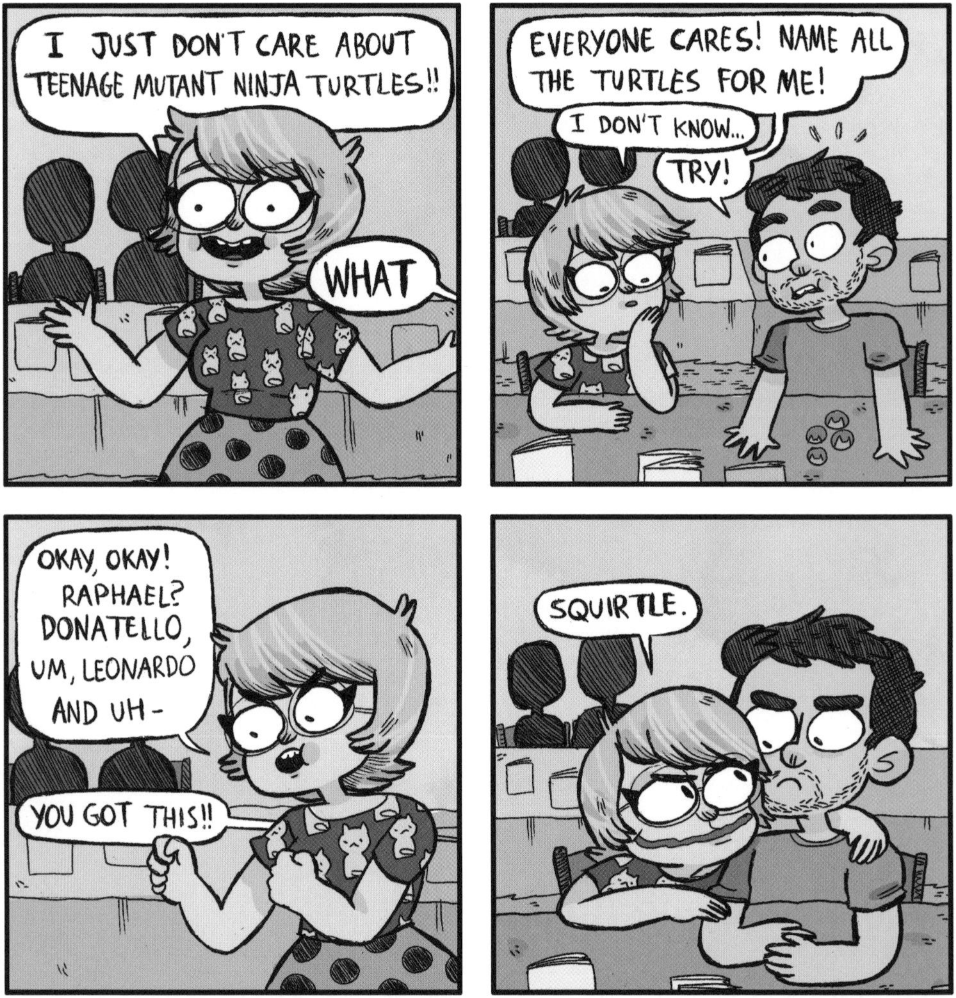
I JUST DON'T CARE ABOUT TEENAGE MUTANT NINJA TURTLES!!
WHAT
EVERYONE CARES! NAME ALL THE TURTLES FOR ME!
I DON'T KNOW...
TRY!
OKAY, OKAY! RAPHAEL? DONATELLO, UM, LEONARDO AND UH-
YOU GOT THIS!!
SQUIRTLE.

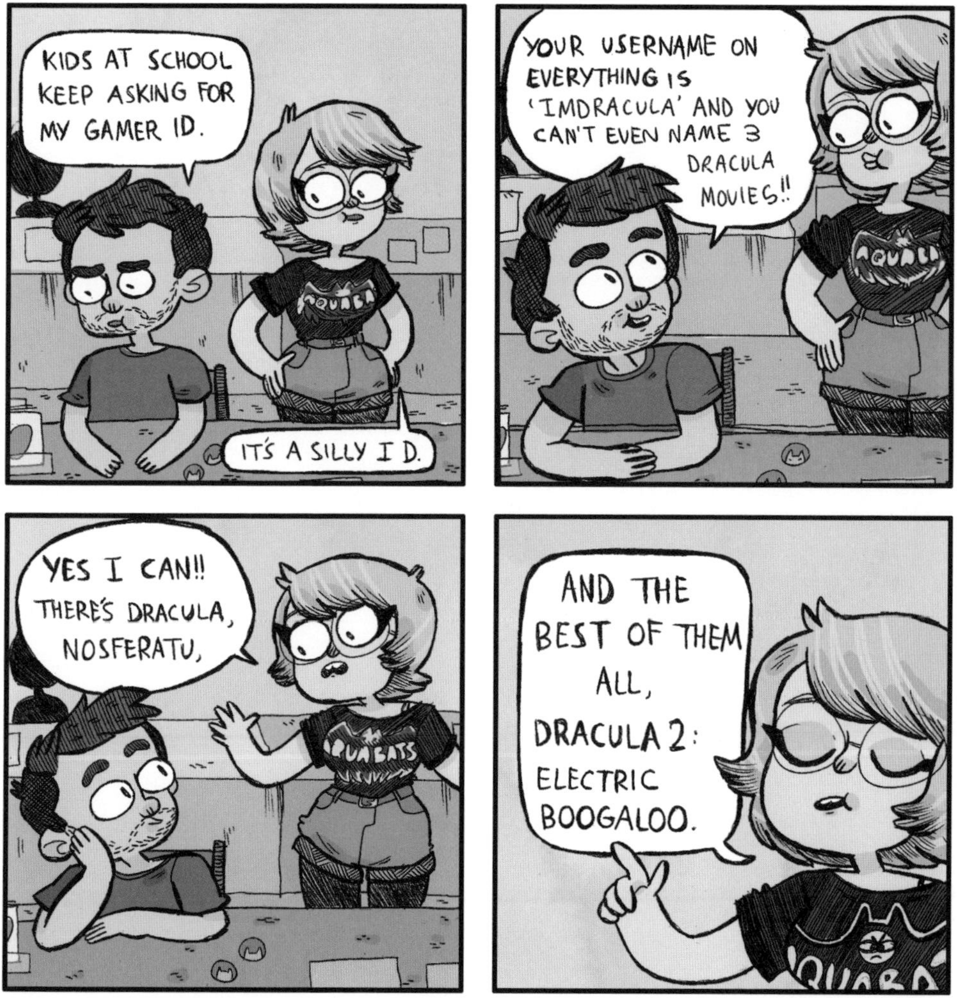
KIDS AT SCHOOL KEEP ASKING FOR MY GAMER ID.
IT'S A SILLY I D.
YOUR USERNAME ON EVERYTHING IS 'IMDRACULA' AND YOU CAN'T EVEN NAME 3 DRACULA MOVIES!!
YES I CAN!! THERE'S DRACULA, NOSFERATU,
AND THE BEST OF THEM ALL, DRACULA 2: ELECTRIC BOOGALOO.

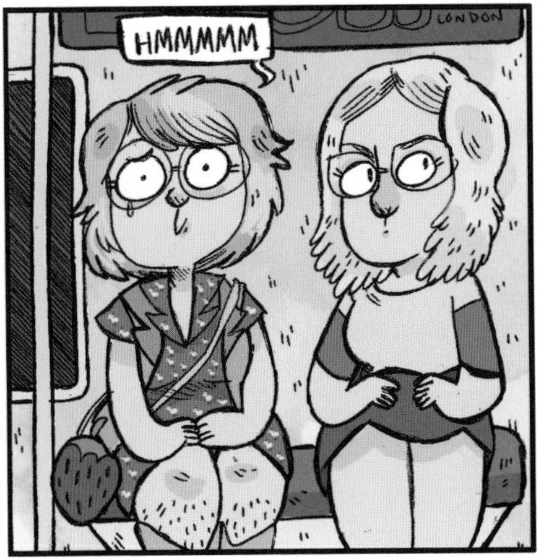
HMMMMM
LONDON

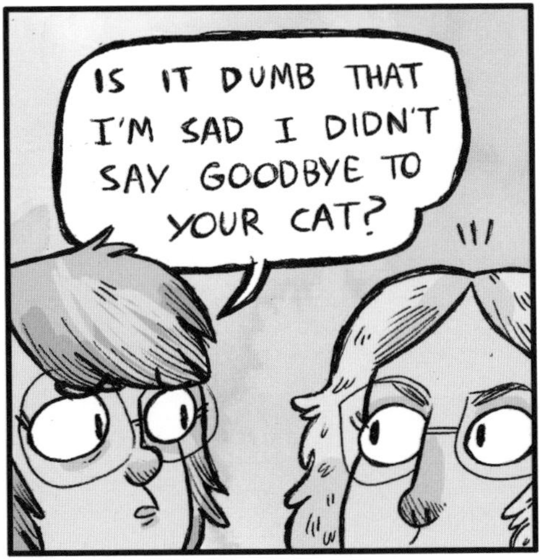
IS IT DUMB THAT I'M SAD I DIDN'T SAY GOODBYE TO YOUR CAT?

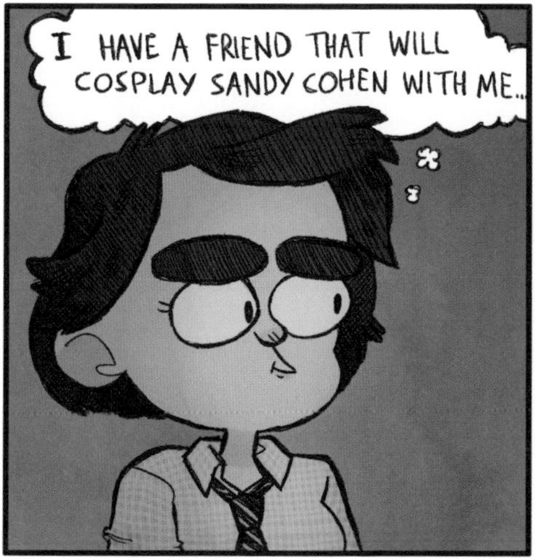
I HAVE A FRIEND THAT WILL COSPLAY SANDY COHEN WITH ME...

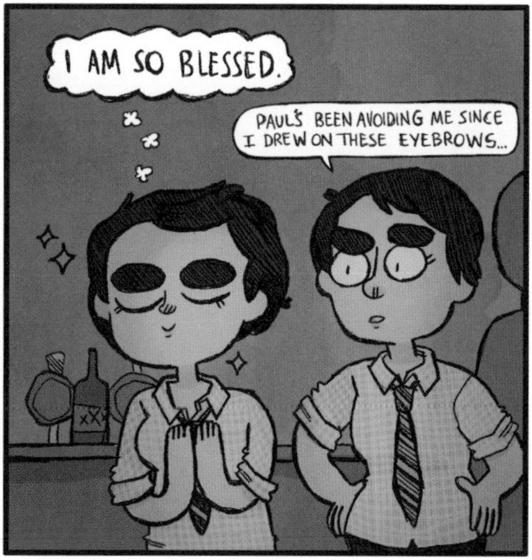
I AM SO BLESSED.
PAUL'S BEEN AVOIDING ME SINCE I DREW ON THESE EYEBROWS...

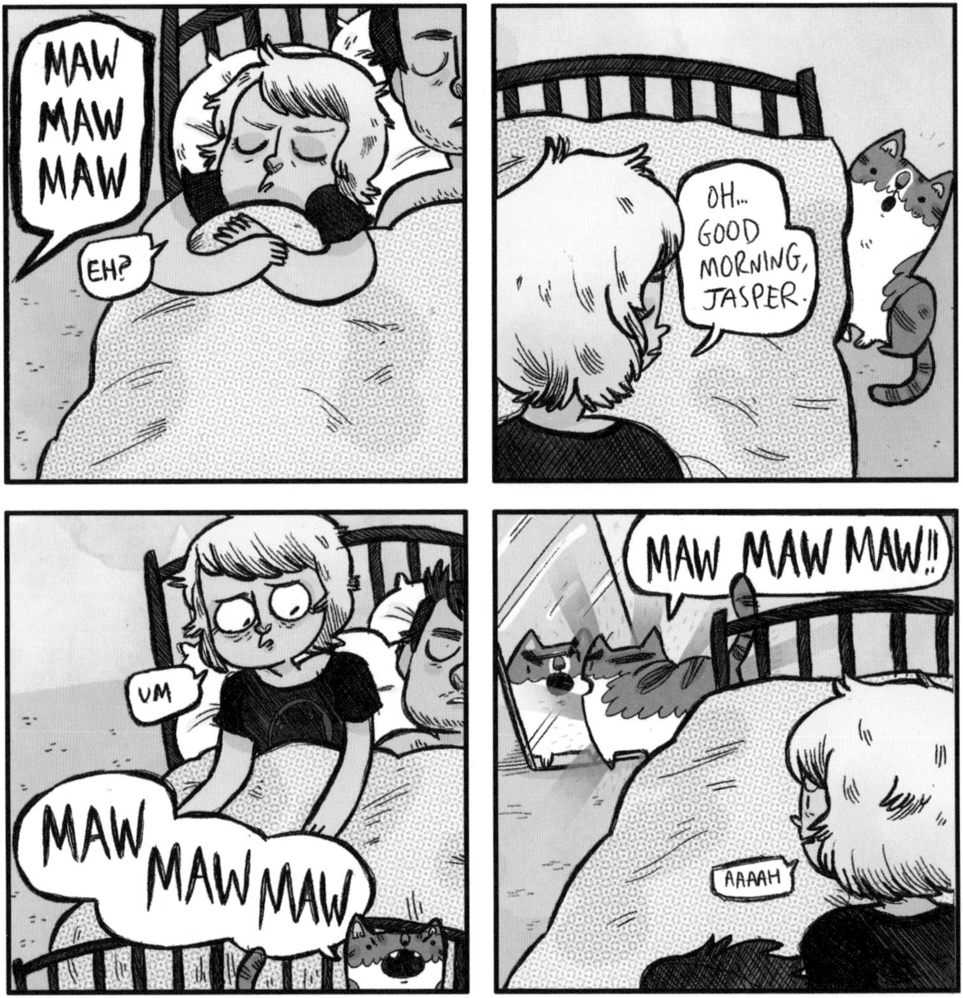
MAW MAW MAW
EH?
OH... GOOD MORNING, JASPER.
UM
MAW MAW MAW
MAW MAW MAW!!
AAAAH

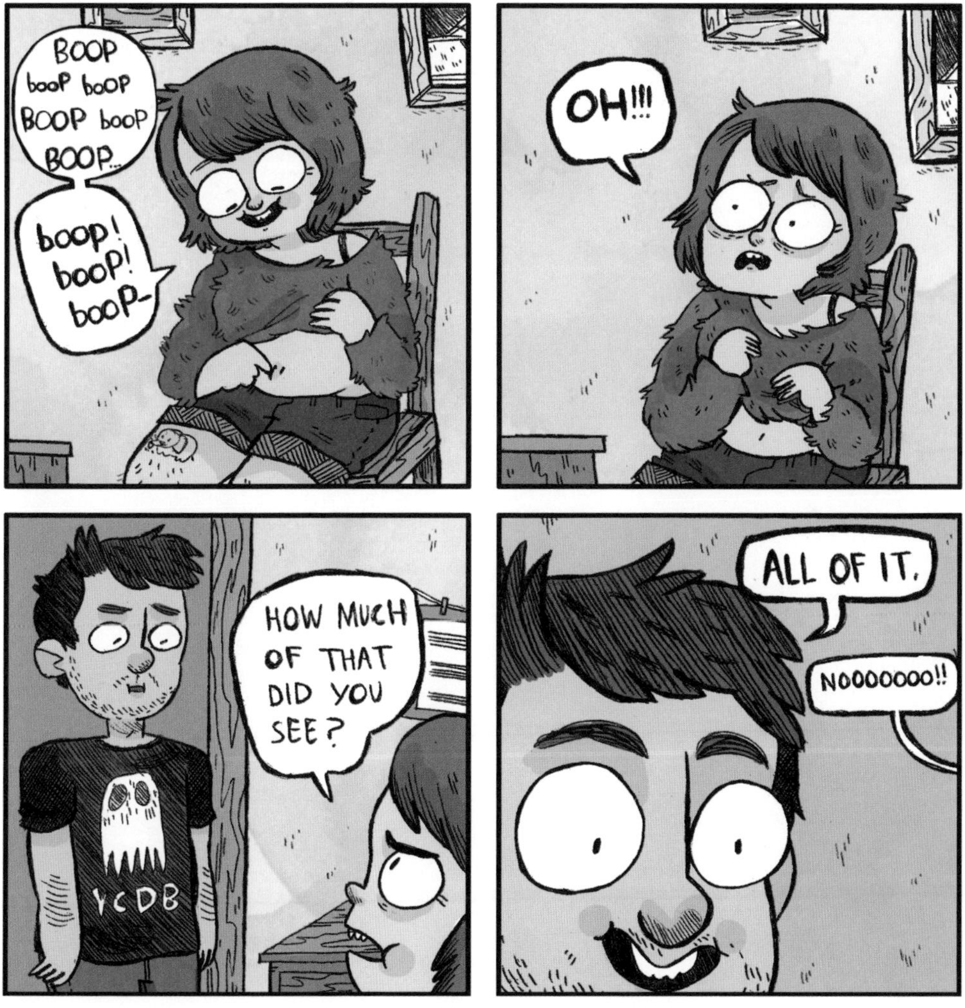
BOOP booP booP BOOP boop BOOP...
boop! booP! booP_
OH!!!
HOW MUCH OF THAT DID YOU SEE?
YCDB
ALL OF IT.
NOOOOOOO!!

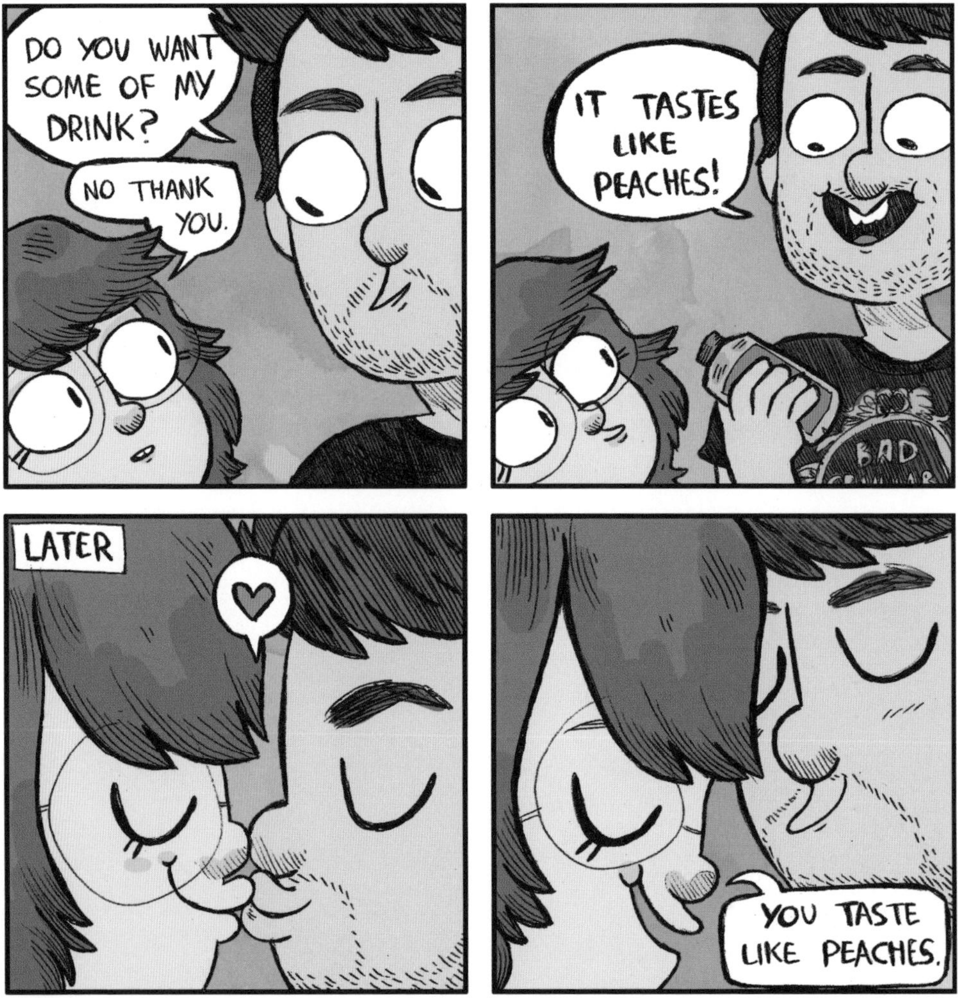
DO YOU WANT SOME OF MY DRINK?
NO THANK YOU.
IT TASTES LIKE PEACHES!
LATER
YOU TASTE LIKE PEACHES.

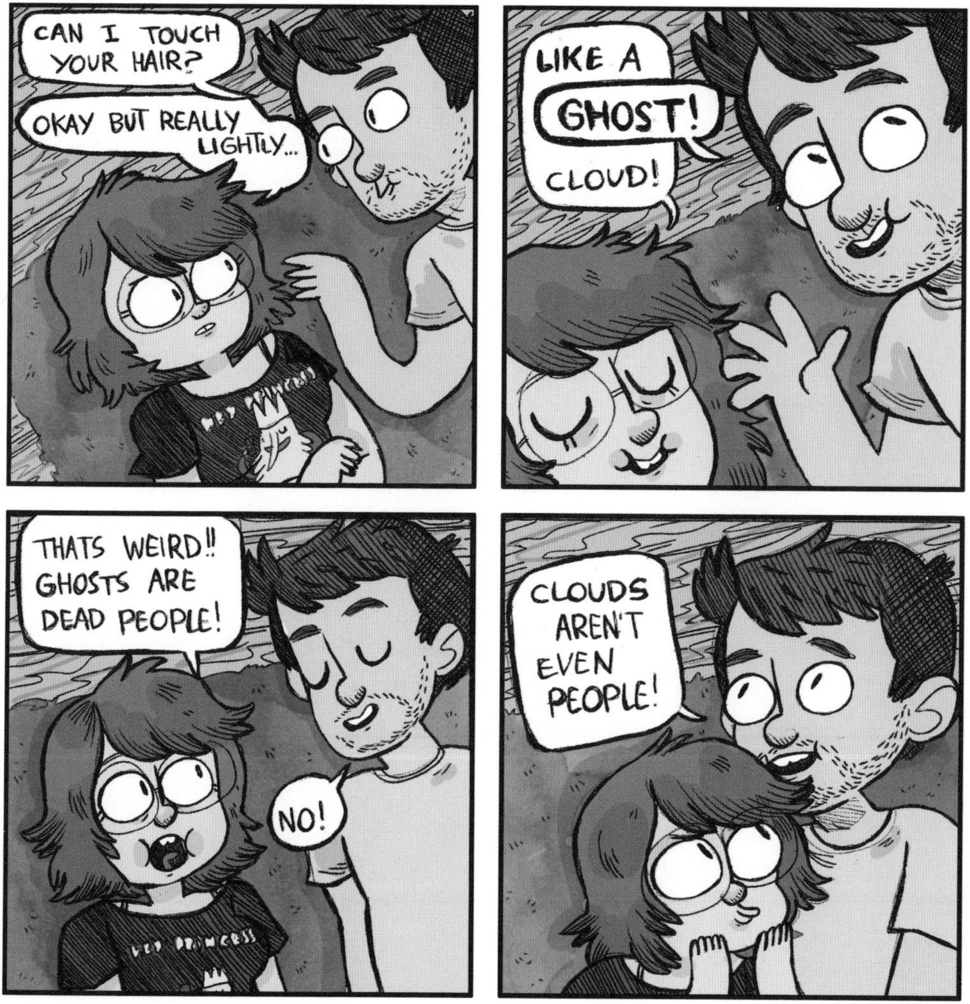
CAN I TOUCH YOUR HAIR?
OKAY BUT REALLY LIGHTLY...
LIKE A GHOST! CLOUD!
THATS WEIRD!! GHOSTS ARE DEAD PEOPLE!
NO!
CLOUDS AREN'T EVEN PEOPLE!

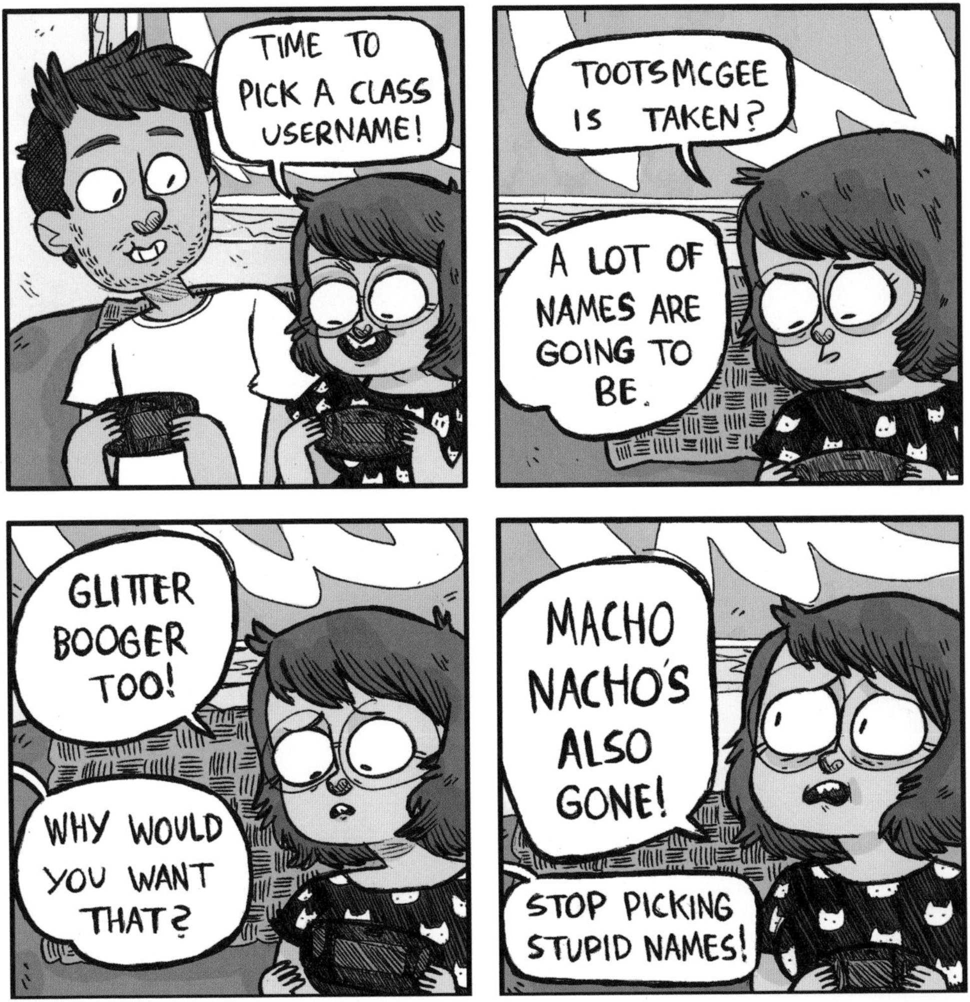
TIME TO PICK A CLASS USERNAME!
TOOTSMCGEE IS TAKEN?
A LOT OF NAMES ARE GOING TO BE.
GLITTER BOOGER TOO!
WHY WOULD YOU WANT THAT?
MACHO NACHO'S ALSO GONE!
STOP PICKING STUPID NAMES!

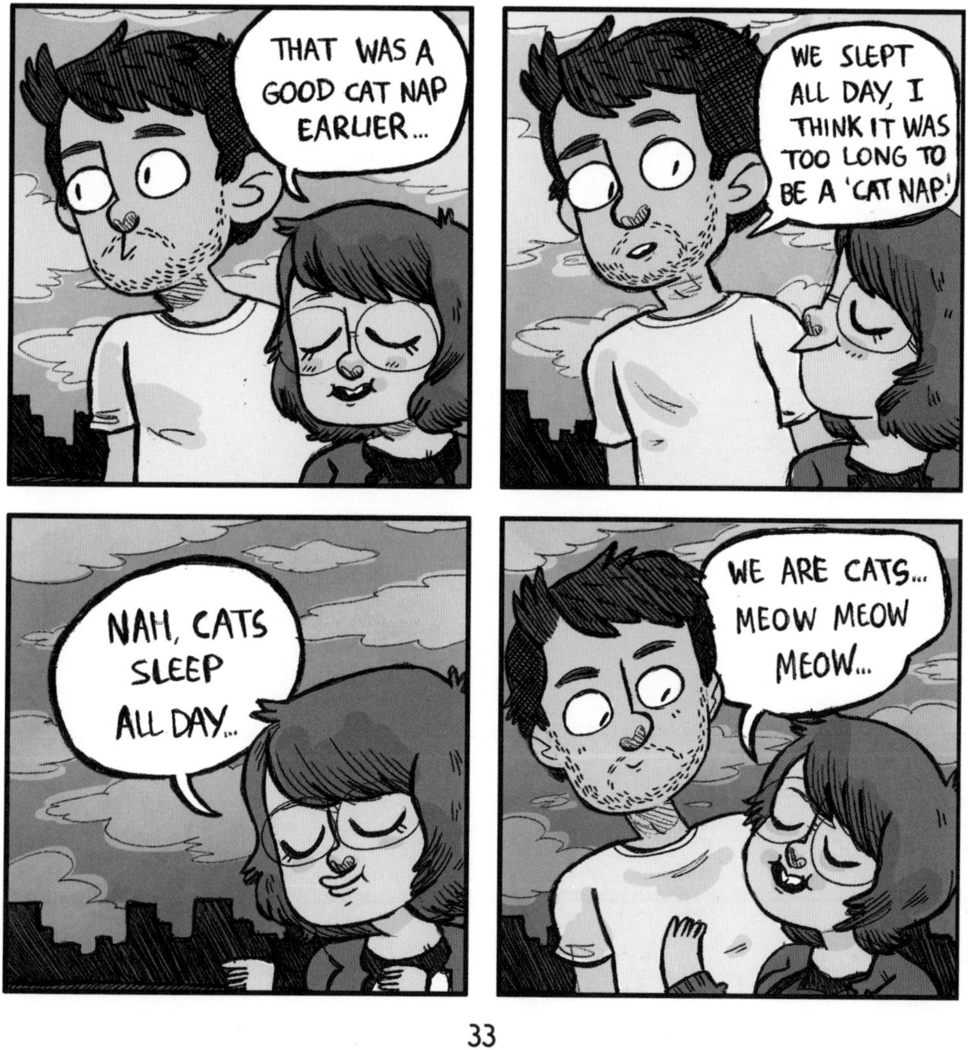
THAT WAS A GOOD CAT NAP EARLIER...
WE SLEPT ALL DAY, I THINK IT WAS TOO LONG TO BE A 'CAT NAP.'
NAH, CATS SLEEP ALL DAY...
WE ARE CATS... MEOW MEOW MEOW...

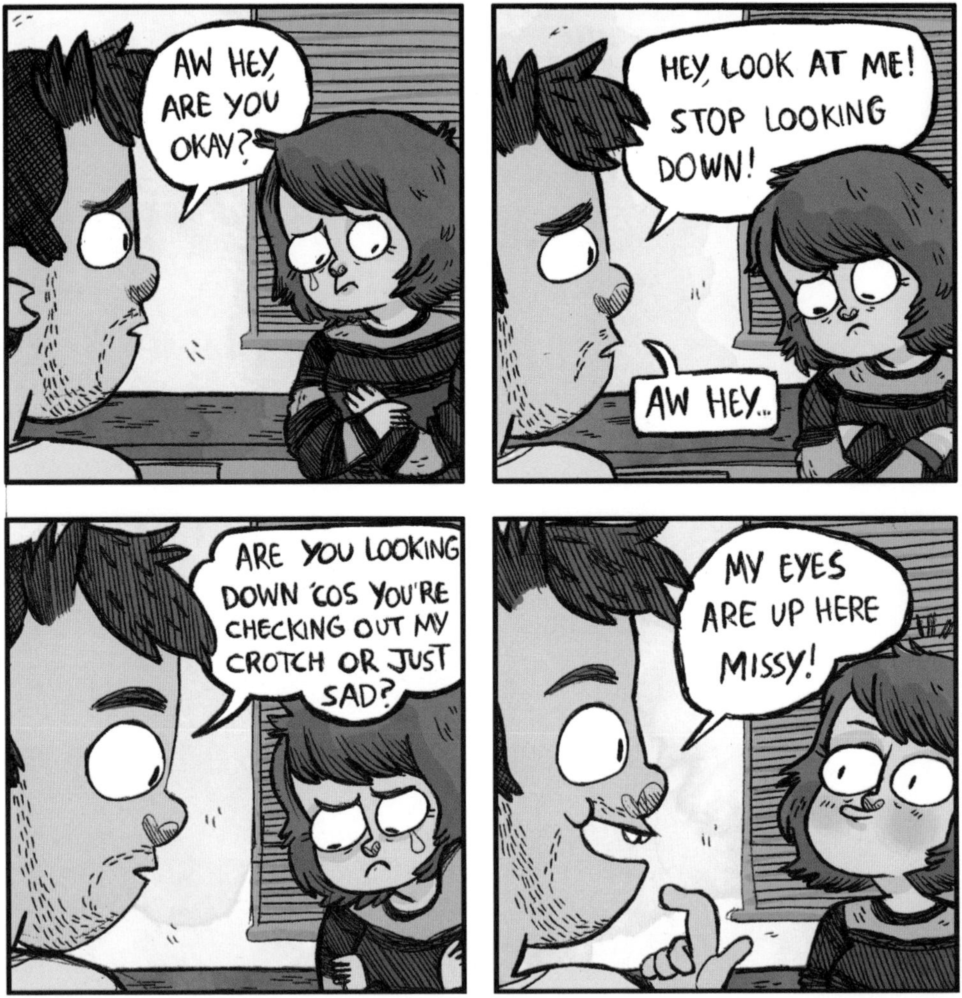
AW HEY, ARE YOU OKAY?
HEY, LOOK AT ME! STOP LOOKING DOWN!
AW HEY...
ARE YOU LOOKING DOWN 'COS YOU'RE CHECKING OUT MY CROTCH OR JUST SAD?
MY EYES ARE UP HERE MISSY!

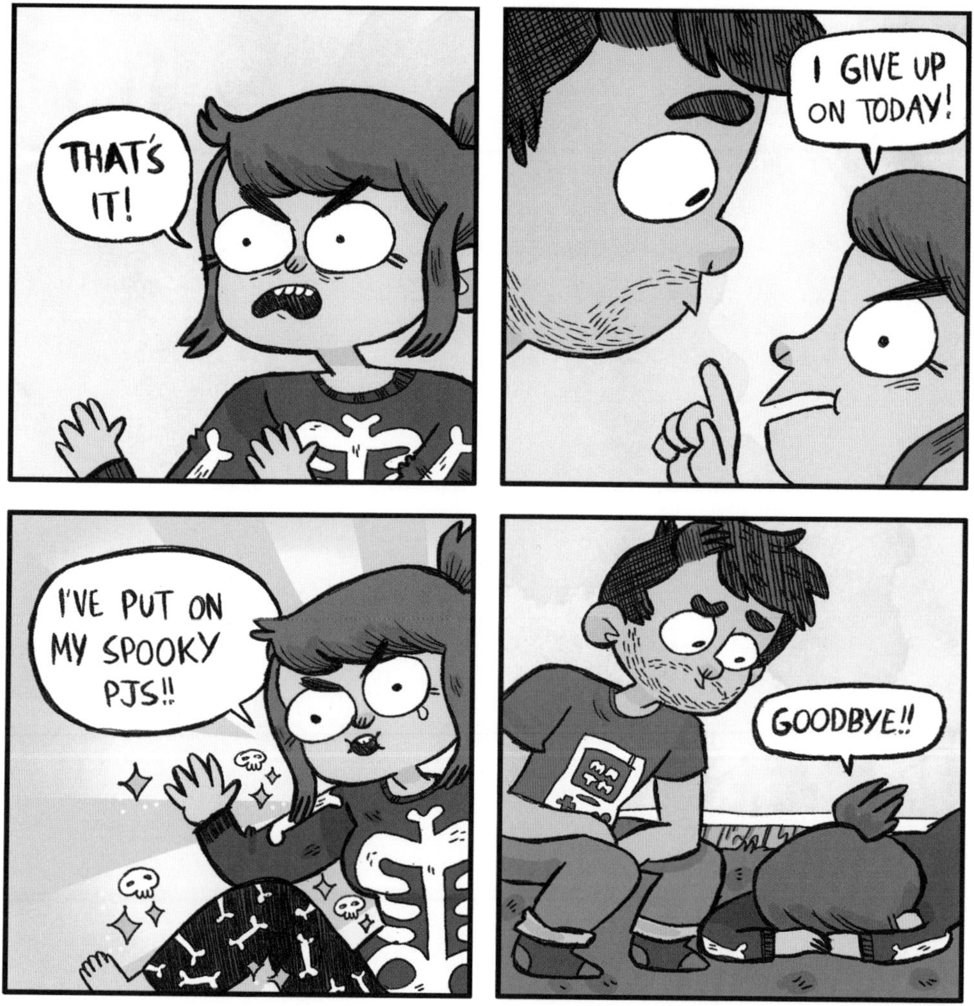
THAT'S IT!
I GIVE UP ON TODAY!
I'VE PUT ON MY SPOOKY PJS!!
GOODBYE!!

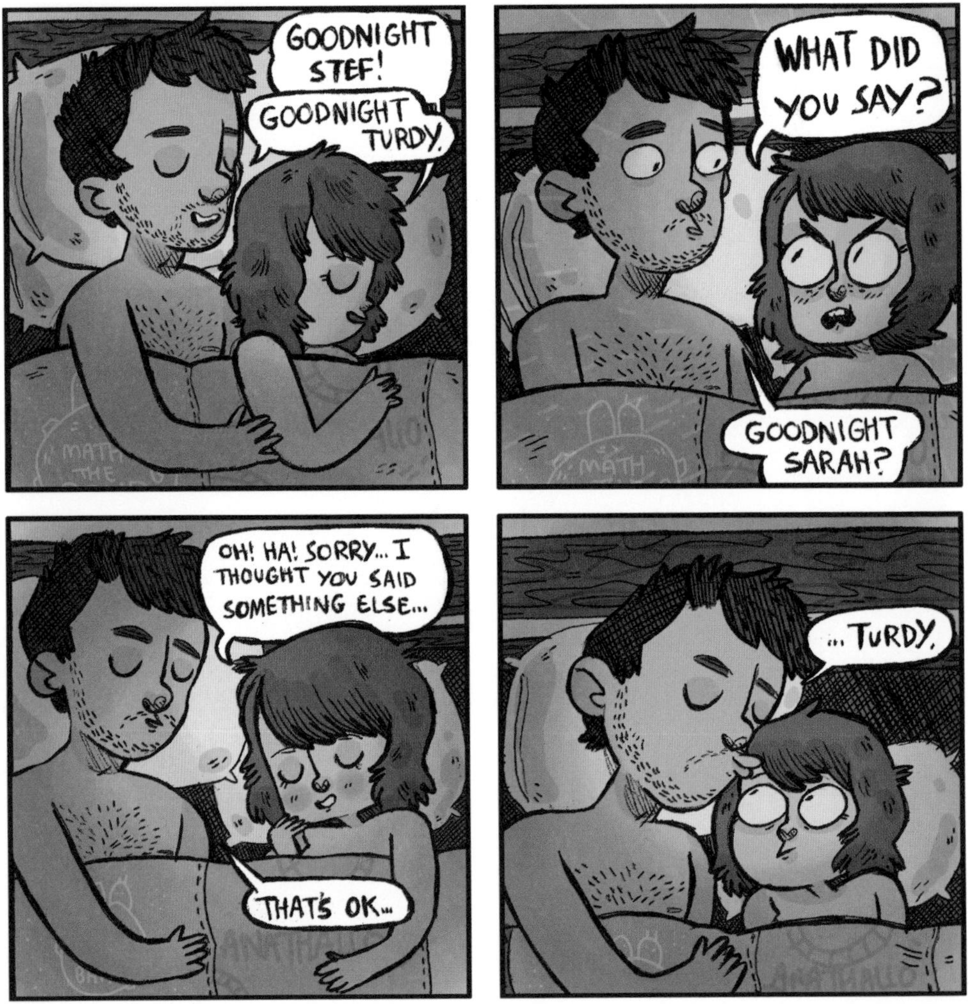
GOODNIGHT STEF!
GOODNIGHT TURDY.
WHAT DID YOU SAY?
GOODNIGHT SARAH?
OH! HA! SORRY... I THOUGHT YOU SAID SOMETHING ELSE...
THAT'S OK...
...TURDY.

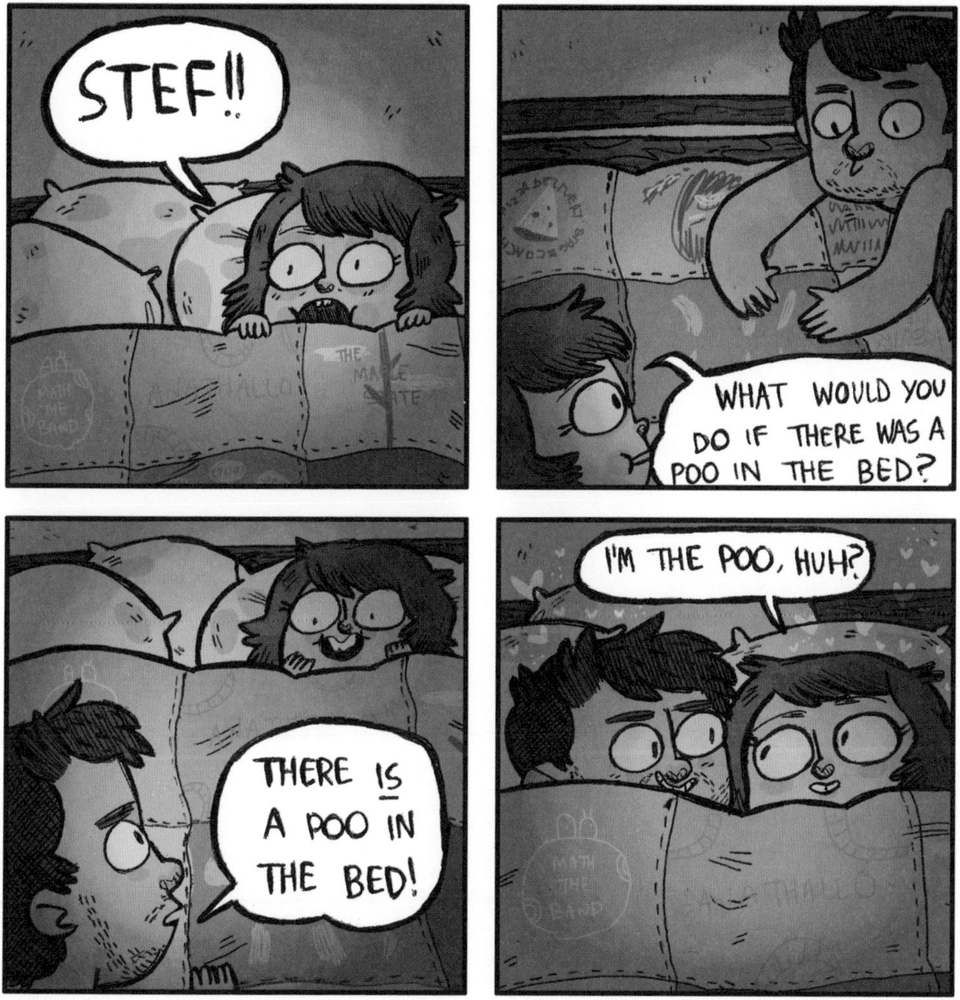
STEF!!
WHAT WOULD YOU DO IF THERE WAS A POO IN THE BED?
THERE IS A POO IN THE BED!
I'M THE POO, HUH?

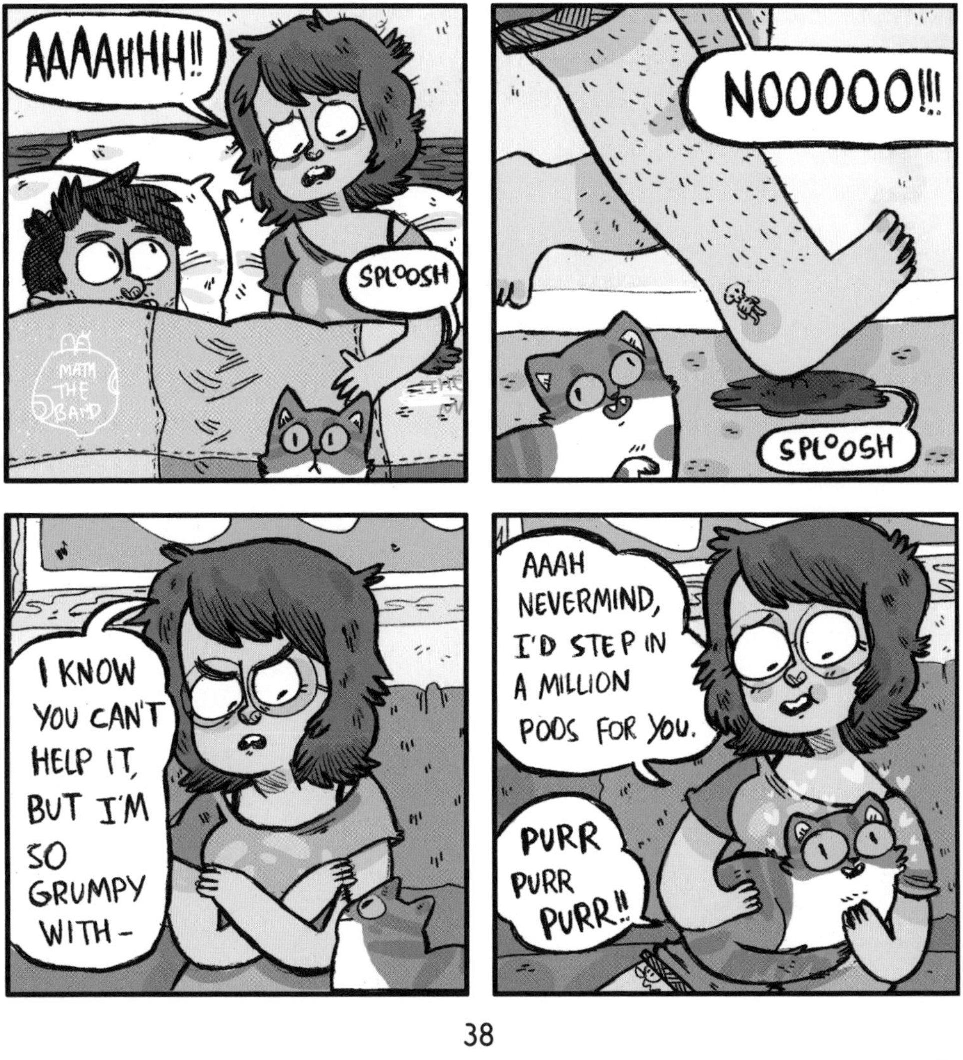
AAAAHHH!!
MATH THE BAND
SPLOOSH
NOOOOO!!!
SPLOOSH
I KNOW YOU CAN'T HELP IT, BUT I'M SO GRUMPY WITH-
AAAH NEVERMIND, I'D STEP IN A MILLION POOS FOR YOU.
PURR PURR PURR!!

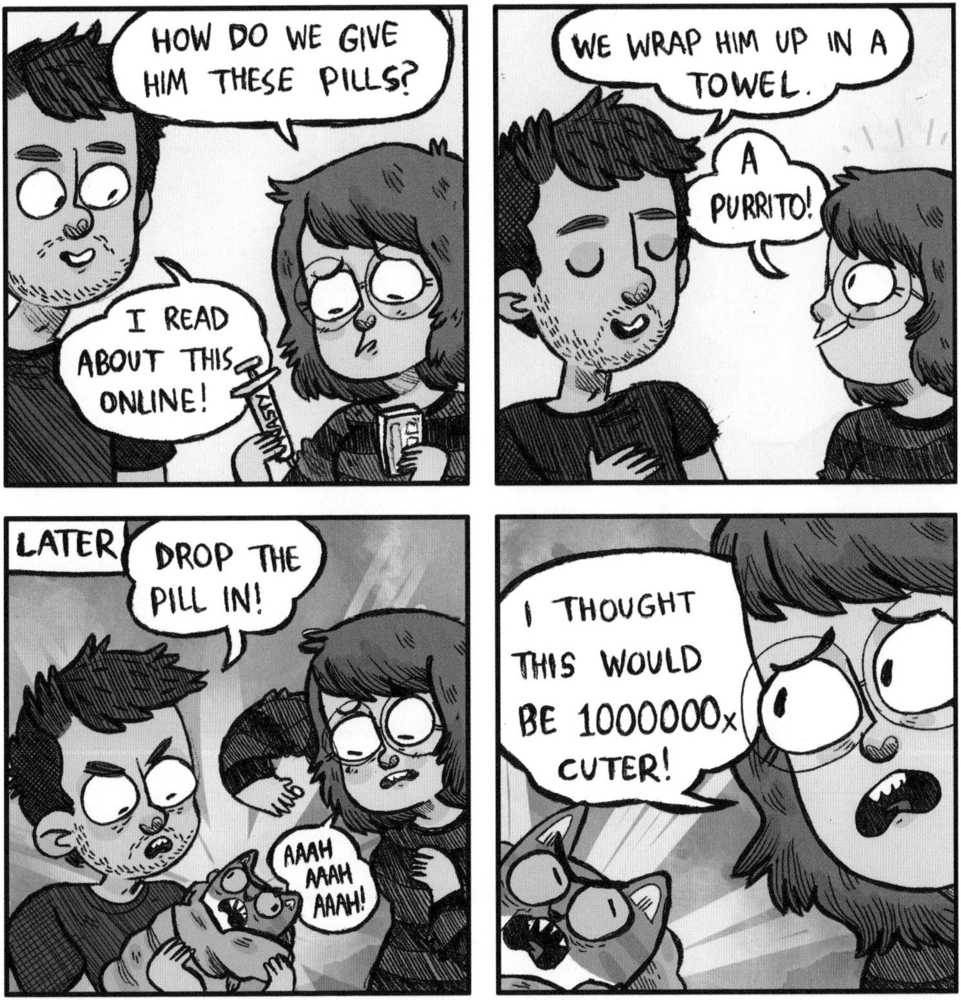
HOW DO WE GIVE HIM THESE PILLS?
I READ ABOUT THIS ONLINE!
WE WRAP HIM UP IN A TOWEL.
A PURRITO!
LATER
DROP THE PILL IN!
AAAH AAAH AAAH!
I THOUGHT THIS WOULD BE 1000000x CUTER!

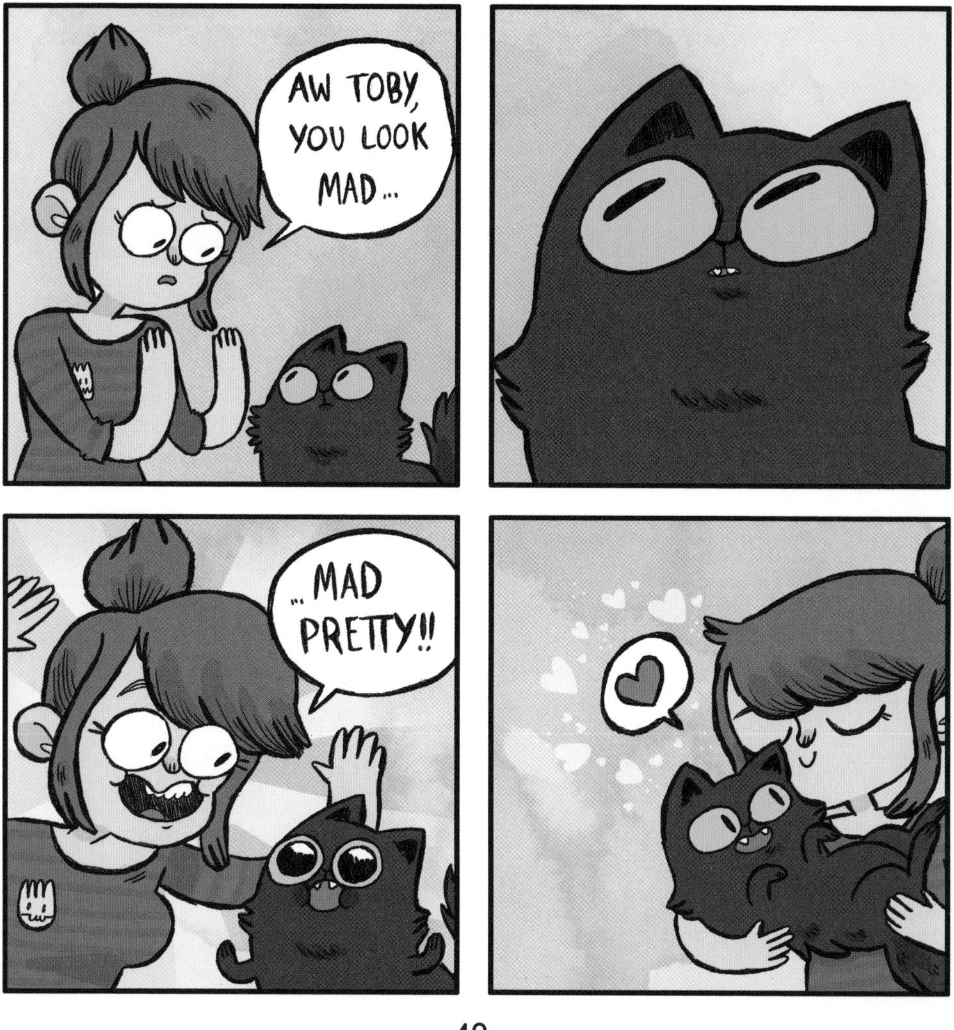
AW TOBY, YOU LOOK MAD...
...MAD PRETTY!!

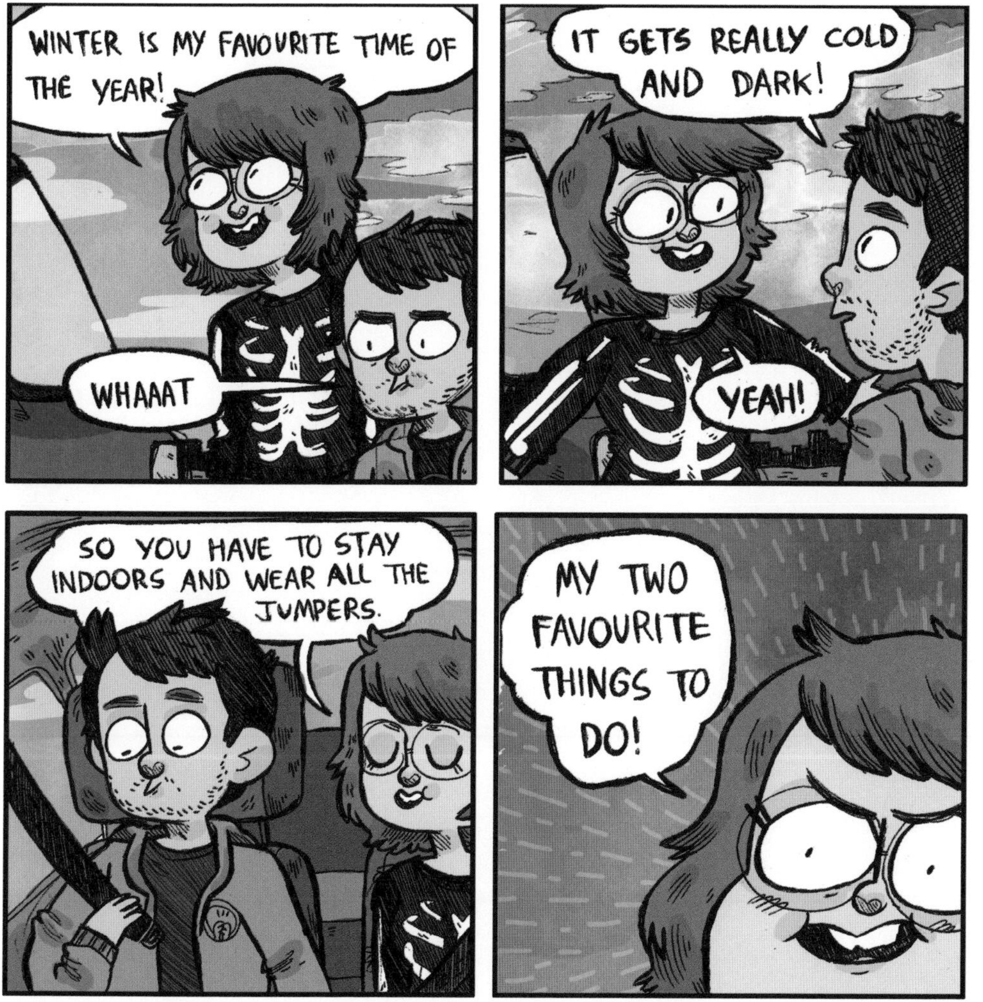
WINTER IS MY FAVOURITE TIME OF THE YEAR!
WHAAAT
IT GETS REALLY COLD AND DARK!
YEAH!
SO YOU HAVE TO STAY INDOORS AND WEAR ALL THE JUMPERS.
MY TWO FAVOURITE THINGS TO DO!

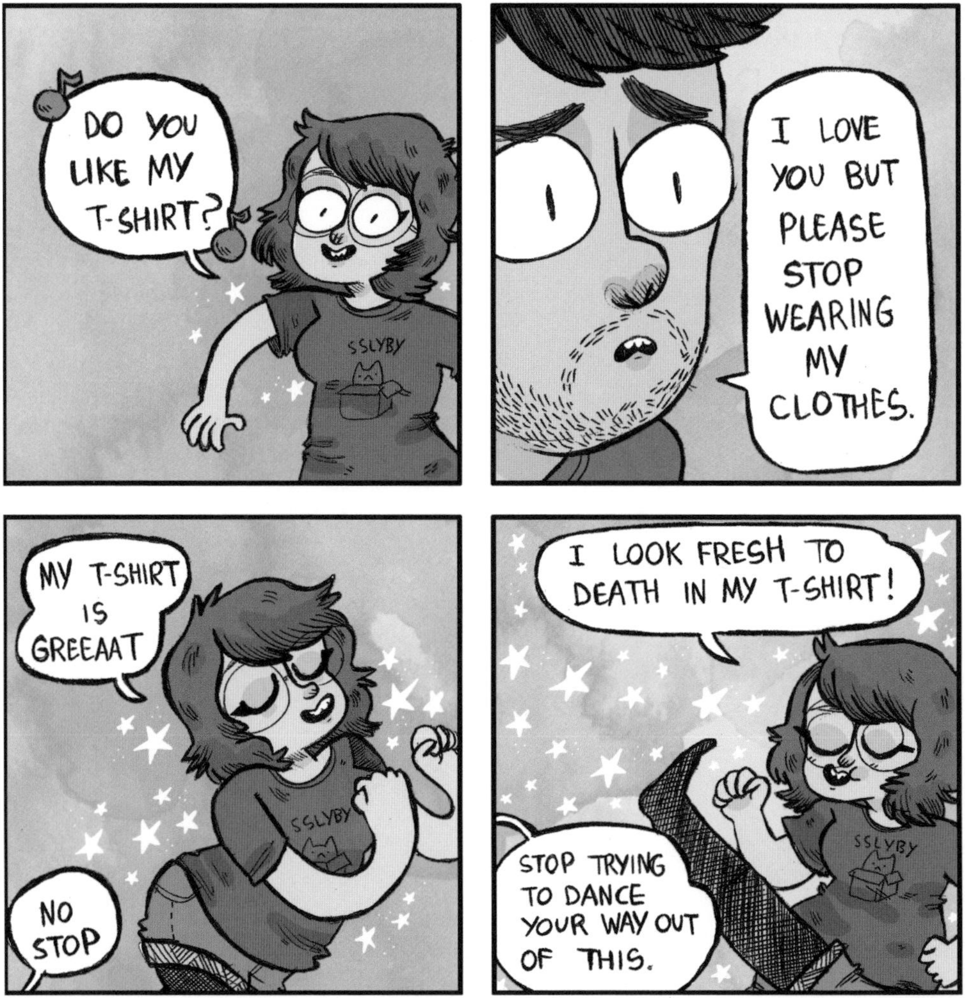
DO YOU LIKE MY T-SHIRT?
SSLYBY
I LOVE YOU BUT PLEASE STOP WEARING MY CLOTHES.
MY T-SHIRT IS GREEAAT
SSLYBY
NO STOP
I LOOK FRESH TO DEATH IN MY T-SHIRT!
SSLYBY
STOP TRYING TO DANCE YOUR WAY OUT OF THIS.

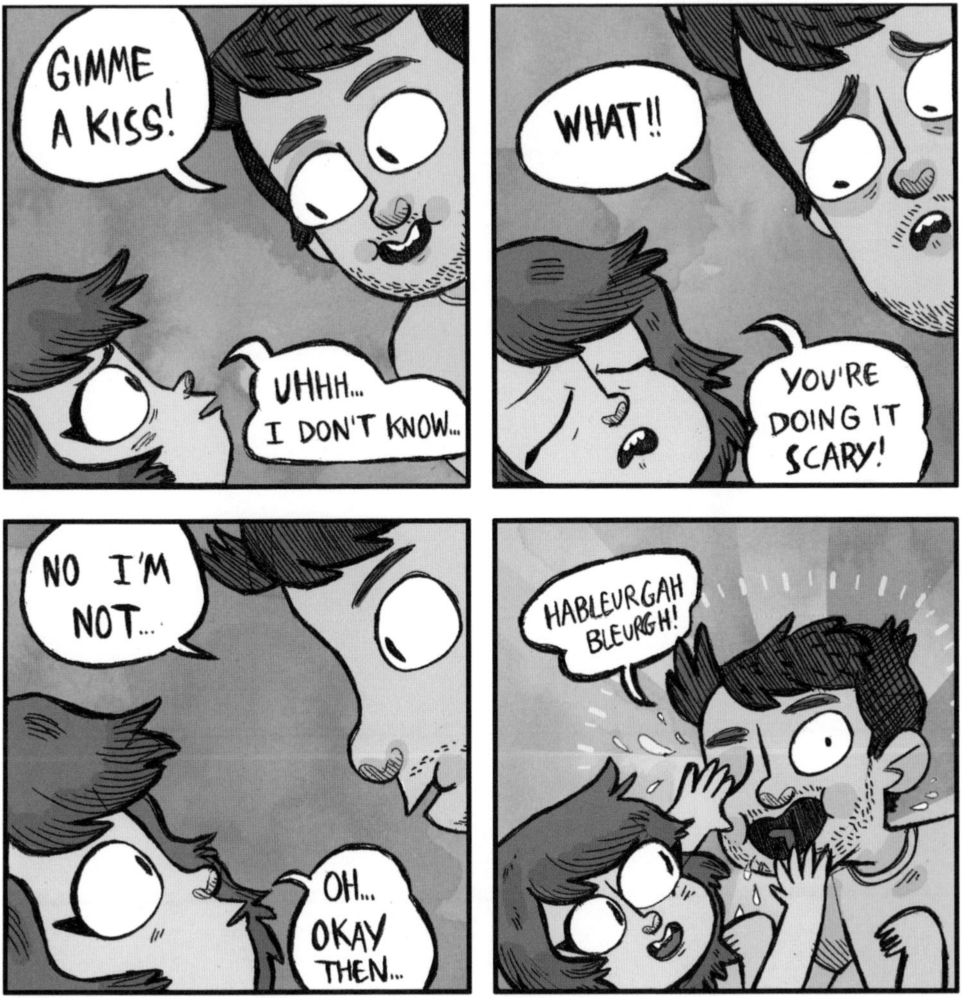
GIMME A KISS!
UHHH... I DON'T KNOW...
WHAT!!
YOU'RE DOING IT SCARY!
NO I'M NOT...
OH... OKAY THEN...
HABLEURGAH BLEURGH!

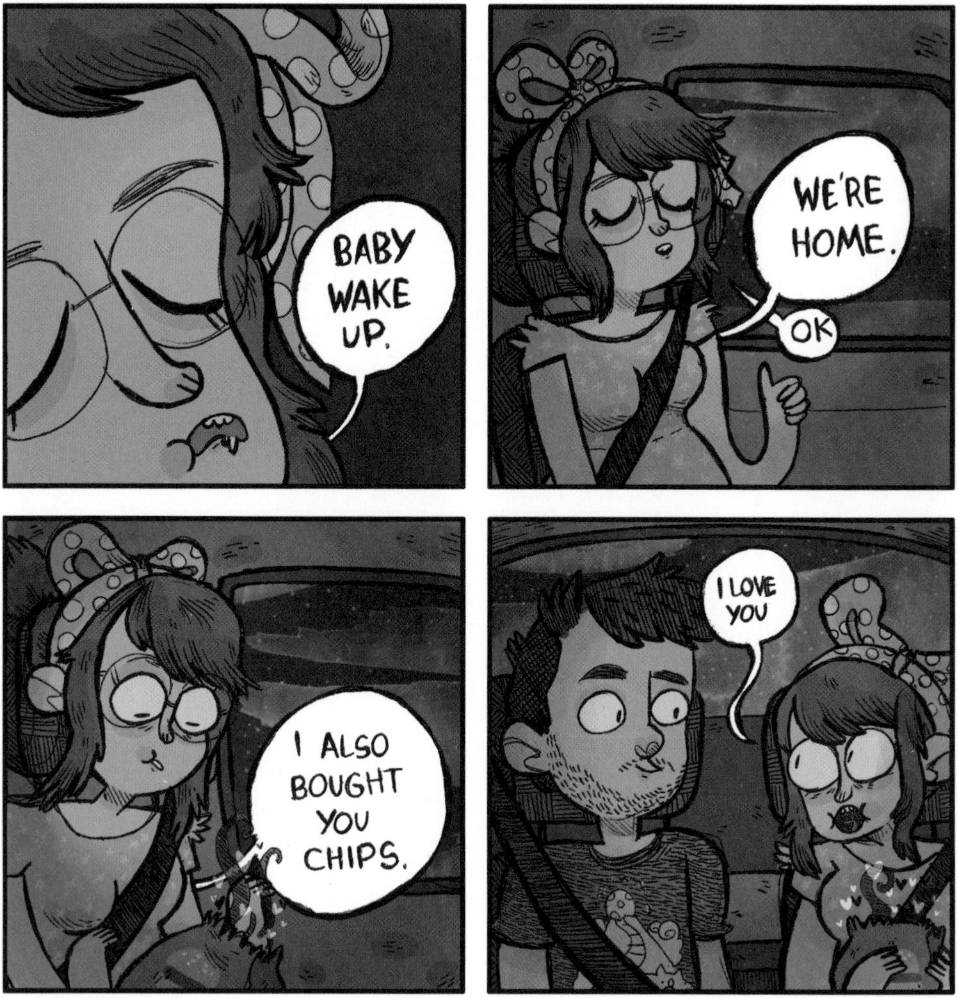
BABY WAKE UP.
WE'RE HOME.
OK
I ALSO BOUGHT YOU CHIPS.
I LOVE YOU

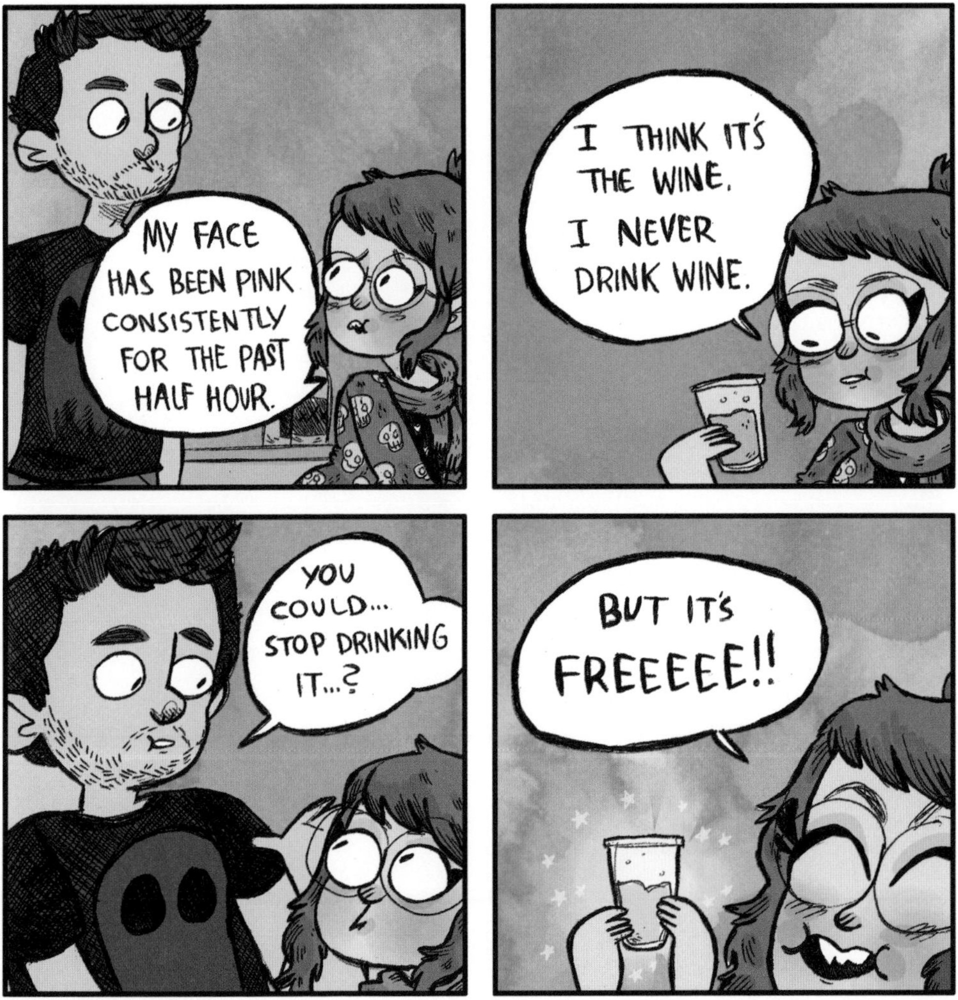
MY FACE HAS BEEN PINK CONSISTENTLY FOR THE PAST HALF HOUR.
I THINK IT'S THE WINE. I NEVER DRINK WINE.
YOU COULD... STOP DRINKING IT...?
BUT IT'S FREEEEE!!

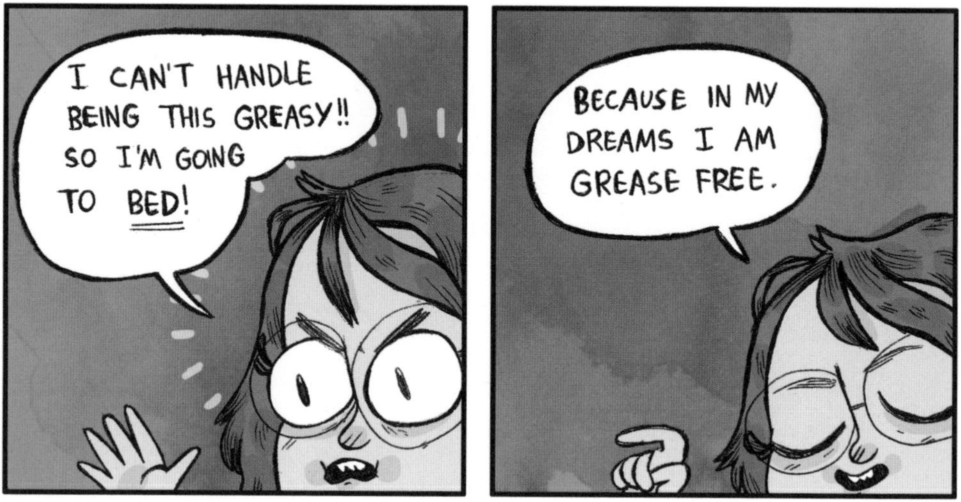
I CAN'T HANDLE BEING THIS GREASY!! SO I'M GOING TO BED!
BECAUSE IN MY DREAMS I AM GREASE FREE.

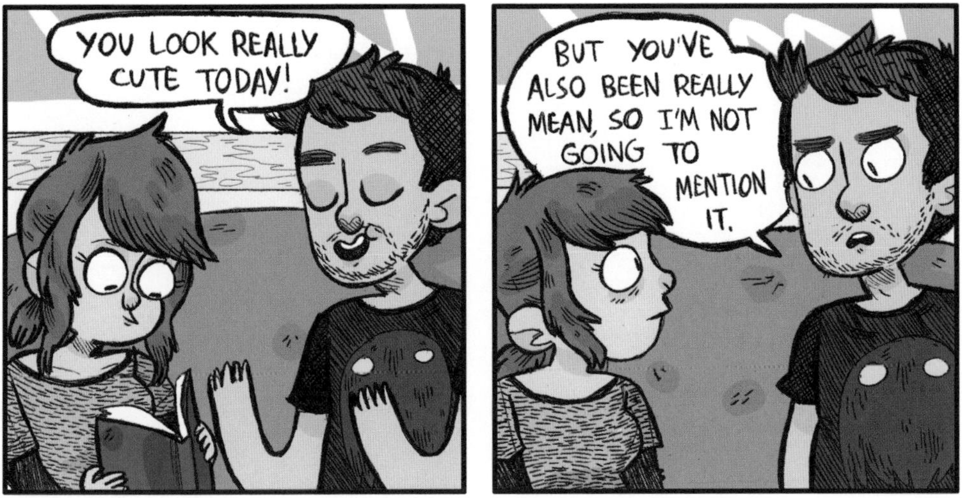
YOU LOOK REALLY CUTE TODAY!
BUT YOU'VE ALSO BEEN REALLY MEAN, SO I'M NOT GOING TO MENTION IT.

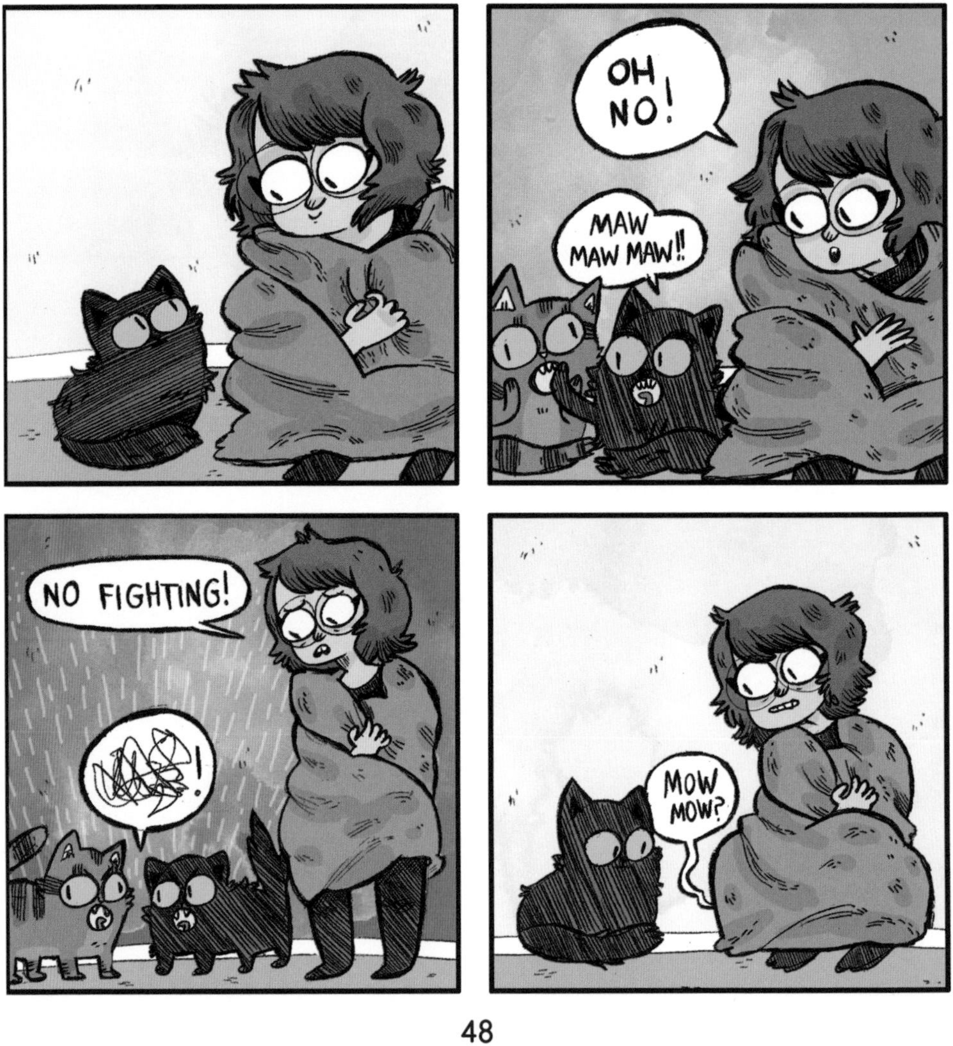
OH NO!
MAW MAW MAW!!
NO FIGHTING!
!
MOW MOW?

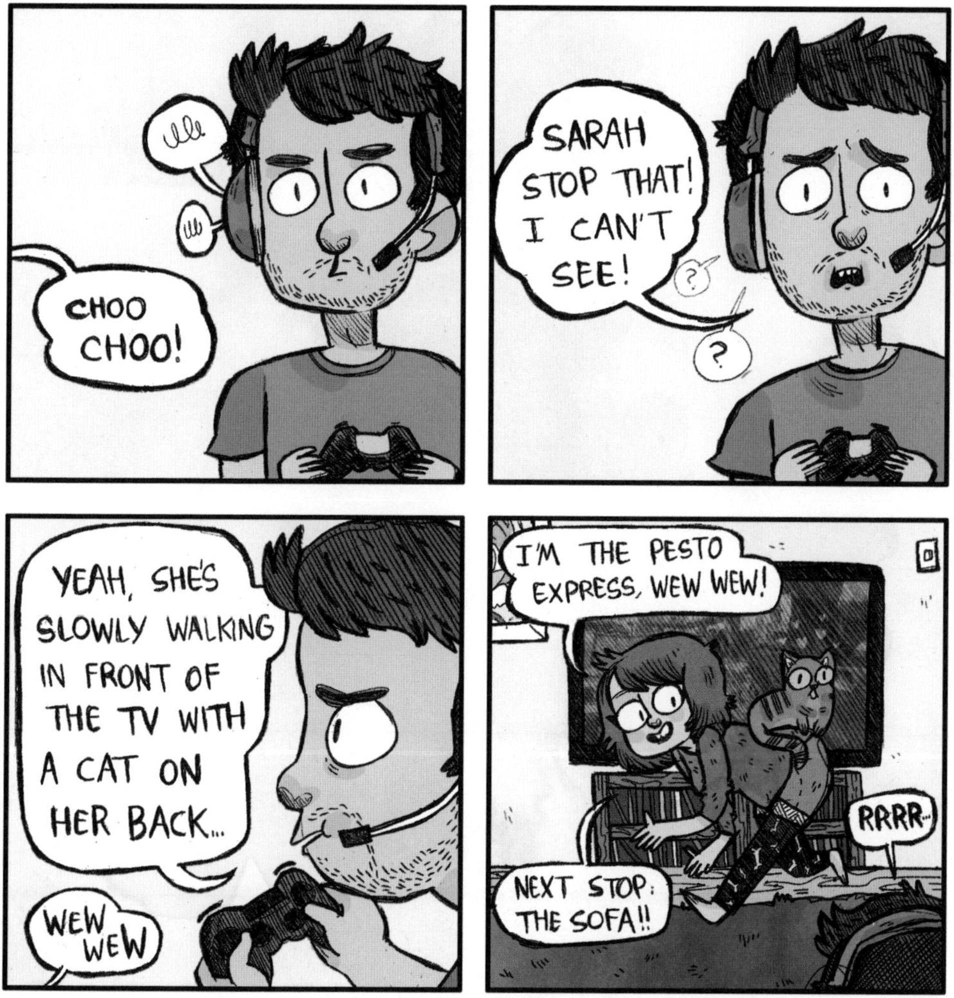
CHOO CHOO!
SARAH STOP THAT! I CAN'T SEE!
?
?
YEAH, SHE'S SLOWLY WALKING IN FRONT OF THE TV WITH A CAT ON HER BACK...
WEW WEW
I'M THE PESTO EXPRESS, WEW WEW!
RRRR...
NEXT STOP: THE SOFA!!

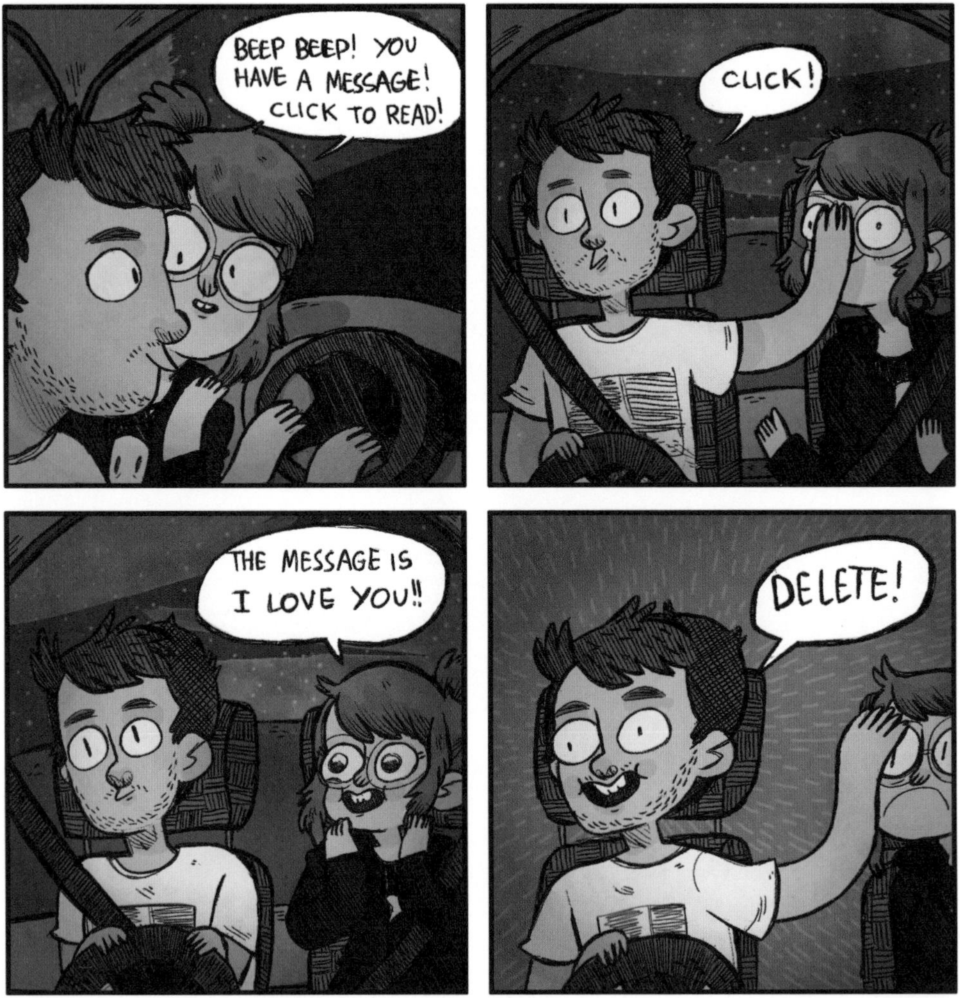
BEEP BEEP! YOU HAVE A MESSAGE! CLICK TO READ!
CLICK!
THE MESSAGE IS I LOVE YOU!!
DELETE!

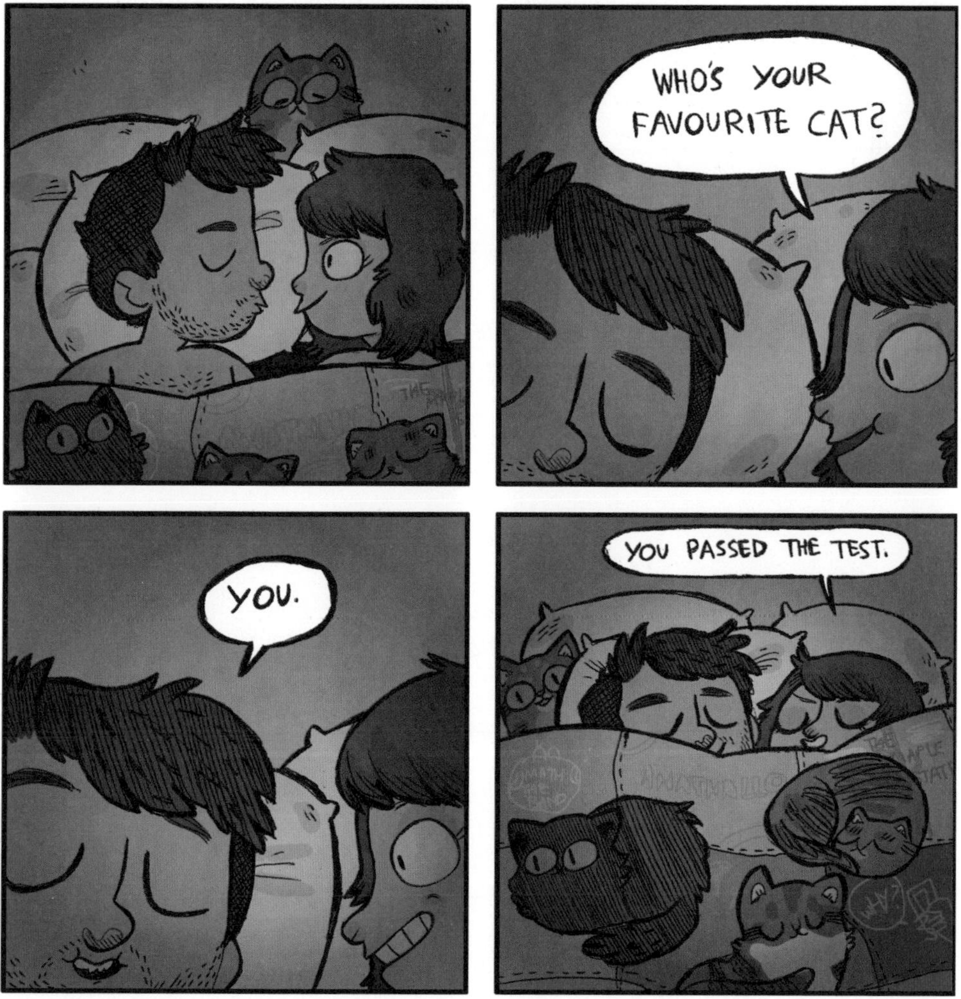
WHO'S YOUR FAVOURITE CAT?
YOU.
YOU PASSED THE TEST.

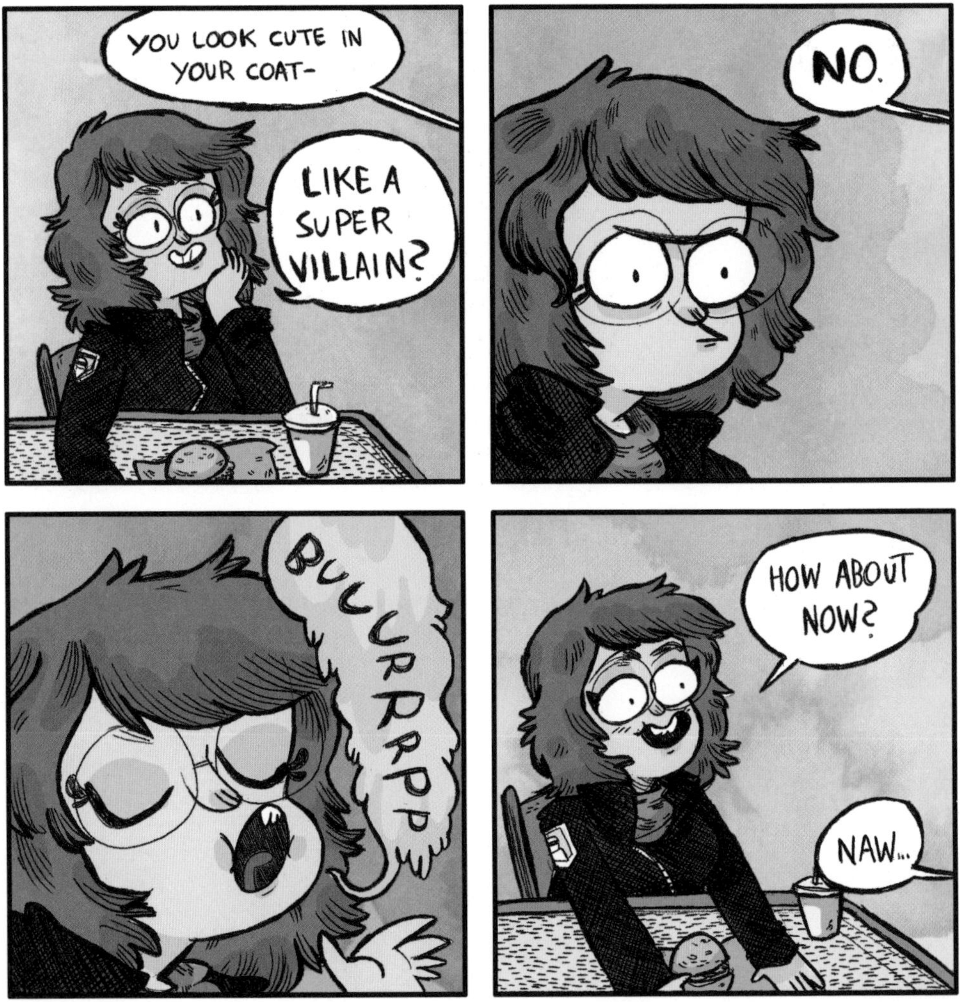
YOU LOOK CUTE IN YOUR COAT-
LIKE A SUPER VILLAIN?
NO.
BUUURRRPP
HOW ABOUT NOW?
NAW...

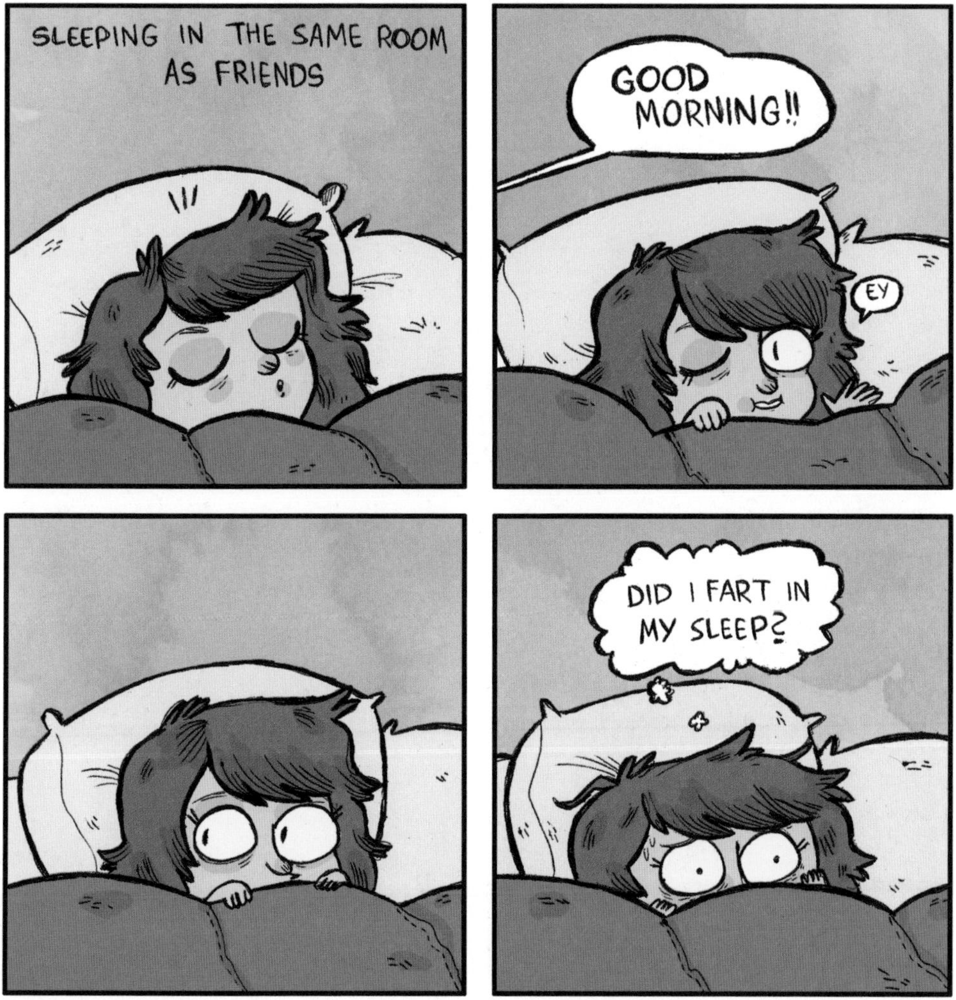
SLEEPING IN THE SAME ROOM AS FRIENDS
GOOD MORNING!!
EY
DID I FART IN MY SLEEP?

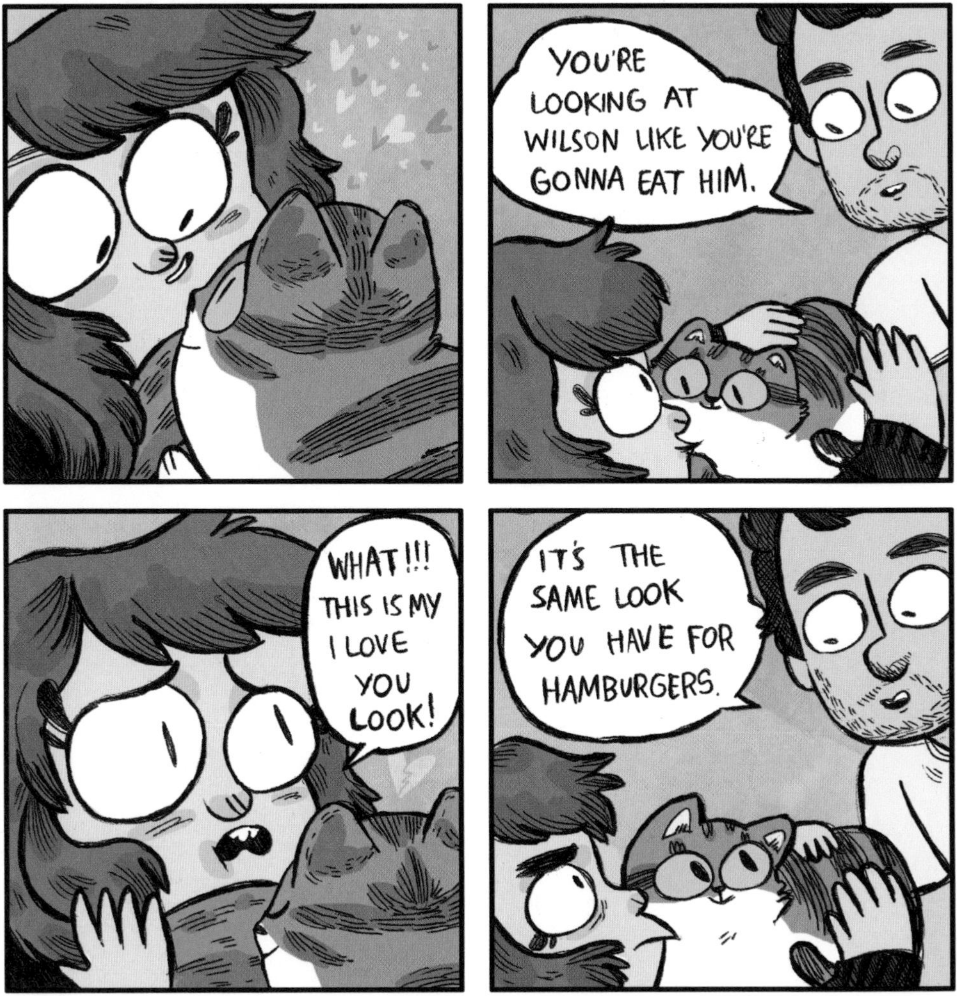
YOU'RE LOOKING AT WILSON LIKE YOU'RE GONNA EAT HIM.
WHAT!!! THIS IS MY I LOVE YOU LOOK!
IT'S THE SAME LOOK YOU HAVE FOR HAMBURGERS.

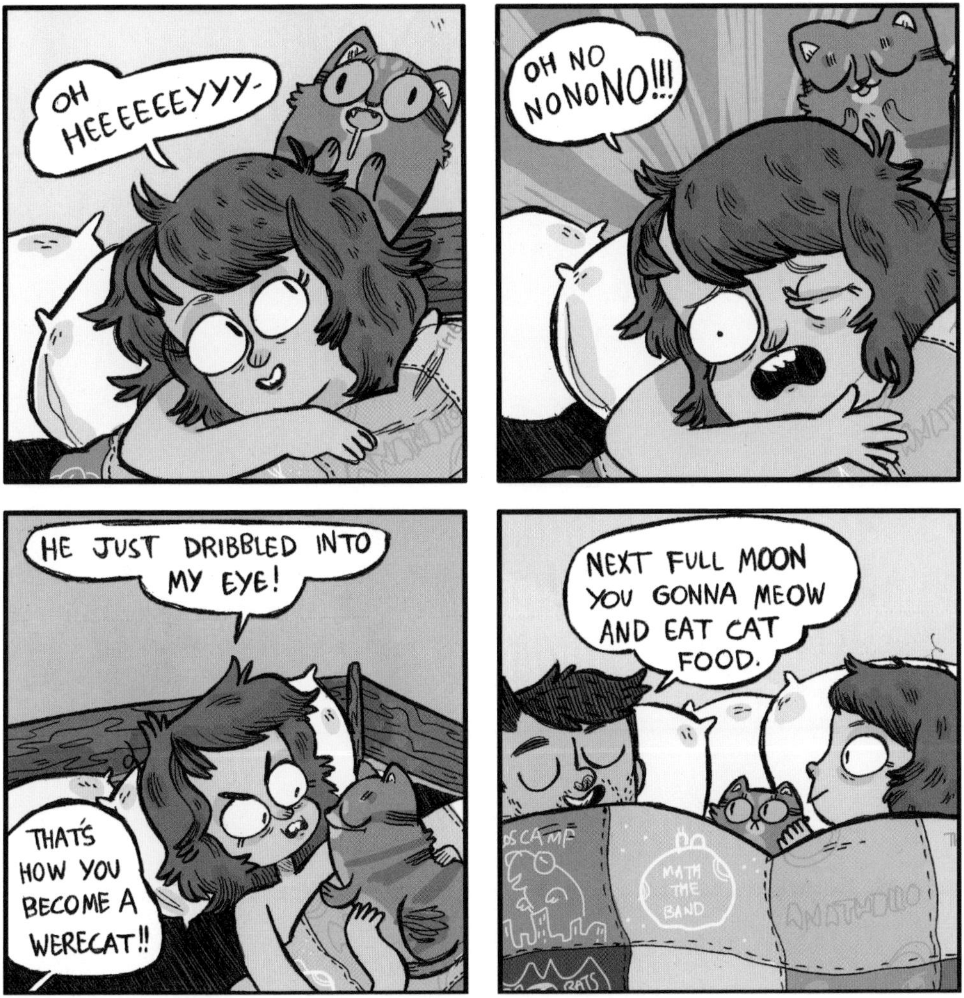
OH HEEEEEEYYY-
OH NO NONONO!!!
HE JUST DRIBBLED INTO MY EYE!
THAT'S HOW YOU BECOME A WERECAT!!
NEXT FULL MOON YOU GONNA MEOW AND EAT CAT FOOD.
MATH THE BAND

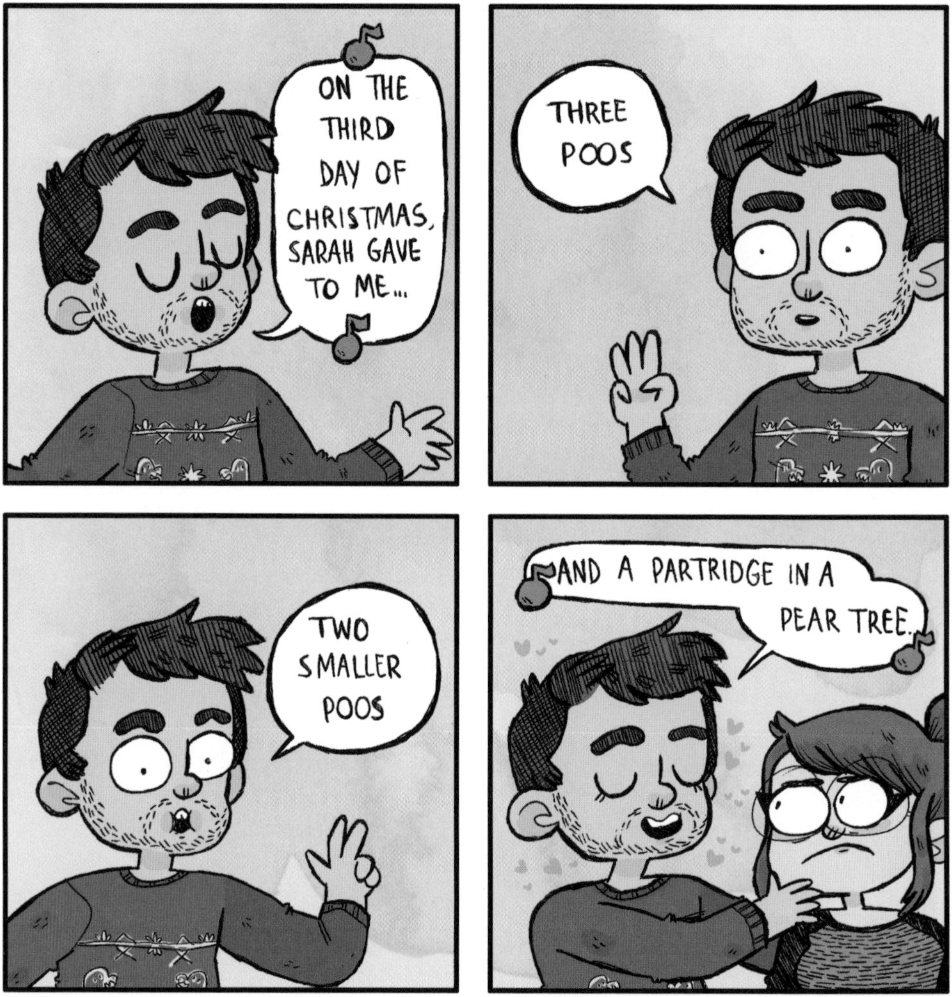
ON THE THIRD DAY OF CHRISTMAS, SARAH GAVE TO ME...
THREE POOS
TWO SMALLER POOS
AND A PARTRIDGE IN A PEAR TREE.

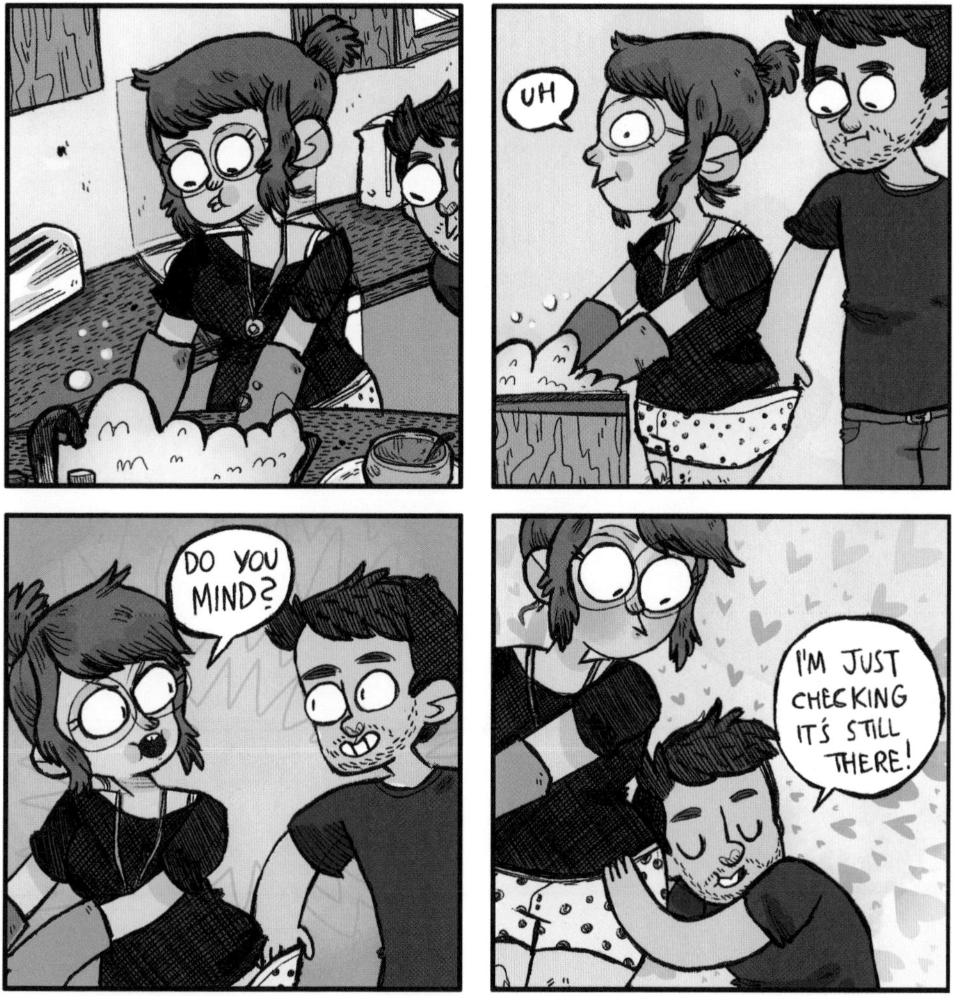
UH
DO YOU MIND?
I'M JUST CHECKING IT'S STILL THERE!

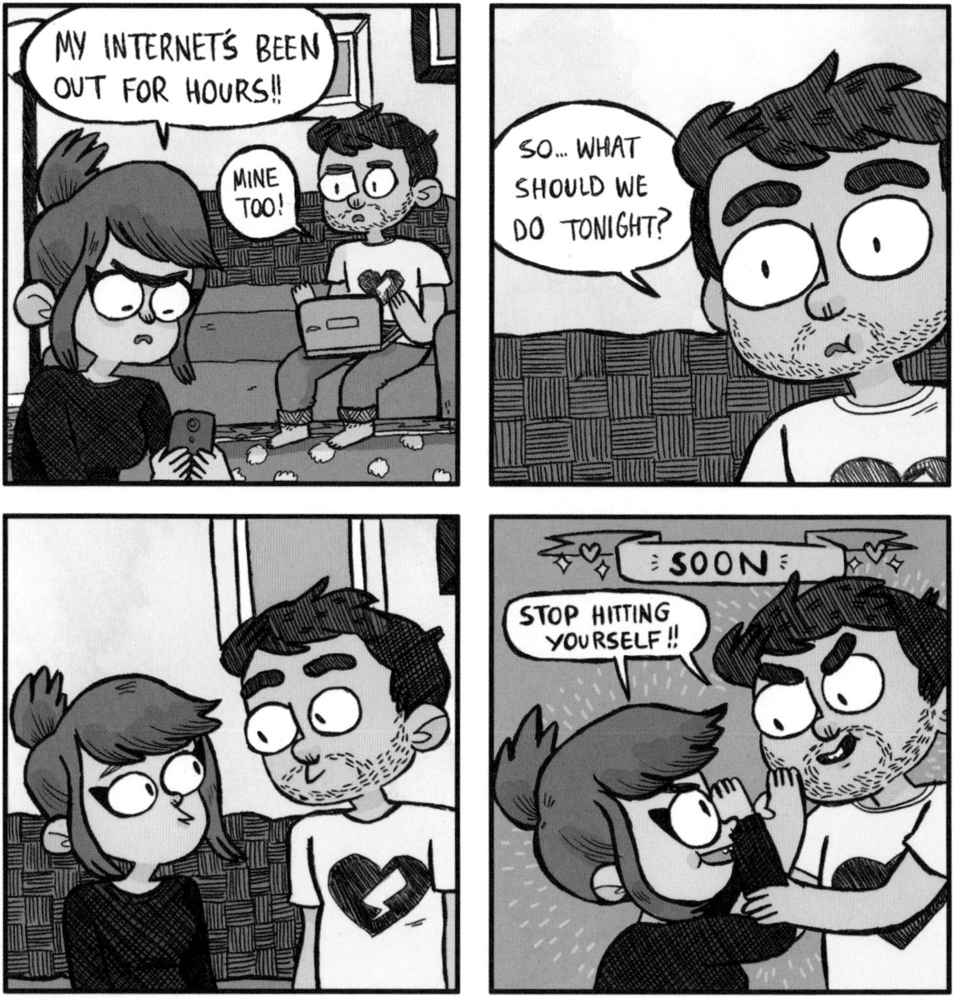
MY INTERNET'S BEEN OUT FOR HOURS!!
MINE TOO!
SO... WHAT SHOULD WE DO TONIGHT?
SOON
STOP HITTING YOURSELF!!

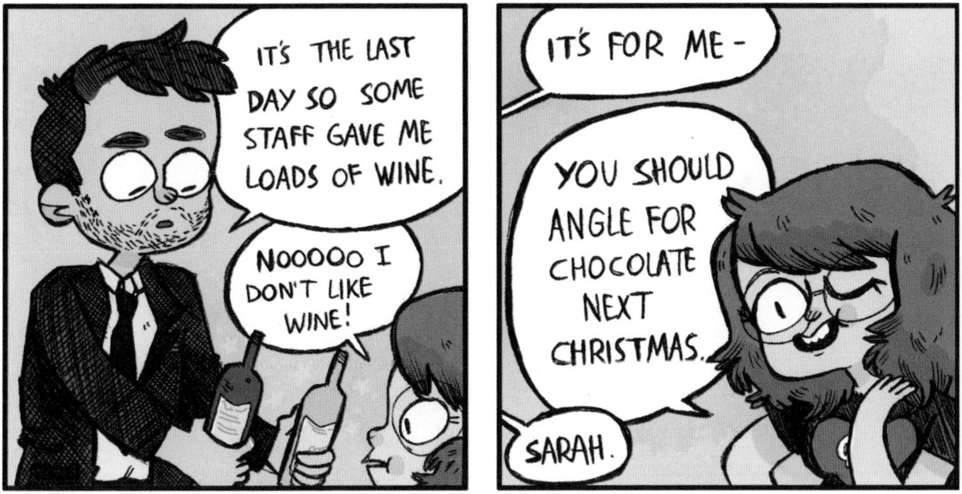
IT'S THE LAST DAY SO SOME STAFF GAVE ME LOADS OF WINE.
NOOOOO I DON'T LIKE WINE!
IT'S FOR ME -
YOU SHOULD ANGLE FOR CHOCOLATE NEXT CHRISTMAS.
SARAH.

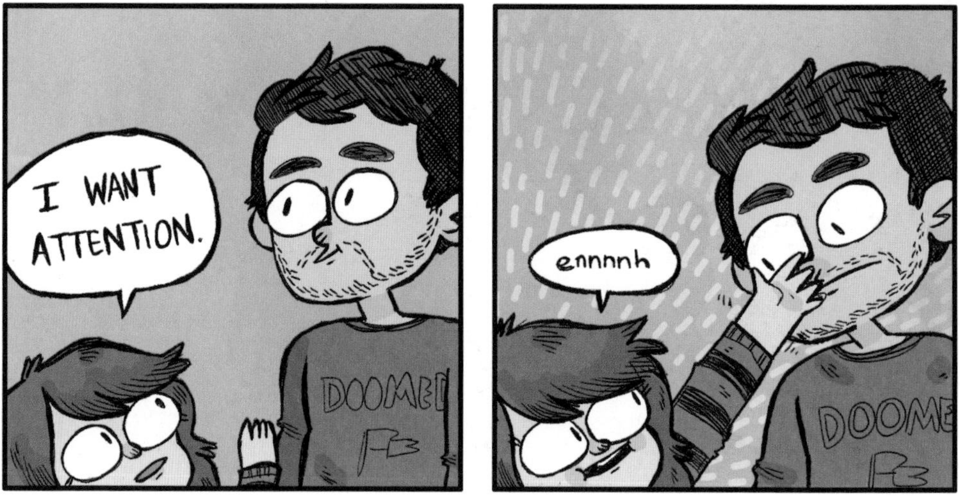
I WANT ATTENTION.
DOOMED
ennnnh
DOOME

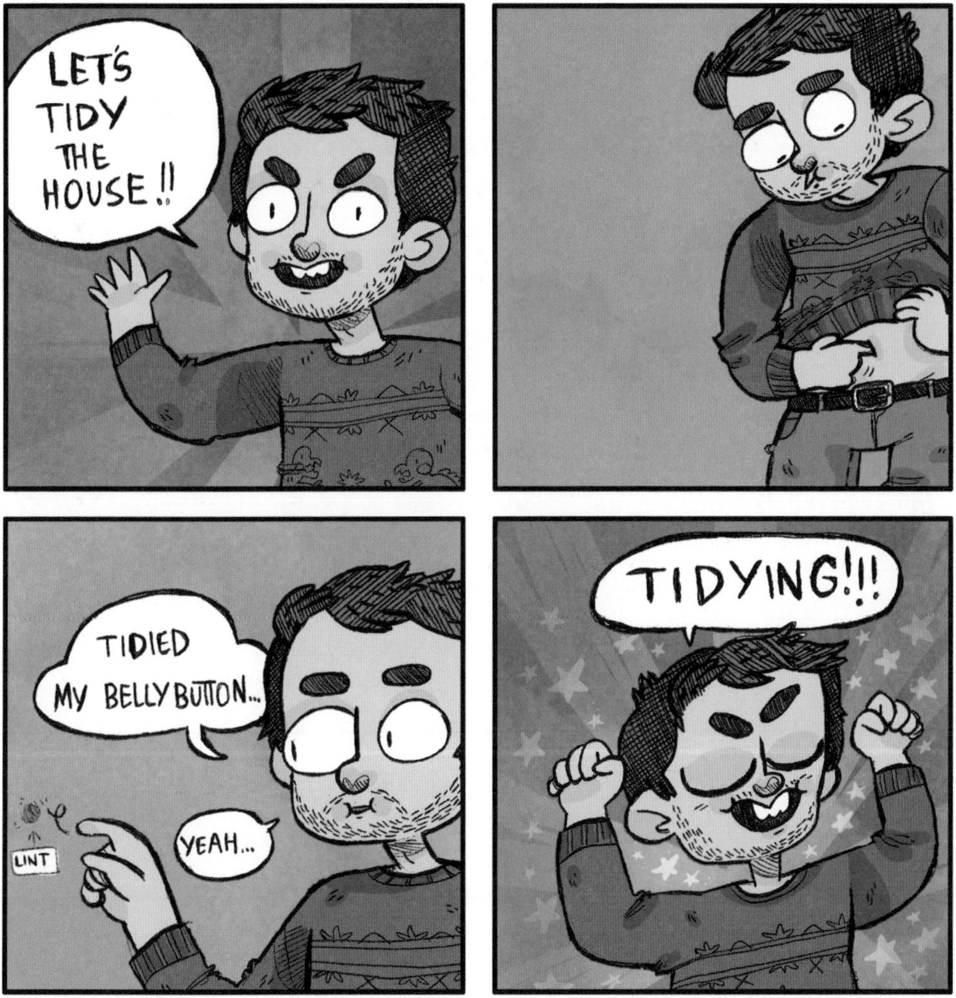
LET'S TIDY THE HOUSE!!
TIDIED MY BELLYBUTTON...
LINT
YEAH...
TIDYING!!!

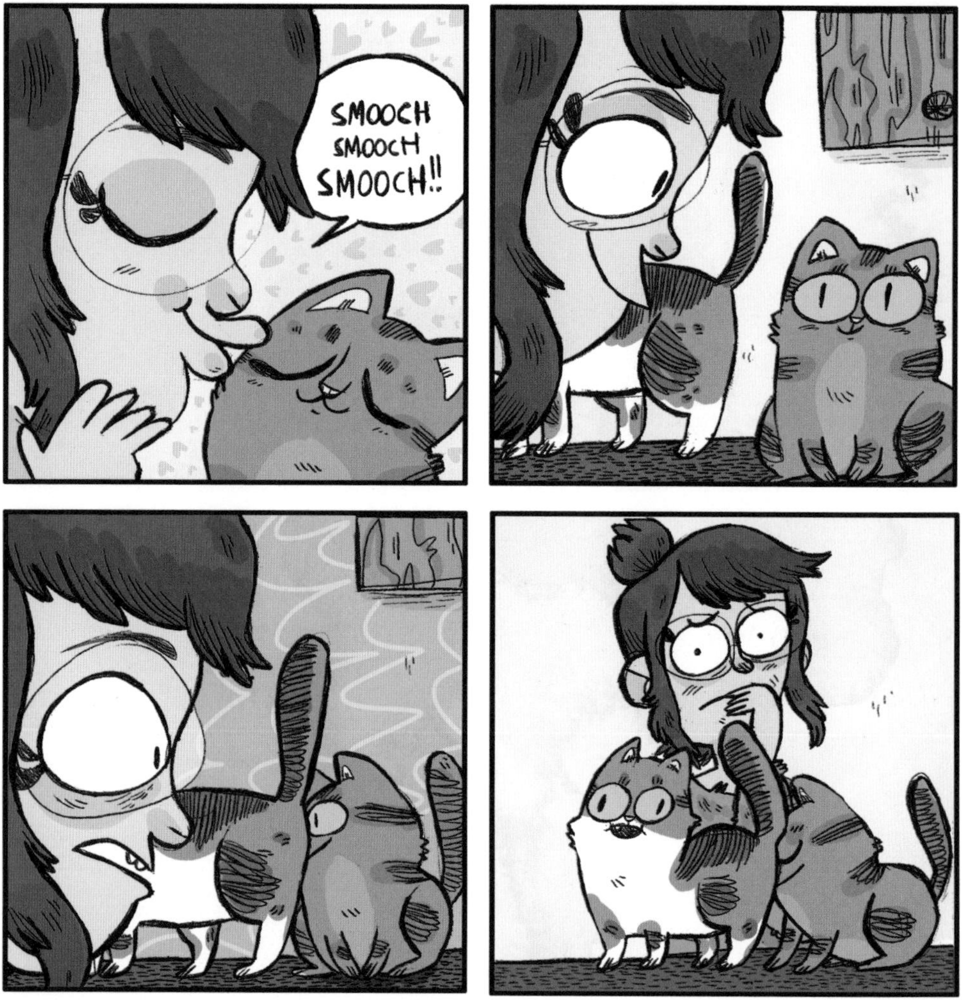
SMOOCH
SMOOCH
SMOOCH!!

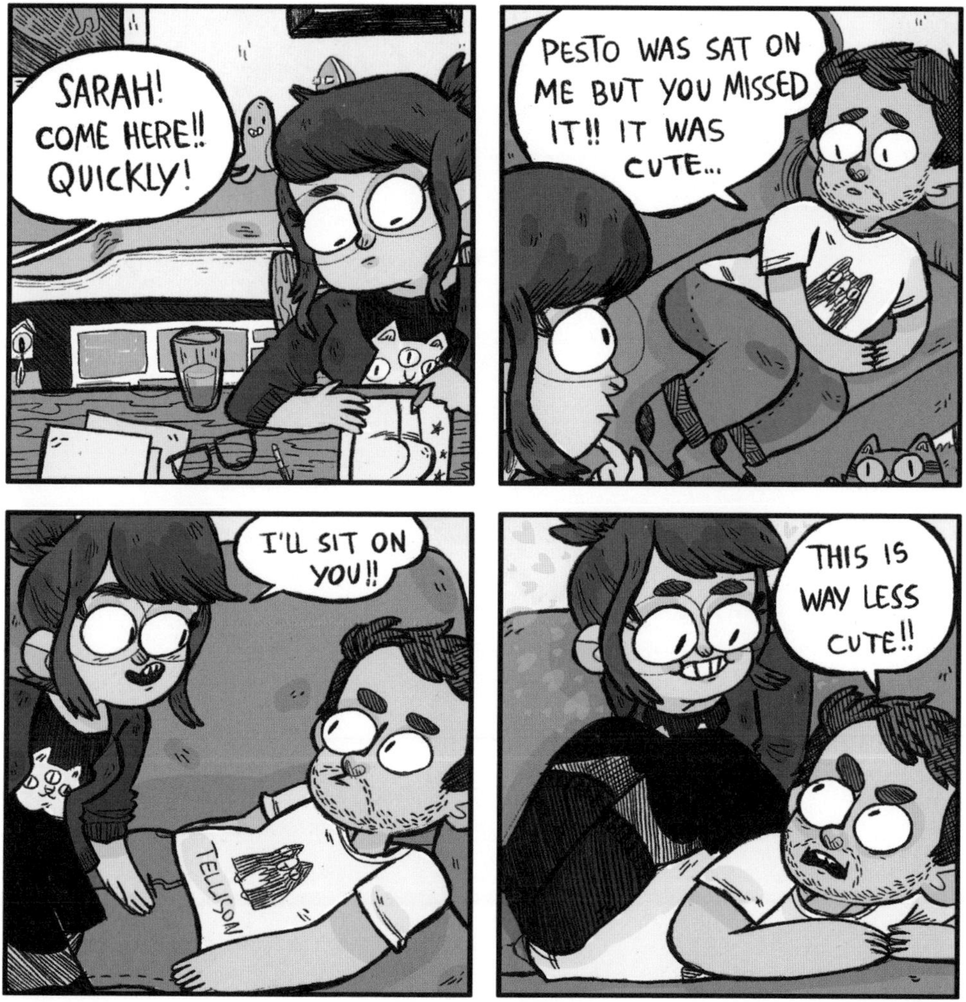
SARAH! COME HERE!! QUICKLY!
PESTO WAS SAT ON ME BUT YOU MISSED IT!! IT WAS CUTE...
I'LL SIT ON YOU!!
TELLISON
THIS IS WAY LESS CUTE!!

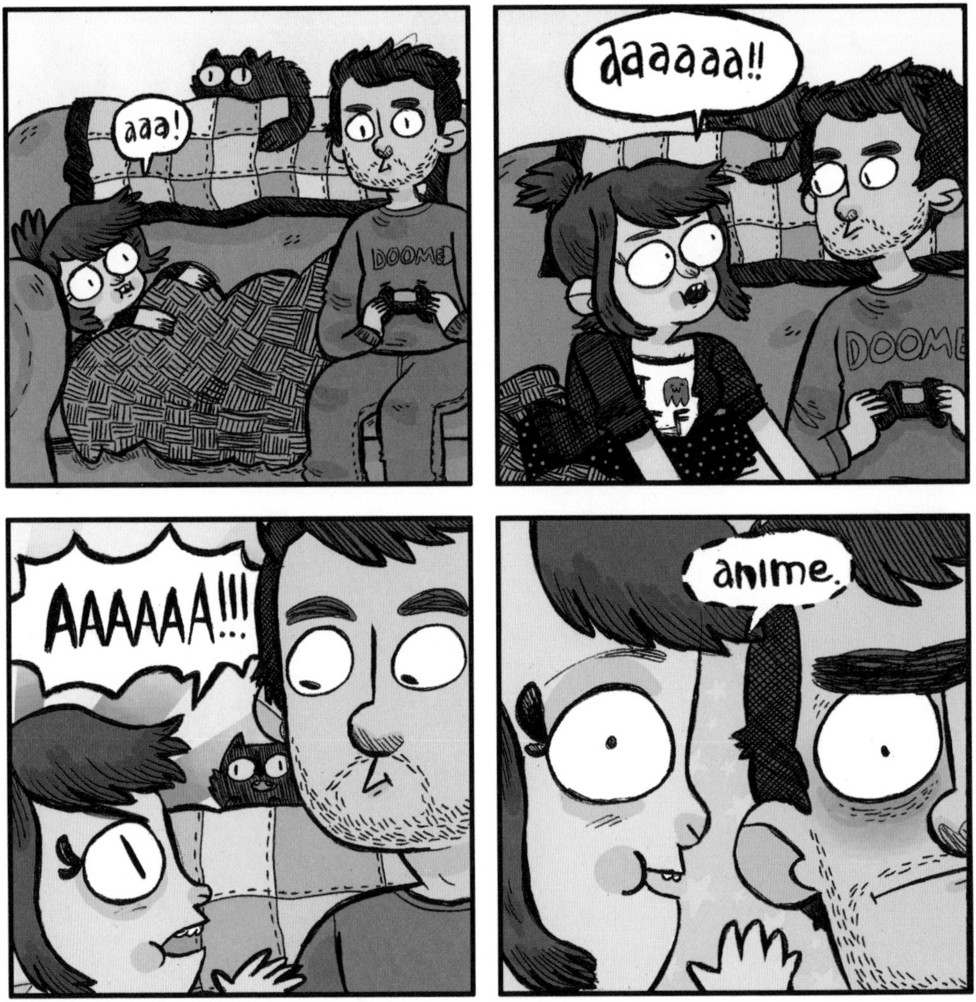
aaa!
aaaaaa!!
AAAAAA!!!
anime.

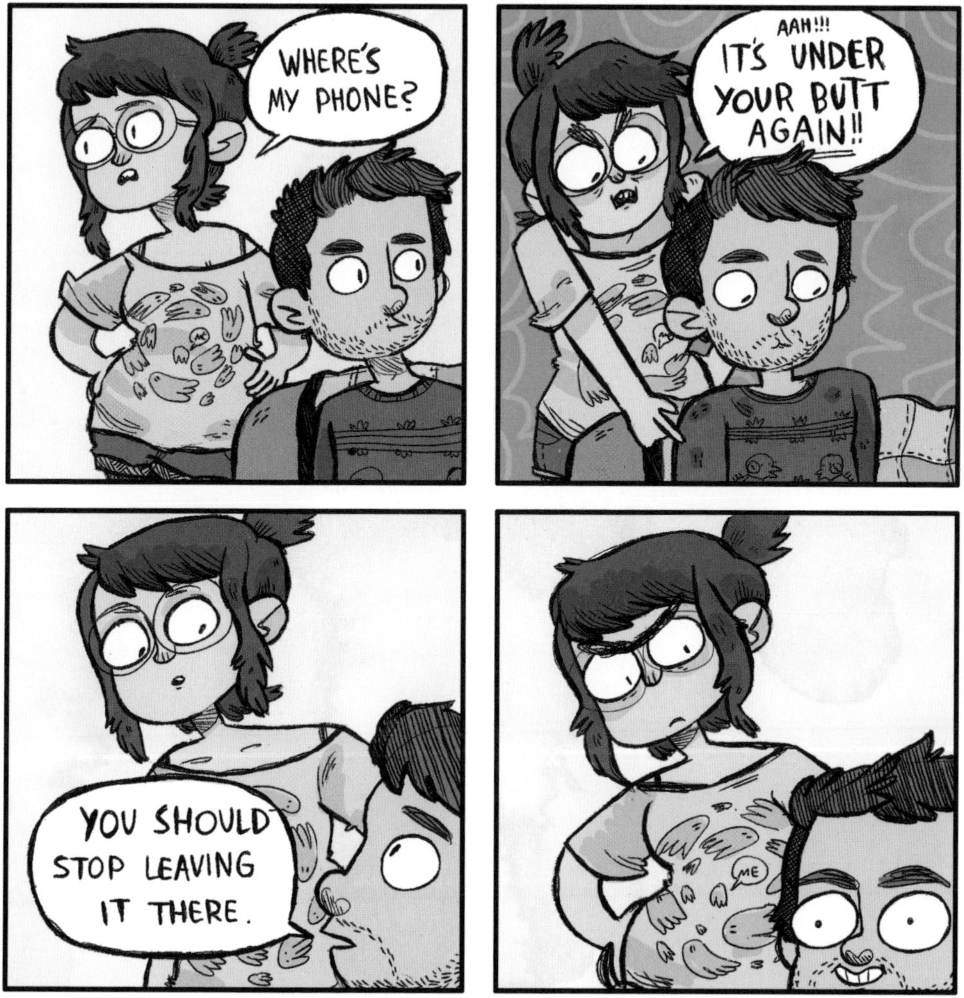
WHERE'S MY PHONE?
AAH!!! IT'S UNDER YOUR BUTT AGAIN!!
YOU SHOULD STOP LEAVING IT THERE.
ME
ME

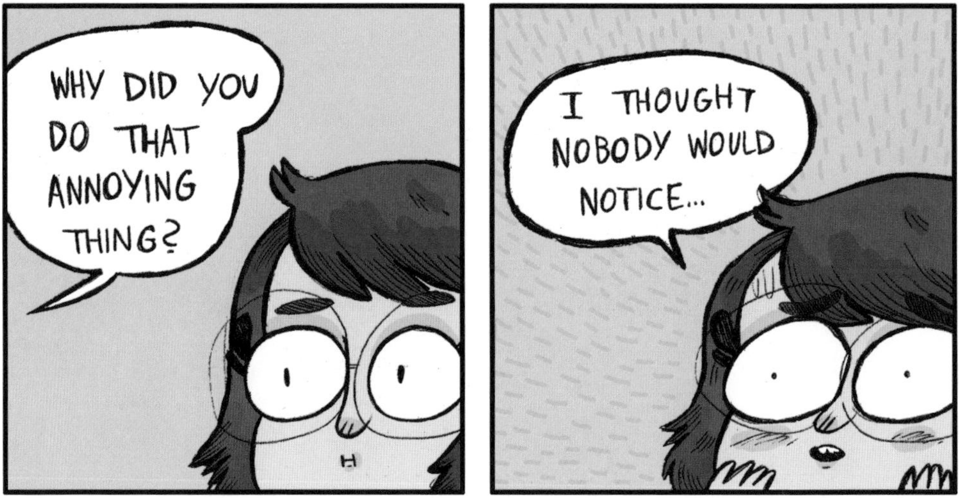
WHY DID YOU DO THAT ANNOYING THING?
I THOUGHT NOBODY WOULD NOTICE...

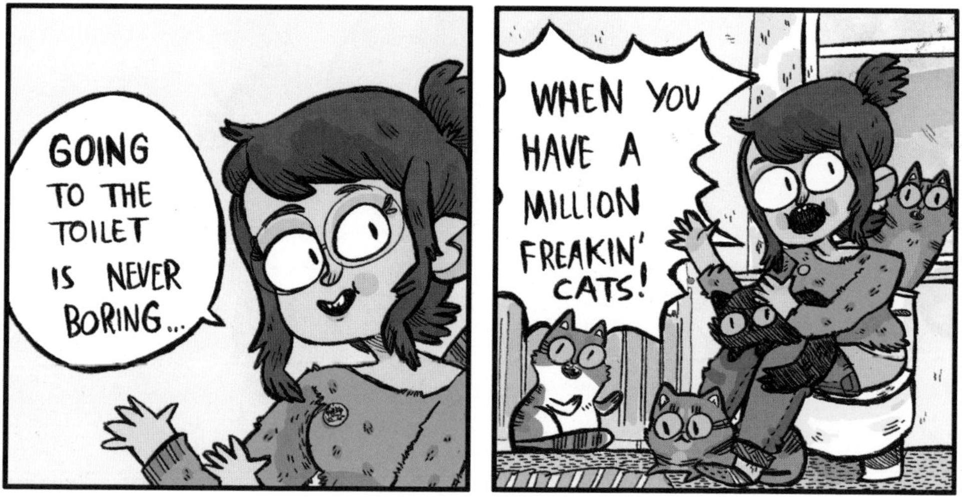
GOING TO THE TOILET IS NEVER BORING...
WHEN YOU HAVE A MILLION FREAKIN' CATS!

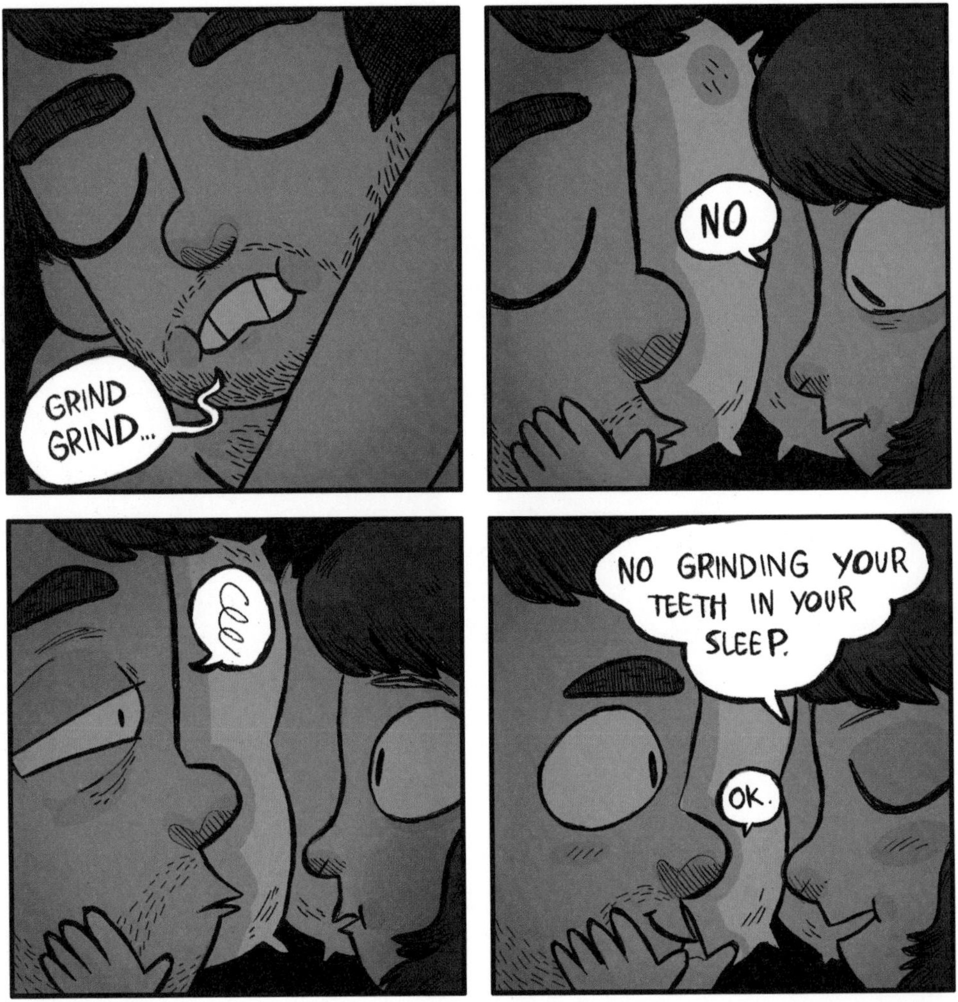
GRIND
GRIND...
NO
NO GRINDING YOUR TEETH IN YOUR SLEEP.
OK.

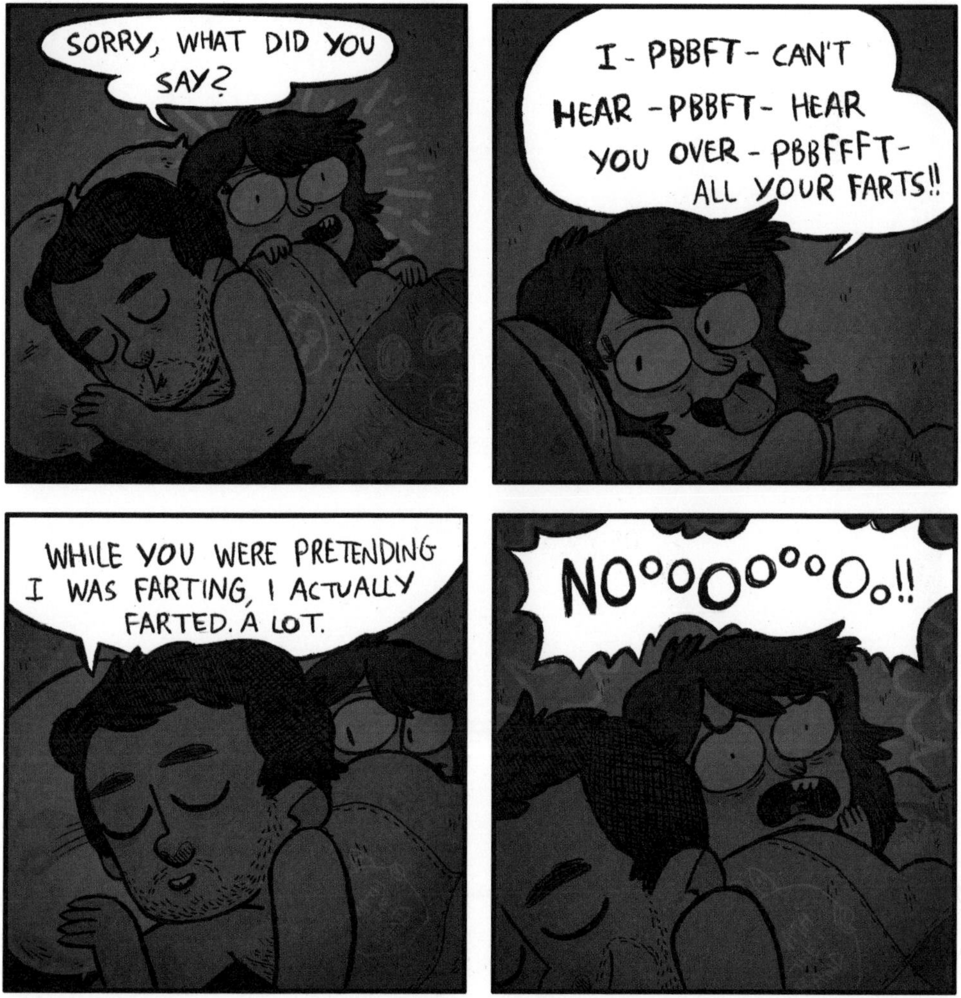
SORRY, WHAT DID YOU SAY?
I- PBBFT- CAN'T HEAR -PBBFT- HEAR YOU OVER - PBBFFFT- ALL YOUR FARTS!!
WHILE YOU WERE PRETENDING I WAS FARTING, I ACTUALLY FARTED. A LOT.
NOoooOoooOo!!

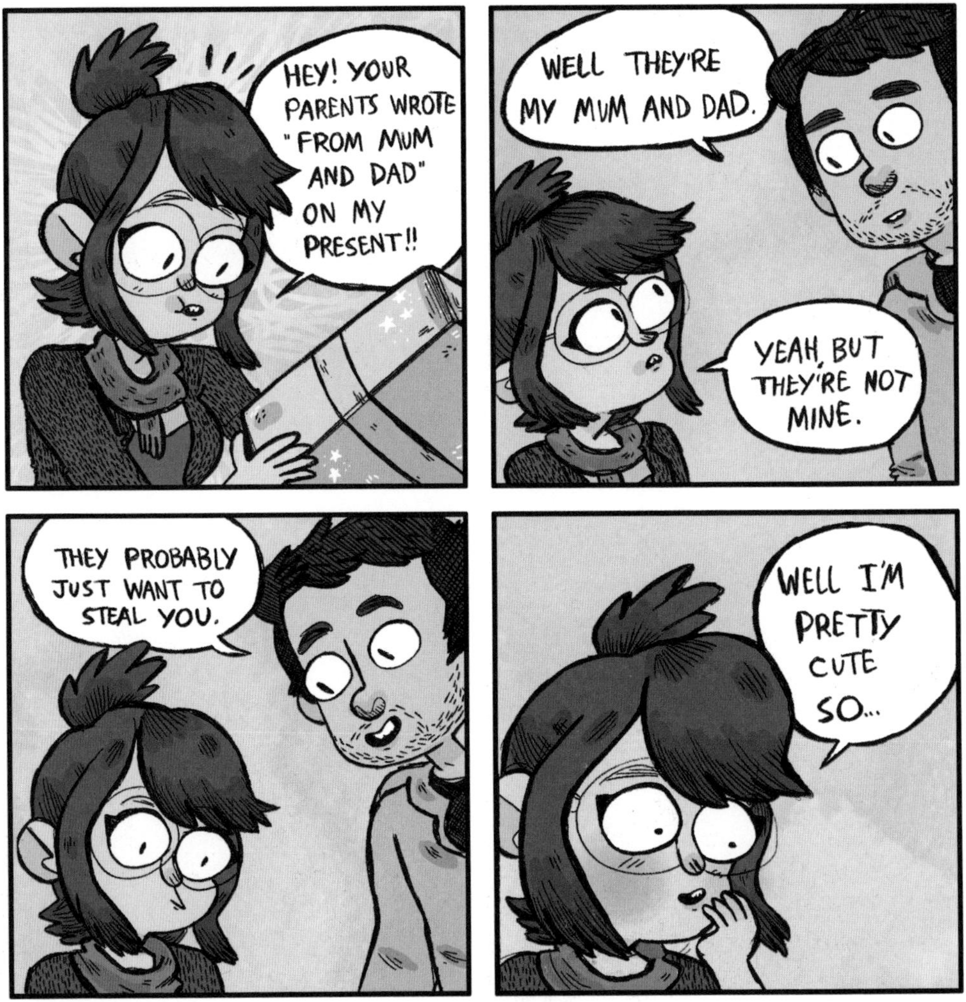
HEY! YOUR PARENTS WROTE "FROM MUM AND DAD" ON MY PRESENT!!
WELL THEY'RE MY MUM AND DAD.
YEAH, BUT THEY'RE NOT MINE.
THEY PROBABLY JUST WANT TO STEAL YOU.
WELL I'M PRETTY CUTE SO...

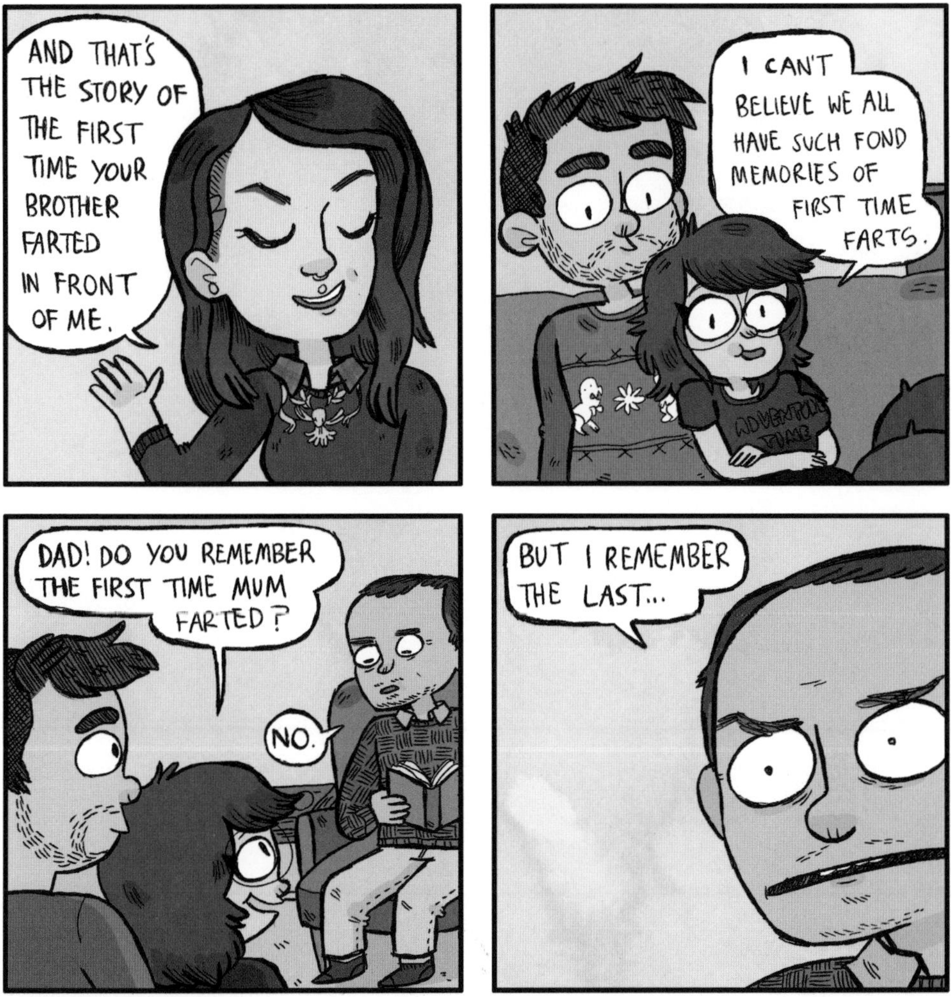
AND THAT'S THE STORY OF THE FIRST TIME YOUR BROTHER FARTED IN FRONT OF ME.
I CAN'T BELIEVE WE ALL HAVE SUCH FOND MEMORIES OF FIRST TIME FARTS.
DAD! DO YOU REMEMBER THE FIRST TIME MUM FARTED?
NO.
BUT I REMEMBER THE LAST...

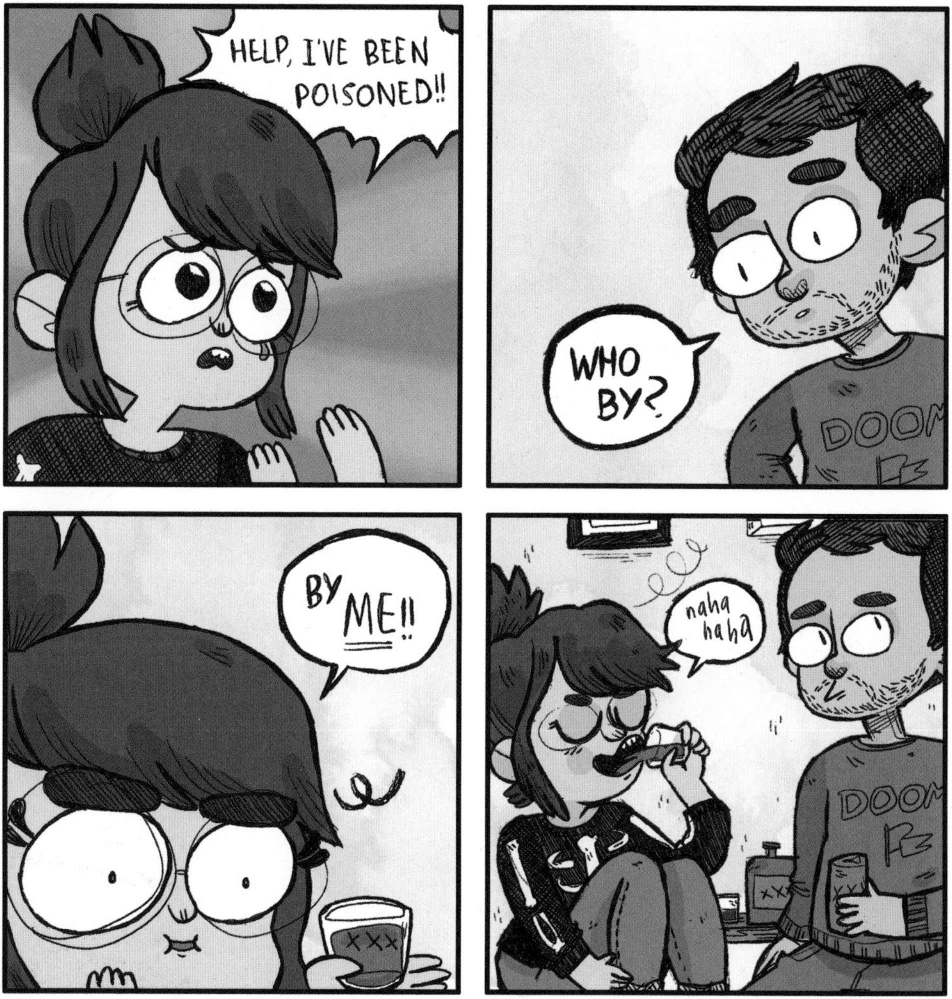
HELP, I'VE BEEN POISONED!!
WHO BY?
BY ME!!
naha haha

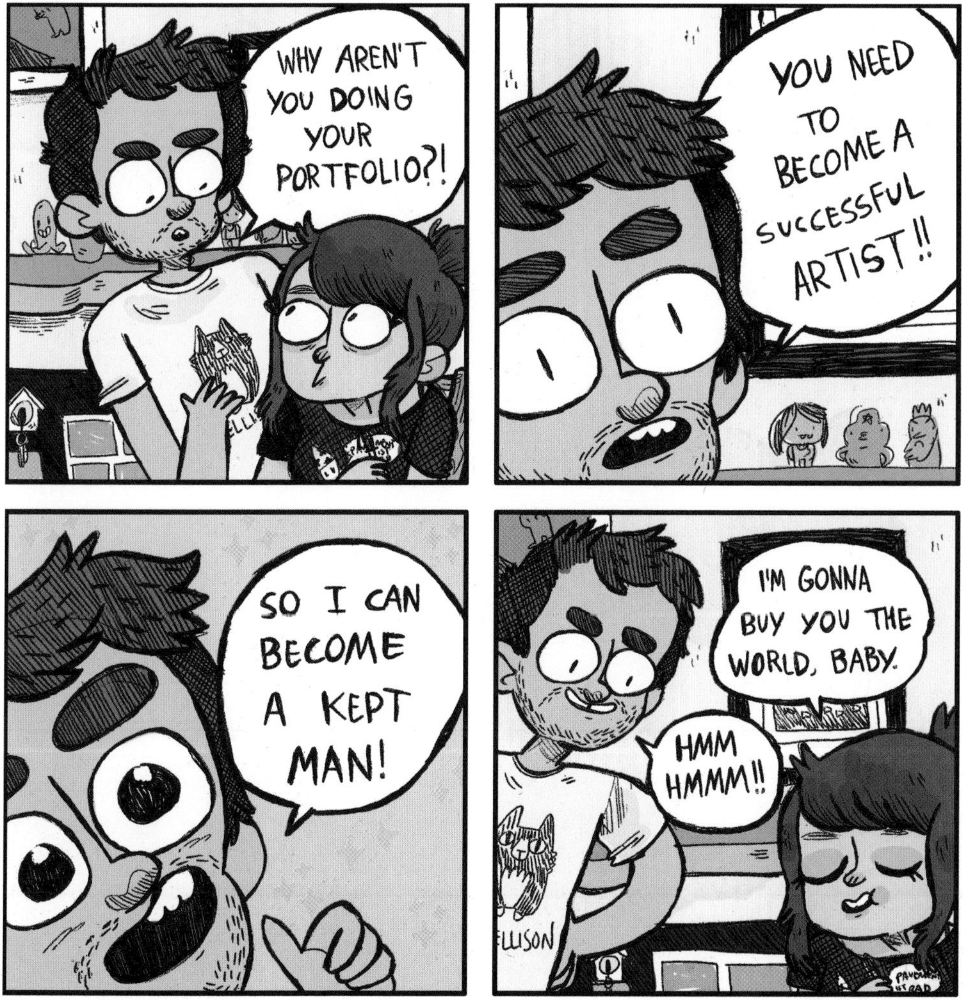
WHY AREN'T YOU DOING YOUR PORTFOLIO?!
YOU NEED TO BECOME A SUCCESSFUL ARTIST!!
SO I CAN BECOME A KEPT MAN!
I'M GONNA BUY YOU THE WORLD, BABY.
HMM HMMM!!

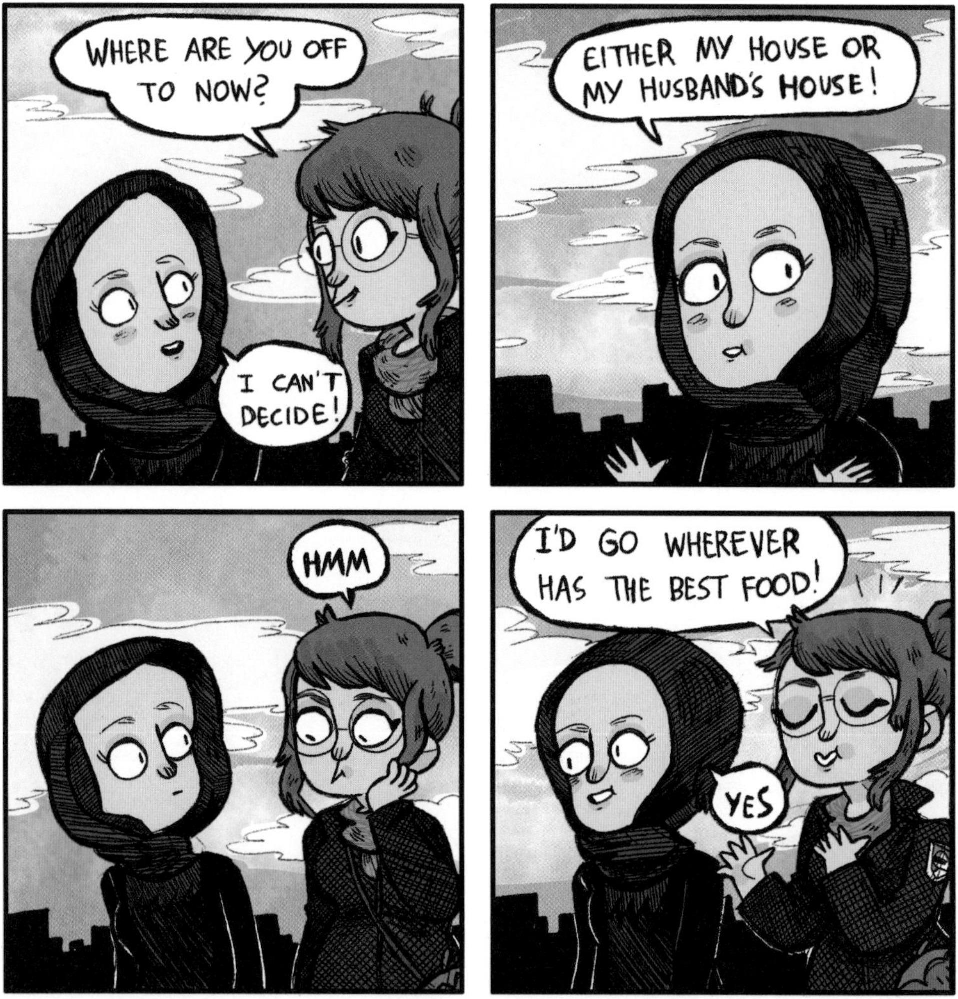
WHERE ARE YOU OFF TO NOW?
I CAN'T DECIDE!
EITHER MY HOUSE OR MY HUSBAND'S HOUSE!
HMM
I'D GO WHEREVER HAS THE BEST FOOD!
YES

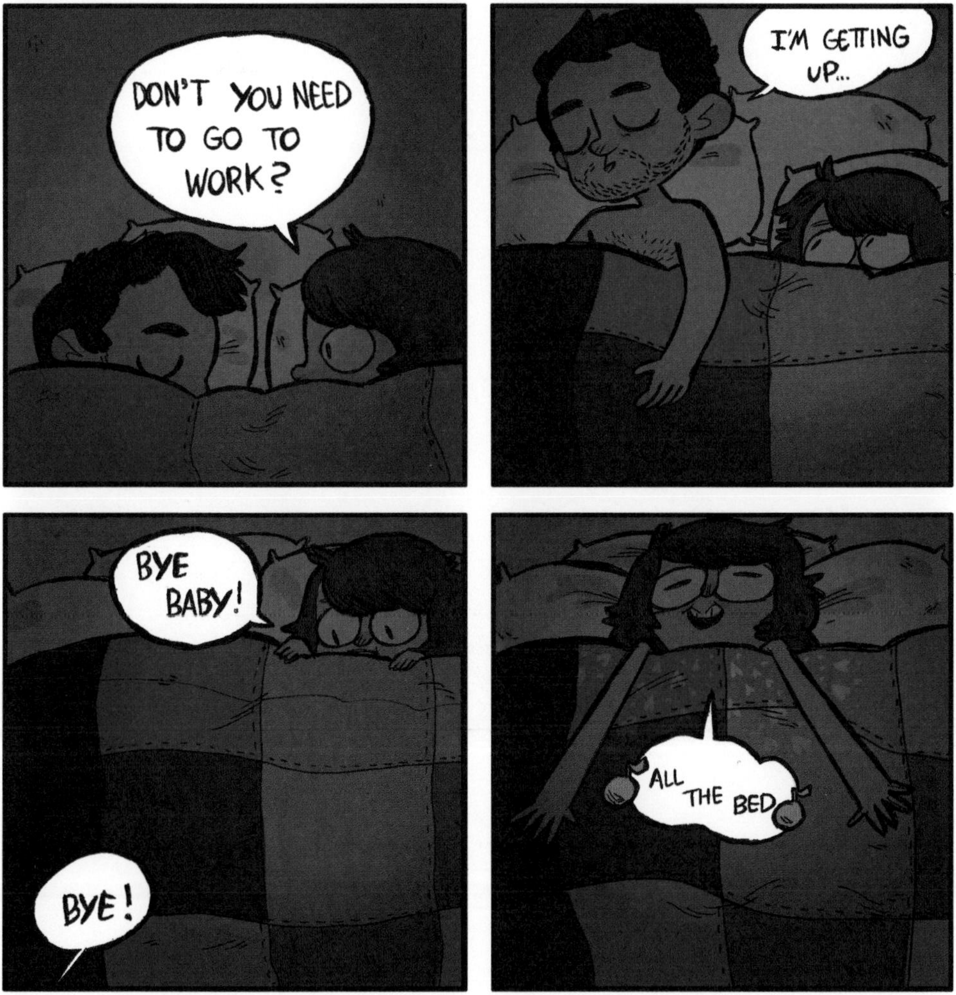
DON'T YOU NEED TO GO TO WORK?
I'M GETTING UP...
BYE BABY!
BYE!
ALL THE BED

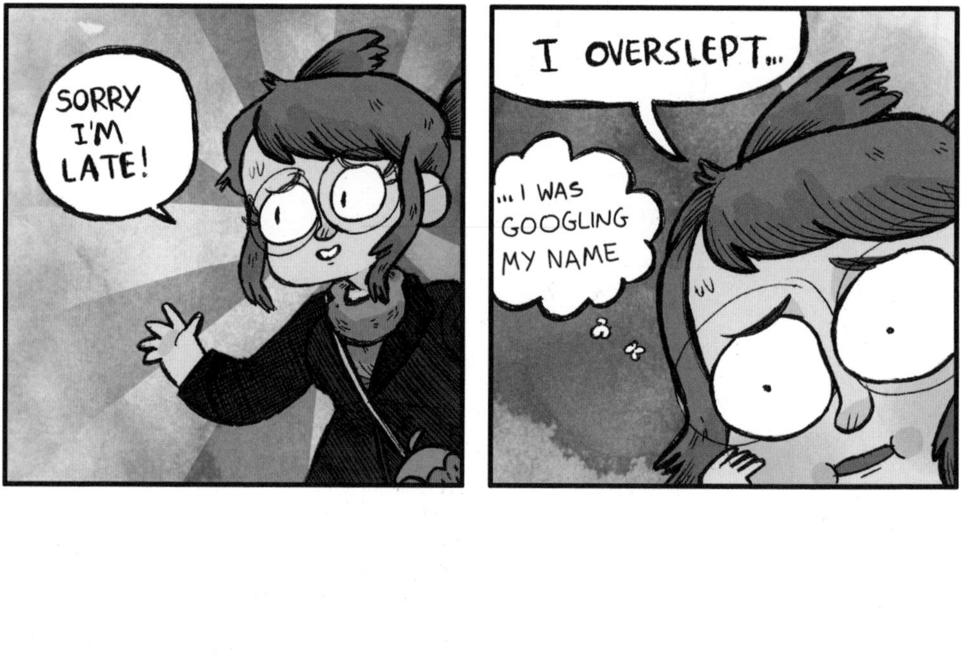
SORRY I'M LATE!
I OVERSLEPT...
...I WAS GOOGLING MY NAME

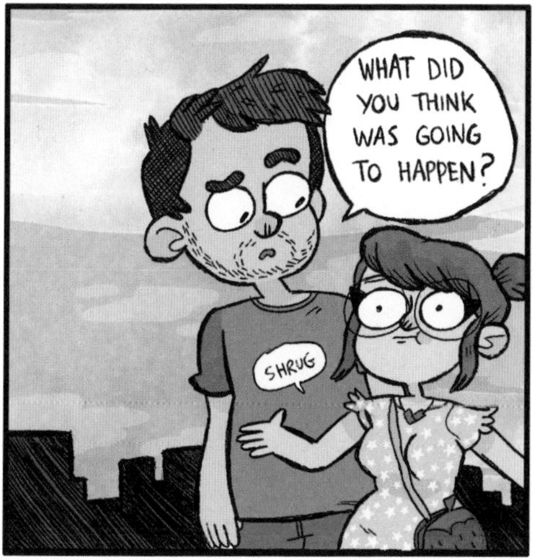
WHAT DID YOU THINK WAS GOING TO HAPPEN?
SHRUG

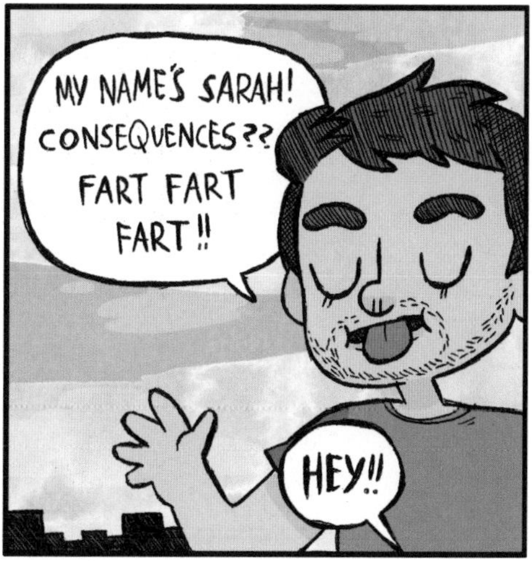
MY NAME'S SARAH! CONSEQUENCES?? FART FART FART!!
HEY!!

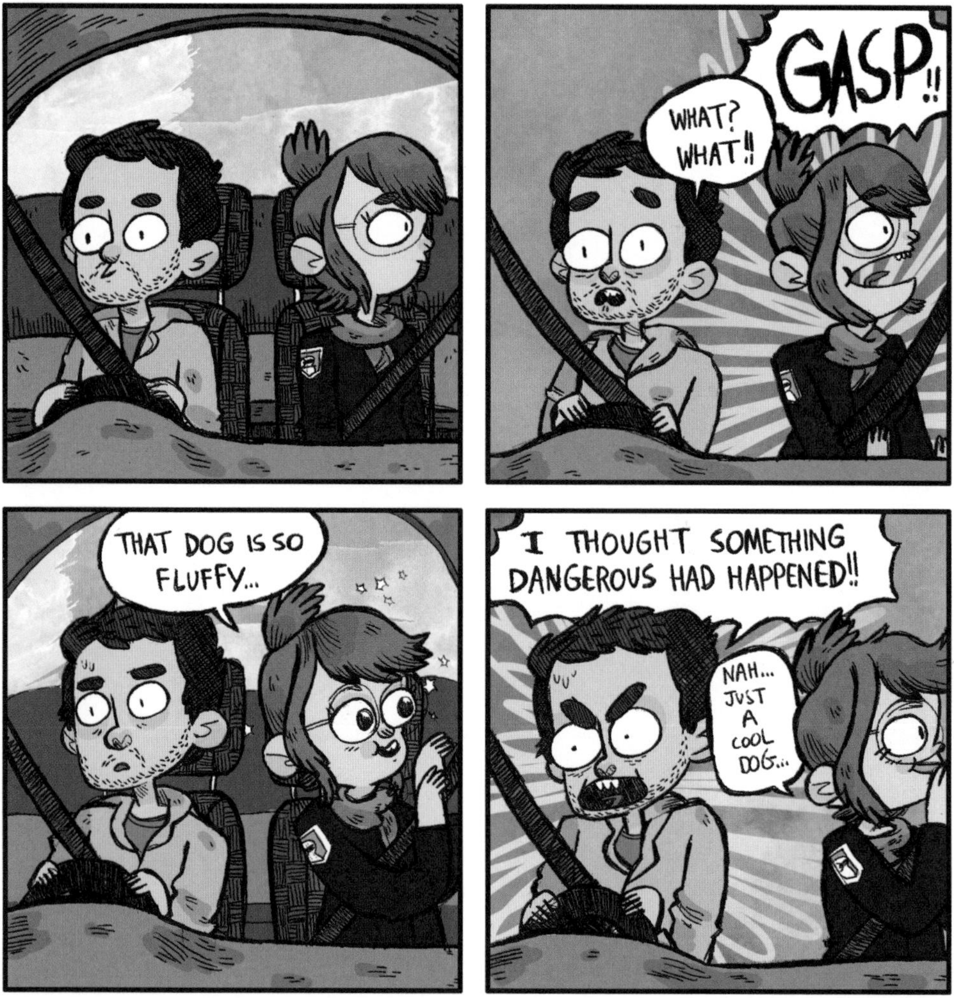
GASP!!
WHAT? WHAT!!
THAT DOG IS SO FLUFFY...
I THOUGHT SOMETHING DANGEROUS HAD HAPPENED!!
NAH... JUST A COOL DOG...

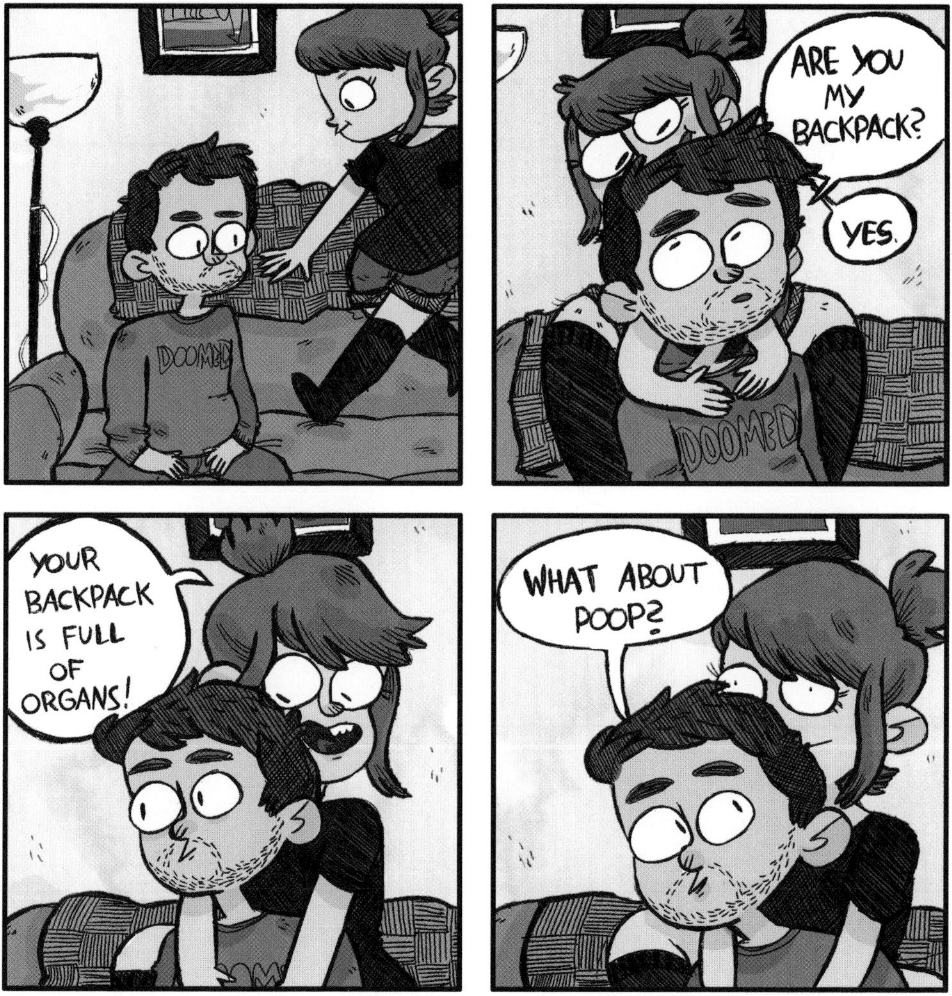
DOOMED
ARE YOU MY BACKPACK?
YES.
DOOMED
YOUR BACKPACK IS FULL OF ORGANS!
WHAT ABOUT POOP?

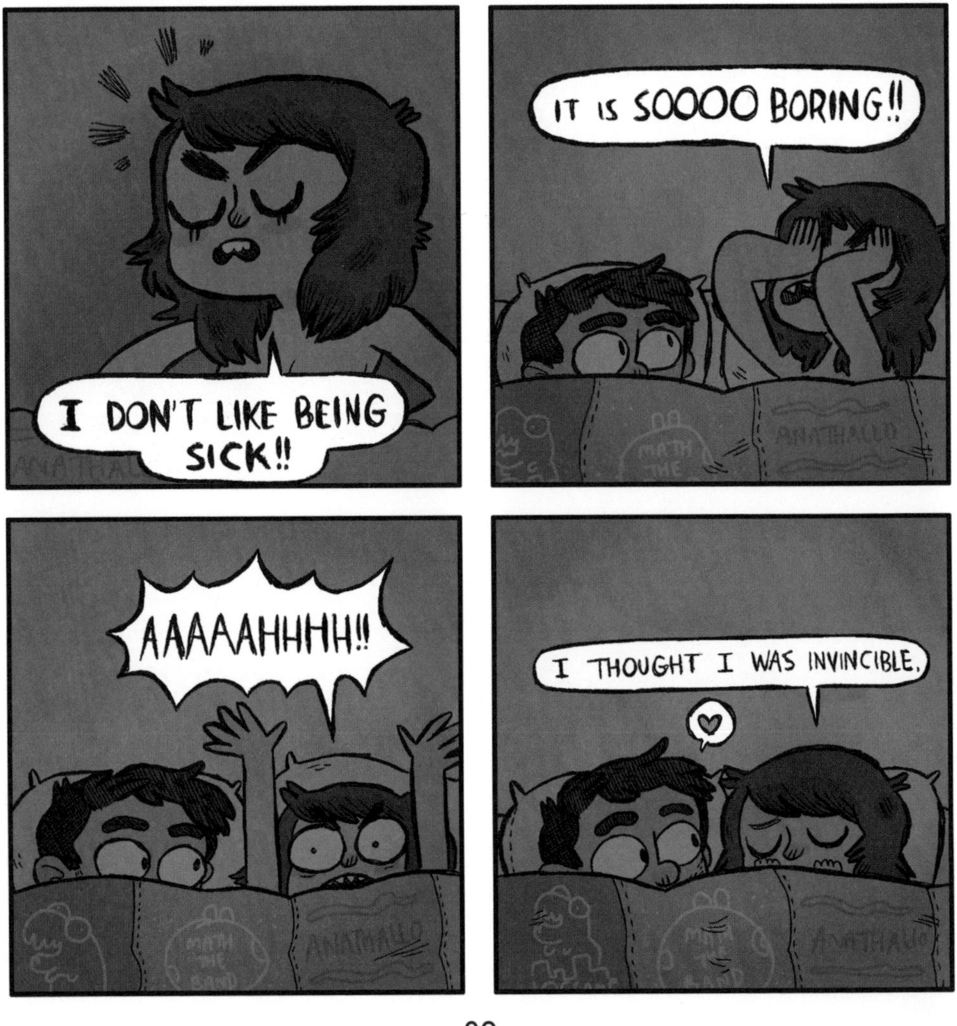
I DON'T LIKE BEING SICK!!
IT IS SOOOO BORING!!
AAAAAHHHH!!
I THOUGHT I WAS INVINCIBLE.

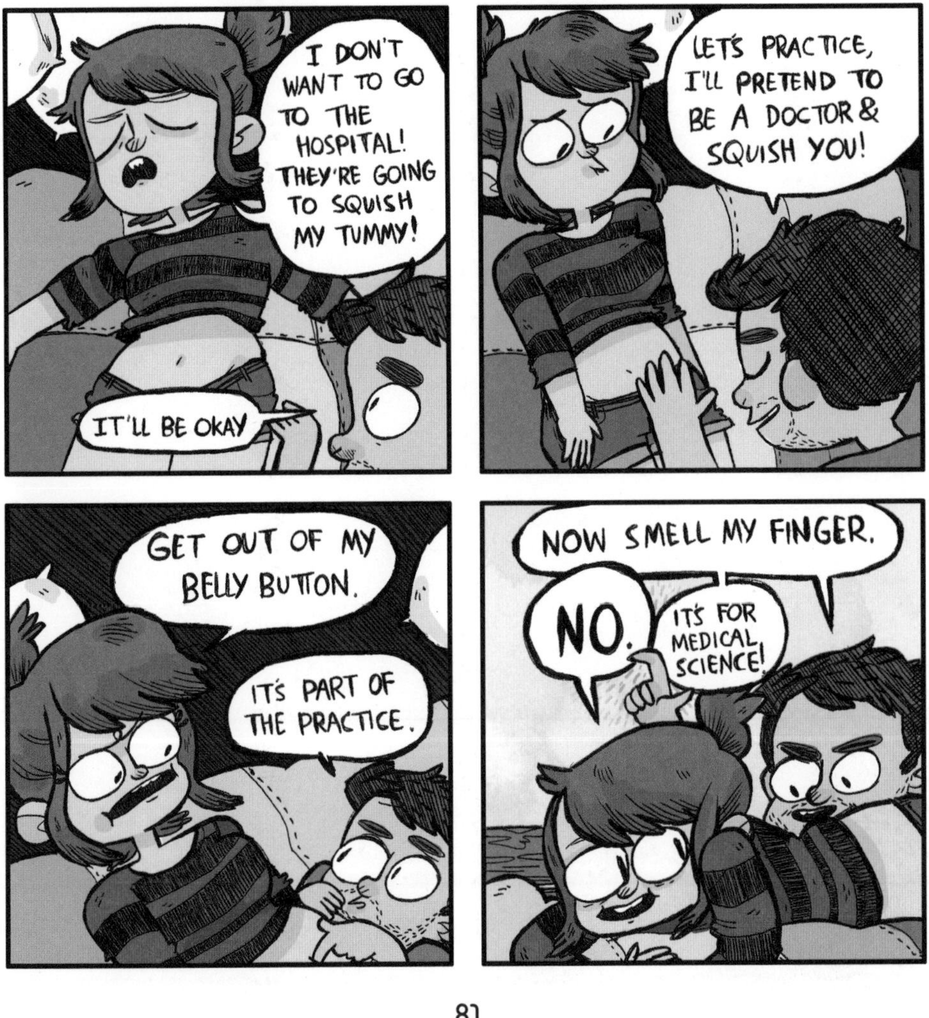
I DON'T WANT TO GO TO THE HOSPITAL! THEY'RE GOING TO SQUISH MY TUMMY!
IT'LL BE OKAY
LET'S PRACTICE, I'LL PRETEND TO BE A DOCTOR & SQUISH YOU!
GET OUT OF MY BELLY BUTTON.
IT'S PART OF THE PRACTICE.
NOW SMELL MY FINGER.
NO.
IT'S FOR MEDICAL SCIENCE!

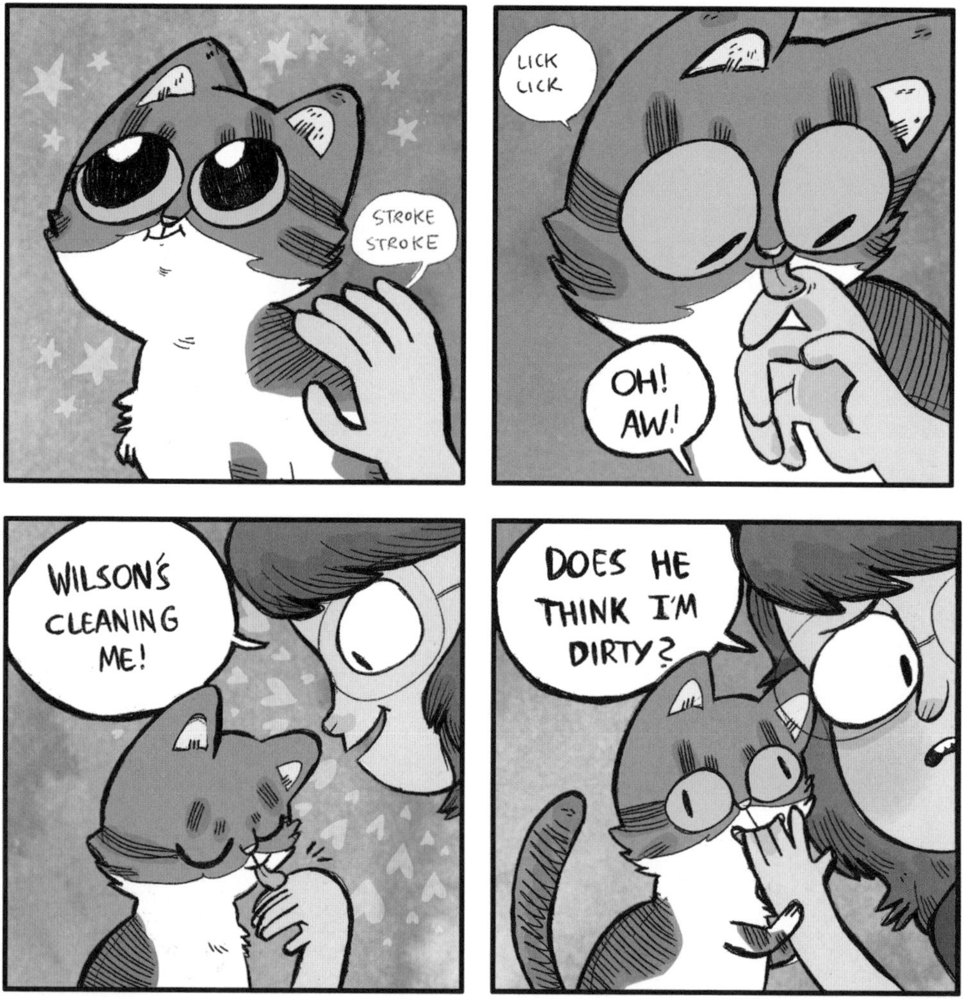
STROKE STROKE
LICK LICK
OH! AW!
WILSON'S CLEANING ME!
DOES HE THINK I'M DIRTY?

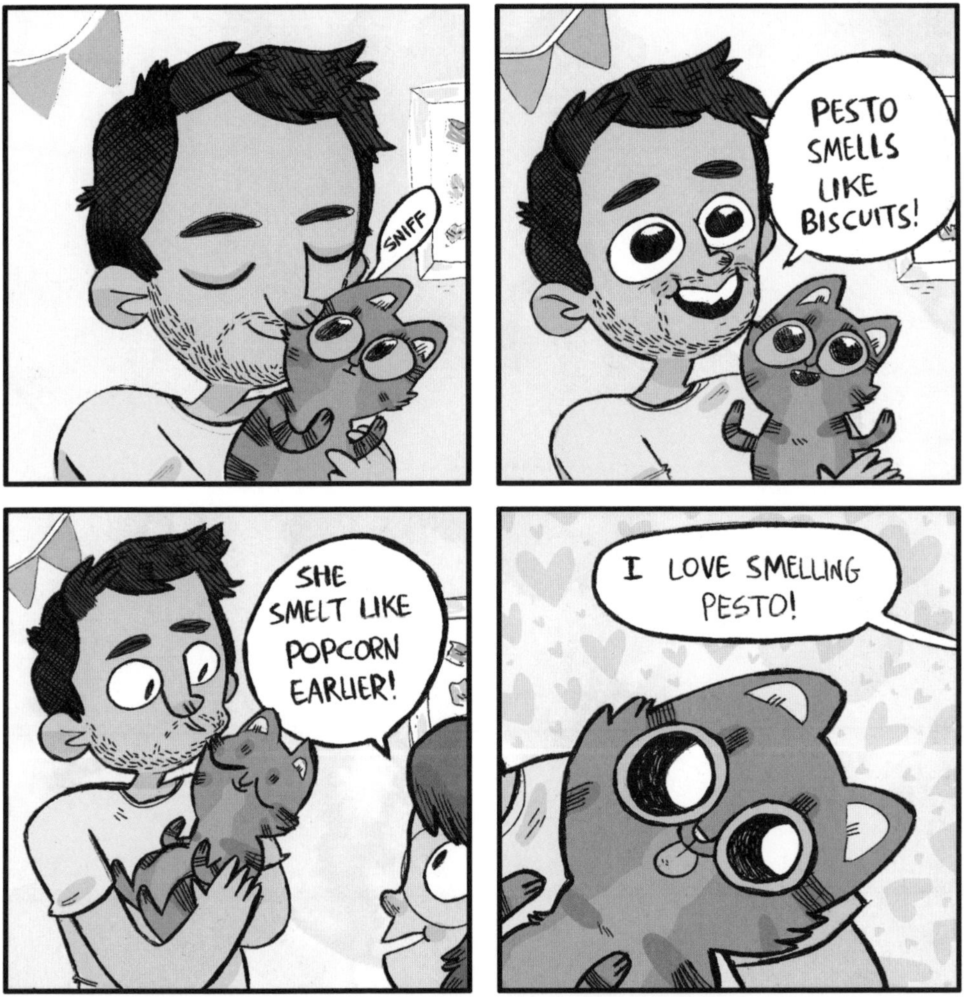
SNIFF
PESTO SMELLS LIKE BISCUITS!
SHE SMELT LIKE POPCORN EARLIER!
I LOVE SMELLING PESTO!

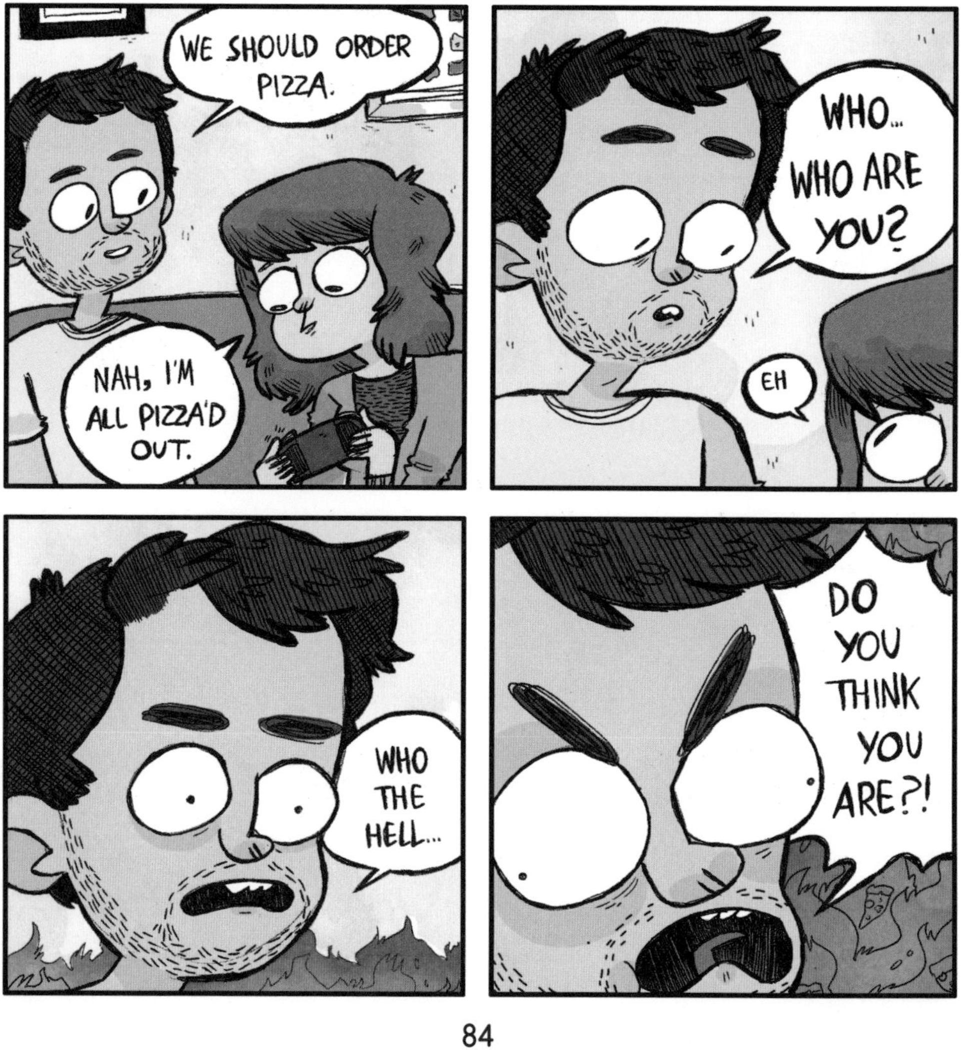
WE SHOULD ORDER PIZZA.
NAH, I'M ALL PIZZA'D OUT.
WHO... WHO ARE YOU?
EH
WHO THE HELL...
DO YOU THINK YOU ARE?!

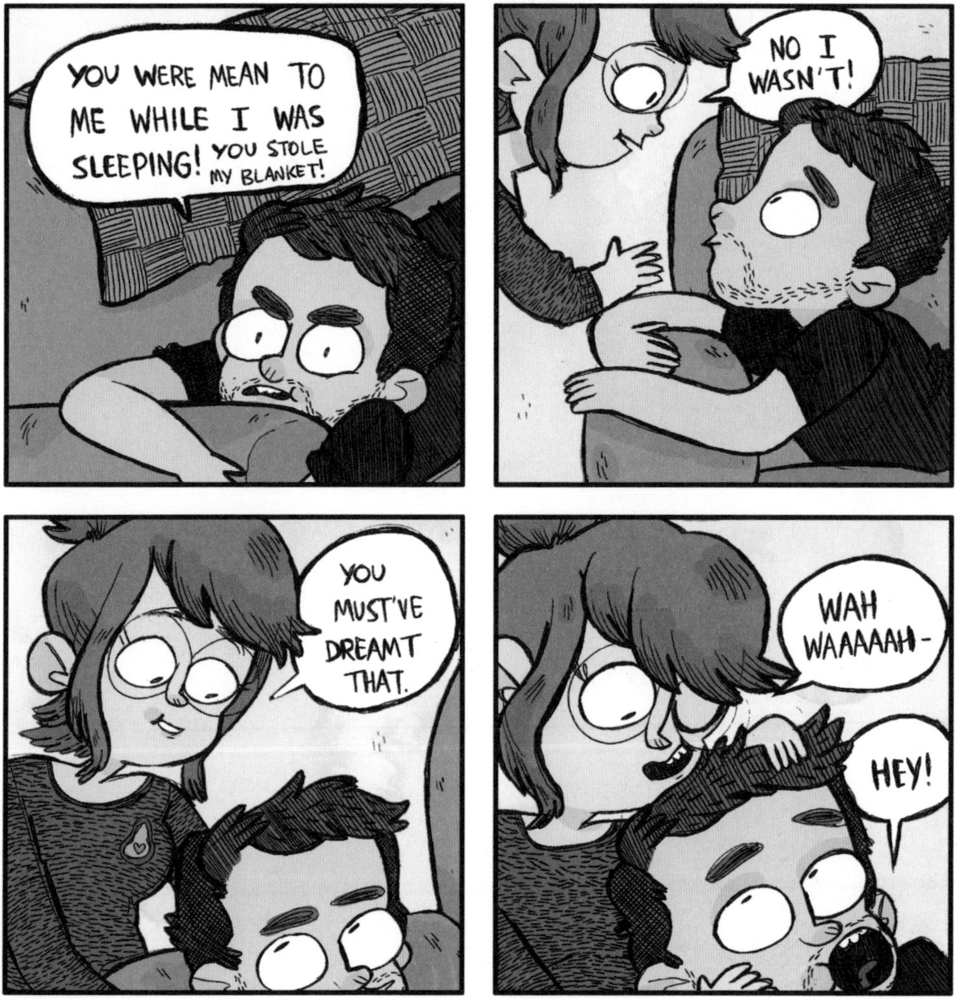
YOU WERE MEAN TO ME WHILE I WAS SLEEPING!
YOU STOLE MY BLANKET!
NO I WASN'T!
YOU MUST'VE DREAMT THAT.
WAH WAAAAAH-
HEY!

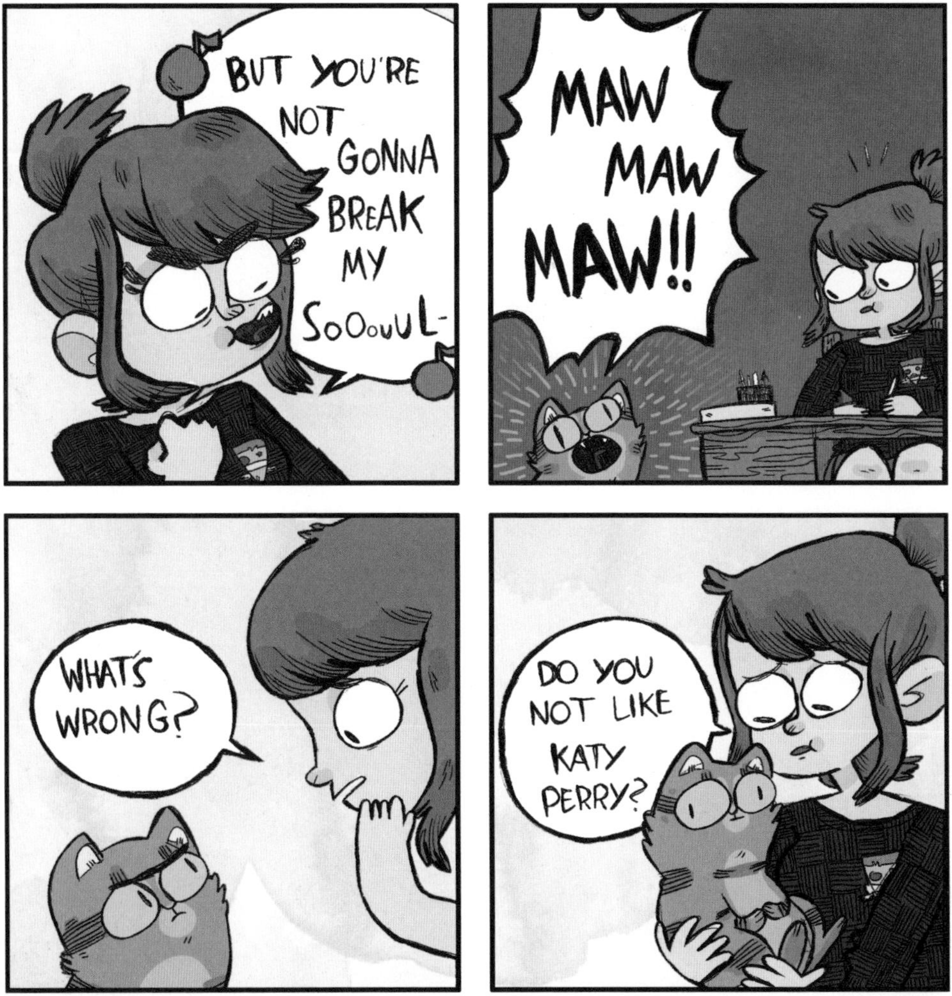
BUT YOU'RE NOT GONNA BREAK MY SoOouuL-
MAW MAW MAW!!
WHAT'S WRONG?
DO YOU NOT LIKE KATY PERRY?

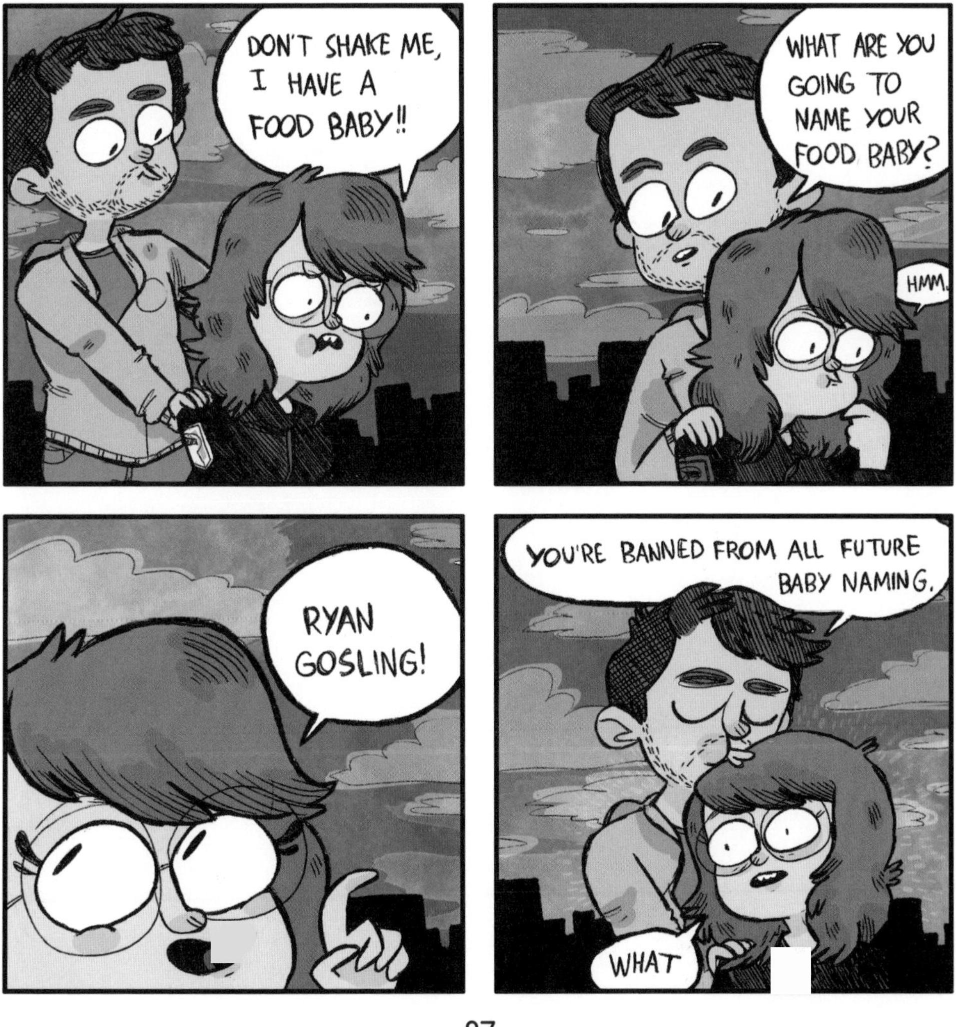
DON'T SHAKE ME, I HAVE A FOOD BABY!!
WHAT ARE YOU GOING TO NAME YOUR FOOD BABY?
HMM.
RYAN GOSLING!
YOU'RE BANNED FROM ALL FUTURE BABY NAMING.
WHAT

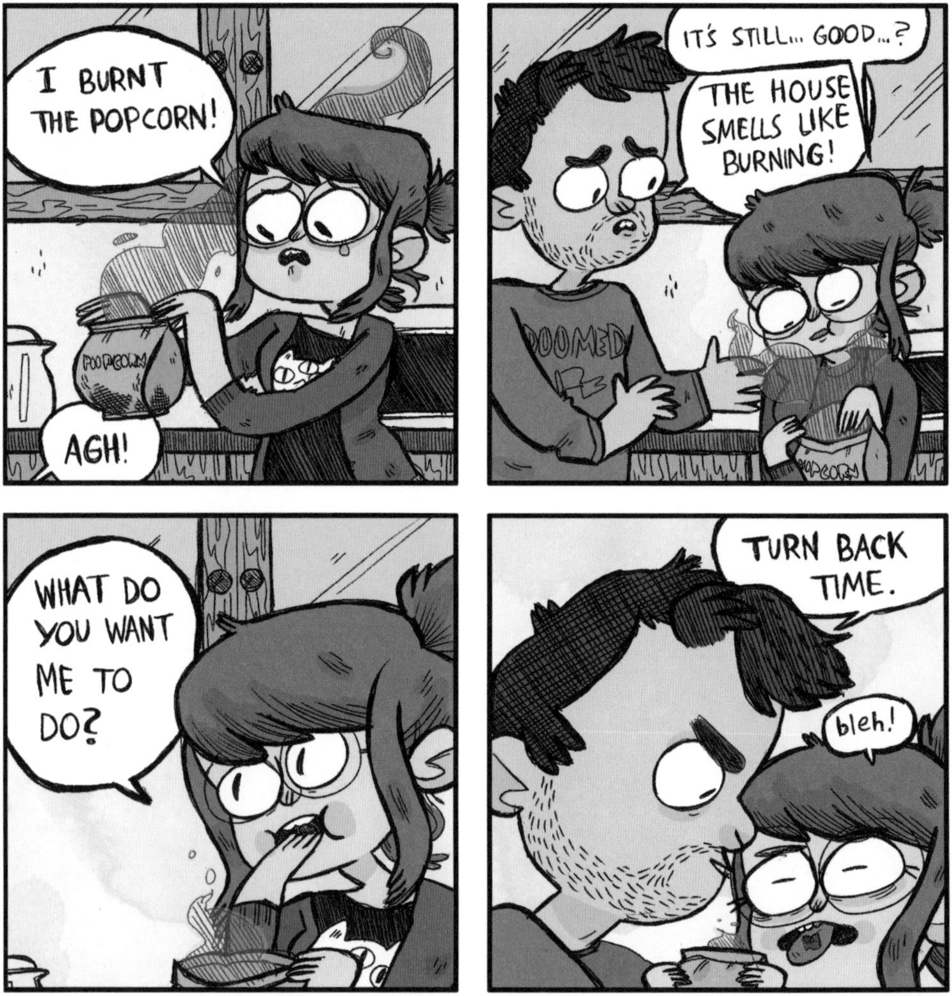
I BURNT THE POPCORN!
POPCORN
AGH!
IT'S STILL... GOOD...?
THE HOUSE SMELLS LIKE BURNING!
DOOMED
POPCORN
WHAT DO YOU WANT ME TO DO?
TURN BACK TIME.
bleh!

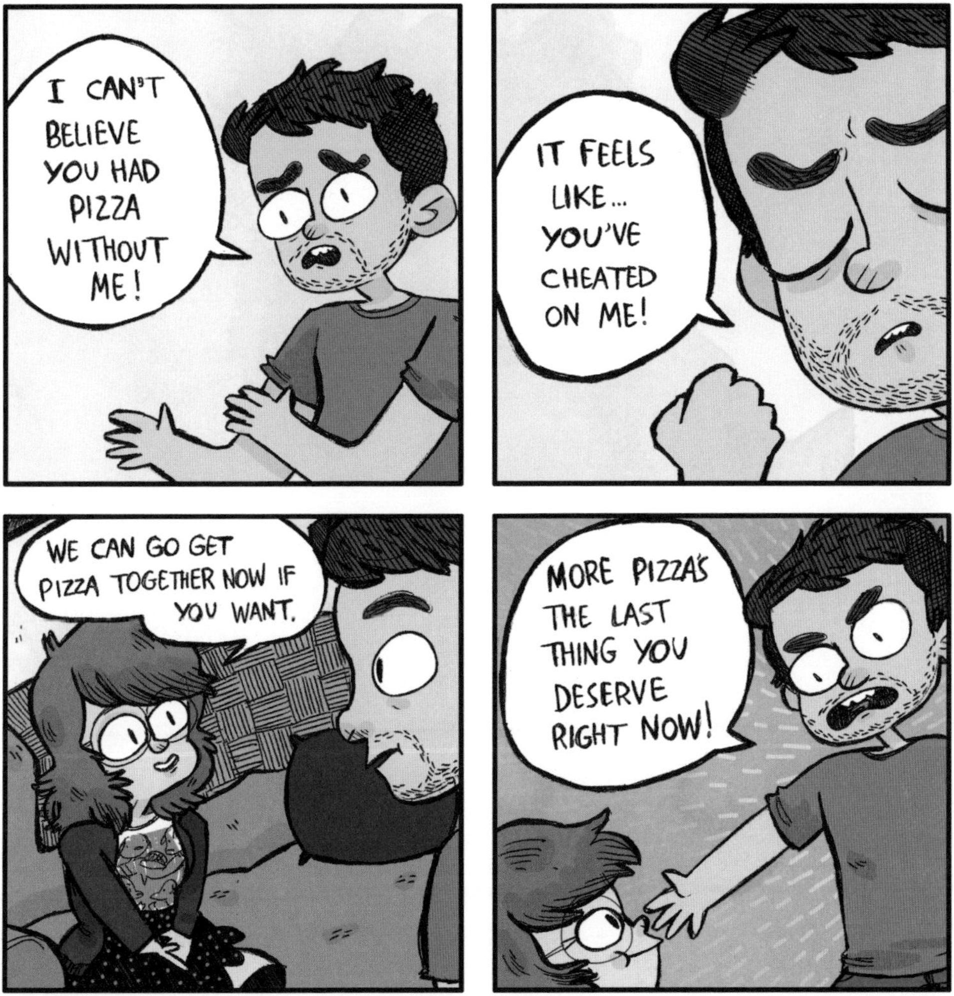
I CAN'T BELIEVE YOU HAD PIZZA WITHOUT ME!
IT FEELS LIKE... YOU'VE CHEATED ON ME!
WE CAN GO GET PIZZA TOGETHER NOW IF YOU WANT.
MORE PIZZA'S THE LAST THING YOU DESERVE RIGHT NOW!

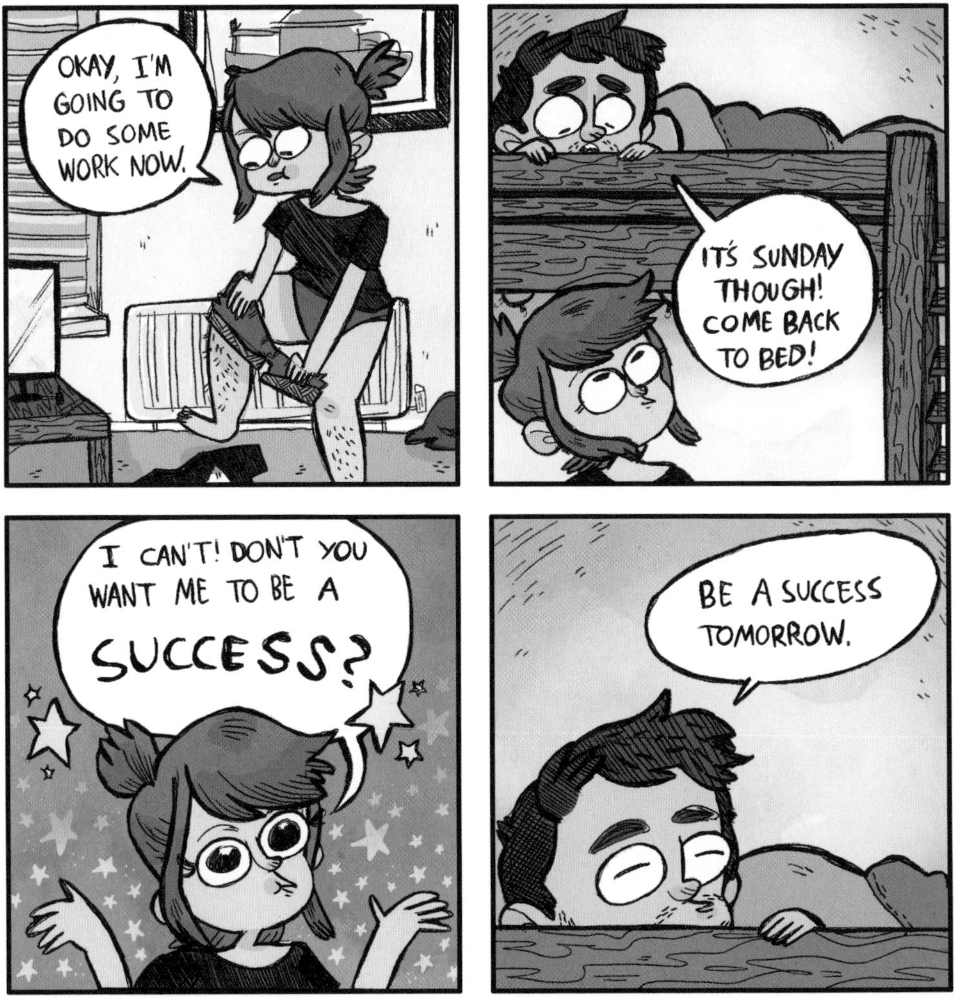
OKAY, I'M GOING TO DO SOME WORK NOW.
IT'S SUNDAY THOUGH! COME BACK TO BED!
I CAN'T! DON'T YOU WANT ME TO BE A SUCCESS?
BE A SUCCESS TOMORROW.

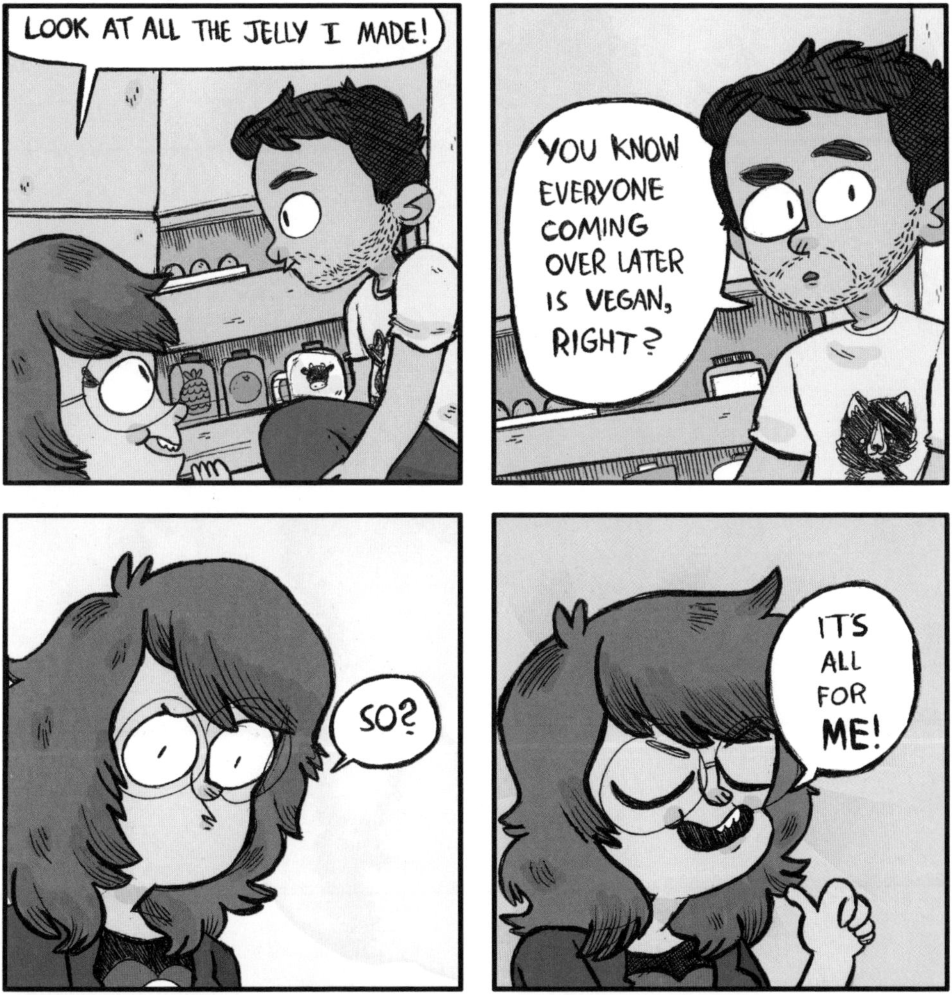
LOOK AT ALL THE JELLY I MADE!
YOU KNOW EVERYONE COMING OVER LATER IS VEGAN, RIGHT?
SO?
IT'S ALL FOR ME!

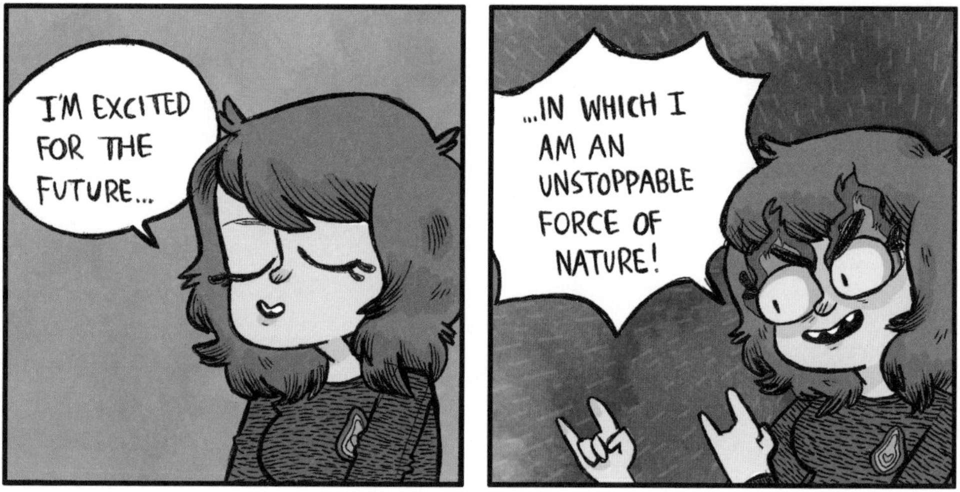
I'M EXCITED FOR THE FUTURE...
...IN WHICH I AM AN UNSTOPPABLE FORCE OF NATURE!

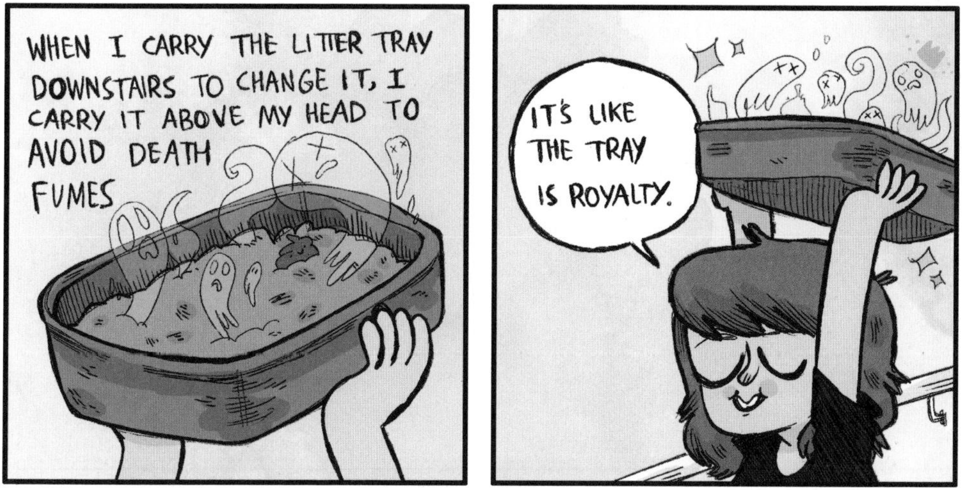
WHEN I CARRY THE LITTER TRAY DOWNSTAIRS TO CHANGE IT, I CARRY IT ABOVE MY HEAD TO AVOID DEATH FUMES
IT'S LIKE THE TRAY IS ROYALTY.

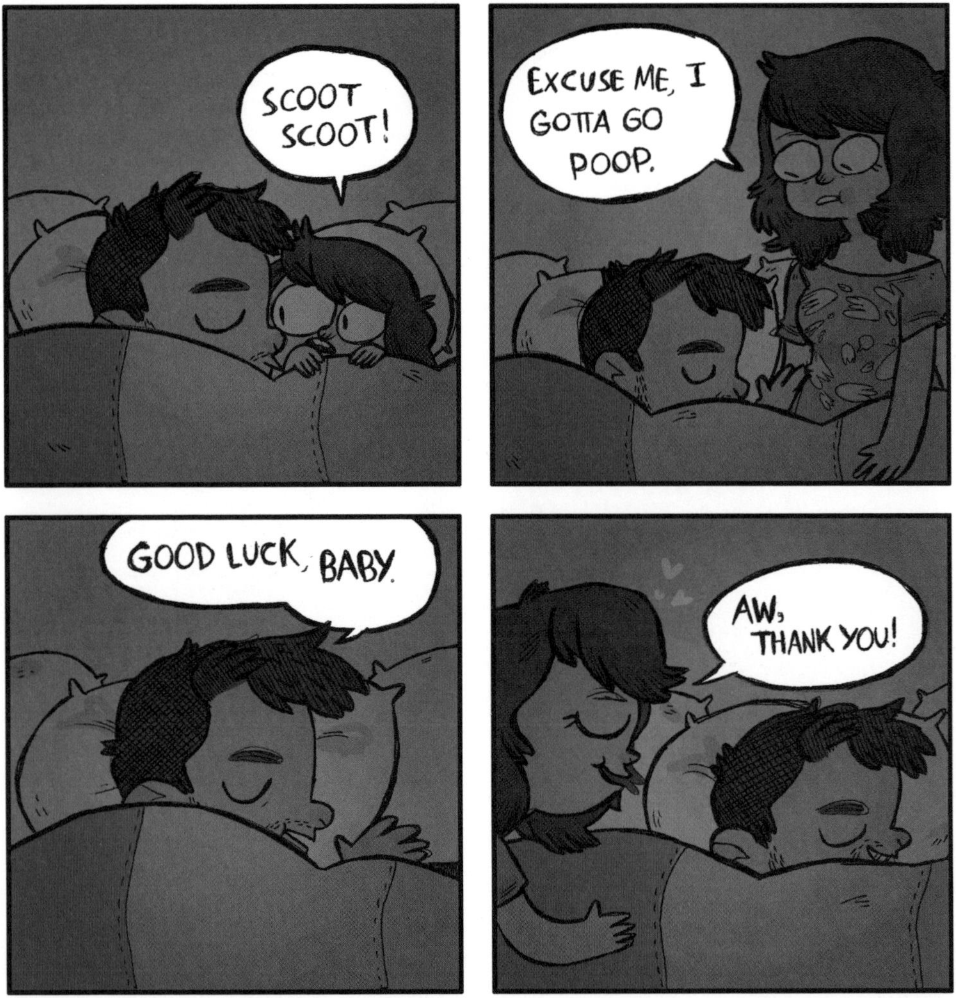
SCOOT SCOOT!
EXCUSE ME, I GOTTA GO POOP.
GOOD LUCK, BABY.
AW, THANK YOU!

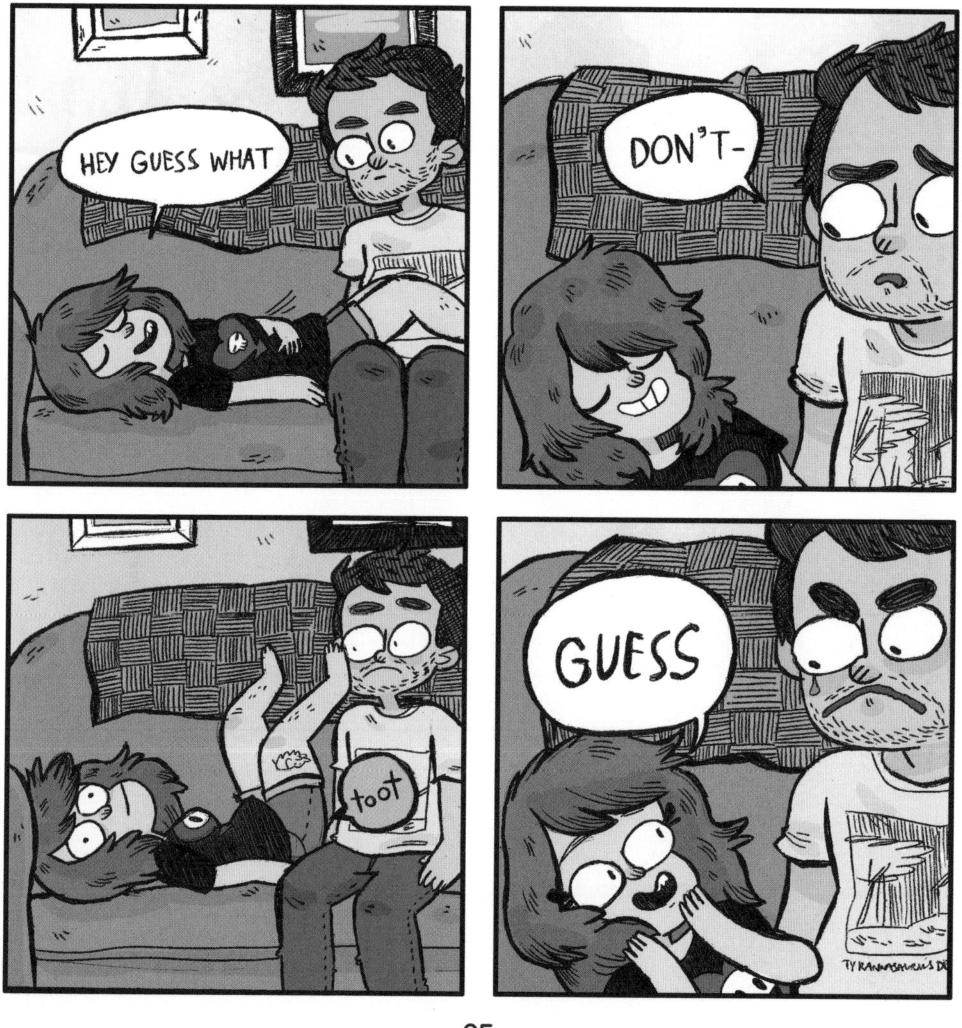
HEY GUESS WHAT
DON'T-
toot
GUESS

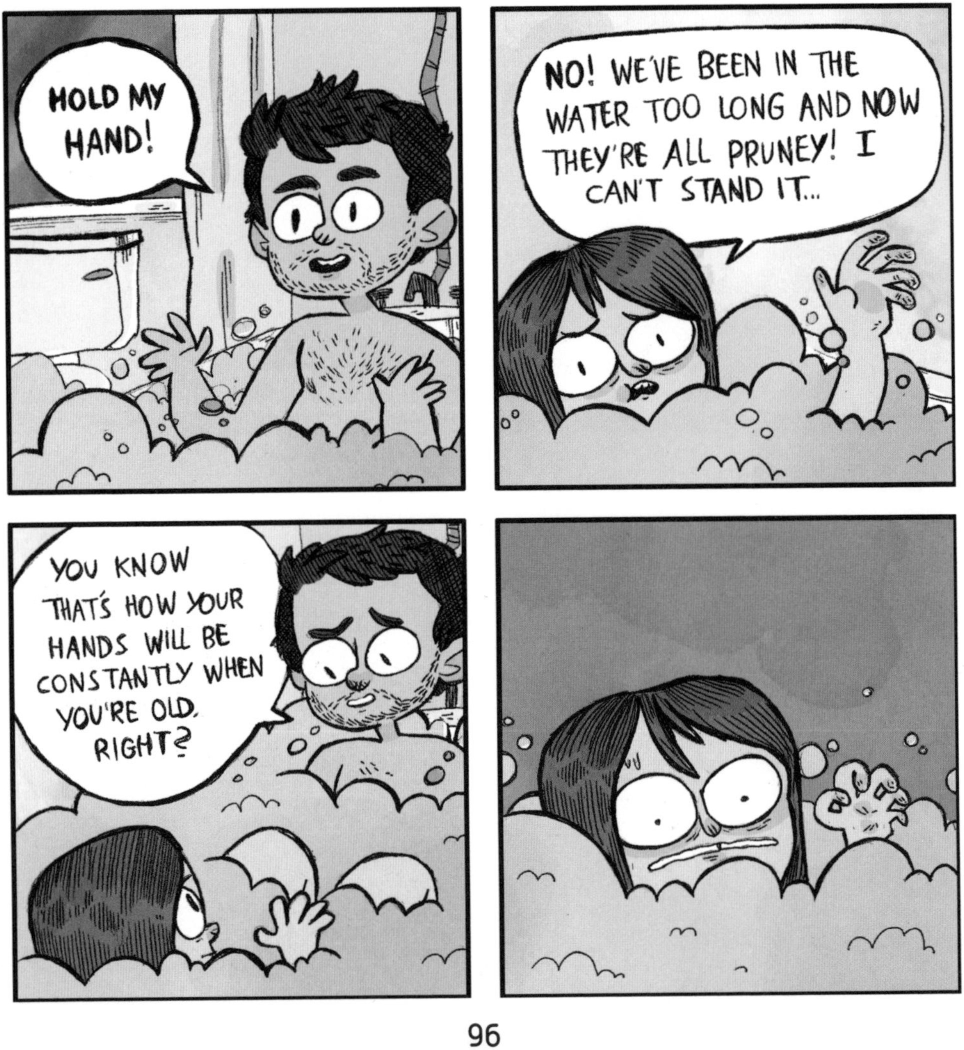
HOLD MY HAND!
NO! WE'VE BEEN IN THE WATER TOO LONG AND NOW THEY'RE ALL PRUNEY! I CAN'T STAND IT...
YOU KNOW THAT'S HOW YOUR HANDS WILL BE CONSTANTLY WHEN YOU'RE OLD, RIGHT?

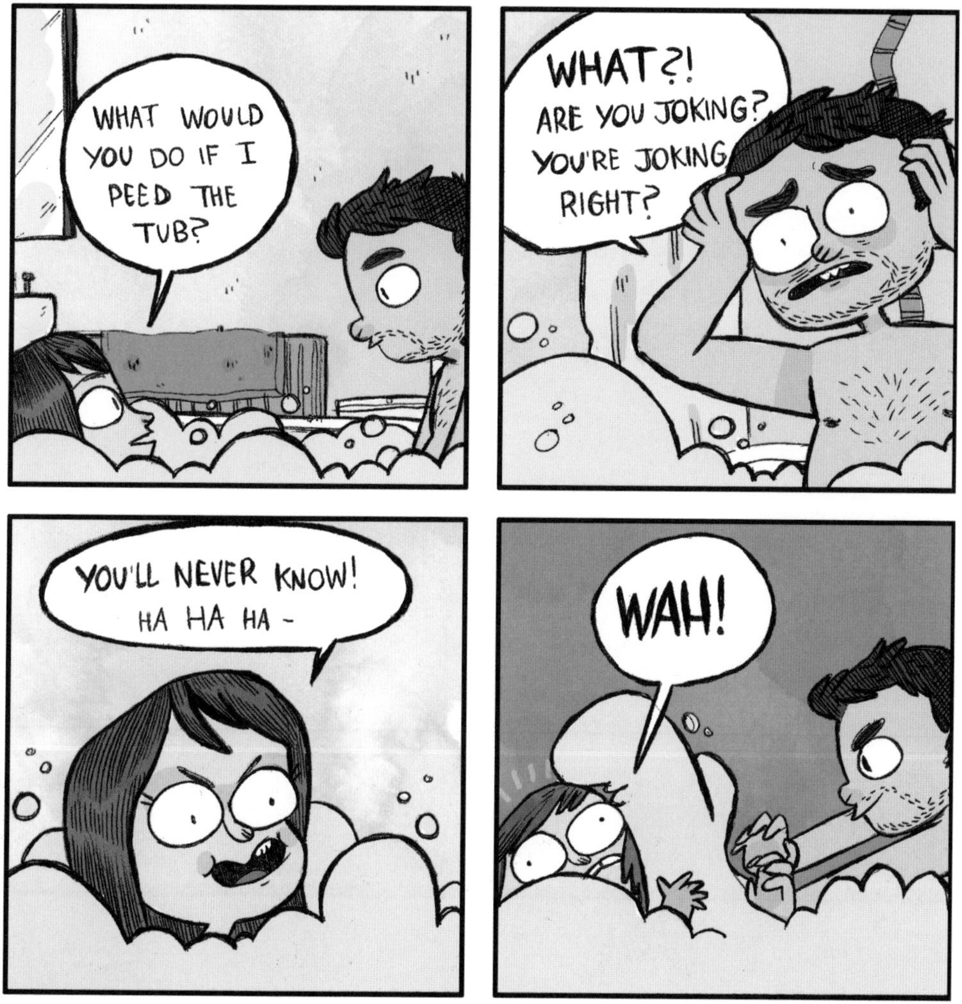
WHAT WOULD YOU DO IF I PEED THE TUB?
WHAT?! ARE YOU JOKING? YOU'RE JOKING RIGHT?
YOU'LL NEVER KNOW! HA HA HA -
WAH!

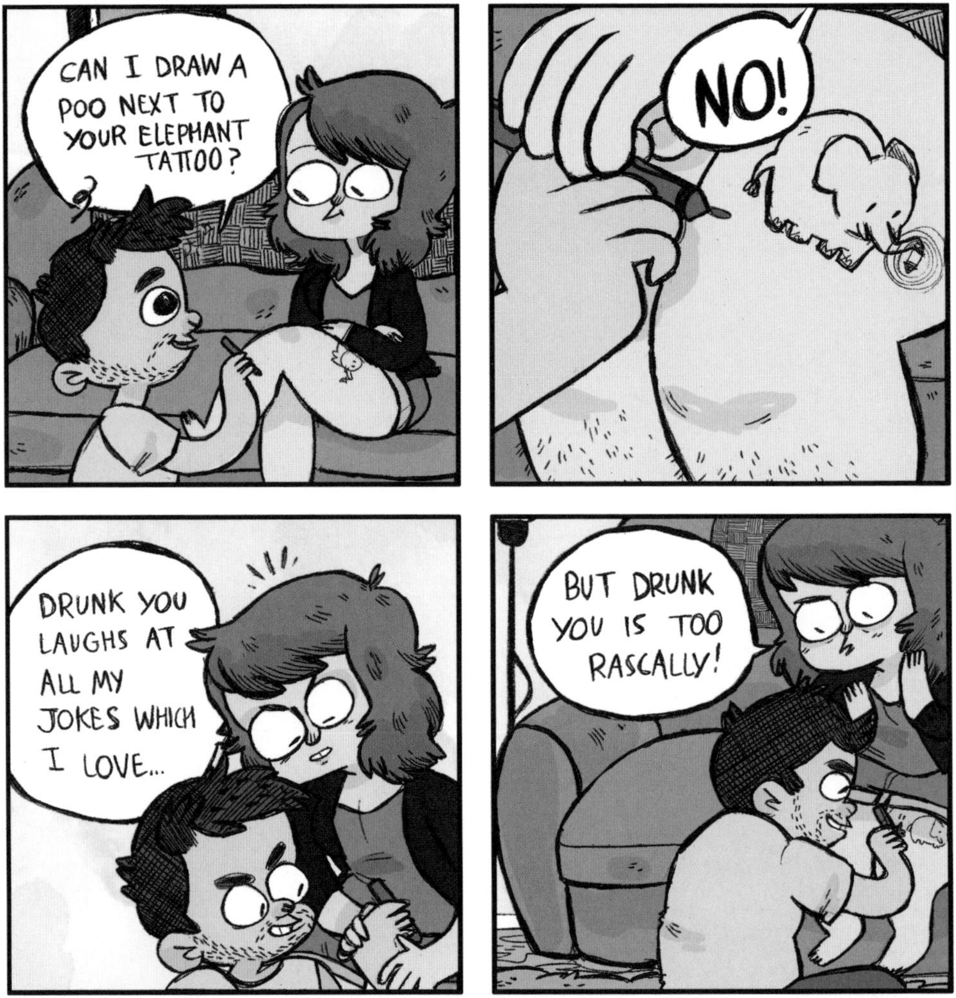
CAN I DRAW A POO NEXT TO YOUR ELEPHANT TATTOO?
NO!
DRUNK YOU LAUGHS AT ALL MY JOKES WHICH I LOVE...
BUT DRUNK YOU IS TOO RASCALLY!

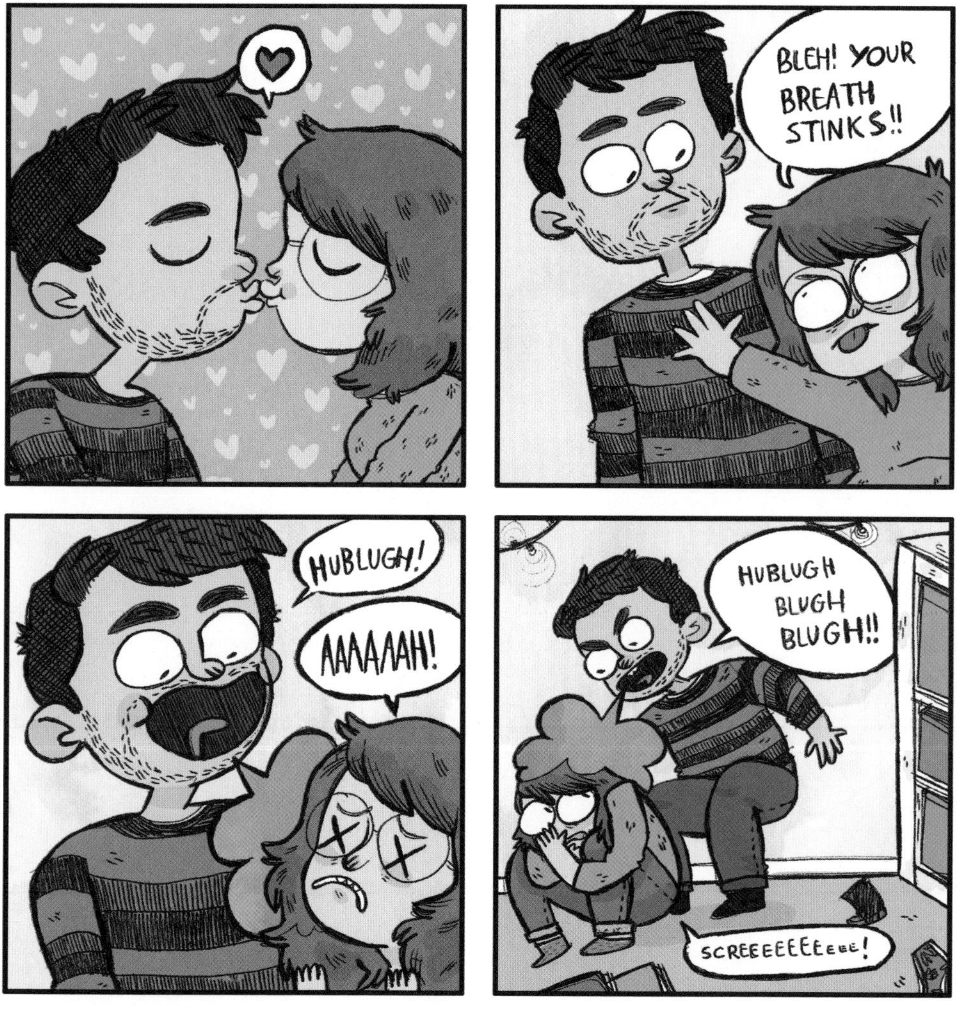
BLEH! YOUR BREATH STINKS!!
HUBLUGH!
AAAAAAH!
HUBLUGH BLUGH BLUGH!!
SCREEEEEEEeeee!

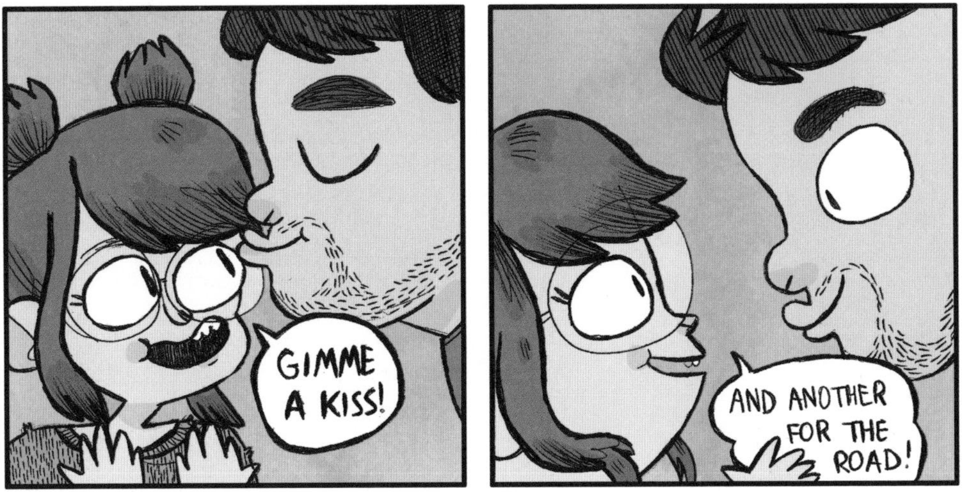
GIMME A KISS!
AND ANOTHER FOR THE ROAD!

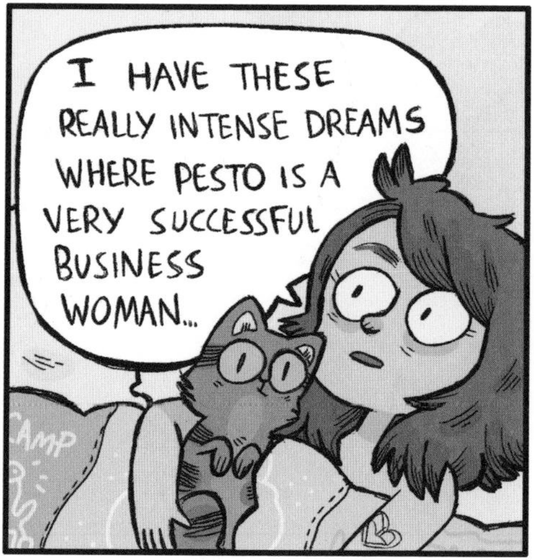
I HAVE THESE REALLY INTENSE DREAMS WHERE PESTO IS A VERY SUCCESSFUL BUSINESS WOMAN...
CAMP

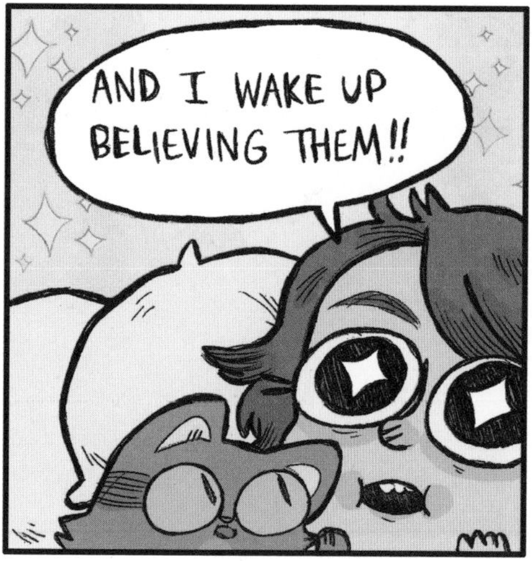
AND I WAKE UP BELIEVING THEM!!

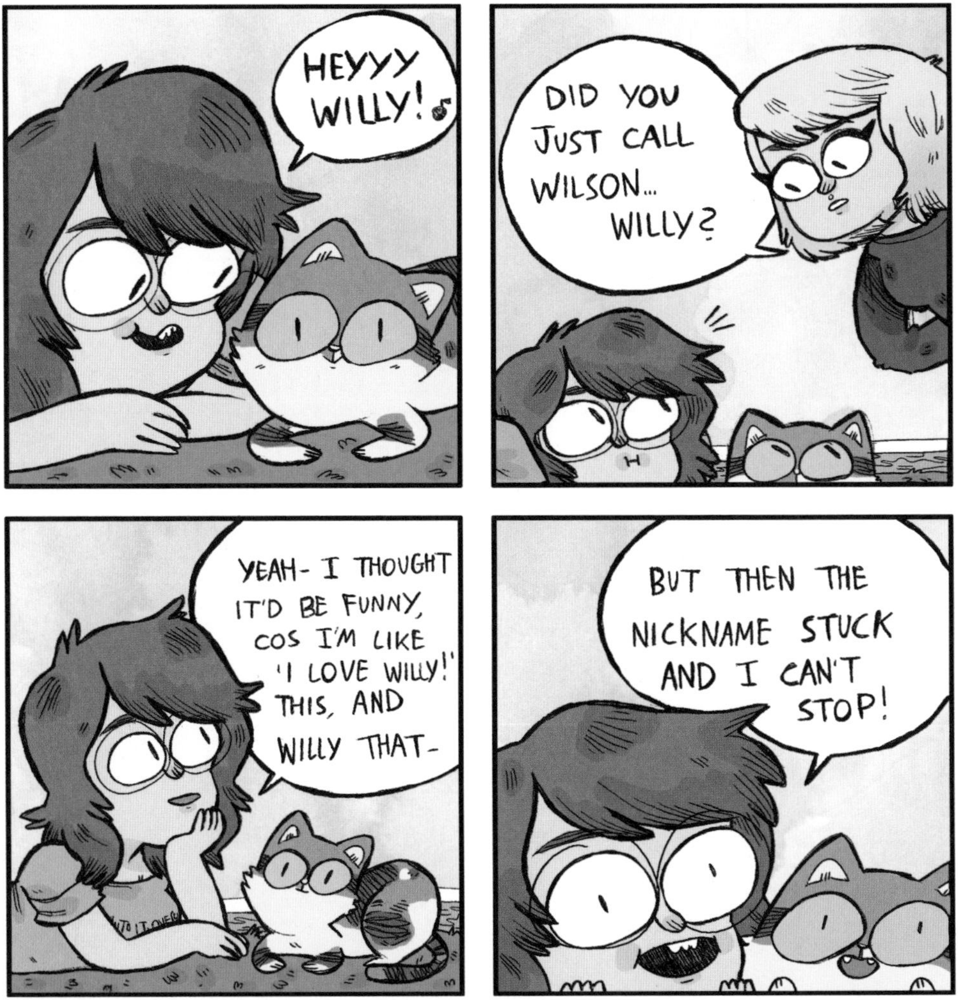
HEYYY WILLY!
DID YOU JUST CALL WILSON... WILLY?
YEAH- I THOUGHT IT'D BE FUNNY, COS I'M LIKE 'I LOVE WILLY!' THIS, AND WILLY THAT-
BUT THEN THE NICKNAME STUCK AND I CAN'T STOP!

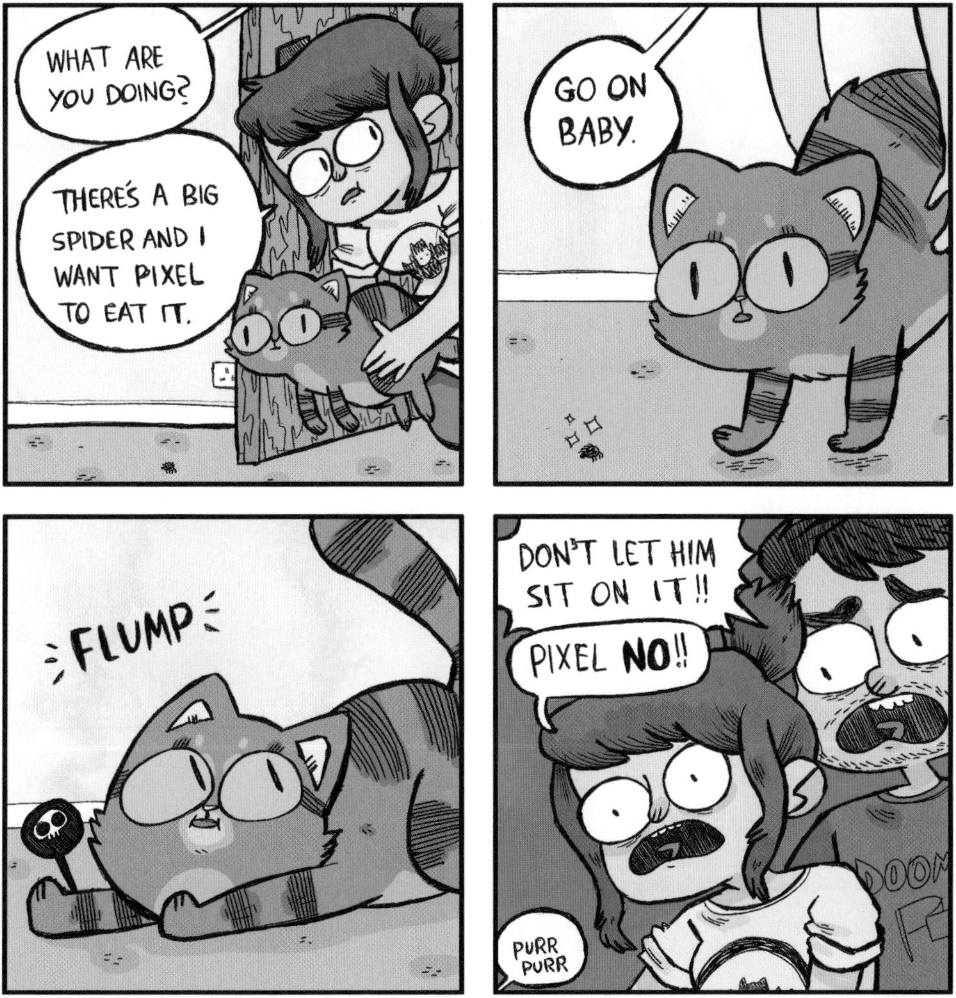
WHAT ARE YOU DOING?
THERE'S A BIG SPIDER AND I WANT PIXEL TO EAT IT.
GO ON BABY.
FLUMP
DON'T LET HIM SIT ON IT!!
PIXEL NO!!
PURR PURR

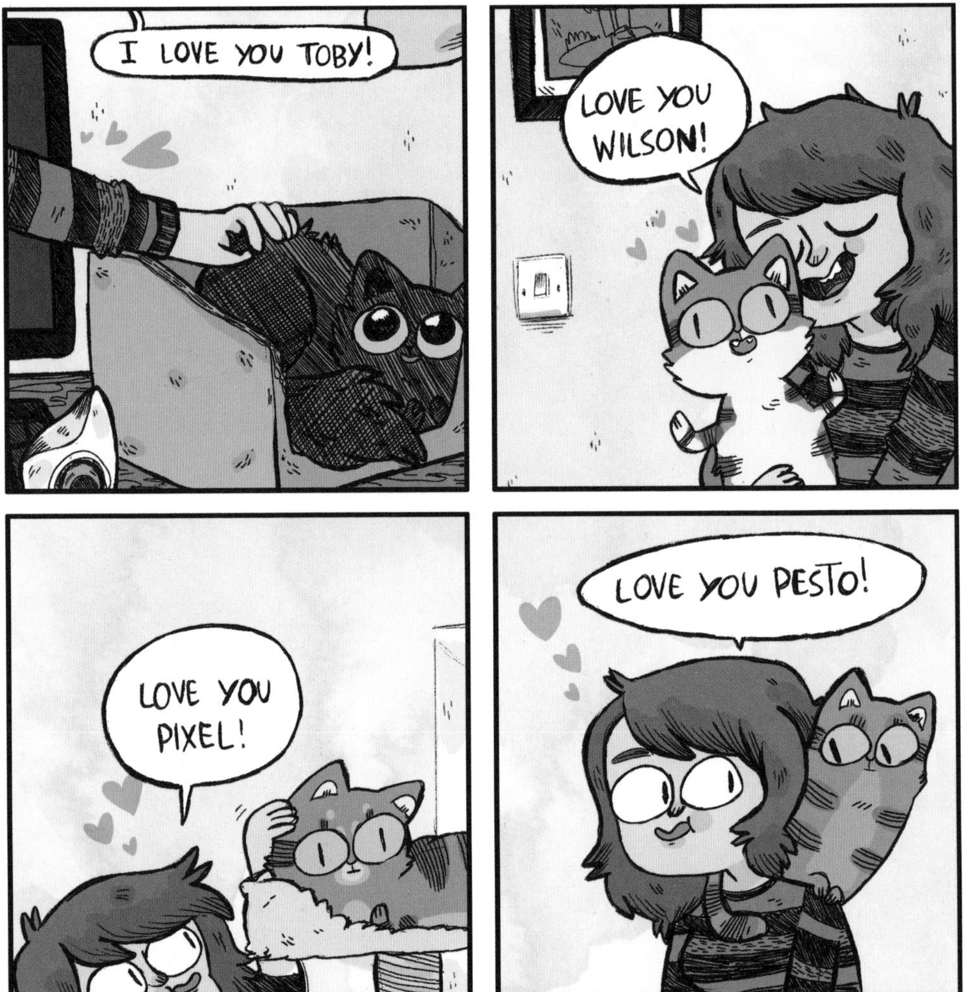
I LOVE YOU TOBY!
LOVE YOU WILSON!
LOVE YOU PIXEL!
LOVE YOU PESTO!

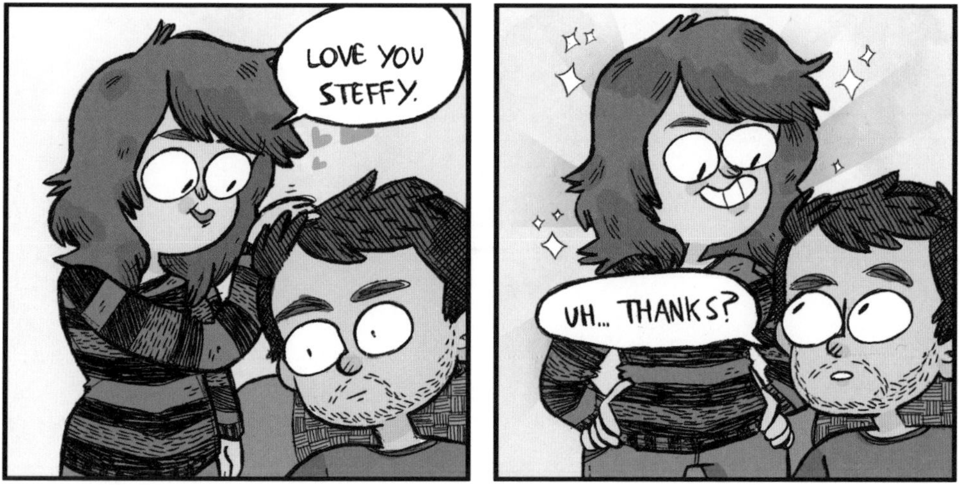
LOVE YOU STEFFY.
UH... THANKS?

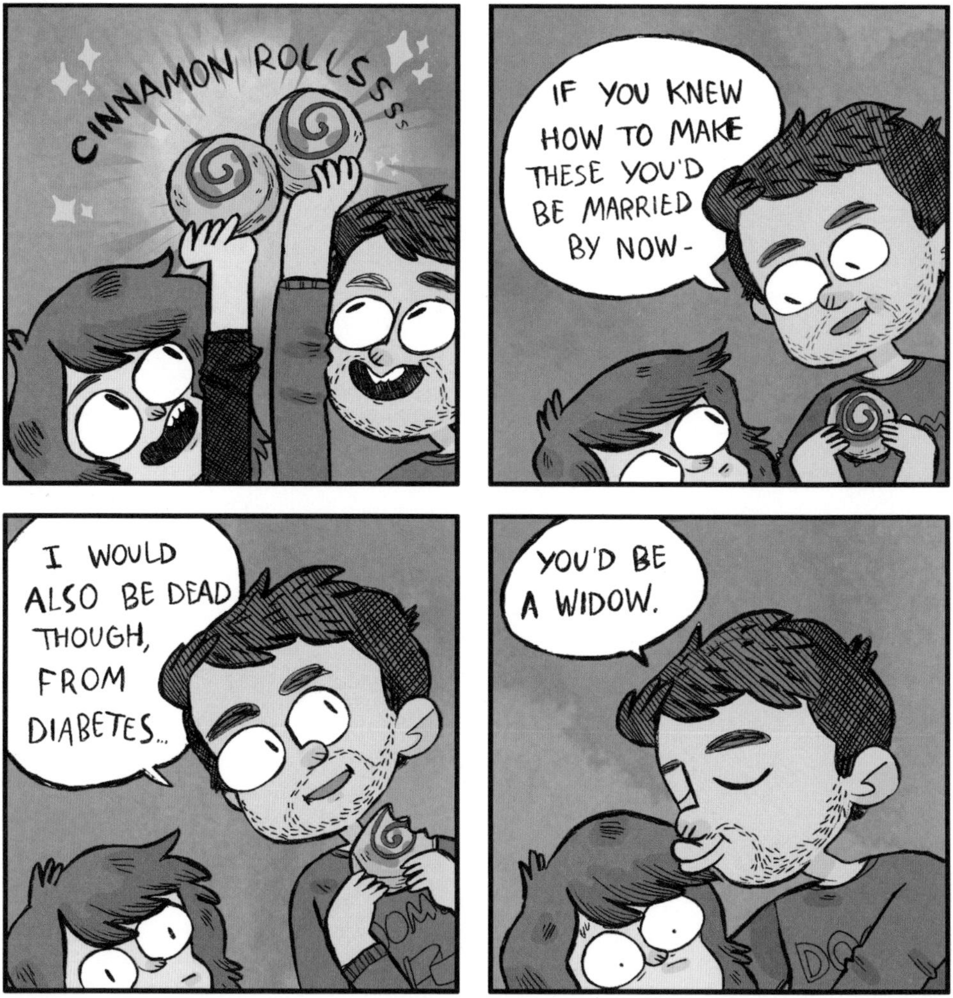
CINNAMON ROLLSSSSS
IF YOU KNEW HOW TO MAKE THESE YOU'D BE MARRIED BY NOW-
I WOULD ALSO BE DEAD THOUGH, FROM DIABETES...
YOU'D BE A WIDOW.

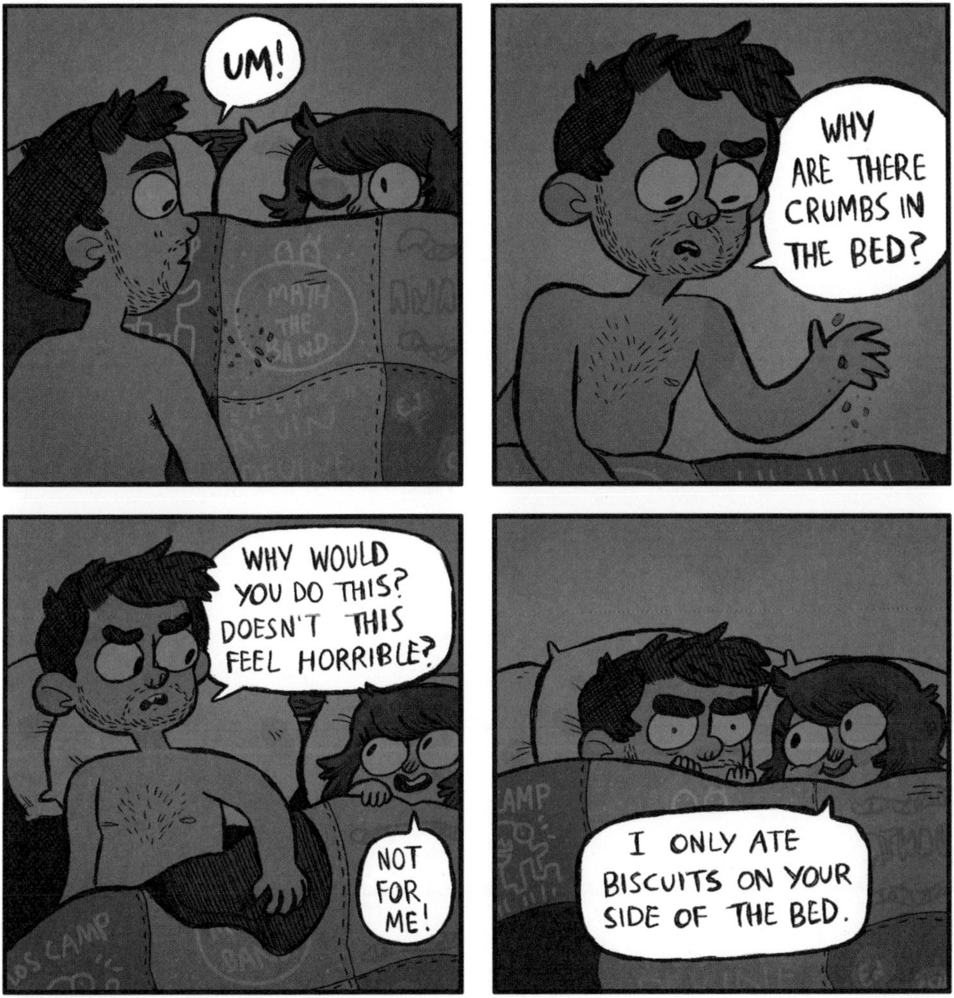
UM!
WHY ARE THERE CRUMBS IN THE BED?
WHY WOULD YOU DO THIS? DOESN'T THIS FEEL HORRIBLE?
NOT FOR ME!
I ONLY ATE BISCUITS ON YOUR SIDE OF THE BED.

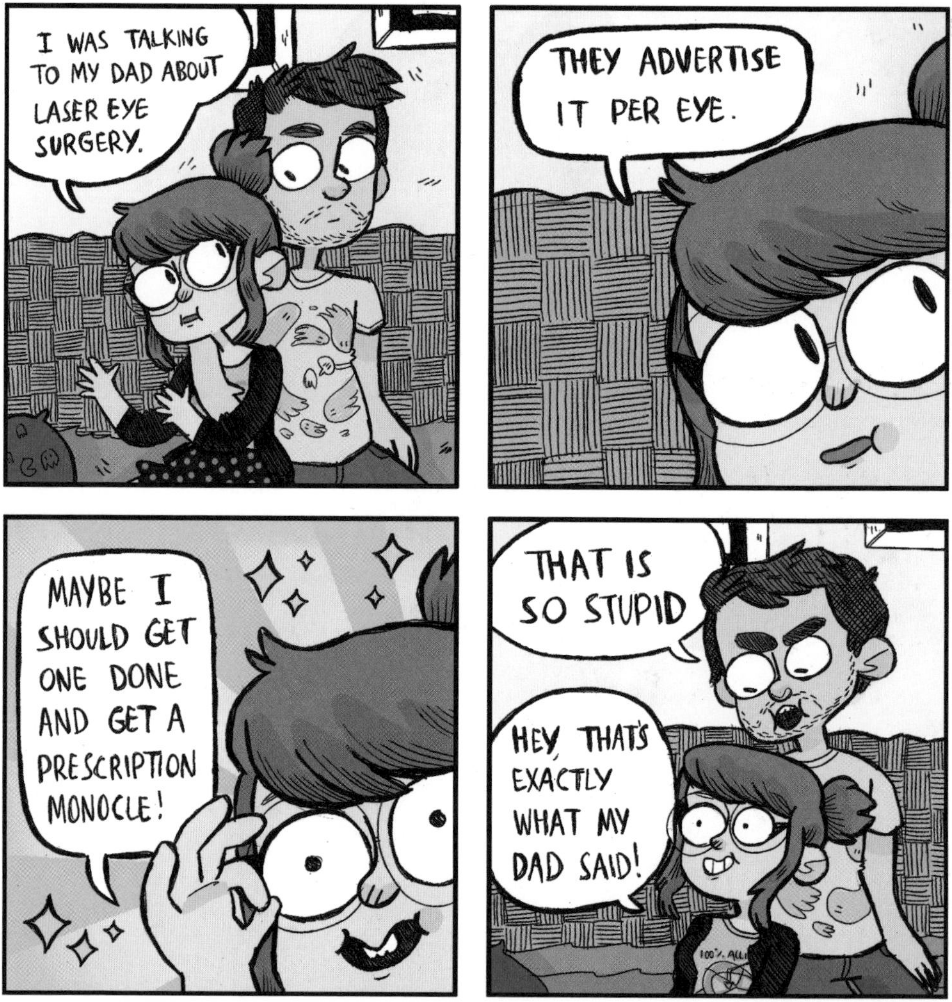
I WAS TALKING TO MY DAD ABOUT LASER EYE SURGERY.
THEY ADVERTISE IT PER EYE.
MAYBE I SHOULD GET ONE DONE AND GET A PRESCRIPTION MONOCLE!
THAT IS SO STUPID
HEY, THAT'S EXACTLY WHAT MY DAD SAID!

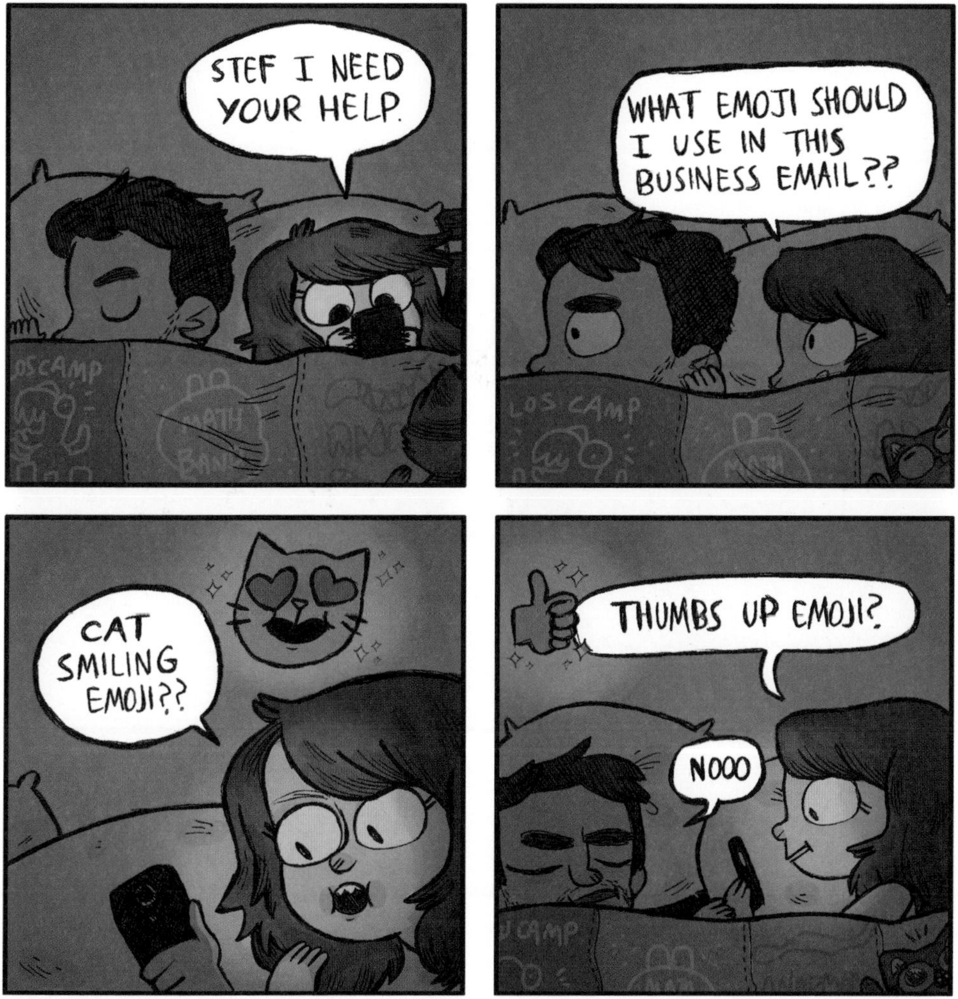
STEF I NEED YOUR HELP.
WHAT EMOJI SHOULD I USE IN THIS BUSINESS EMAIL??
CAT SMILING EMOJI??
THUMBS UP EMOJI?
NOOO

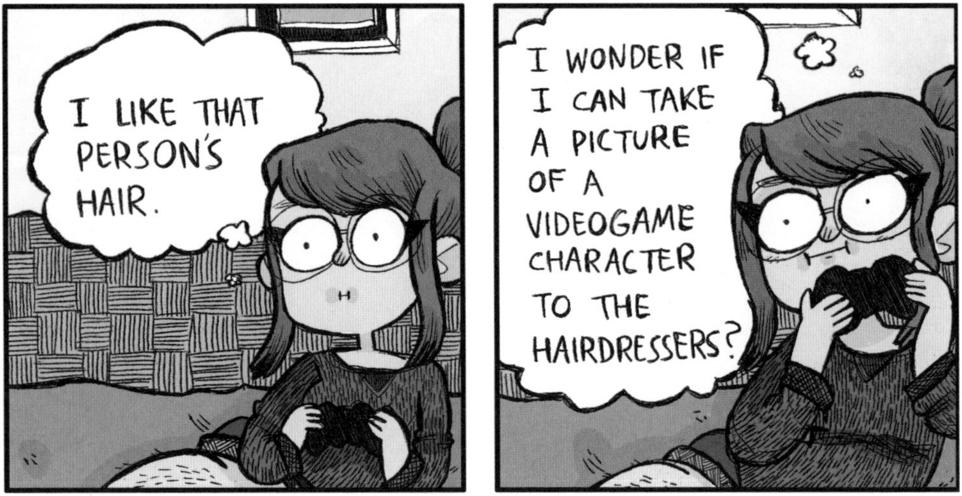
I LIKE THAT PERSON'S HAIR.
I WONDER IF I CAN TAKE A PICTURE OF A VIDEOGAME CHARACTER TO THE HAIRDRESSERS?

THAT WAS NICE OF YOUR DAD TO GIVE US GARDENING TOOLS.
AND NOW WE HAVE WEAPONS FOR THE IMPENDING ZOMBIE APOCALYPSE!!!

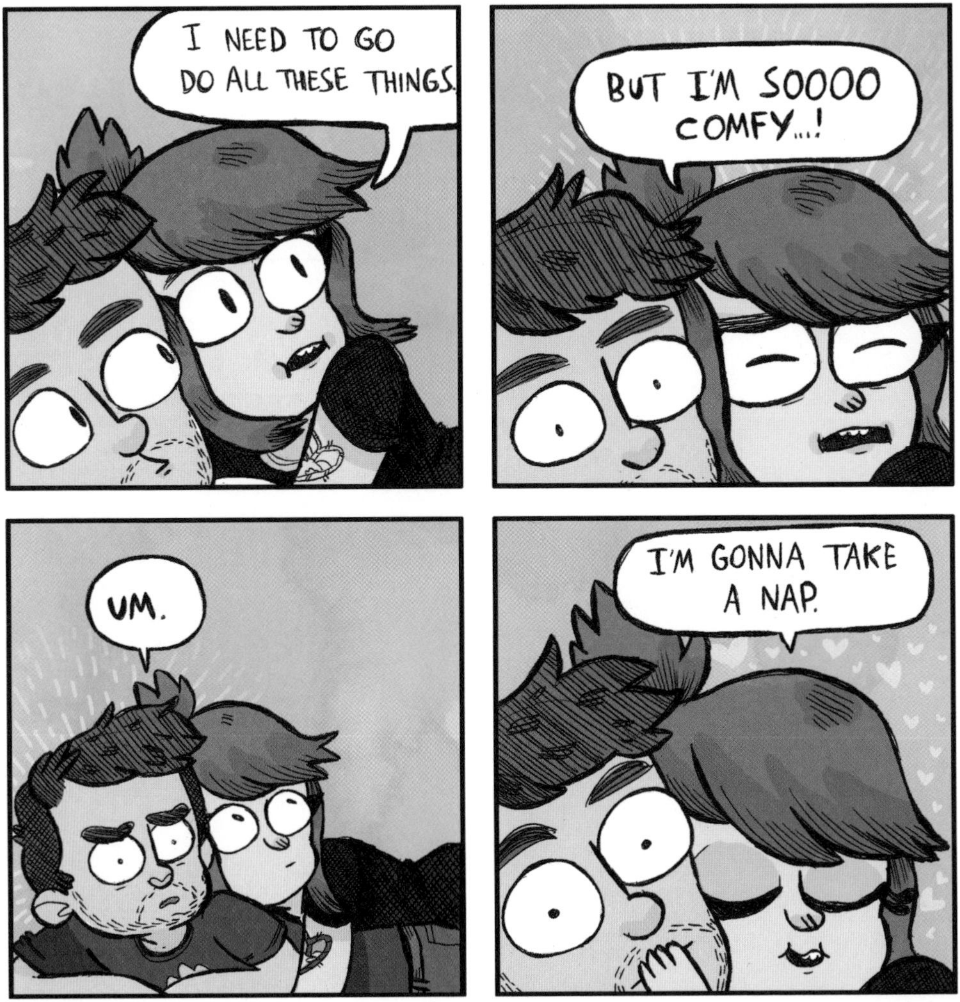
I NEED TO GO DO ALL THESE THINGS.
BUT I'M SOOOO COMFY...!
UM.
I'M GONNA TAKE A NAP.

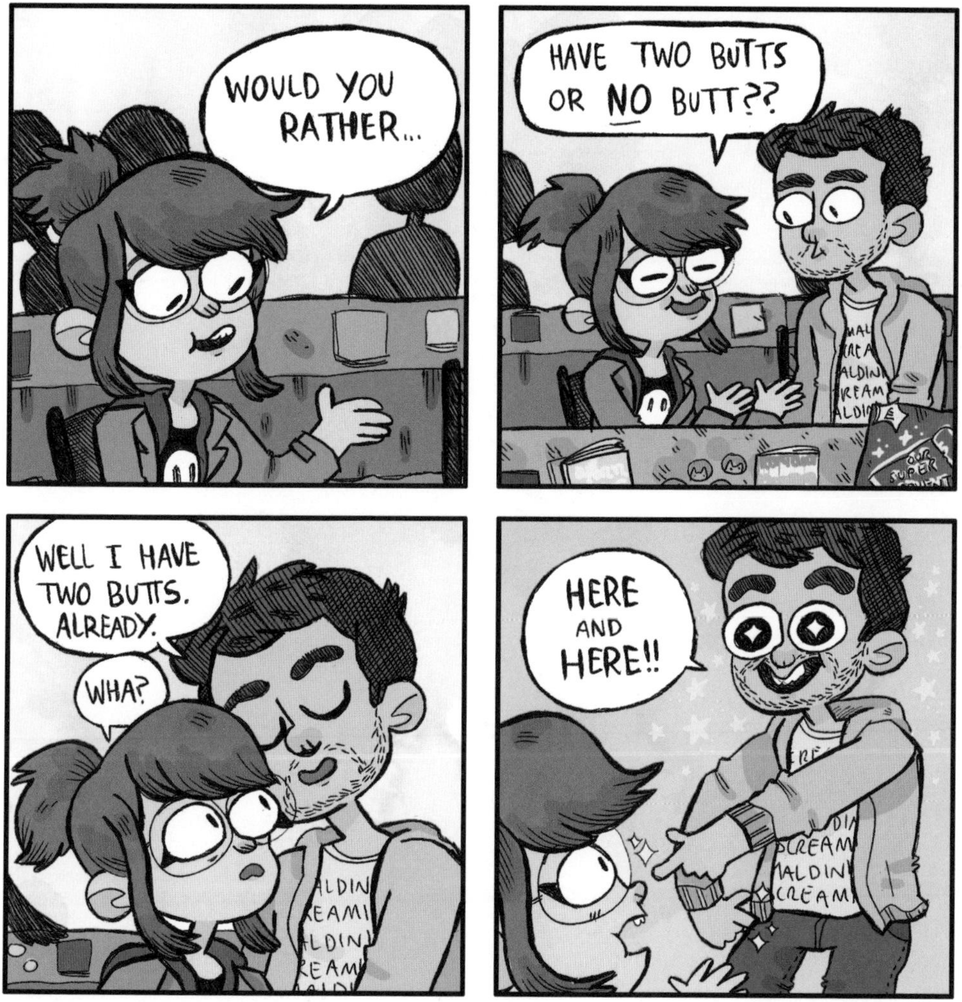
WOULD YOU RATHER...
HAVE TWO BUTTS OR NO BUTT??
WELL I HAVE TWO BUTTS. ALREADY.
WHA?
HERE AND HERE!!

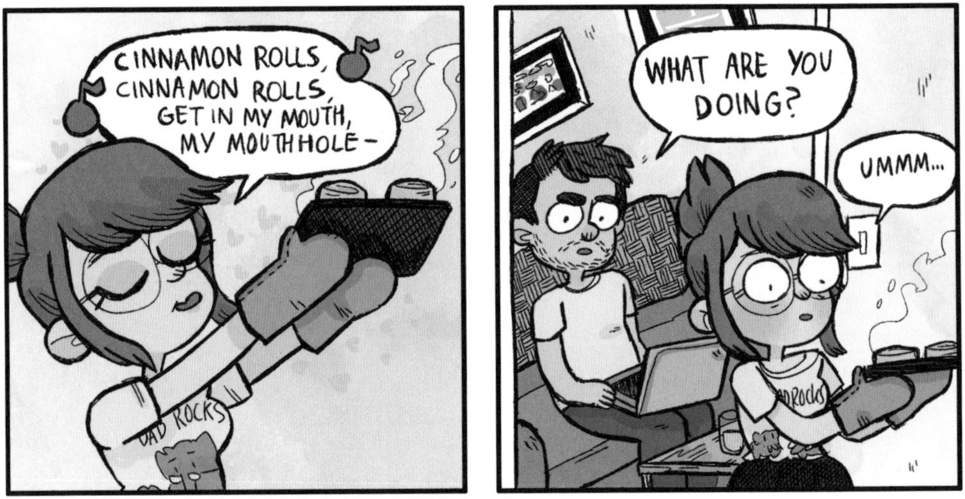
CINNAMON ROLLS, CINNAMON ROLLS, GET IN MY MOUTH, MY MOUTHHOLE-
DAD ROCKS
WHAT ARE YOU DOING?
UMMM...

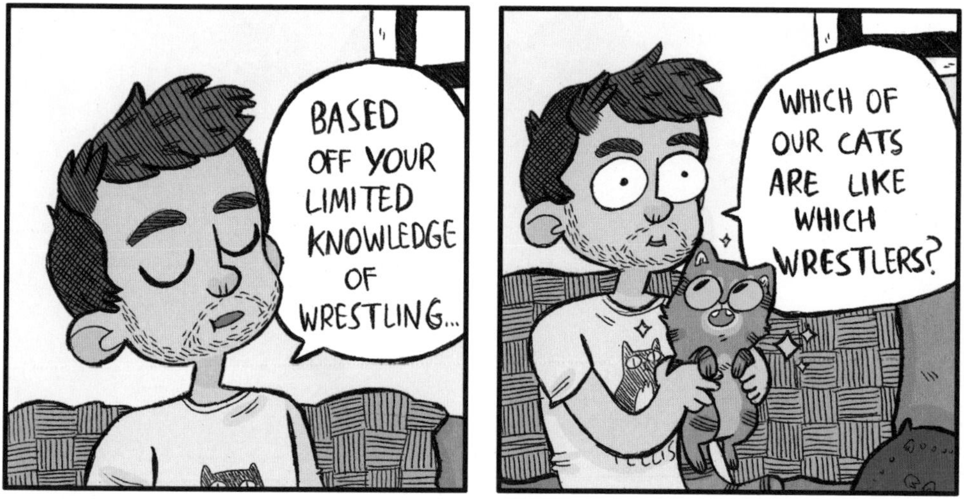
BASED OFF YOUR LIMITED KNOWLEDGE OF WRESTLING...
WHICH OF OUR CATS ARE LIKE WHICH WRESTLERS?

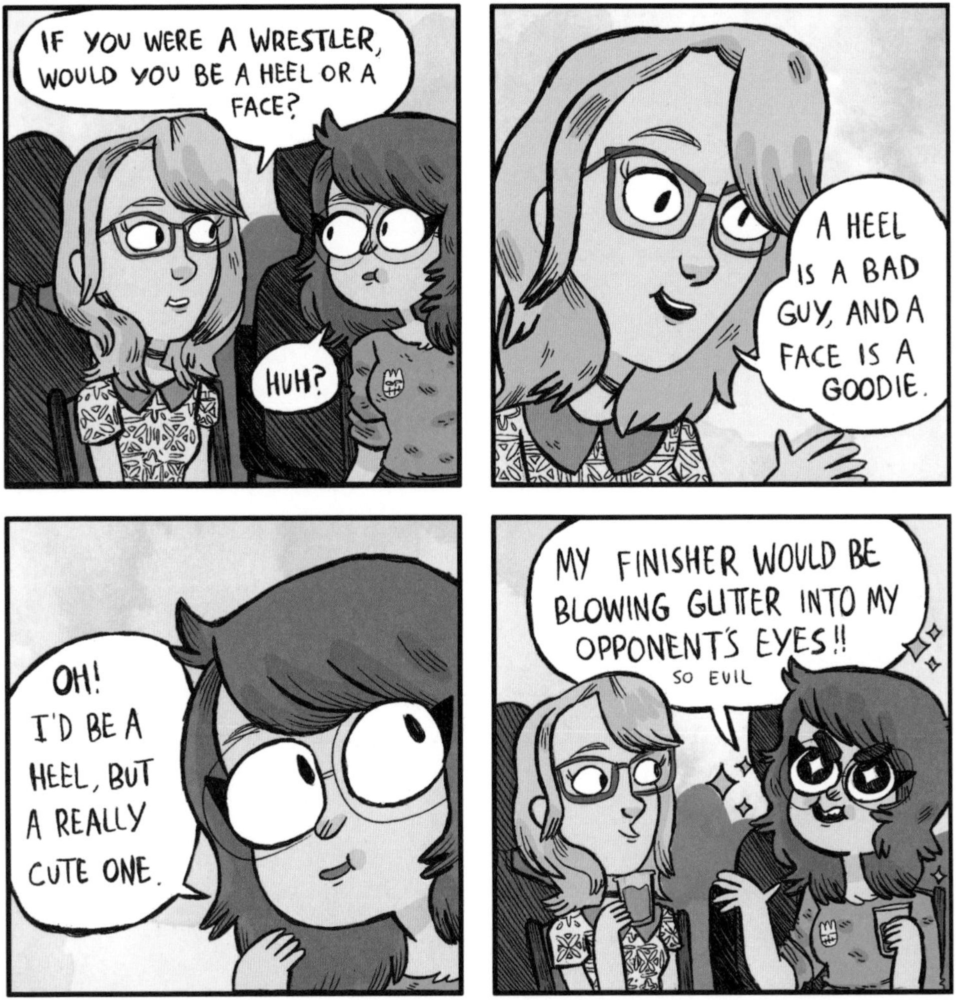
IF YOU WERE A WRESTLER, WOULD YOU BE A HEEL OR A FACE?
HUH?
A HEEL IS A BAD GUY, AND A FACE IS A GOODIE.
OH! I'D BE A HEEL, BUT A REALLY CUTE ONE.
MY FINISHER WOULD BE BLOWING GLITTER INTO MY OPPONENT'S EYES!!
SO EVIL

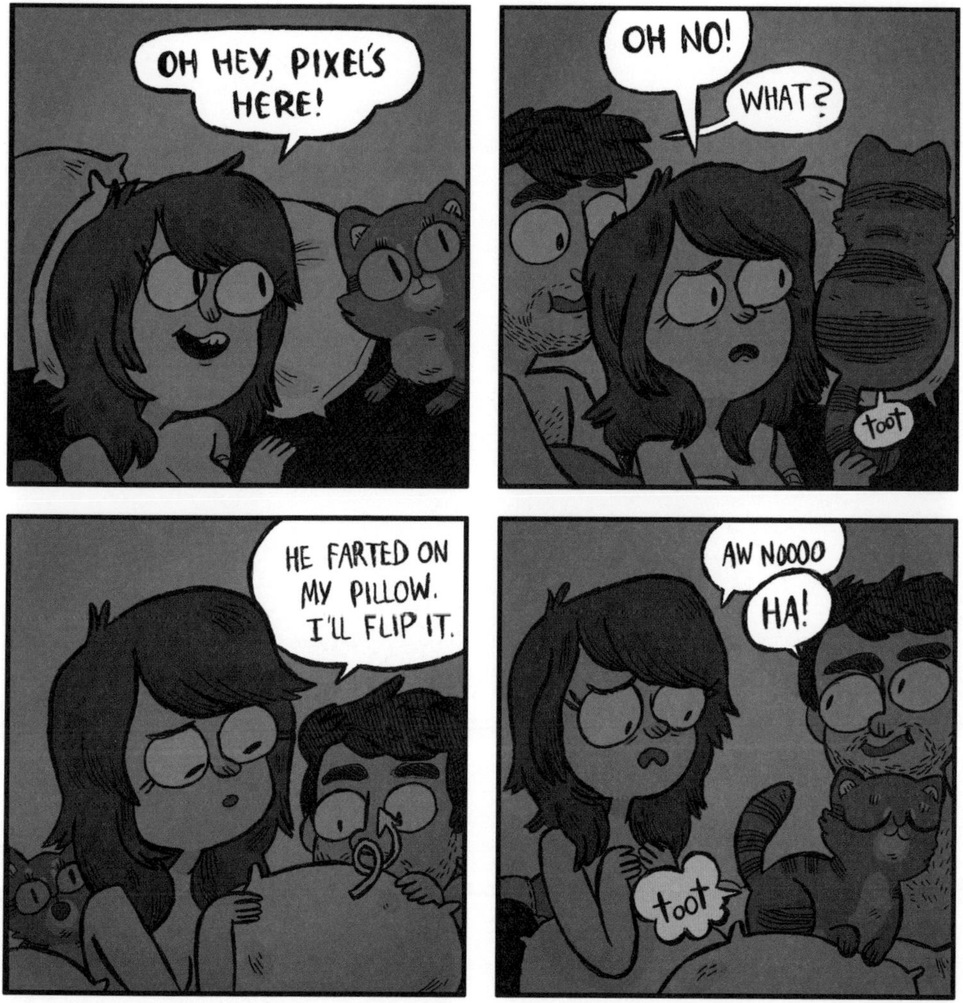

OH HEY, PIXEL'S HERE!
OH NO!
WHAT?
toot
HE FARTED ON MY PILLOW. I'LL FLIP IT.
AW NOOOO
HA!
toot

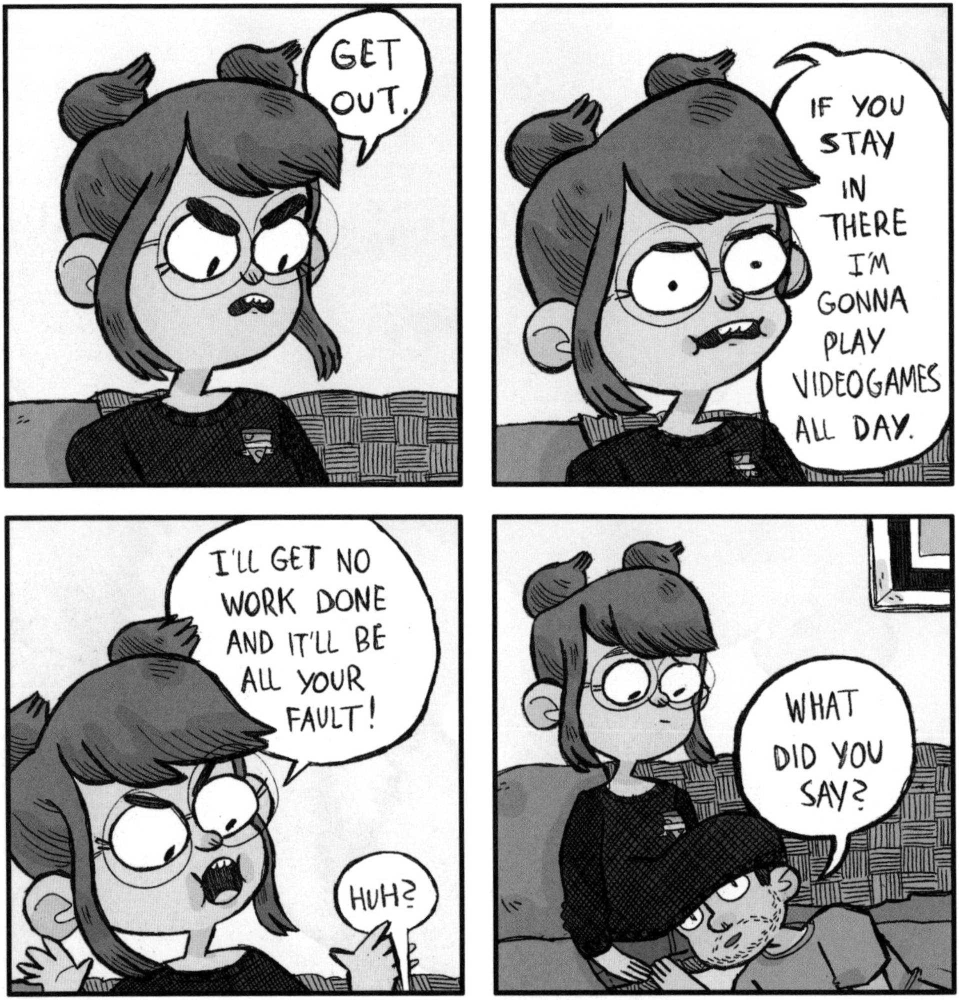
GET OUT.
IF YOU STAY IN THERE I'M GONNA PLAY VIDEOGAMES ALL DAY.
I'LL GET NO WORK DONE AND IT'LL BE ALL YOUR FAULT!
HUH?
WHAT DID YOU SAY?

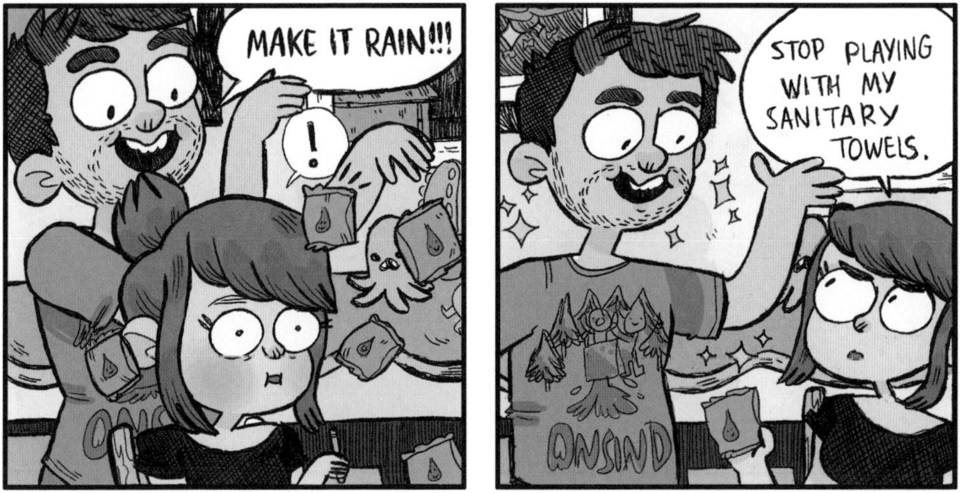
MAKE IT RAIN!!!
!
STOP PLAYING WITH MY SANITARY TOWELS.
ONSIND

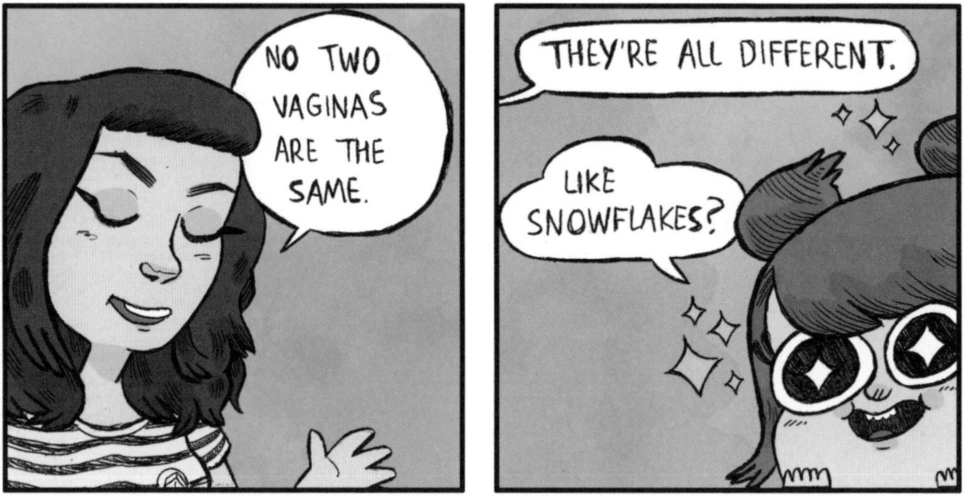
NO TWO VAGINAS ARE THE SAME.
THEY'RE ALL DIFFERENT.
LIKE SNOWFLAKES?

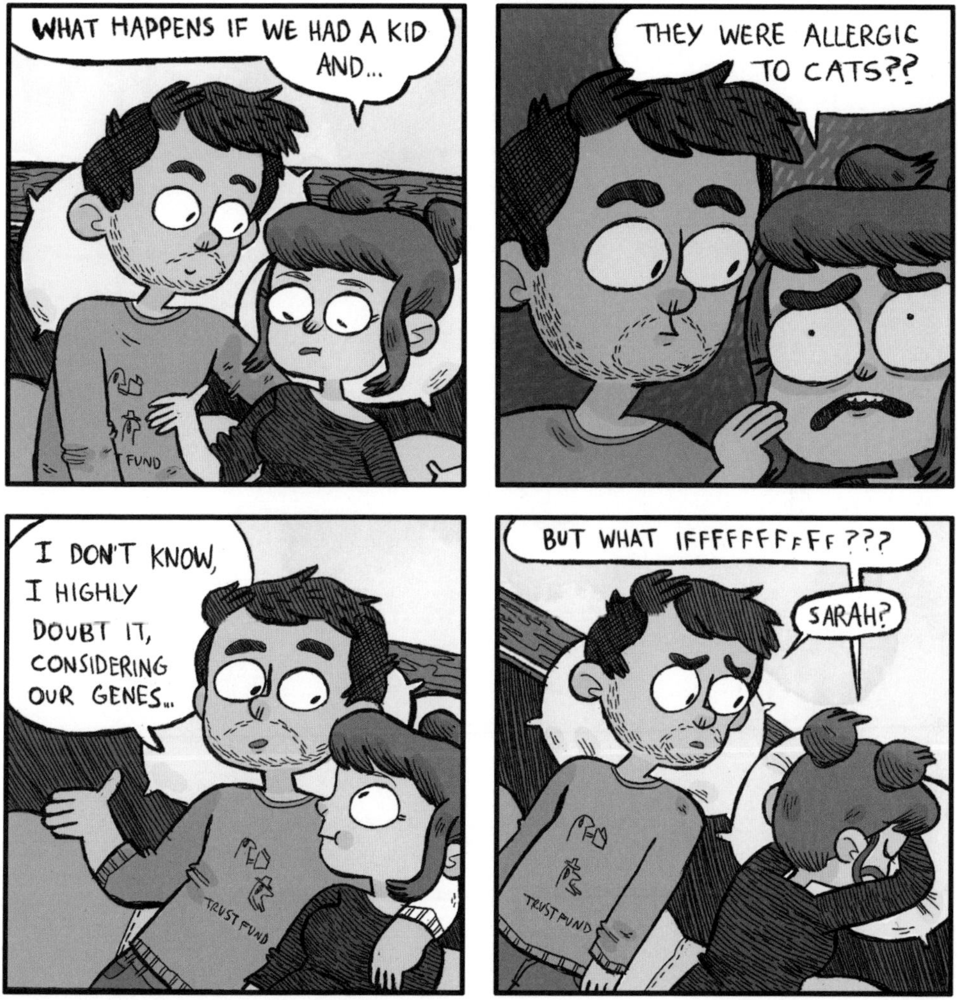
WHAT HAPPENS IF WE HAD A KID AND...
THEY WERE ALLERGIC TO CATS??
I DON'T KNOW, I HIGHLY DOUBT IT, CONSIDERING OUR GENES...
TRUST FUND
BUT WHAT IFFFFFFFFFF???
SARAH?
TRUST FUND

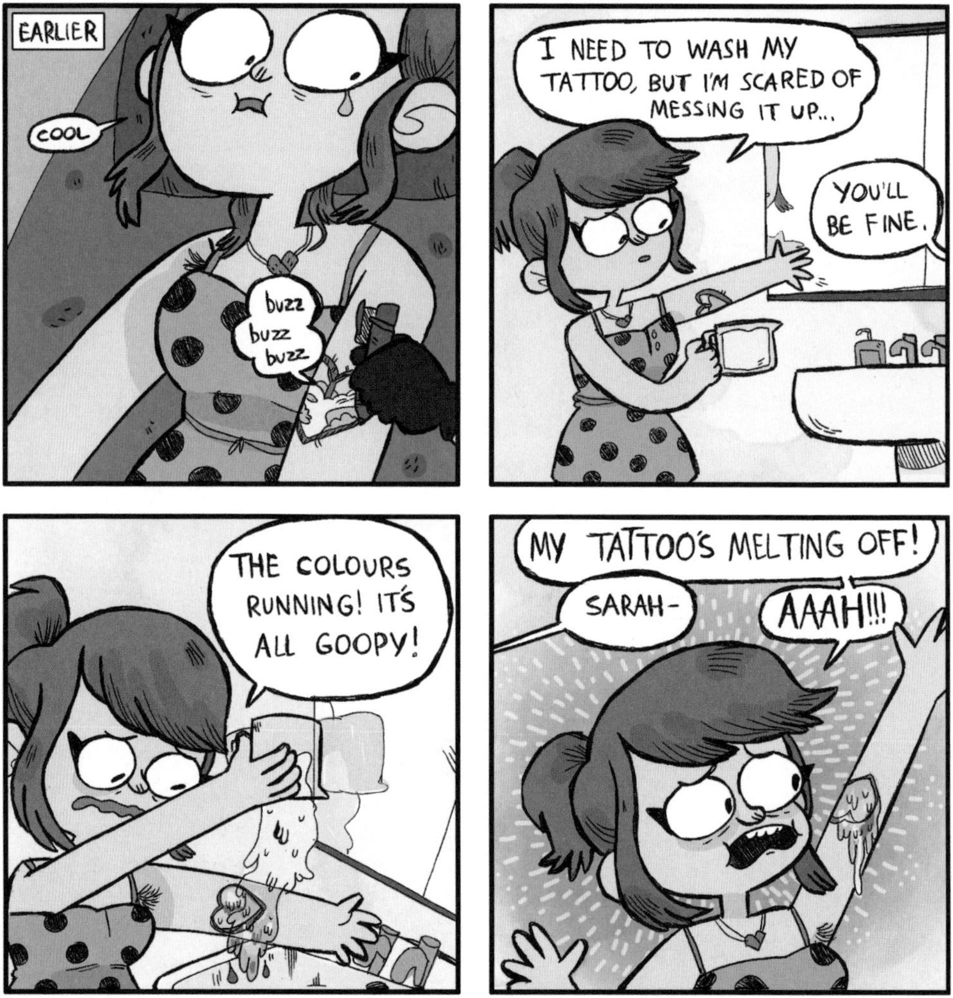
EARLIER
COOL
buzz
buzz
buzz
I NEED TO WASH MY TATTOO, BUT I'M SCARED OF MESSING IT UP...
YOU'LL BE FINE.
THE COLOURS RUNNING! IT'S ALL GOOPY!
MY TATTOO'S MELTING OFF!
SARAH-
AAAH!!!

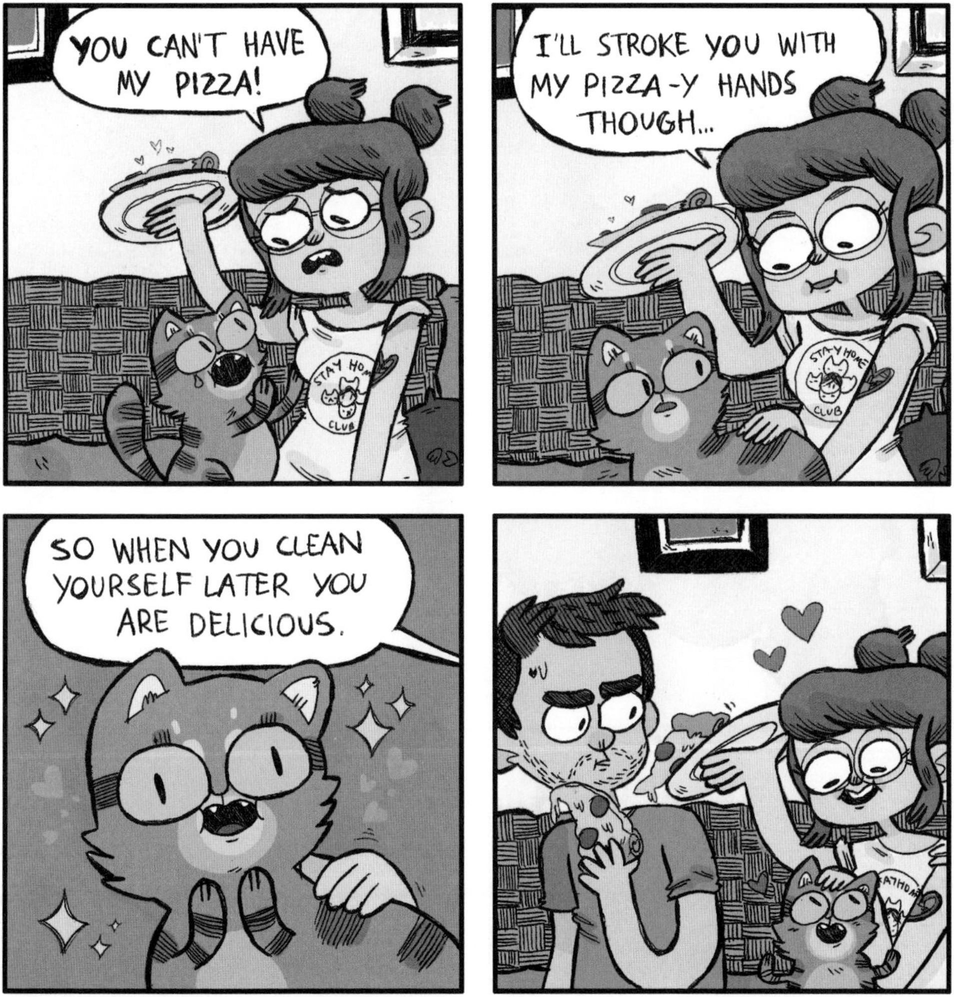
YOU CAN'T HAVE MY PIZZA!
I'LL STROKE YOU WITH MY PIZZA-Y HANDS THOUGH...
SO WHEN YOU CLEAN YOURSELF LATER YOU ARE DELICIOUS.

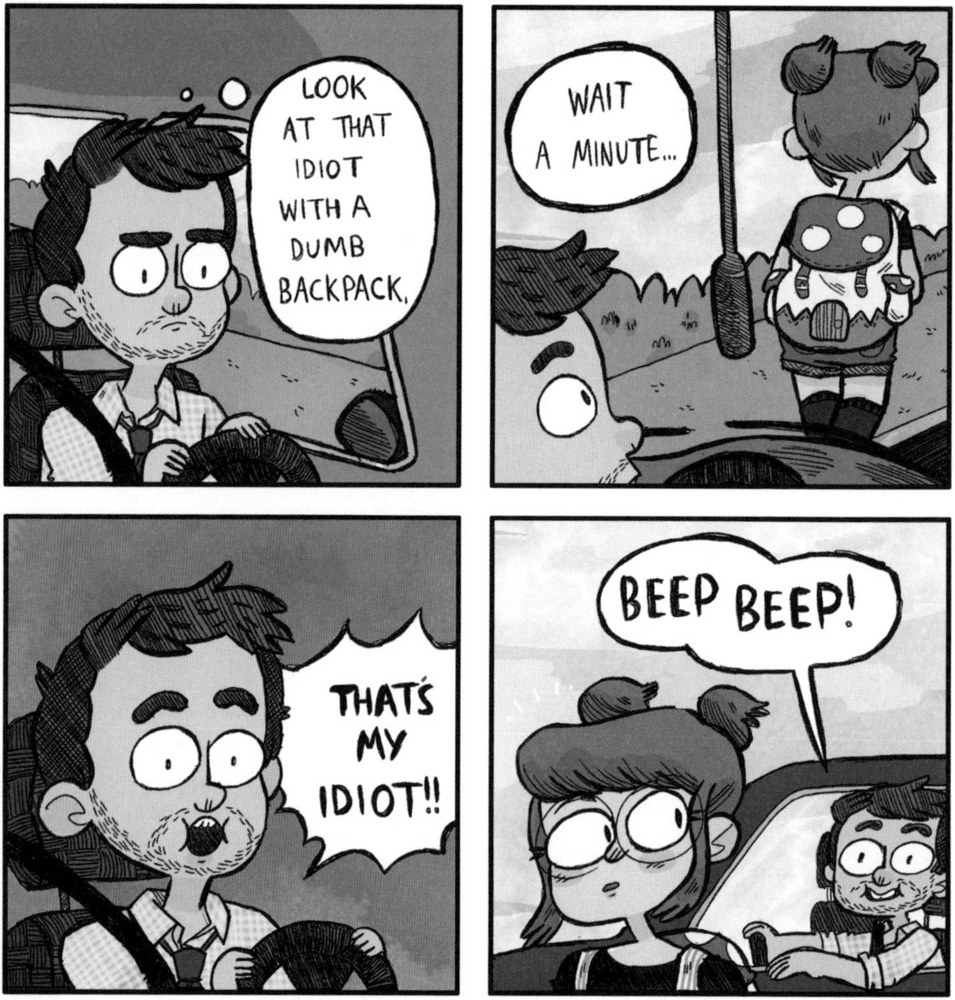
LOOK AT THAT IDIOT WITH A DUMB BACKPACK.
WAIT A MINUTE...
THAT'S MY IDIOT!!
BEEP BEEP!

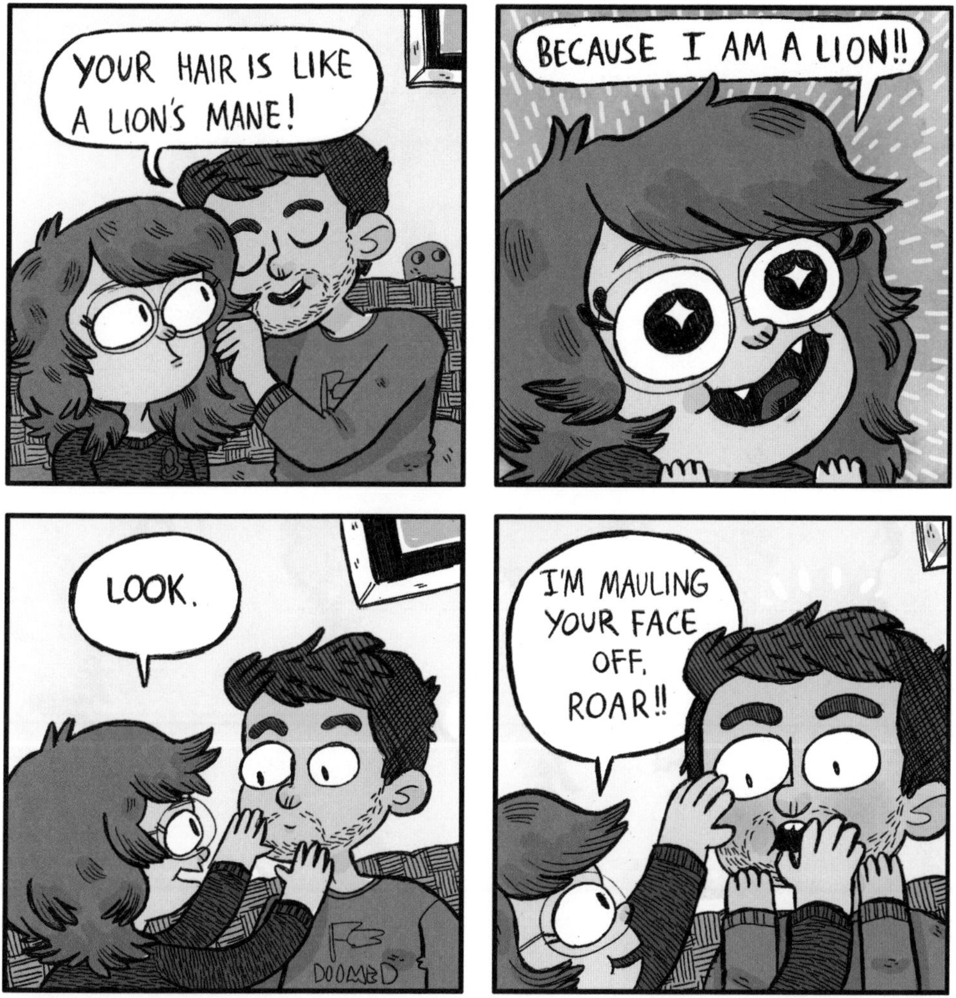
YOUR HAIR IS LIKE A LION'S MANE!
BECAUSE I AM A LION!!
LOOK.
DOOMED
I'M MAULING YOUR FACE OFF. ROAR!!

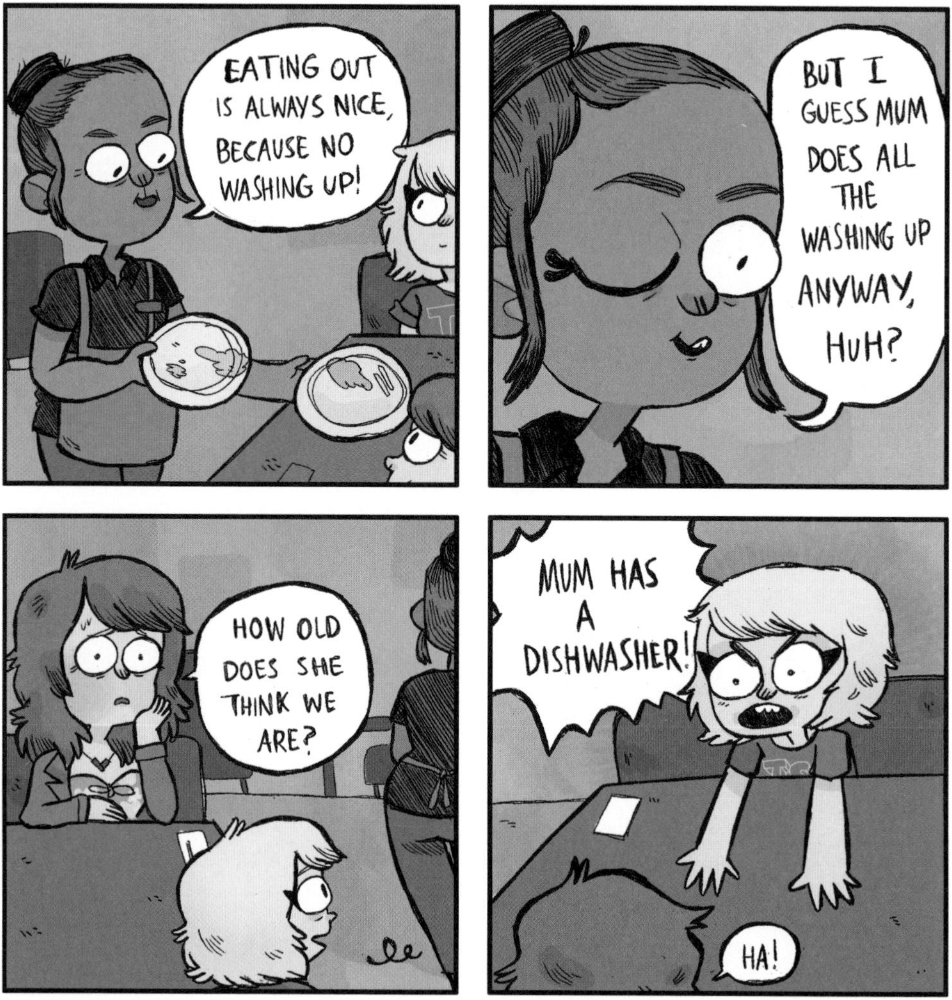
EATING OUT IS ALWAYS NICE, BECAUSE NO WASHING UP!
BUT I GUESS MUM DOES ALL THE WASHING UP ANYWAY, HUH?
HOW OLD DOES SHE THINK WE ARE?
MUM HAS A DISHWASHER!
HA!

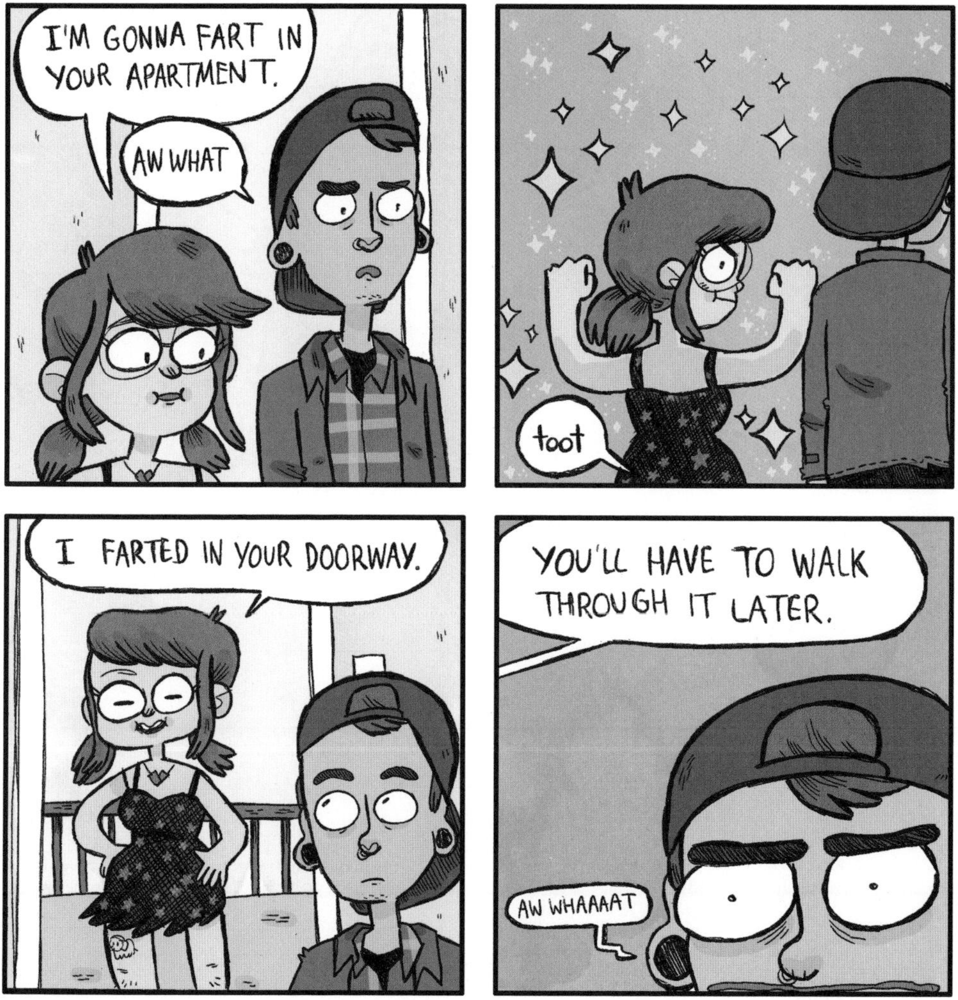
I'M GONNA FART IN YOUR APARTMENT.
AW WHAT
toot
I FARTED IN YOUR DOORWAY.
YOU'LL HAVE TO WALK THROUGH IT LATER.
AW WHAAAAT

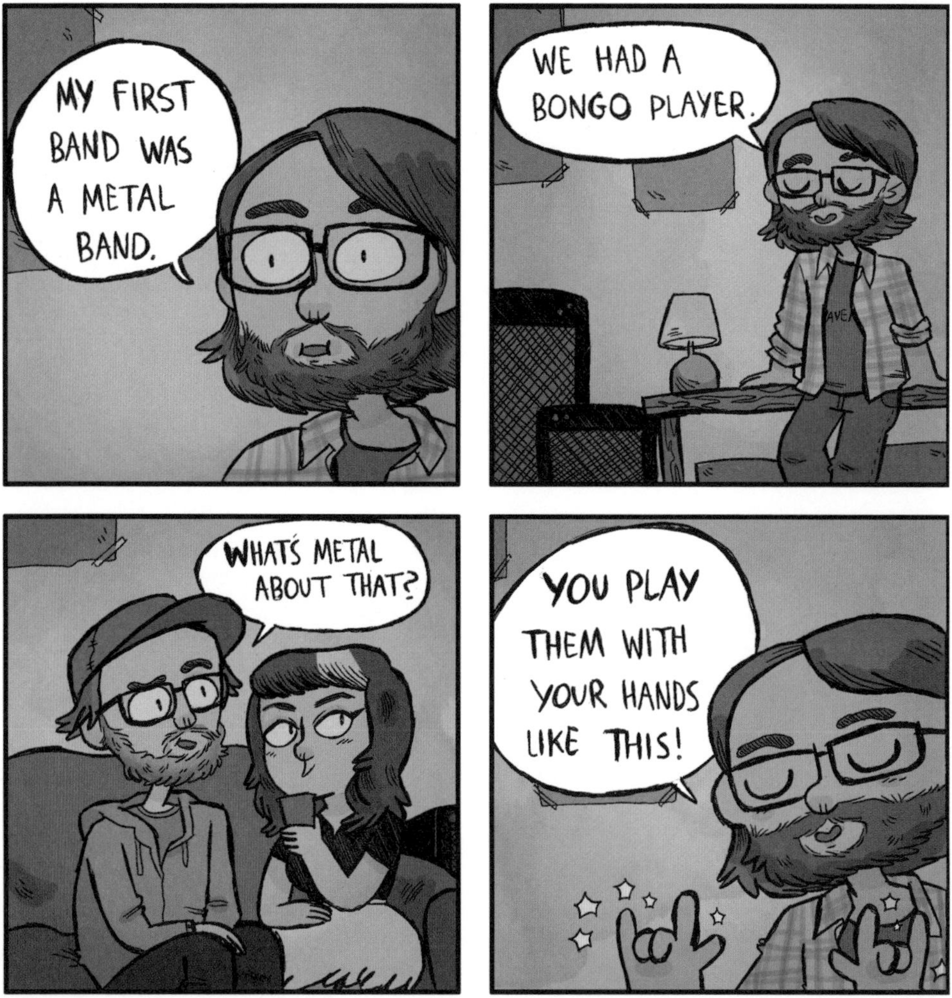
MY FIRST BAND WAS A METAL BAND.
WE HAD A BONGO PLAYER.
WHAT'S METAL ABOUT THAT?
YOU PLAY THEM WITH YOUR HANDS LIKE THIS!

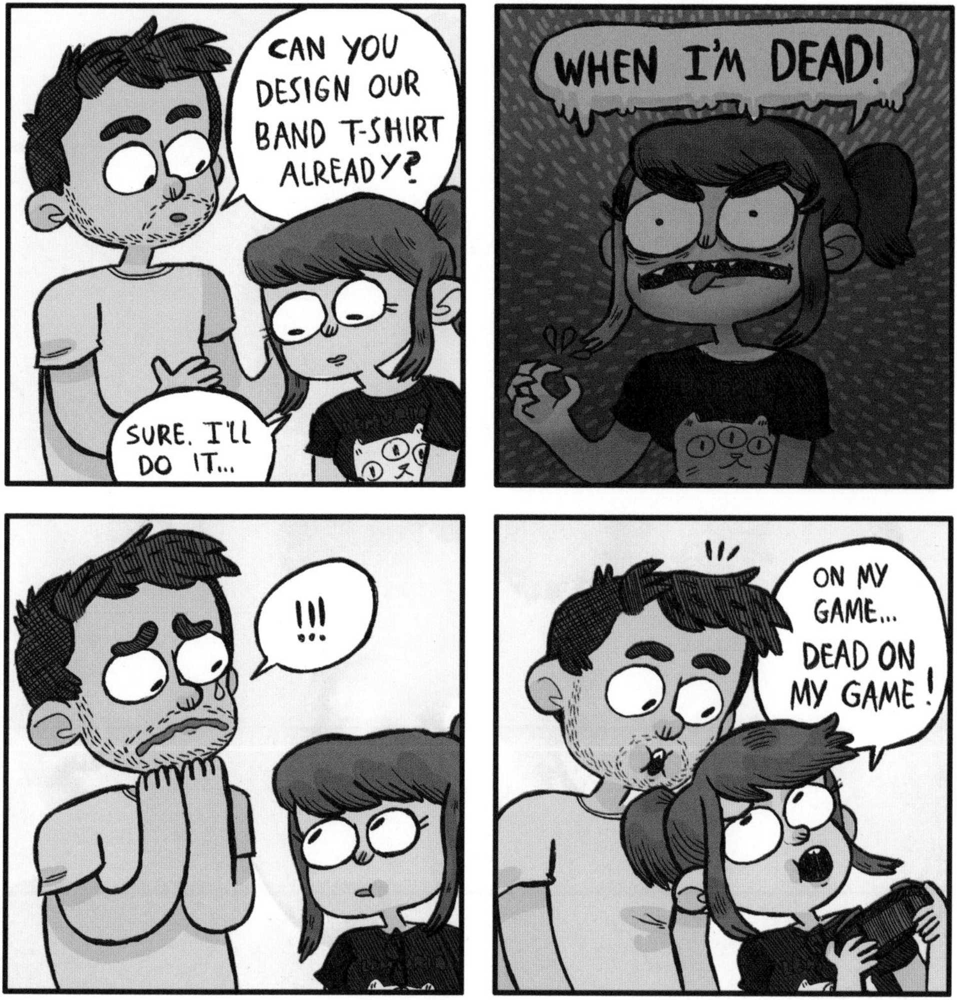
CAN YOU DESIGN OUR BAND T-SHIRT ALREADY?
SURE. I'LL DO IT...
WHEN I'M DEAD!
!!!
ON MY GAME...
DEAD ON MY GAME!

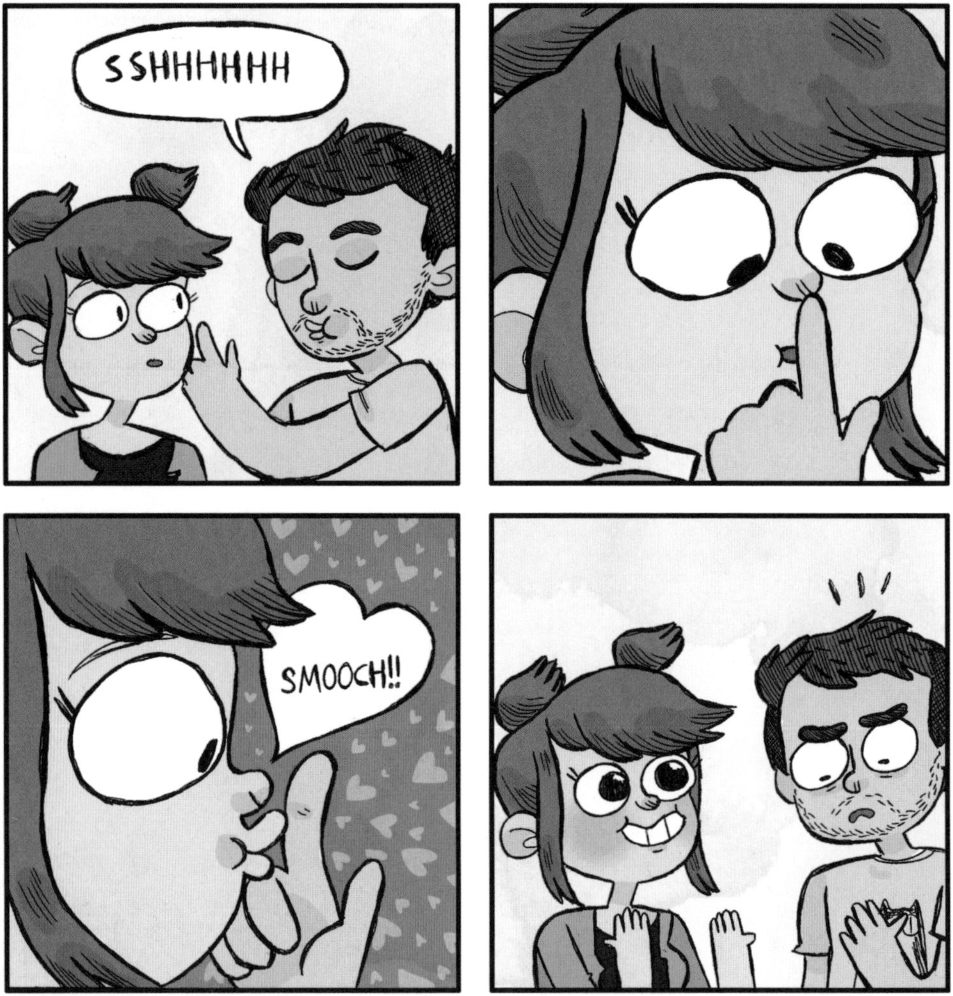
SSHHHHHH
SMOOCH!!

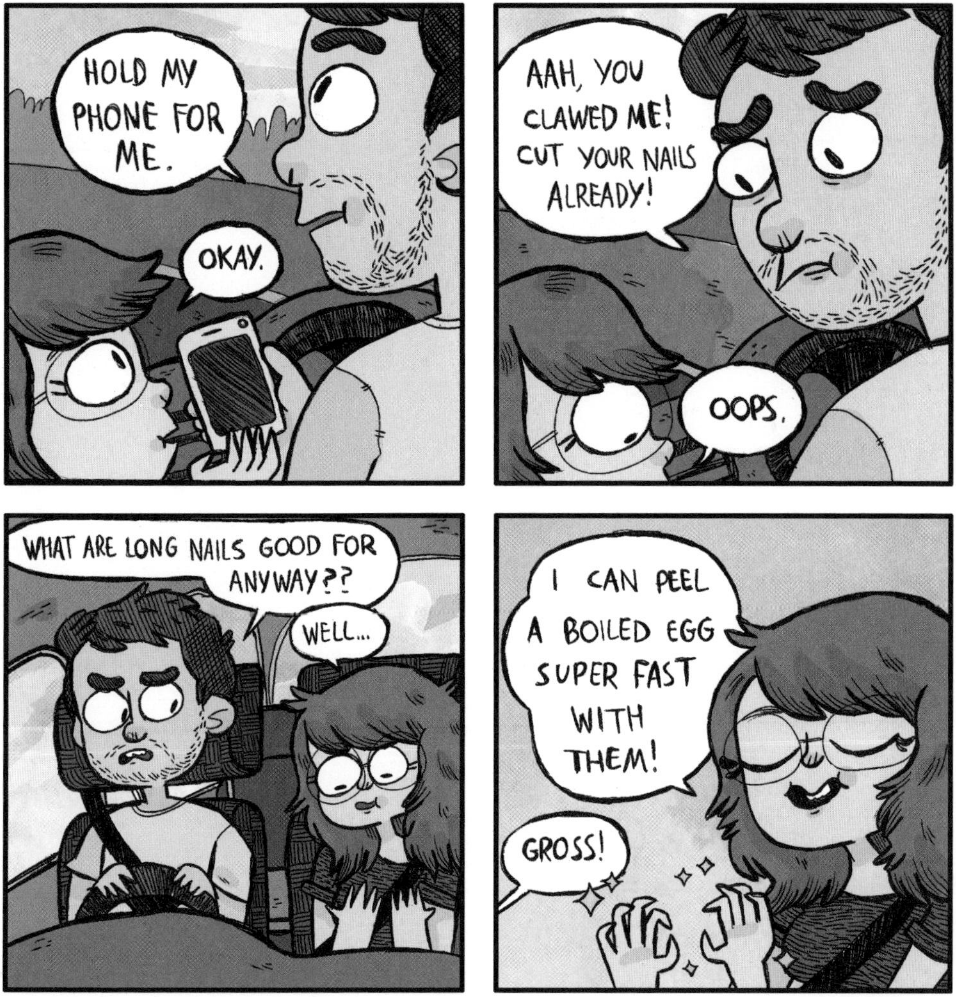
HOLD MY PHONE FOR ME.
OKAY.
AAH, YOU CLAWED ME! CUT YOUR NAILS ALREADY!
OOPS.
WHAT ARE LONG NAILS GOOD FOR ANYWAY??
WELL...
I CAN PEEL A BOILED EGG SUPER FAST WITH THEM!
GROSS!

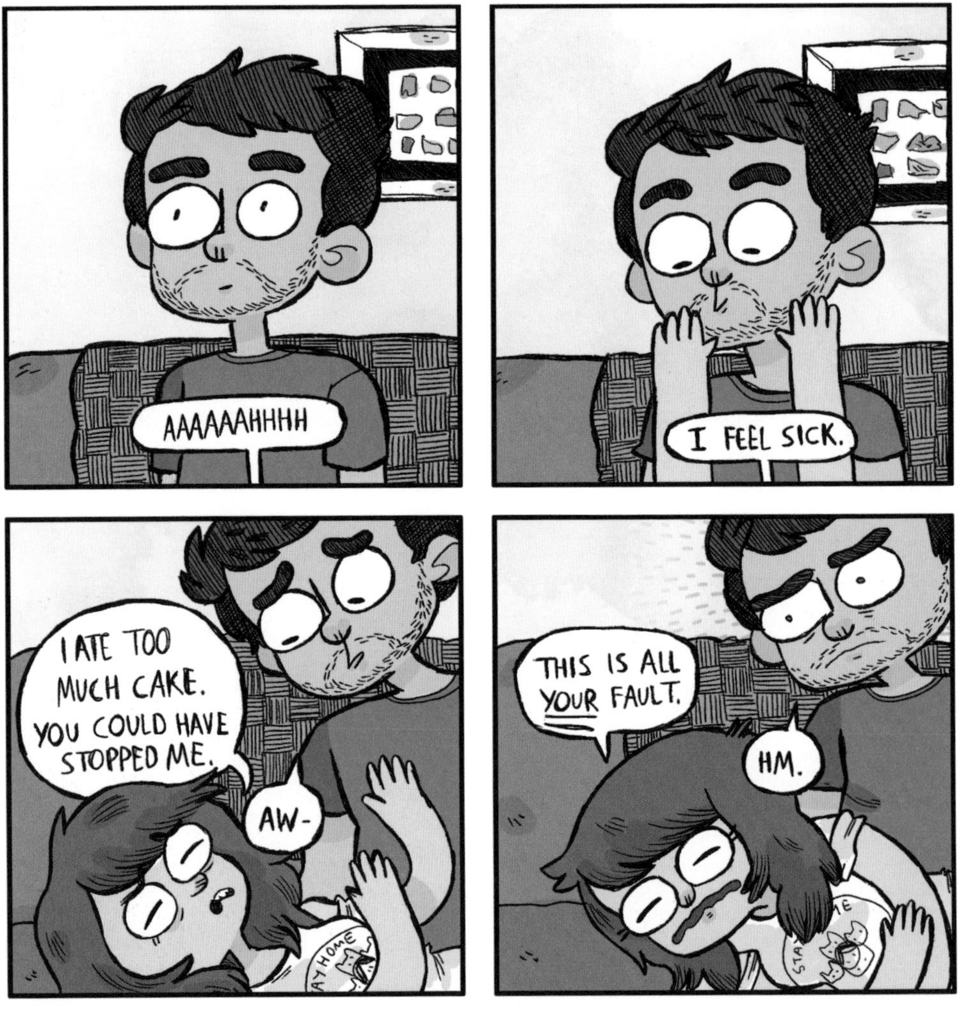
AAAAAAHHHH
I FEEL SICK.
I ATE TOO MUCH CAKE. YOU COULD HAVE STOPPED ME.
AW-
THIS IS ALL YOUR FAULT.
HM.

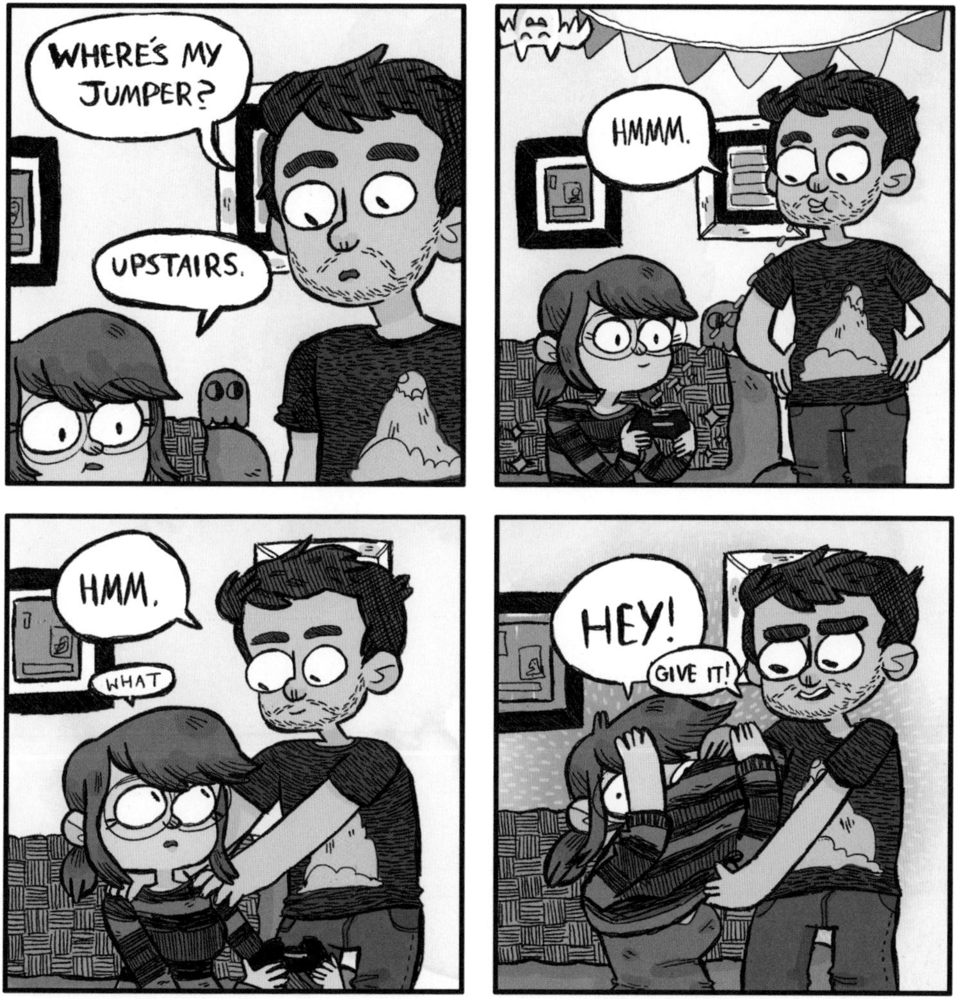
WHERE'S MY JUMPER?
UPSTAIRS.
HMMM.
HMM.
WHAT
HEY!
GIVE IT!

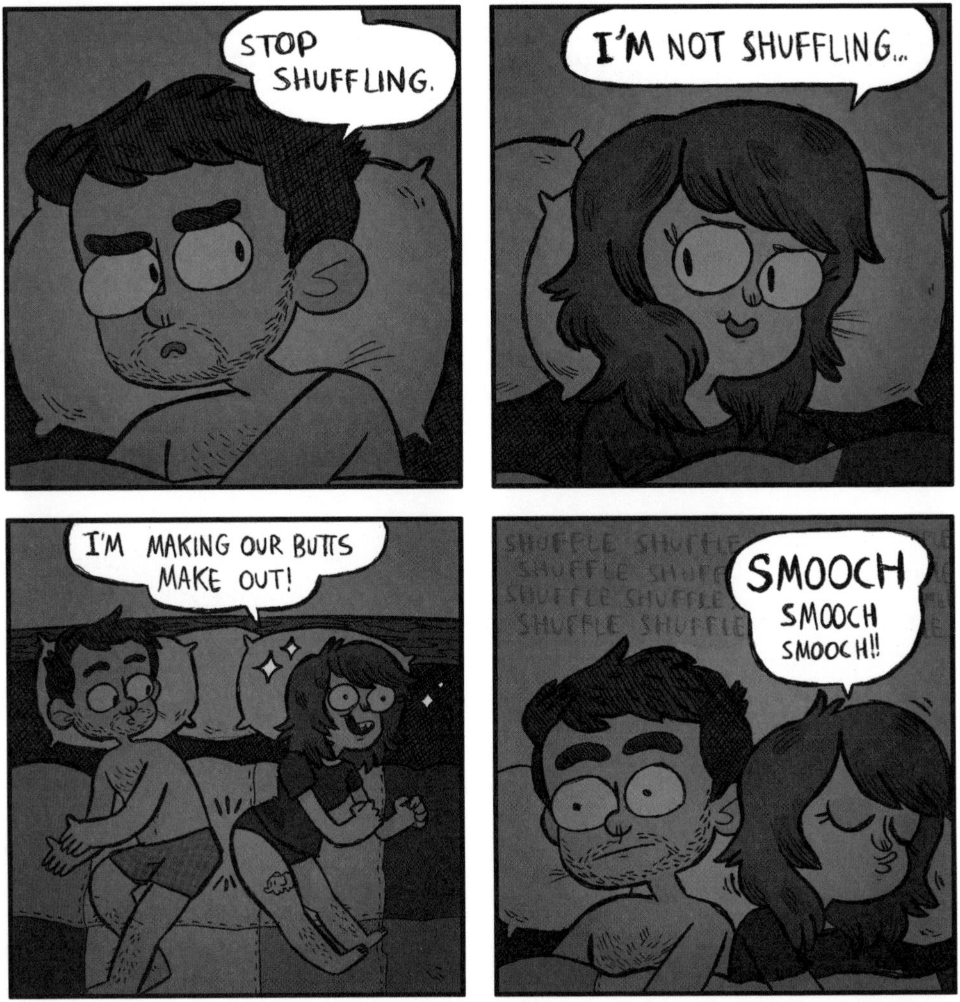
STOP SHUFFLING.
I'M NOT SHUFFLING...
I'M MAKING OUR BUTTS MAKE OUT!
SHUFFLE SHUFFLE SHUFFLE SHUFFLE SHUFFLE SHUFFLE SHUFFLE SHUFFLE
SMOOCH SMOOCH SMOOCH!!

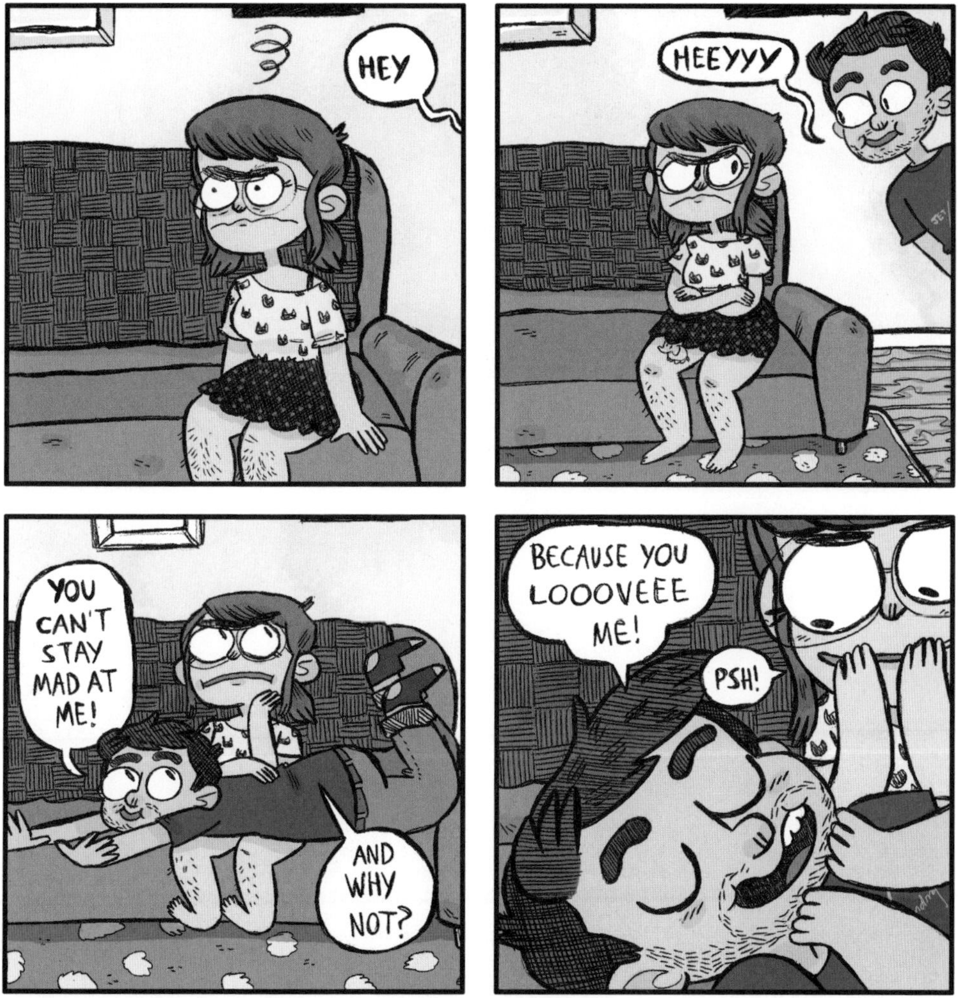

HEY
HEEYYY
YOU CAN'T STAY MAD AT ME!
AND WHY NOT?
BECAUSE YOU LOOOVEEE ME!
PSH!

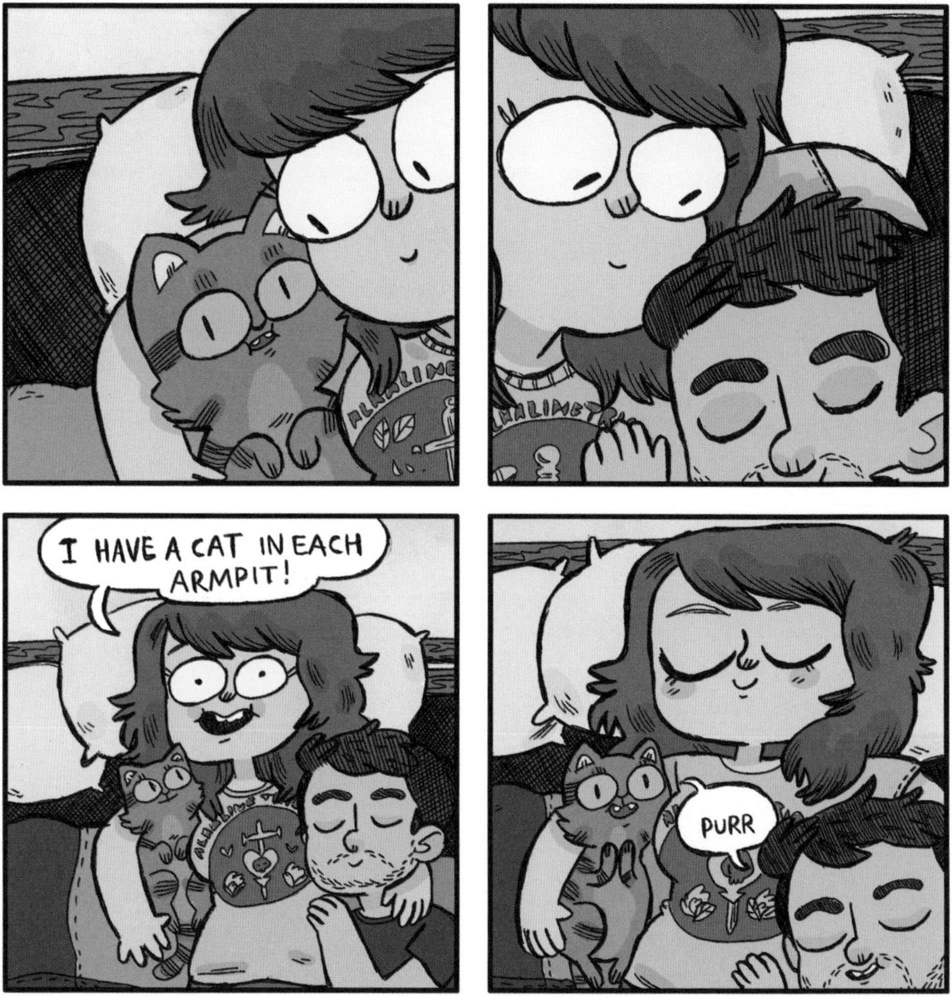
I HAVE A CAT IN EACH ARMPIT!
PURR

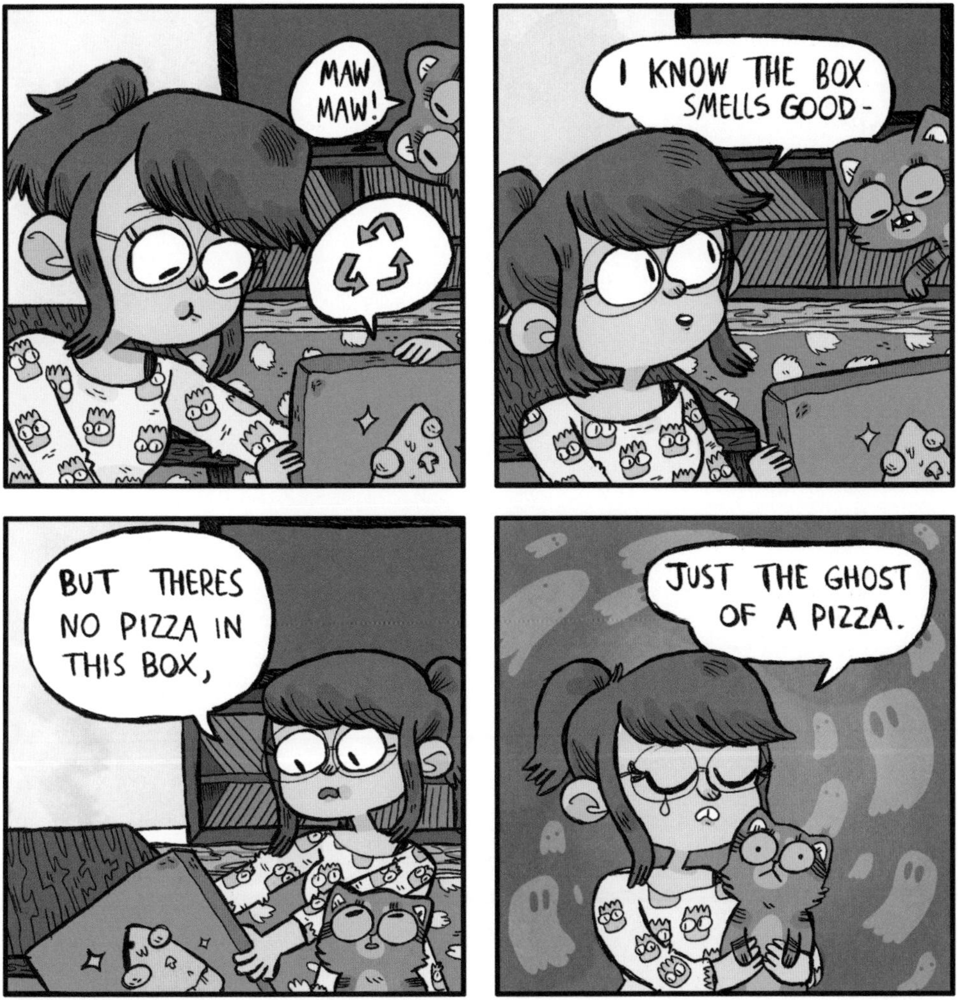
MAW MAW!
I KNOW THE BOX SMELLS GOOD -
BUT THERES NO PIZZA IN THIS BOX,
JUST THE GHOST OF A PIZZA.

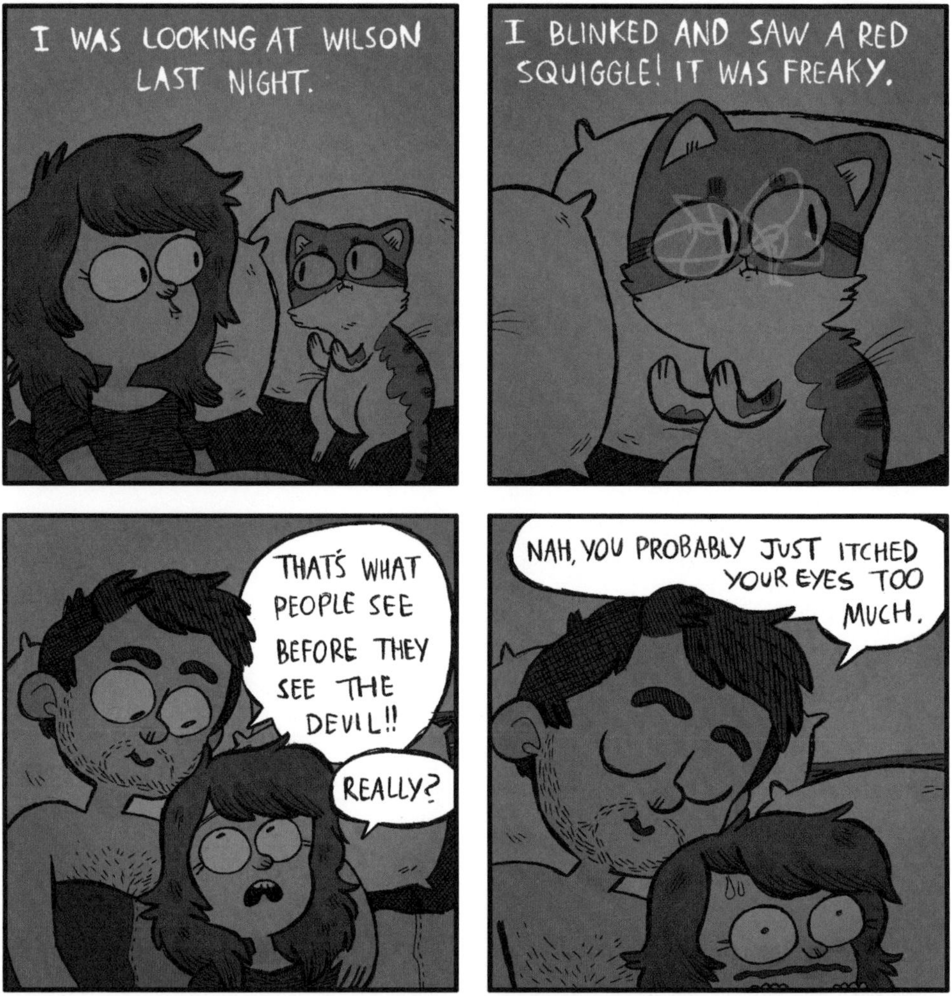
I WAS LOOKING AT WILSON LAST NIGHT.
I BLINKED AND SAW A RED SQUIGGLE! IT WAS FREAKY.
THAT'S WHAT PEOPLE SEE BEFORE THEY SEE THE DEVIL!!
REALLY?
NAH, YOU PROBABLY JUST ITCHED YOUR EYES TOO MUCH.

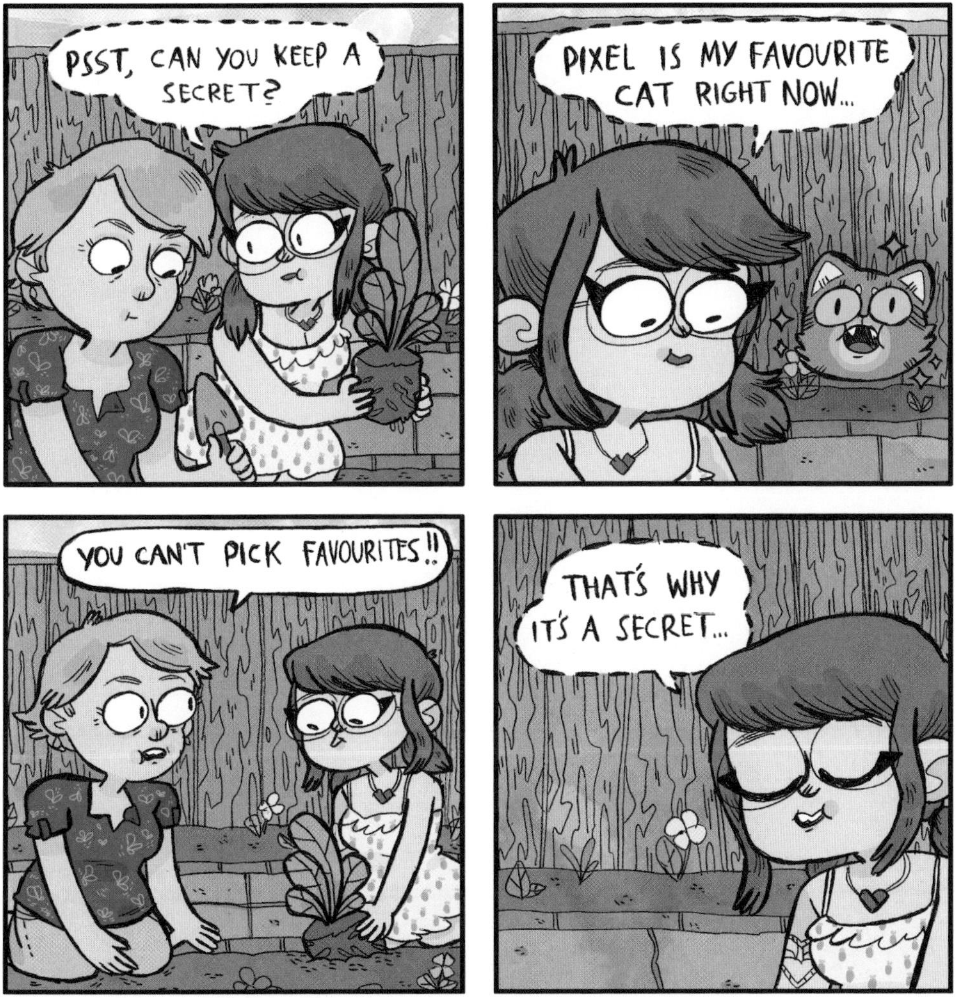
PSST, CAN YOU KEEP A SECRET?
PIXEL IS MY FAVOURITE CAT RIGHT NOW...
YOU CAN'T PICK FAVOURITES!!
THAT'S WHY IT'S A SECRET...

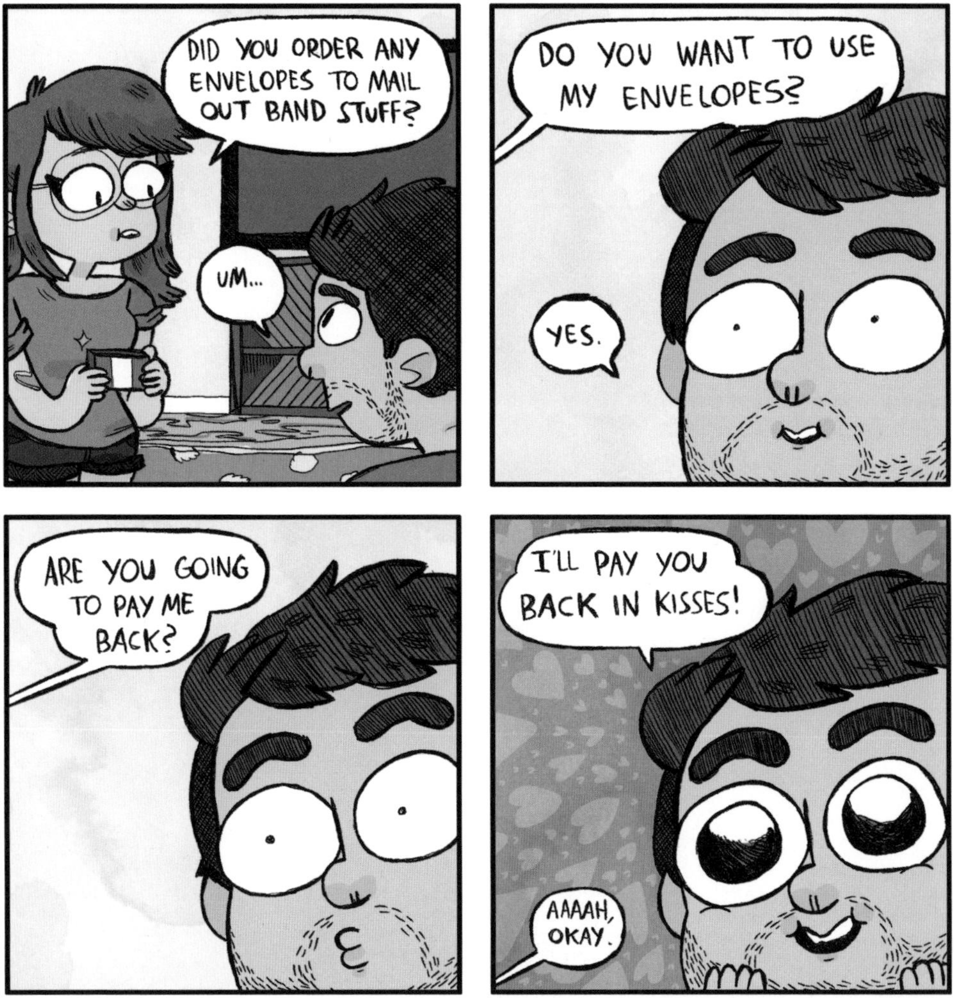
DID YOU ORDER ANY ENVELOPES TO MAIL OUT BAND STUFF?
UM...
DO YOU WANT TO USE MY ENVELOPES?
YES.
ARE YOU GOING TO PAY ME BACK?
I'LL PAY YOU BACK IN KISSES!
AAAAH, OKAY.

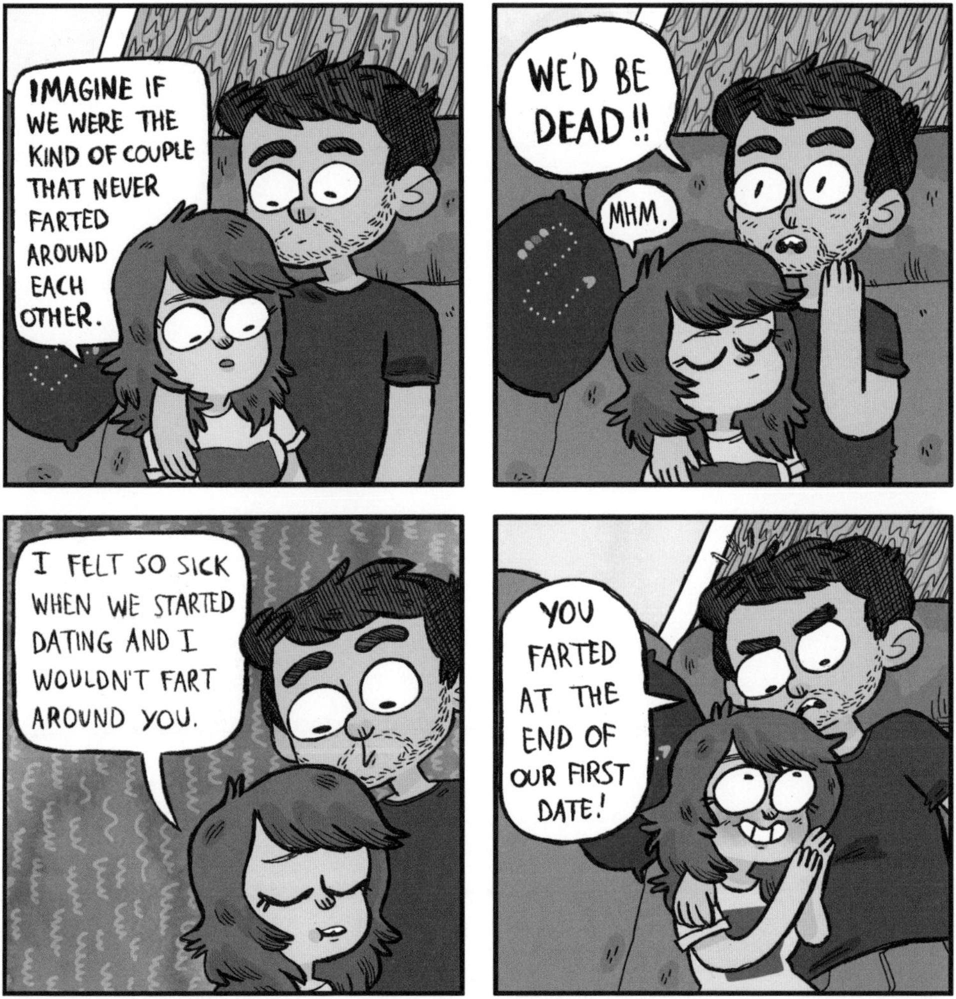
IMAGINE IF WE WERE THE KIND OF COUPLE THAT NEVER FARTED AROUND EACH OTHER.
WE'D BE DEAD!!
MHM.
I FELT SO SICK WHEN WE STARTED DATING AND I WOULDN'T FART AROUND YOU.
YOU FARTED AT THE END OF OUR FIRST DATE!

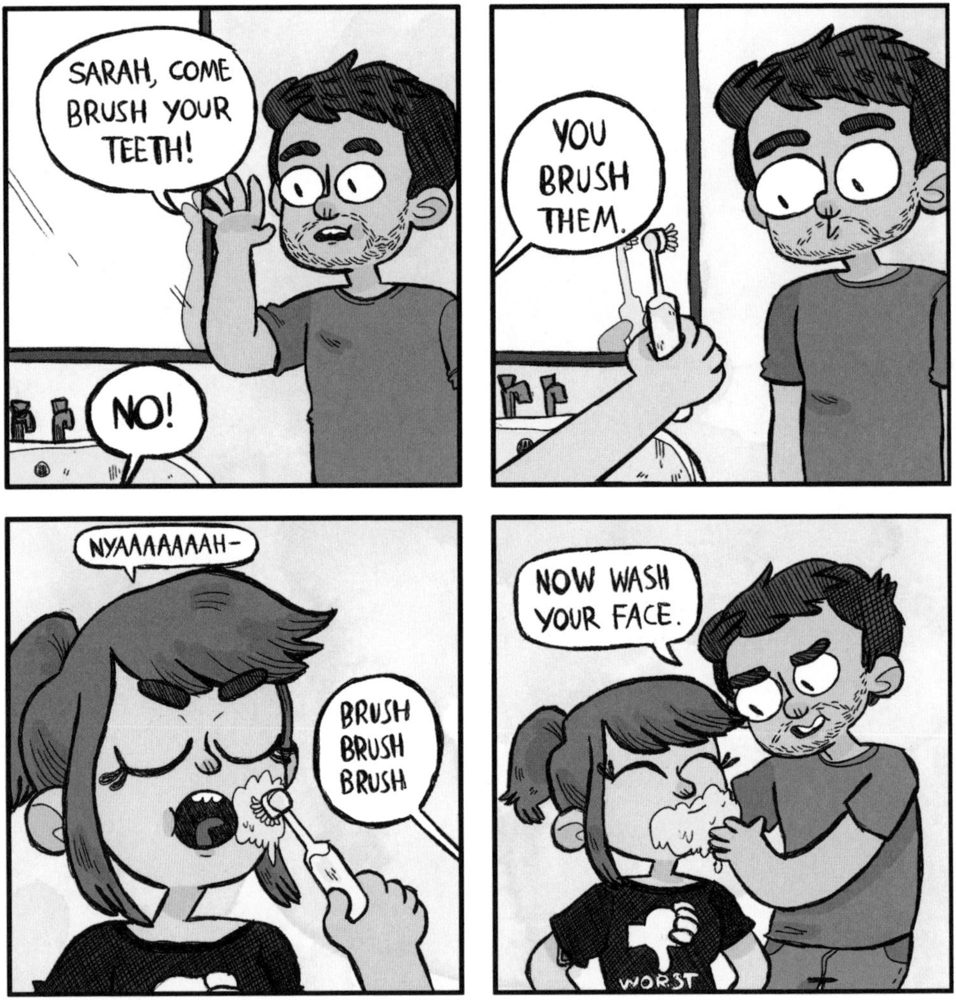
SARAH, COME BRUSH YOUR TEETH!
NO!
YOU BRUSH THEM.
NYAAAAAAAH-
BRUSH BRUSH BRUSH
NOW WASH YOUR FACE.
WORST

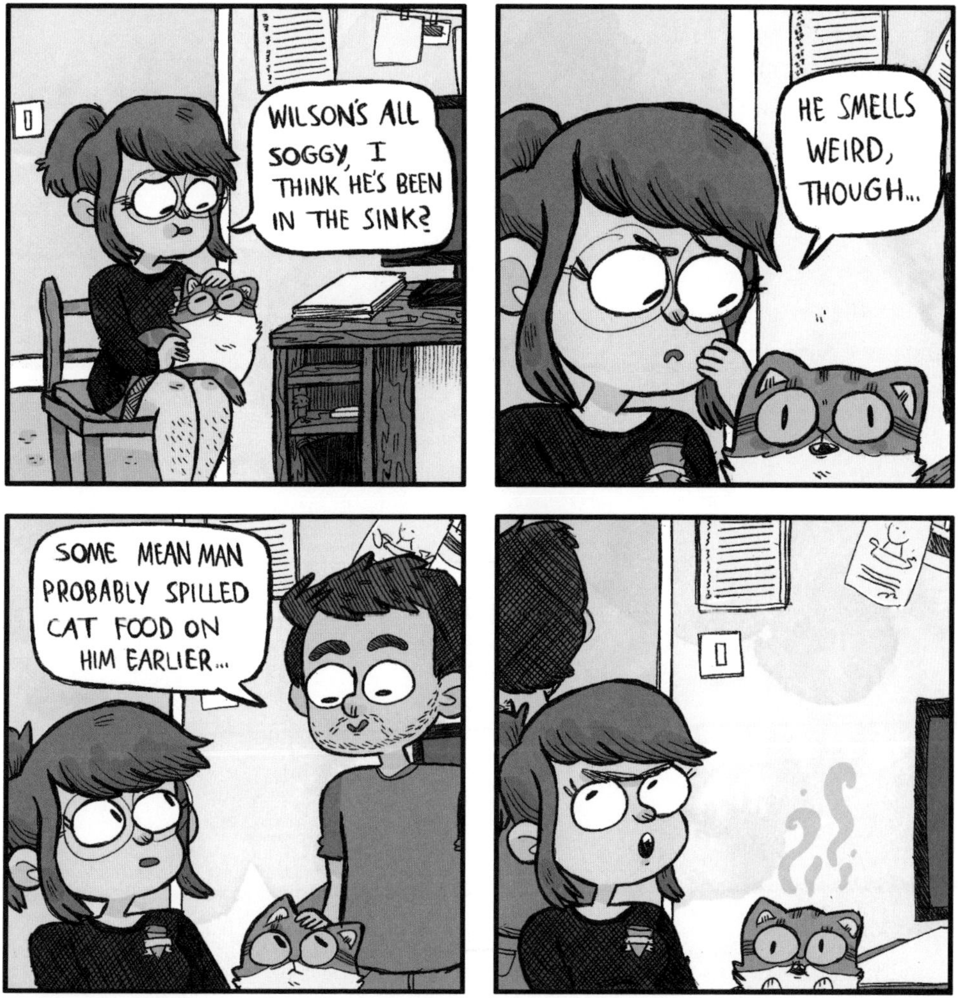
WILSON'S ALL SOGGY, I THINK HE'S BEEN IN THE SINK?
HE SMELLS WEIRD, THOUGH...
SOME MEAN MAN PROBABLY SPILLED CAT FOOD ON HIM EARLIER...

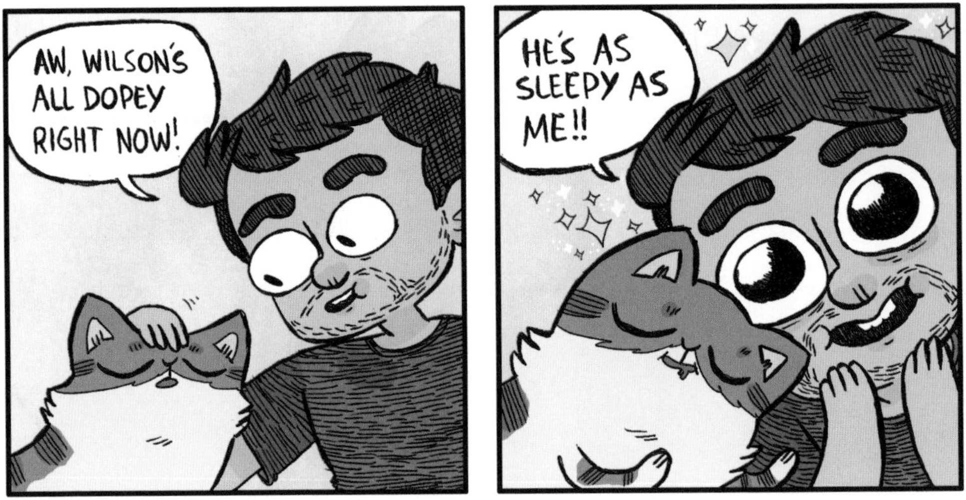
AW, WILSON'S ALL DOPEY RIGHT NOW!
HE'S AS SLEEPY AS ME!!

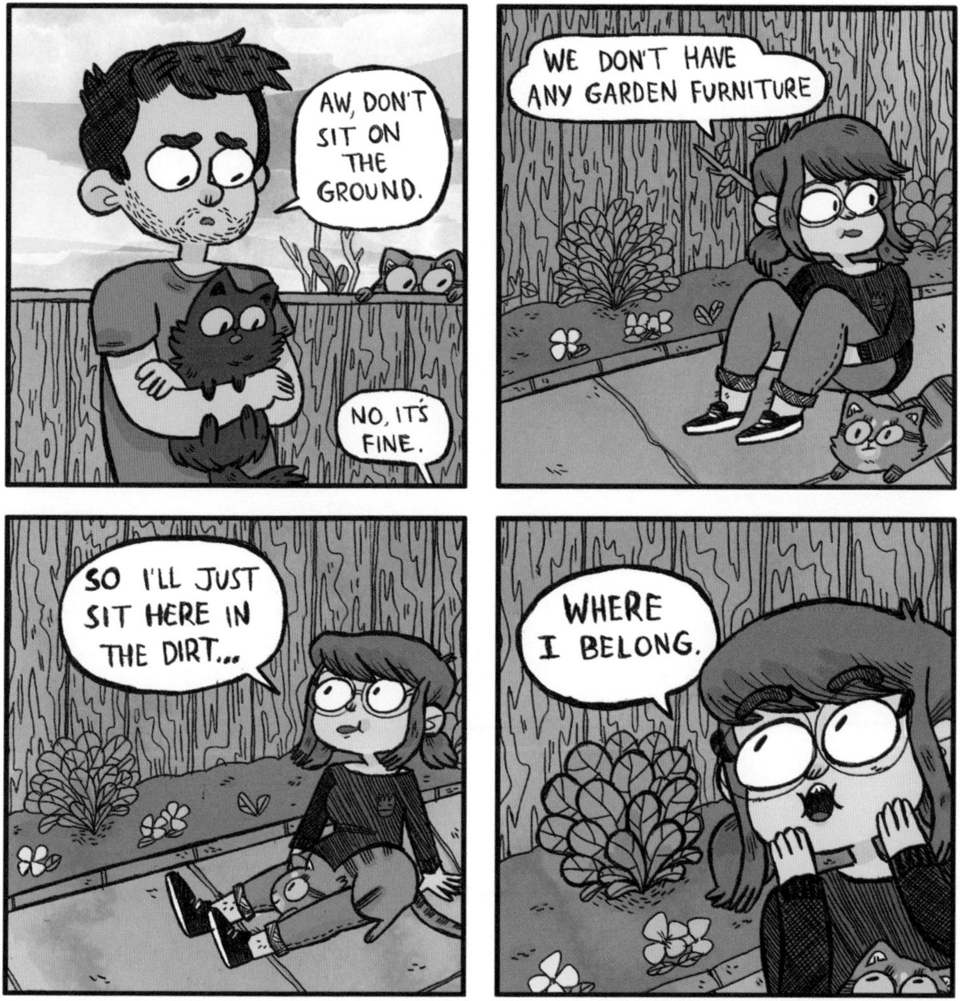
AW, DON'T SIT ON THE GROUND.
NO, IT'S FINE.
WE DON'T HAVE ANY GARDEN FURNITURE
SO I'LL JUST SIT HERE IN THE DIRT...
WHERE I BELONG.

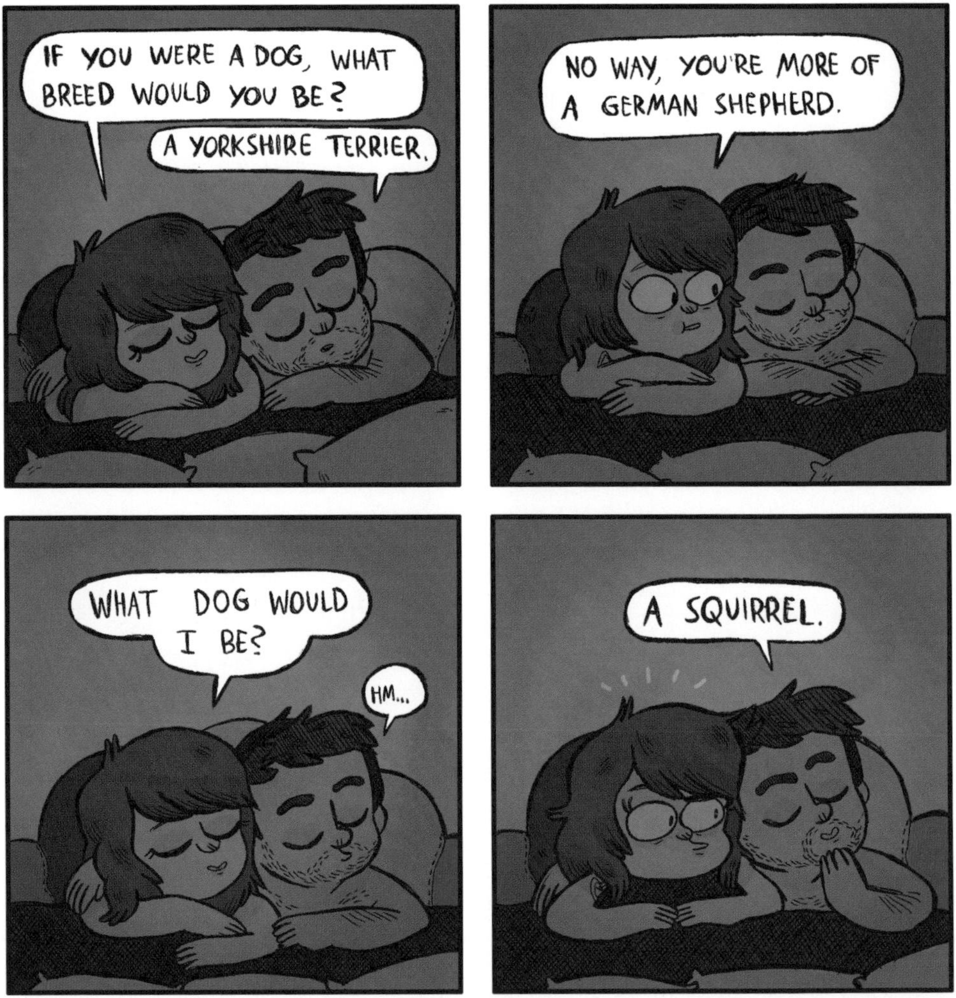
IF YOU WERE A DOG, WHAT BREED WOULD YOU BE?
A YORKSHIRE TERRIER.
NO WAY, YOU'RE MORE OF A GERMAN SHEPHERD.
WHAT DOG WOULD I BE?
HM...
A SQUIRREL.

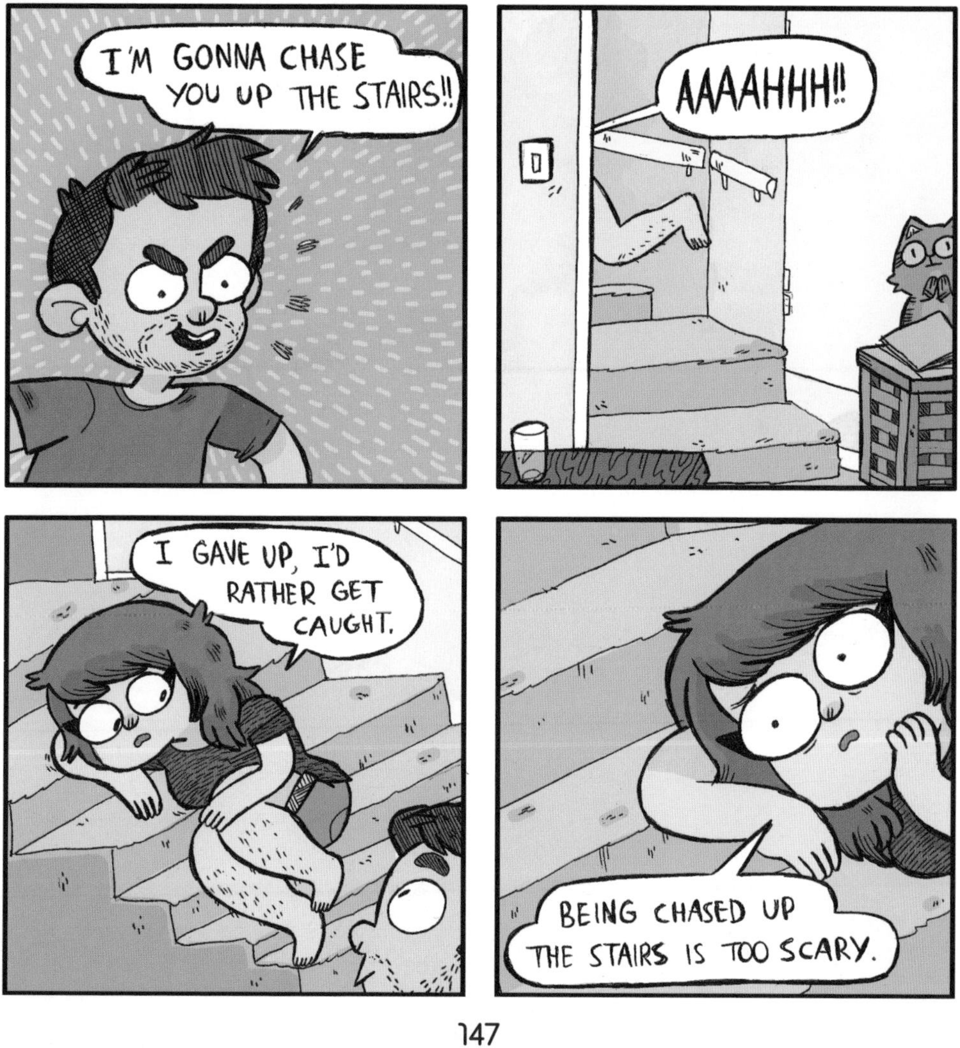
I'M GONNA CHASE YOU UP THE STAIRS!!
AAAAHHH!!
I GAVE UP, I'D RATHER GET CAUGHT.
BEING CHASED UP THE STAIRS IS TOO SCARY.

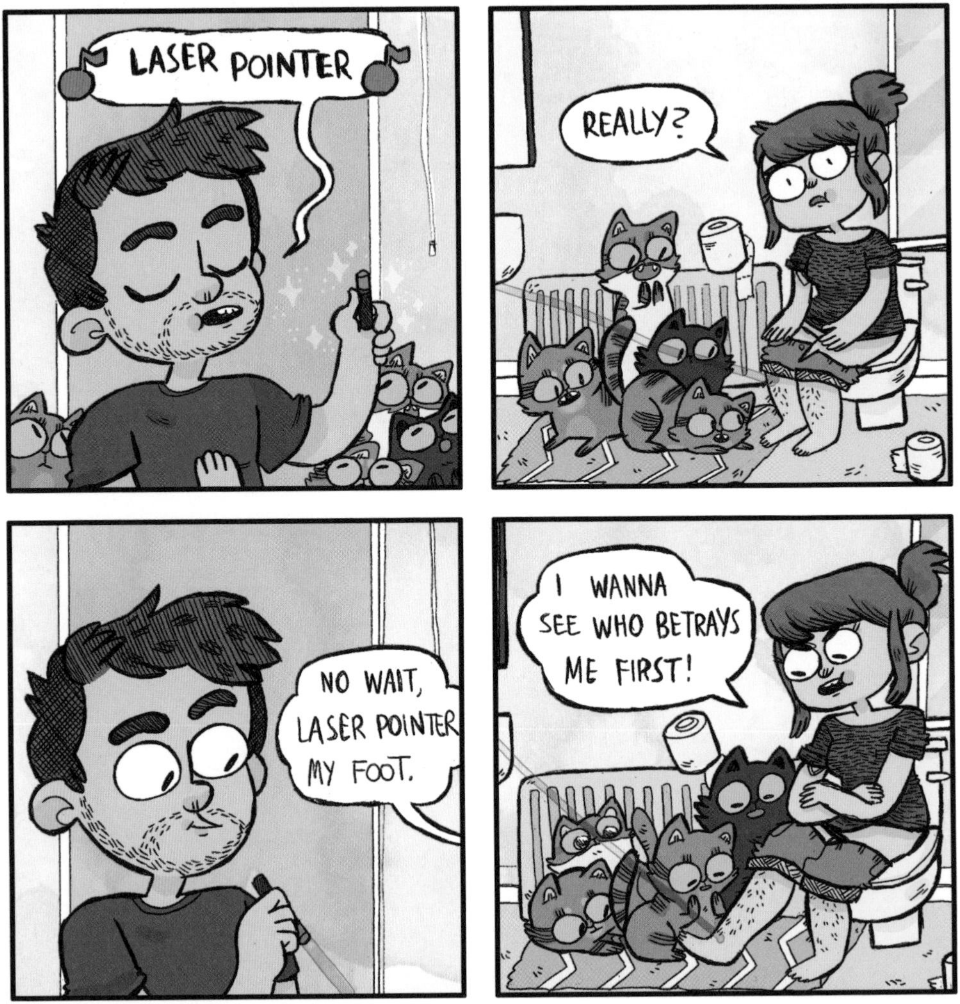
LASER POINTER
REALLY?
NO WAIT, LASER POINTER MY FOOT.
I WANNA SEE WHO BETRAYS ME FIRST!

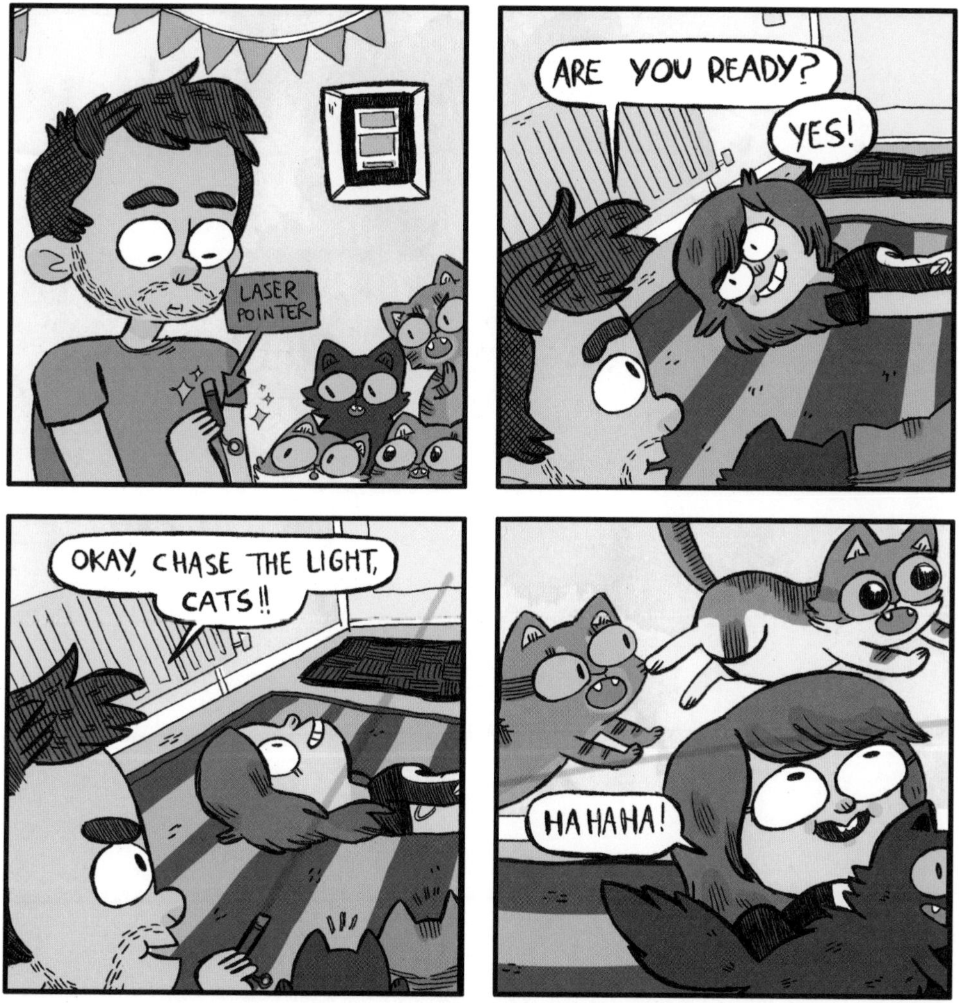
LASER POINTER
ARE YOU READY?
YES!
OKAY, CHASE THE LIGHT, CATS!!
HAHAHA!

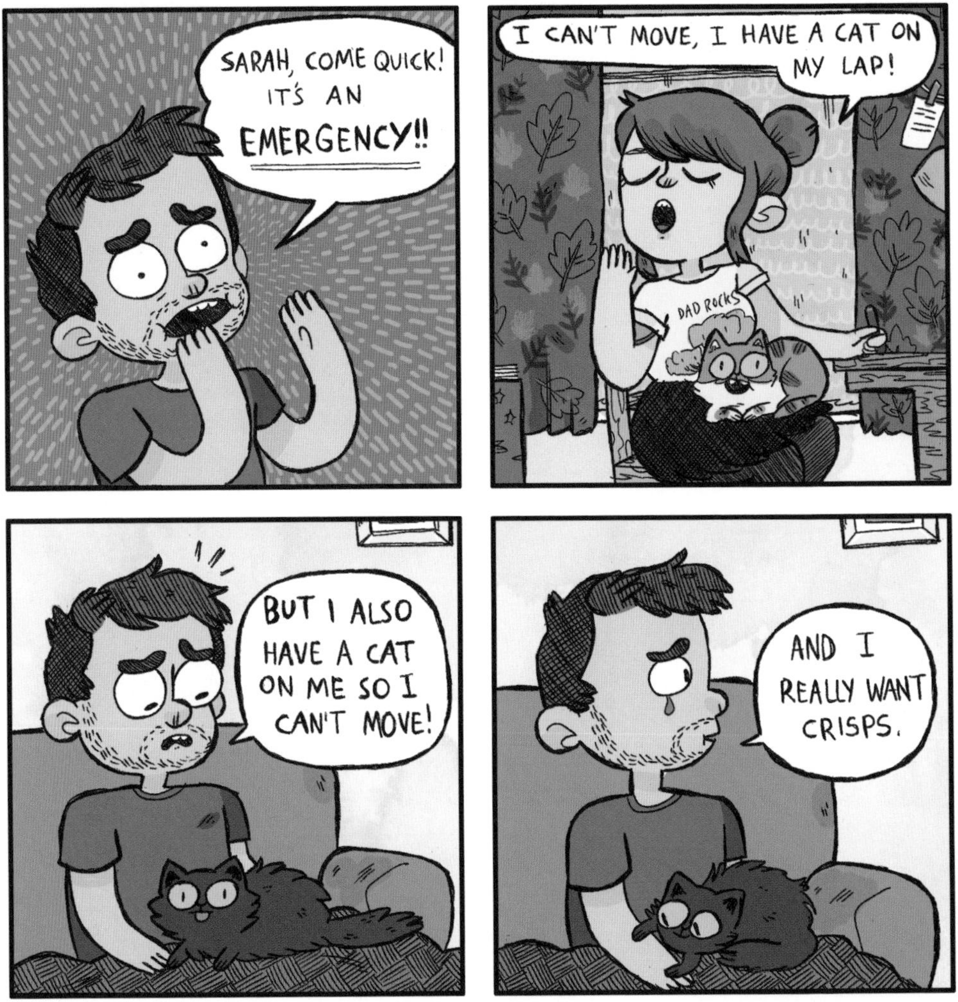
SARAH, COME QUICK! IT'S AN EMERGENCY!!
I CAN'T MOVE, I HAVE A CAT ON MY LAP!
DAD ROCKS
BUT I ALSO HAVE A CAT ON ME SO I CAN'T MOVE!
AND I REALLY WANT CRISPS.

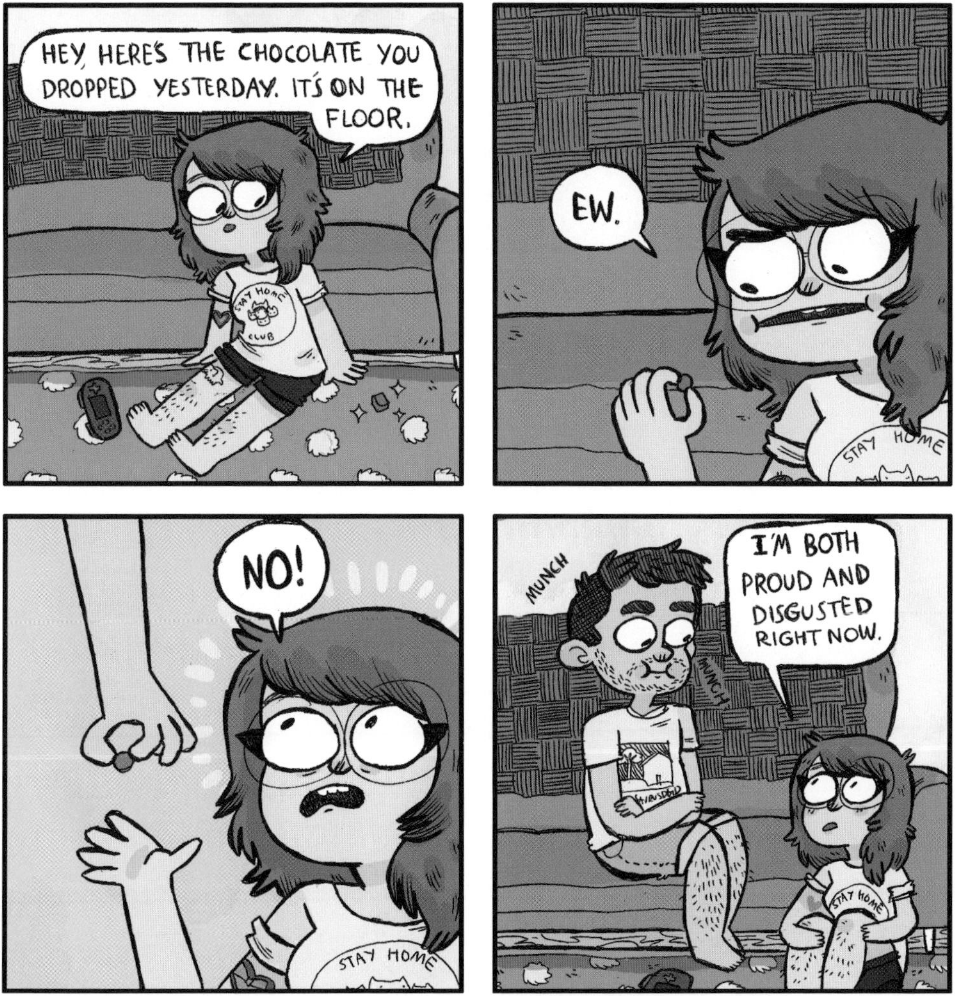
HEY, HERE'S THE CHOCOLATE YOU DROPPED YESTERDAY. IT'S ON THE FLOOR.
EW.
NO!
MUNCH
MUNCH
I'M BOTH PROUD AND DISGUSTED RIGHT NOW.

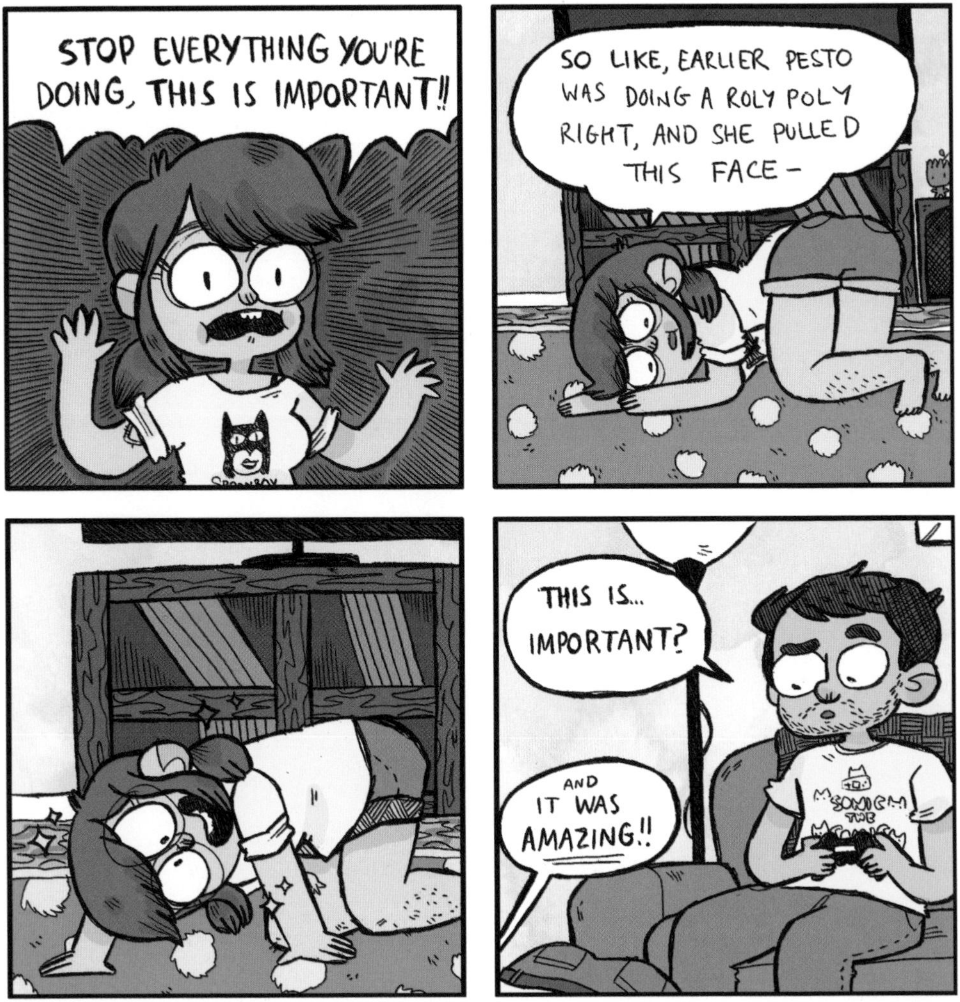
STOP EVERYTHING YOU'RE DOING, THIS IS IMPORTANT!!
SO LIKE, EARLIER PESTO WAS DOING A ROLY POLY RIGHT, AND SHE PULLED THIS FACE-
THIS IS... IMPORTANT?
AND IT WAS AMAZING!!

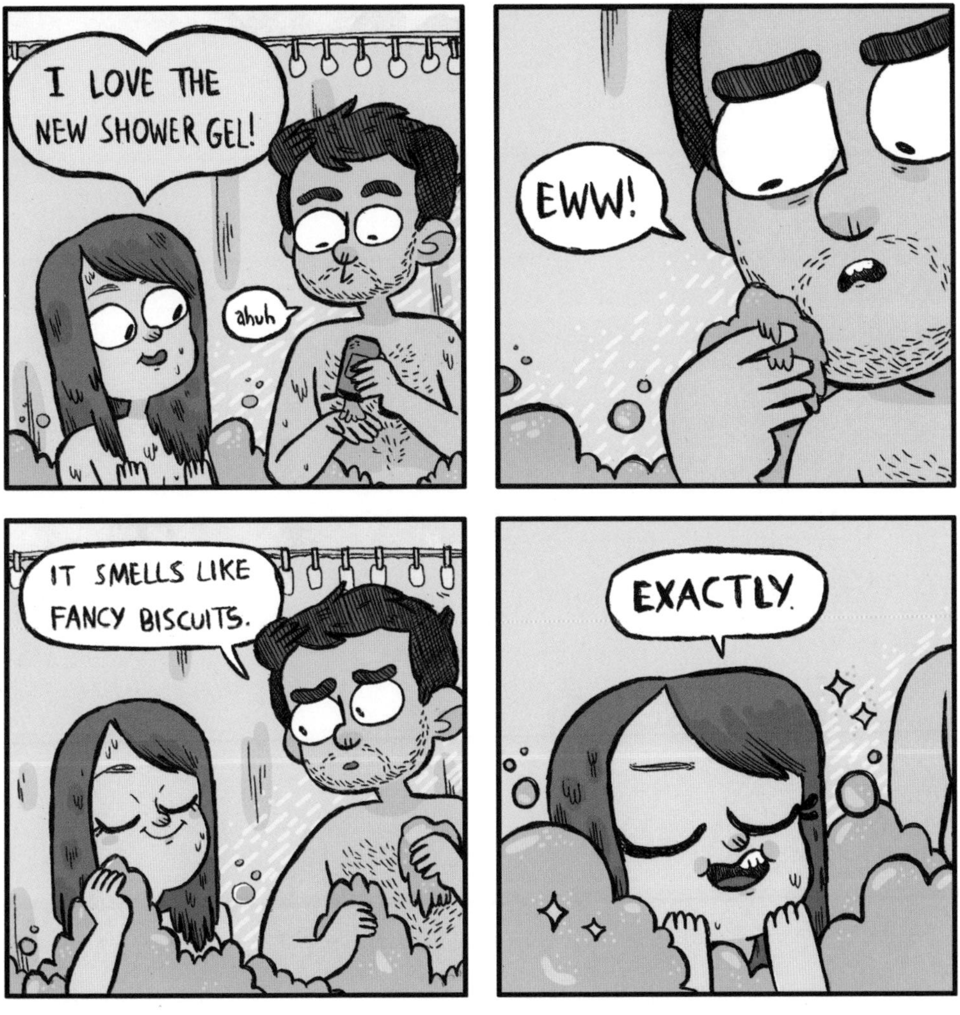
I LOVE THE NEW SHOWER GEL!
ahuh
EWW!
IT SMELLS LIKE FANCY BISCUITS.
EXACTLY.

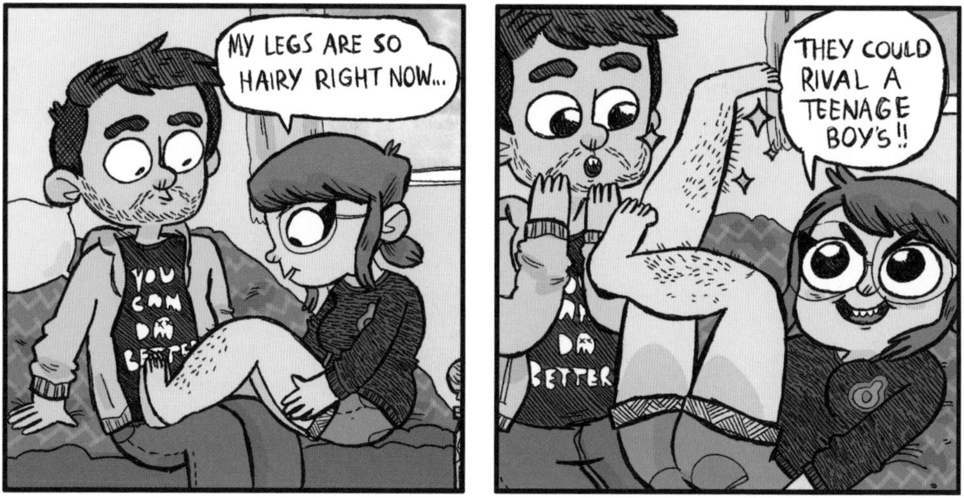
MY LEGS ARE SO HAIRY RIGHT NOW...
THEY COULD RIVAL A TEENAGE BOY'S!!

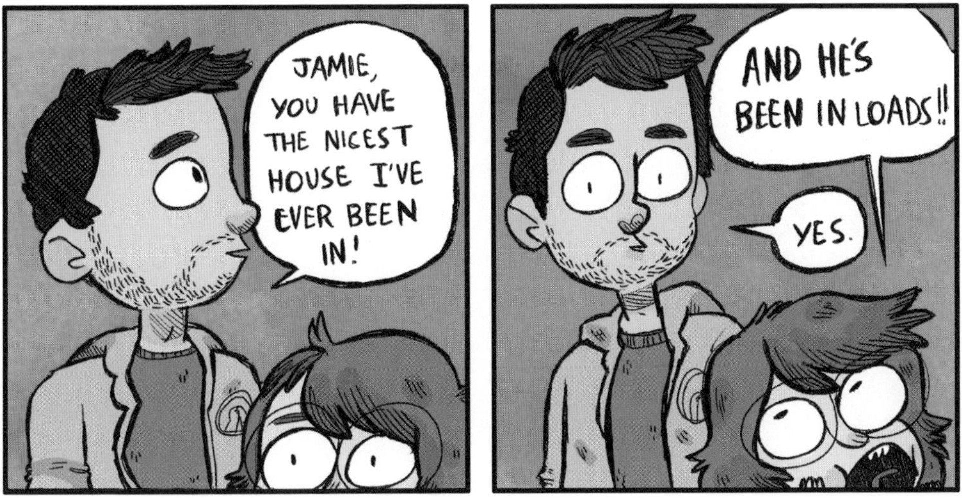
JAMIE, YOU HAVE THE NICEST HOUSE I'VE EVER BEEN IN!
AND HE'S BEEN IN LOADS!!
YES.

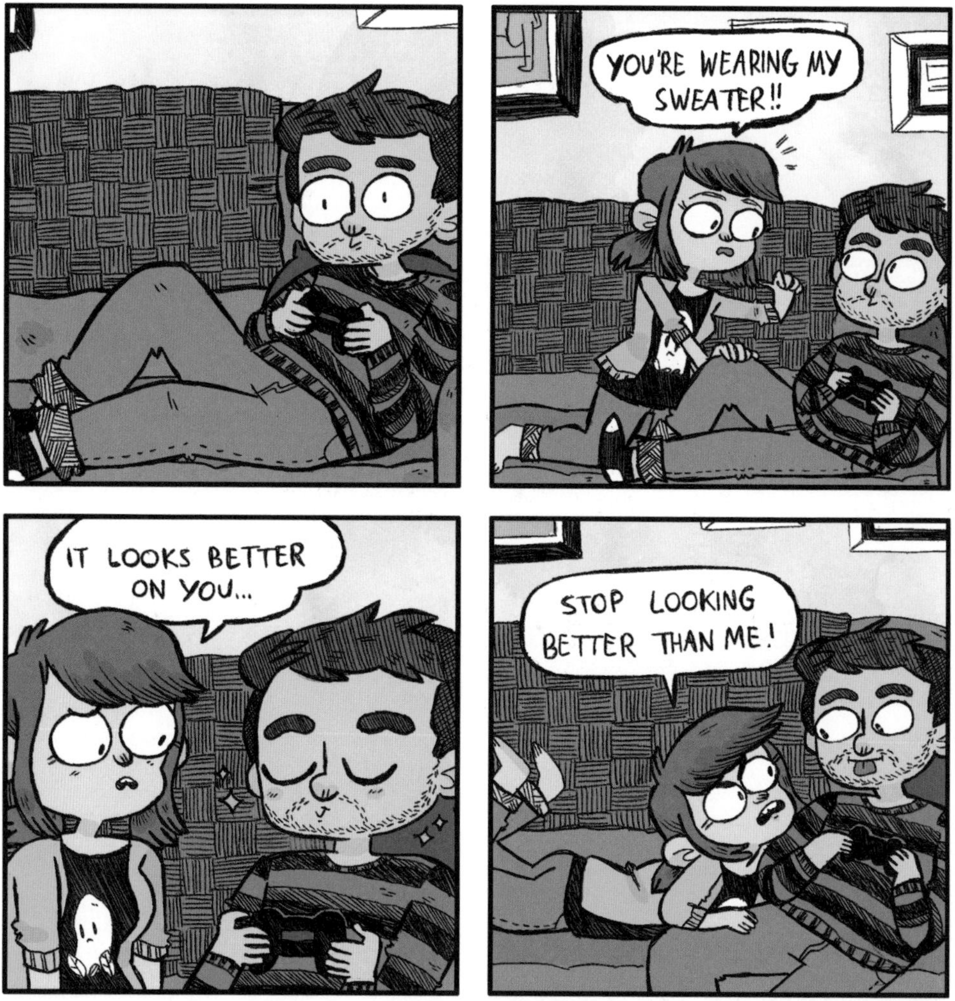
YOU'RE WEARING MY SWEATER!!
IT LOOKS BETTER ON YOU...
STOP LOOKING BETTER THAN ME!

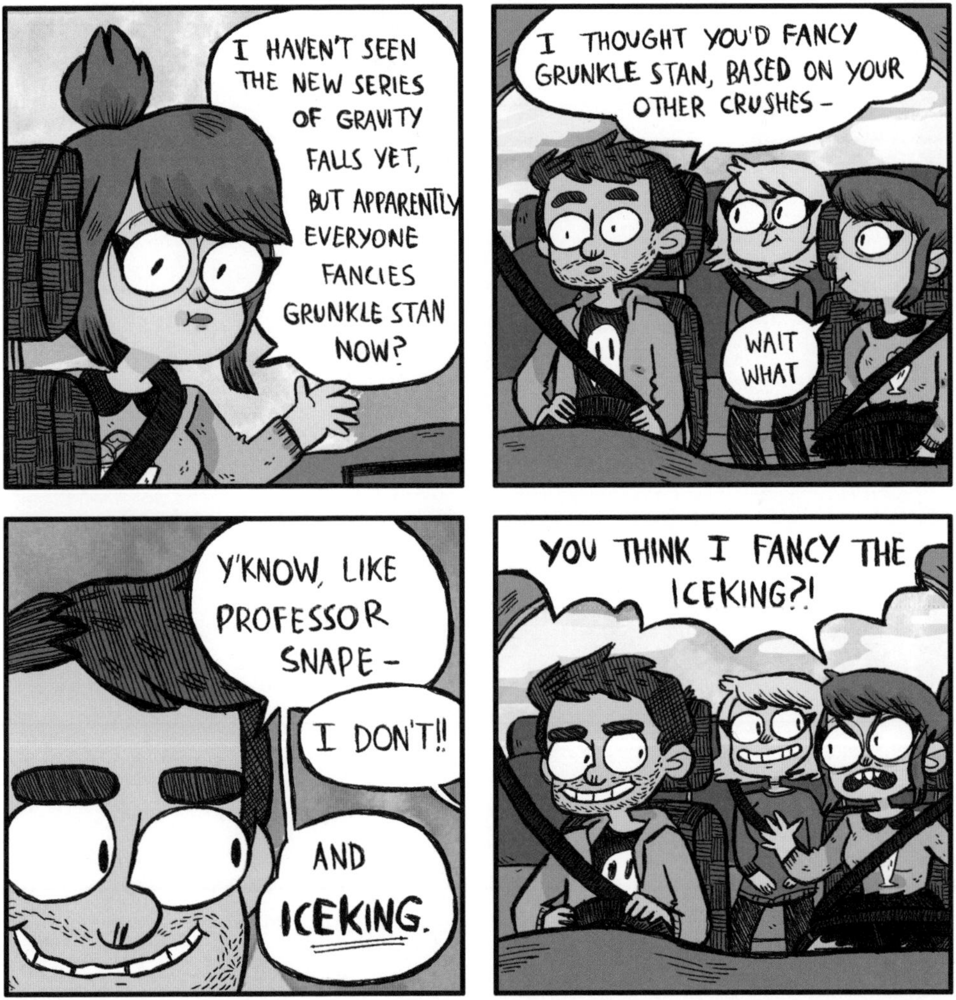
I HAVEN'T SEEN THE NEW SERIES OF GRAVITY FALLS YET, BUT APPARENTLY EVERYONE FANCIES GRUNKLE STAN NOW?
I THOUGHT YOU'D FANCY GRUNKLE STAN, BASED ON YOUR OTHER CRUSHES -
WAIT WHAT
Y'KNOW, LIKE PROFESSOR SNAPE -
I DON'T!!
AND ICEKING.
YOU THINK I FANCY THE ICEKING?!

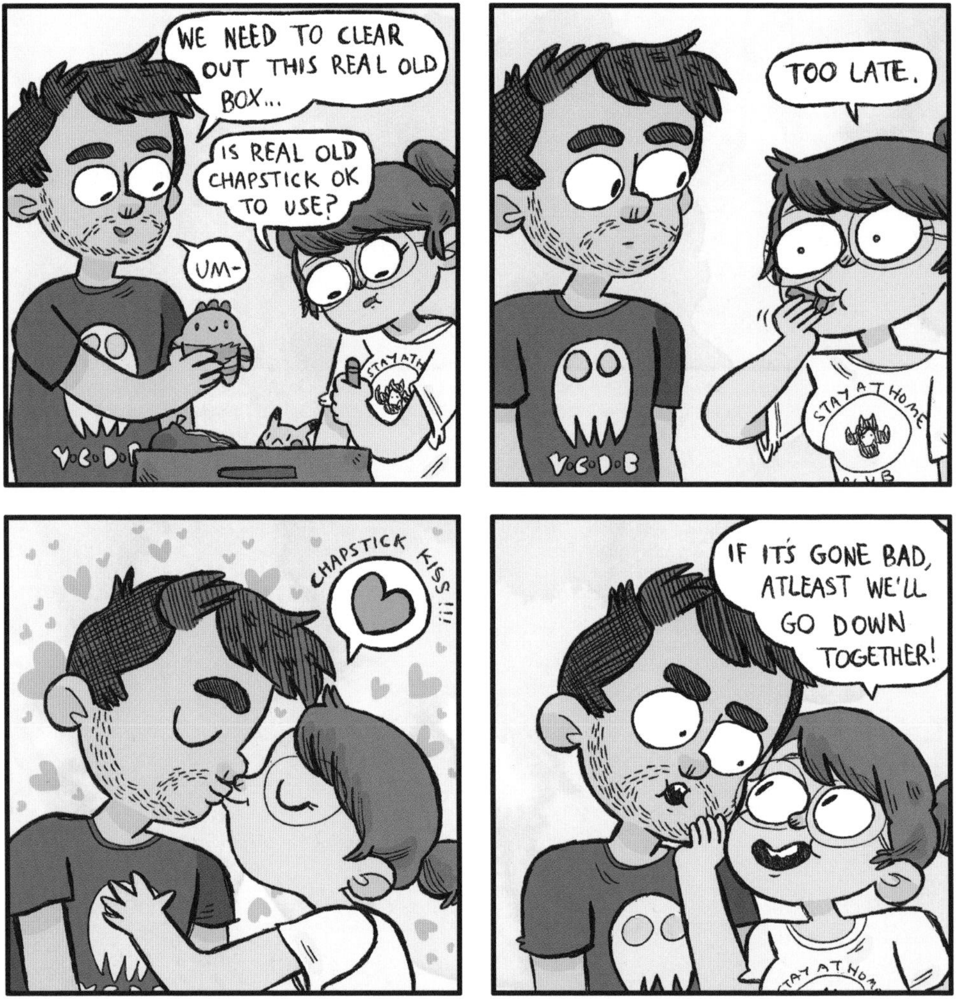
WE NEED TO CLEAR OUT THIS REAL OLD BOX...
IS REAL OLD CHAPSTICK OK TO USE?
UM-
TOO LATE.
CHAPSTICK KISS!!!
IF IT'S GONE BAD, ATLEAST WE'LL GO DOWN TOGETHER!

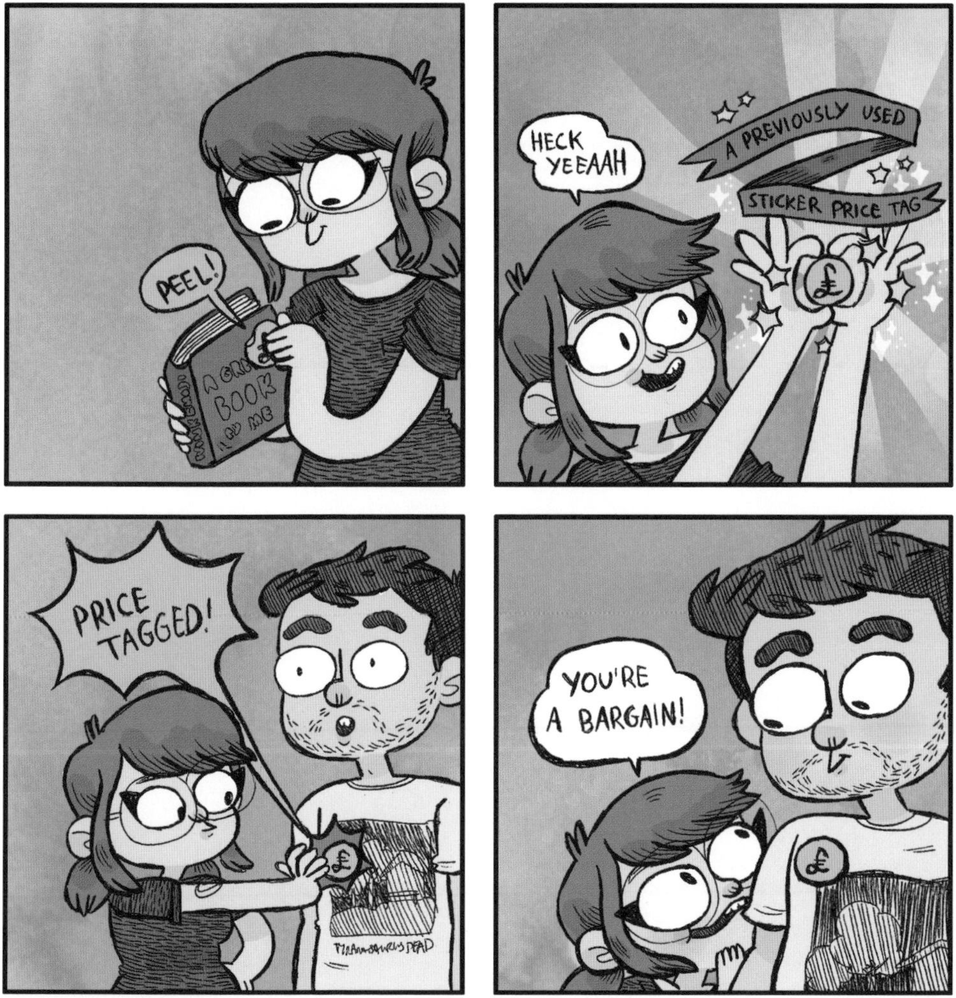
PEEL!
HECK YEEAAH
A PREVIOUSLY USED
STICKER PRICE TAG
PRICE TAGGED!
YOU'RE A BARGAIN!

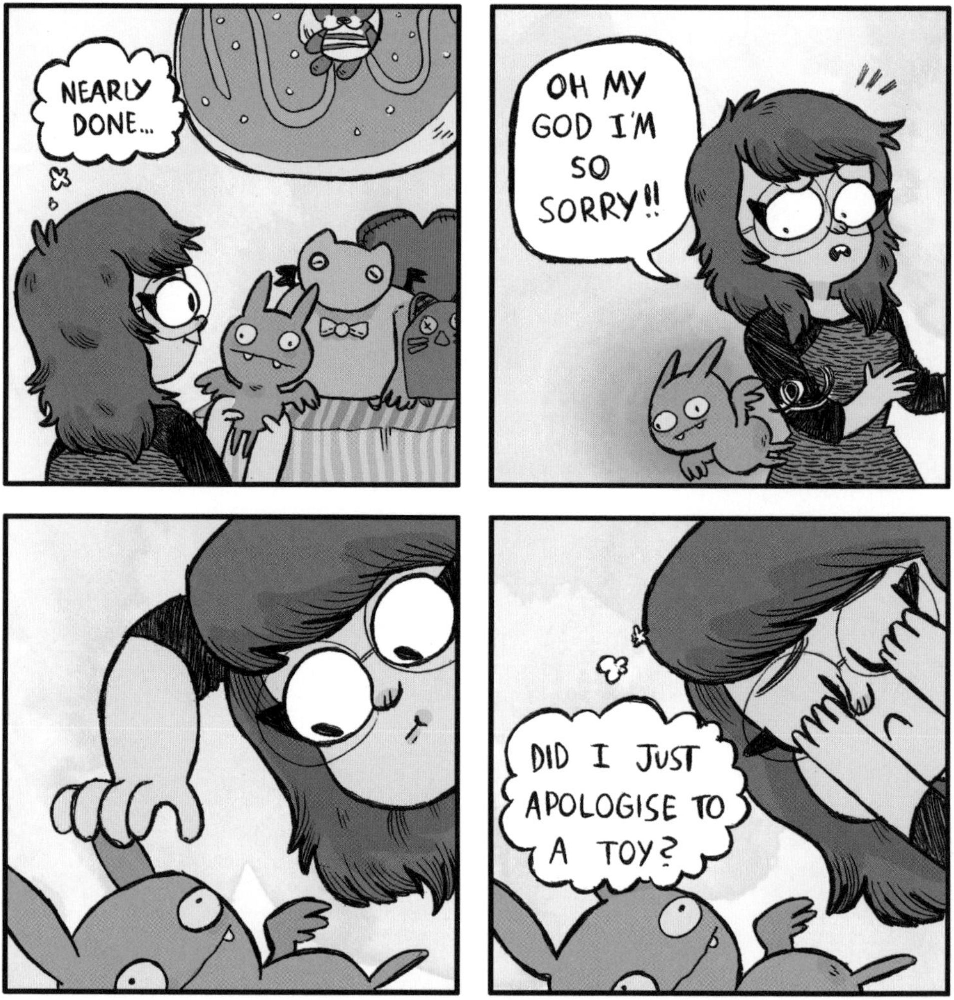
NEARLY DONE...
OH MY GOD I'M SO SORRY!!
DID I JUST APOLOGISE TO A TOY?

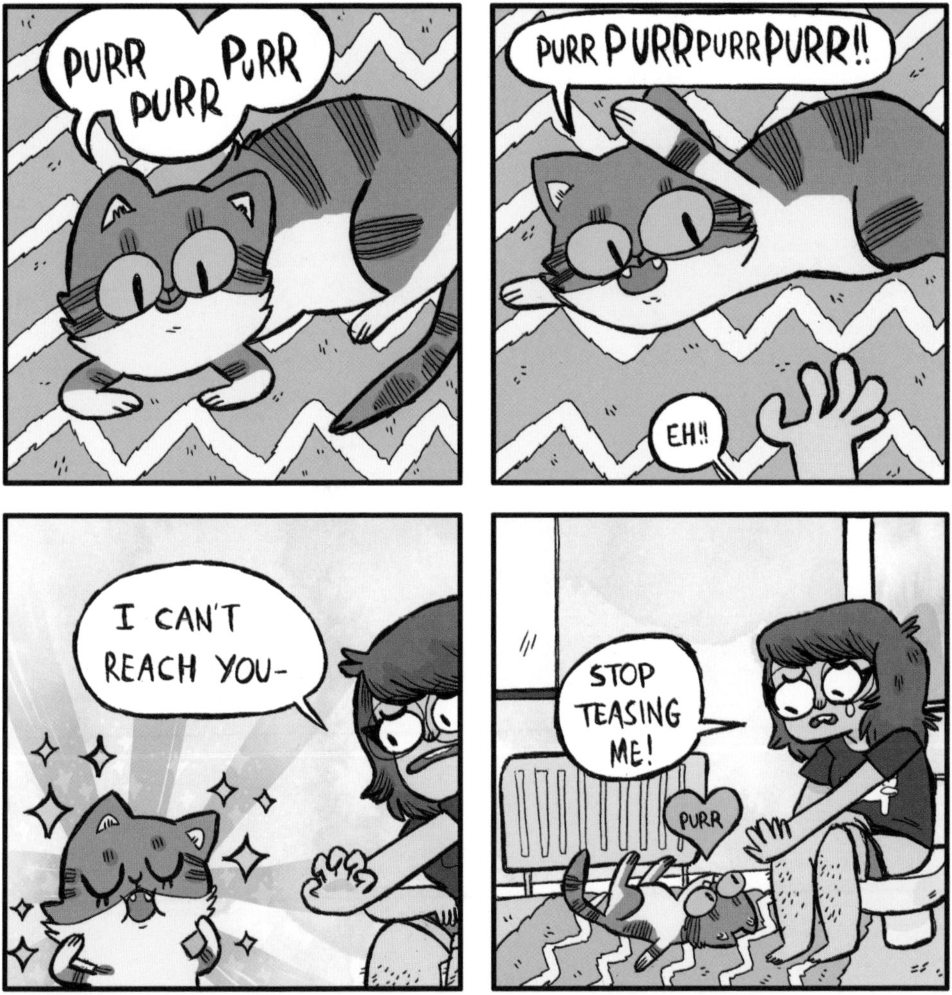
PURR PURR PURR
PURR PURR PURR PURR!!
EH!!
I CAN'T REACH YOU-
STOP TEASING ME!
PURR

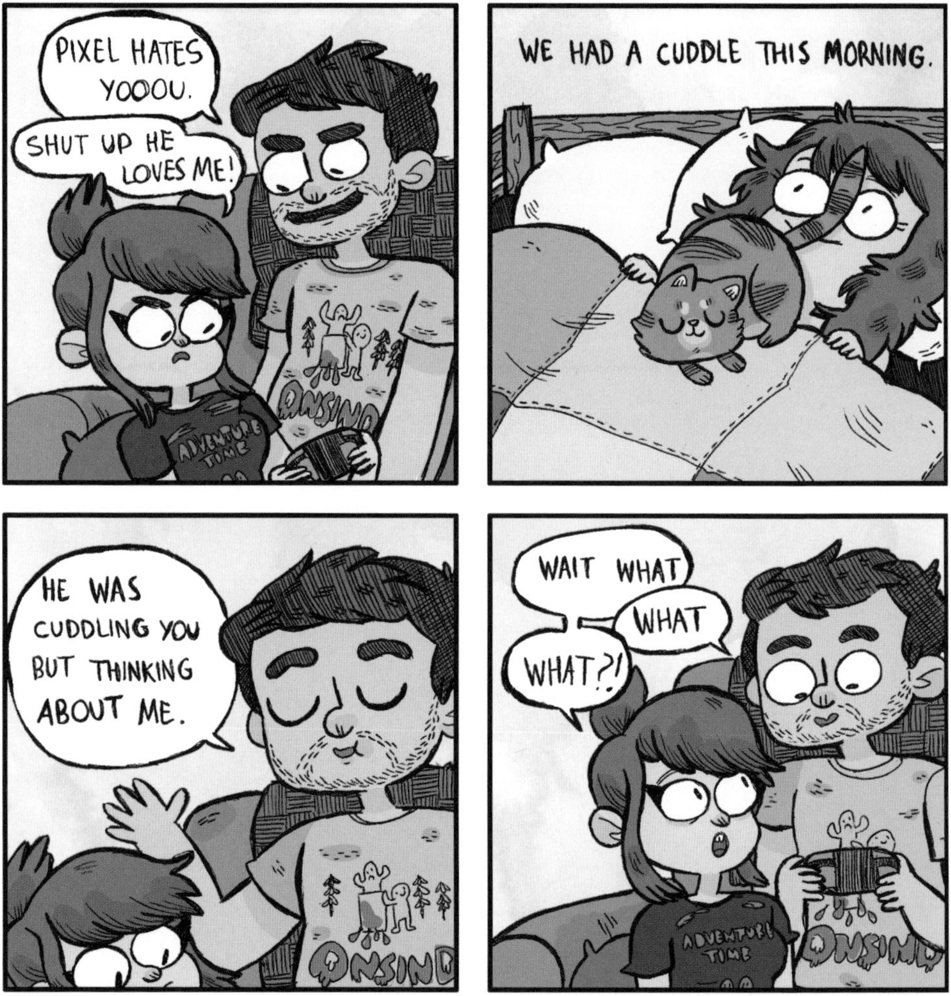

PIXEL HATES YOOOU.
SHUT UP HE LOVES ME!
WE HAD A CUDDLE THIS MORNING.
HE WAS CUDDLING YOU BUT THINKING ABOUT ME.
WAIT WHAT
WHAT
WHAT?!

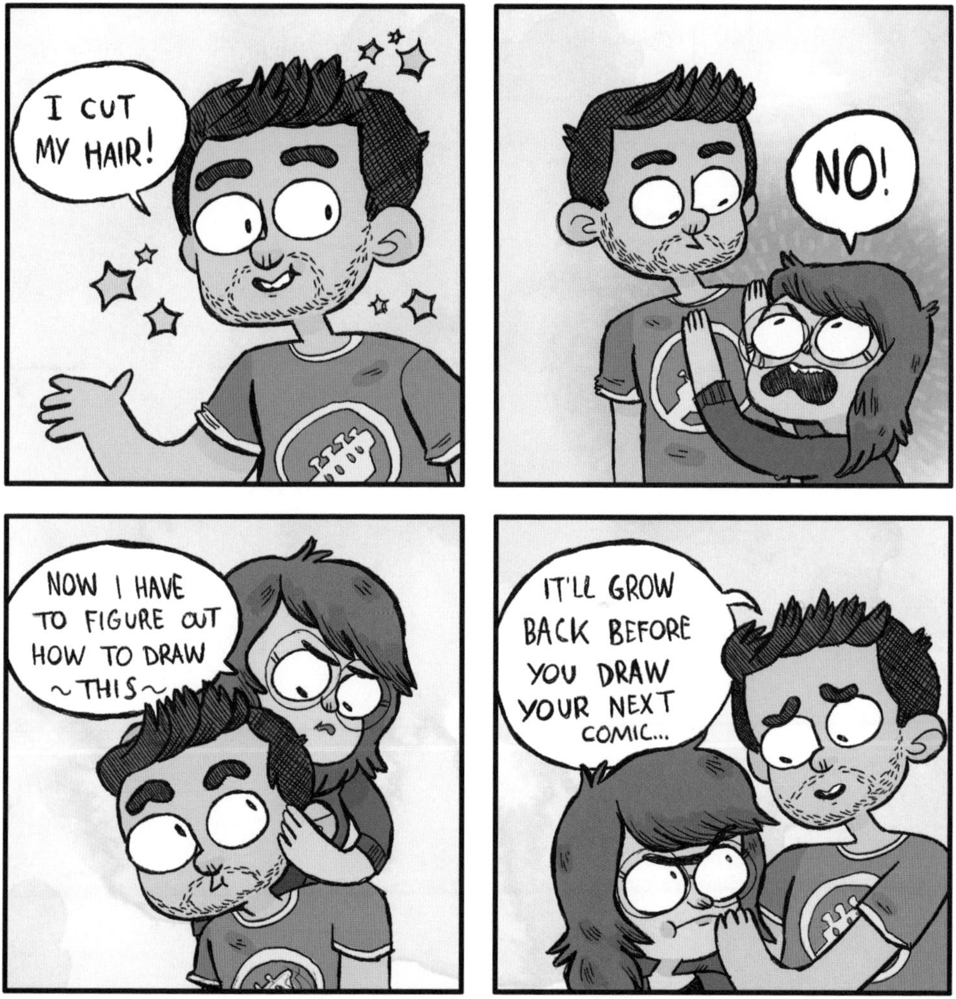
I CUT MY HAIR!
NO!
NOW I HAVE TO FIGURE OUT HOW TO DRAW ~THIS~
IT'LL GROW BACK BEFORE YOU DRAW YOUR NEXT COMIC...

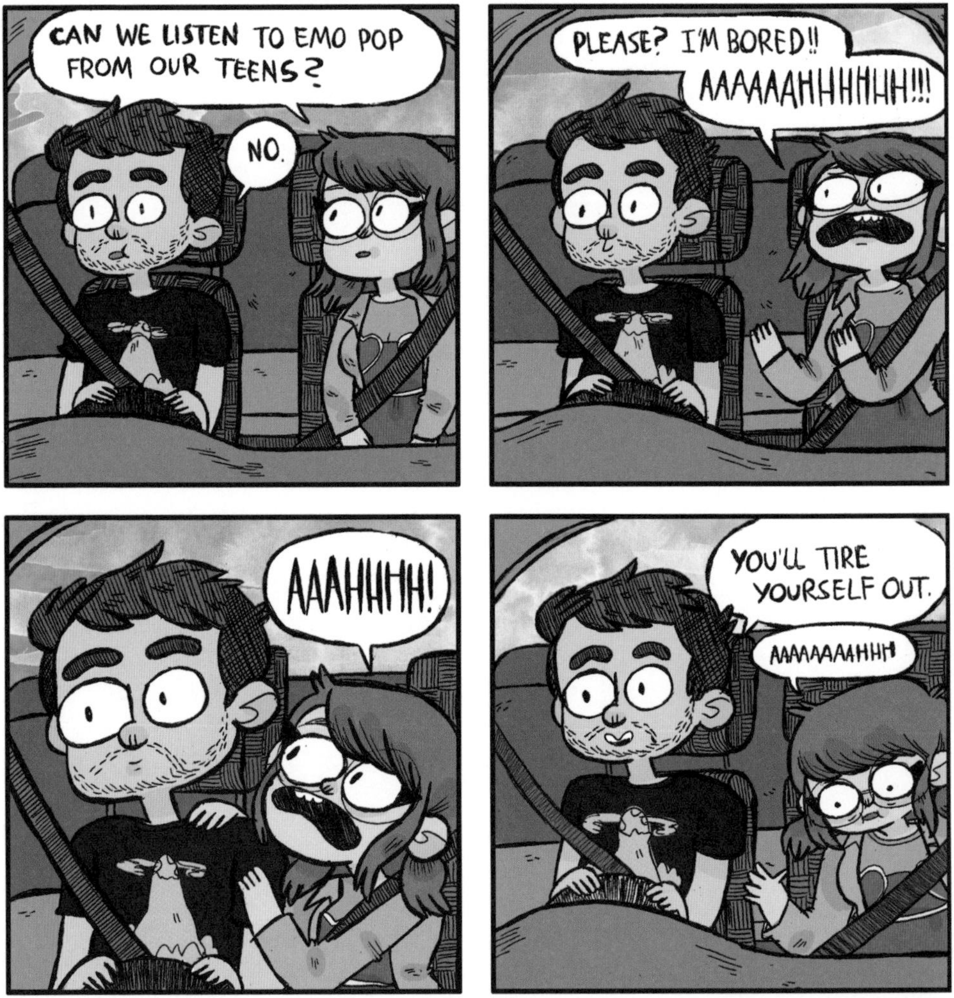
CAN WE LISTEN TO EMO POP FROM OUR TEENS?
NO.
PLEASE? I'M BORED!!
AAAAAAHHHHHH!!!
AAAHHHH!
YOU'LL TIRE YOURSELF OUT.
AAAAAAAAHHH

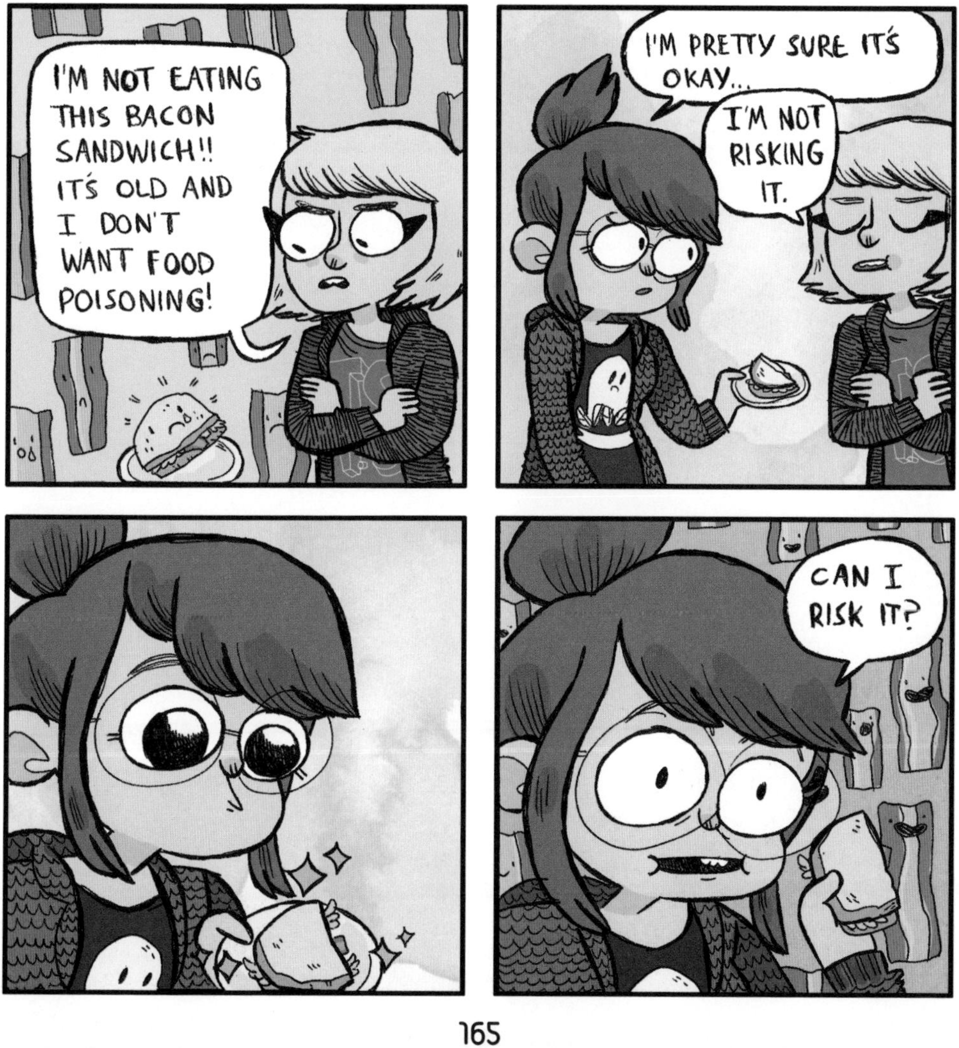
I'M NOT EATING THIS BACON SANDWICH!! IT'S OLD AND I DON'T WANT FOOD POISONING!
I'M PRETTY SURE IT'S OKAY...
I'M NOT RISKING IT.
CAN I RISK IT?

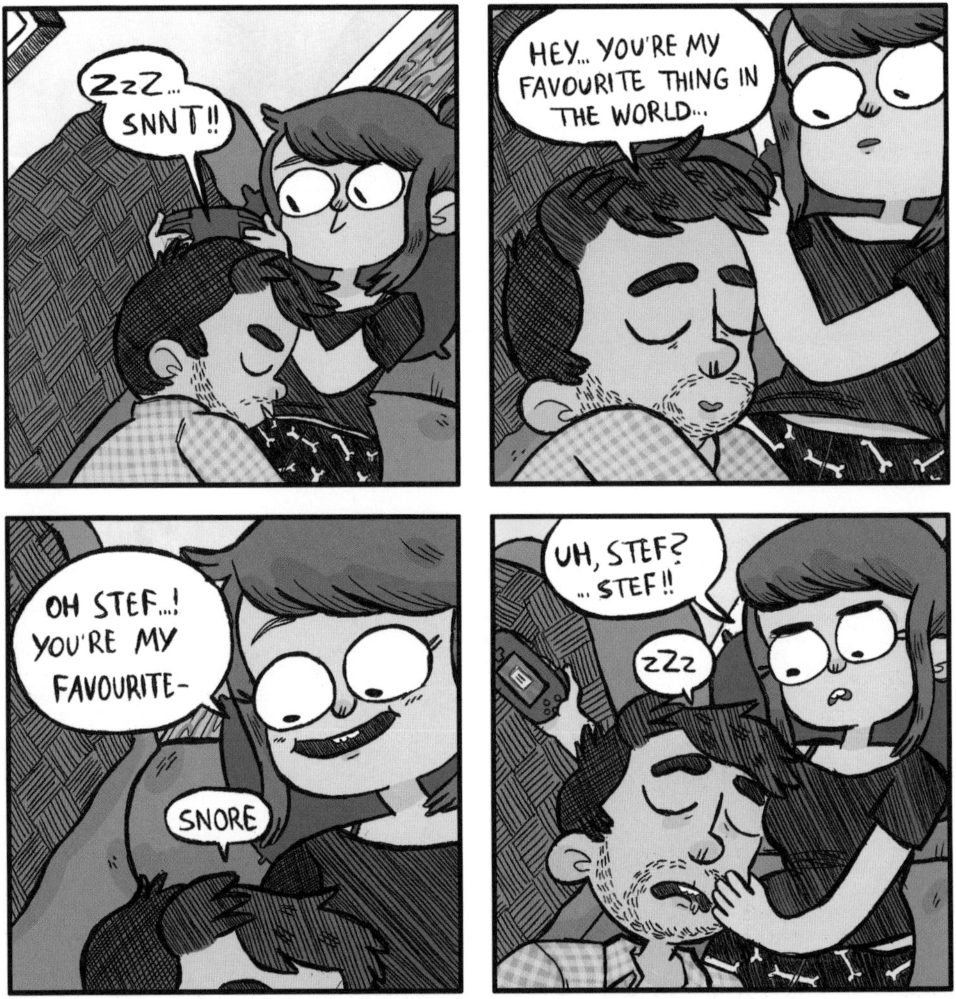
ZzZ... SNNT!!
HEY... YOU'RE MY FAVOURITE THING IN THE WORLD...
OH STEF...! YOU'RE MY FAVOURITE-
SNORE
UH, STEF? ...STEF!!
zZz

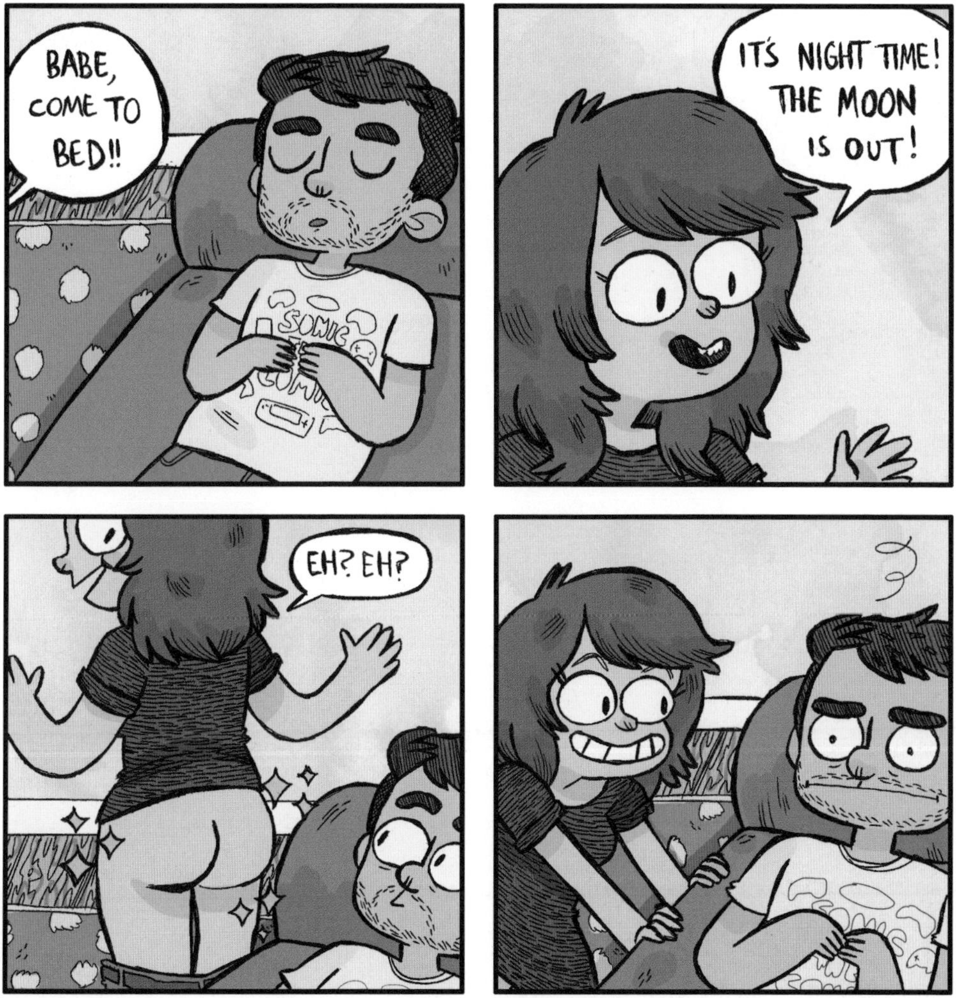
BABE, COME TO BED!!
IT'S NIGHT TIME! THE MOON IS OUT!
EH? EH?

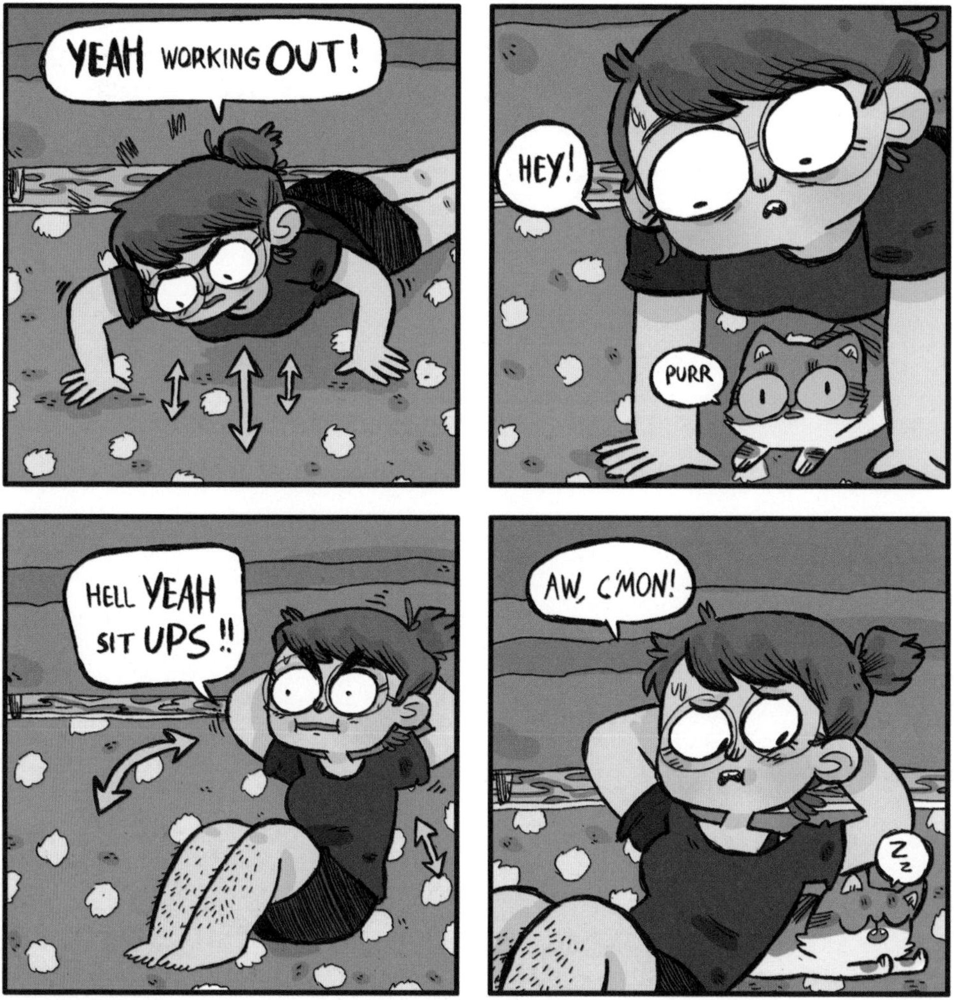
YEAH WORKING OUT!
HEY!
PURR
HELL YEAH SIT UPS!!
AW, C'MON!
Z Z

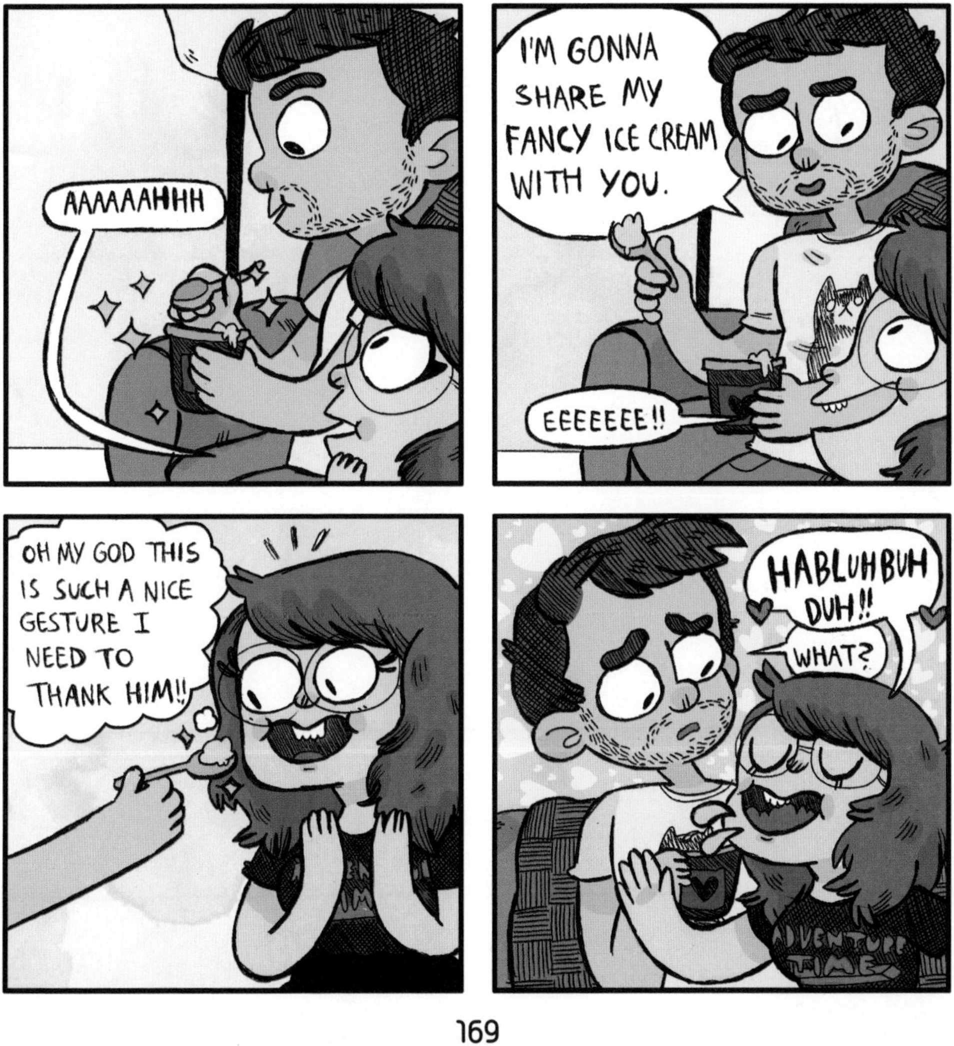
AAAAAAHHH
I'M GONNA SHARE MY FANCY ICE CREAM WITH YOU.
EEEEEEE!!
OH MY GOD THIS IS SUCH A NICE GESTURE I NEED TO THANK HIM!!
HABLUHBUH DUH!!
WHAT?
ADVENTURE TIME

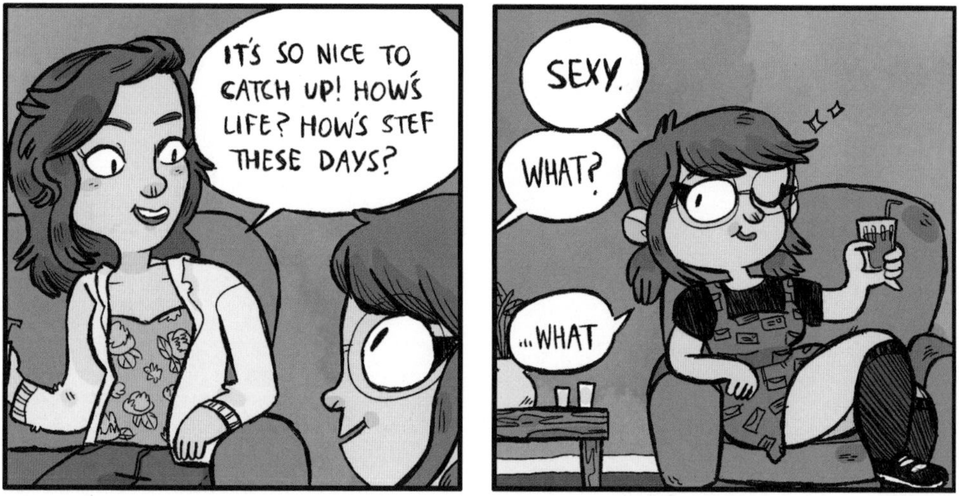
IT'S SO NICE TO CATCH UP! HOW'S LIFE? HOW'S STEF THESE DAYS?
SEXY.
WHAT?
...WHAT

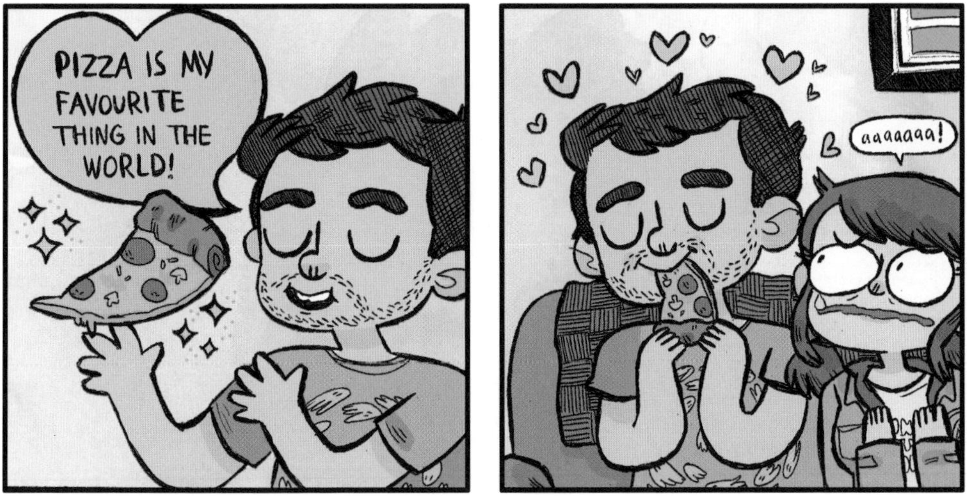
PIZZA IS MY FAVOURITE THING IN THE WORLD!
aaaaaaa!

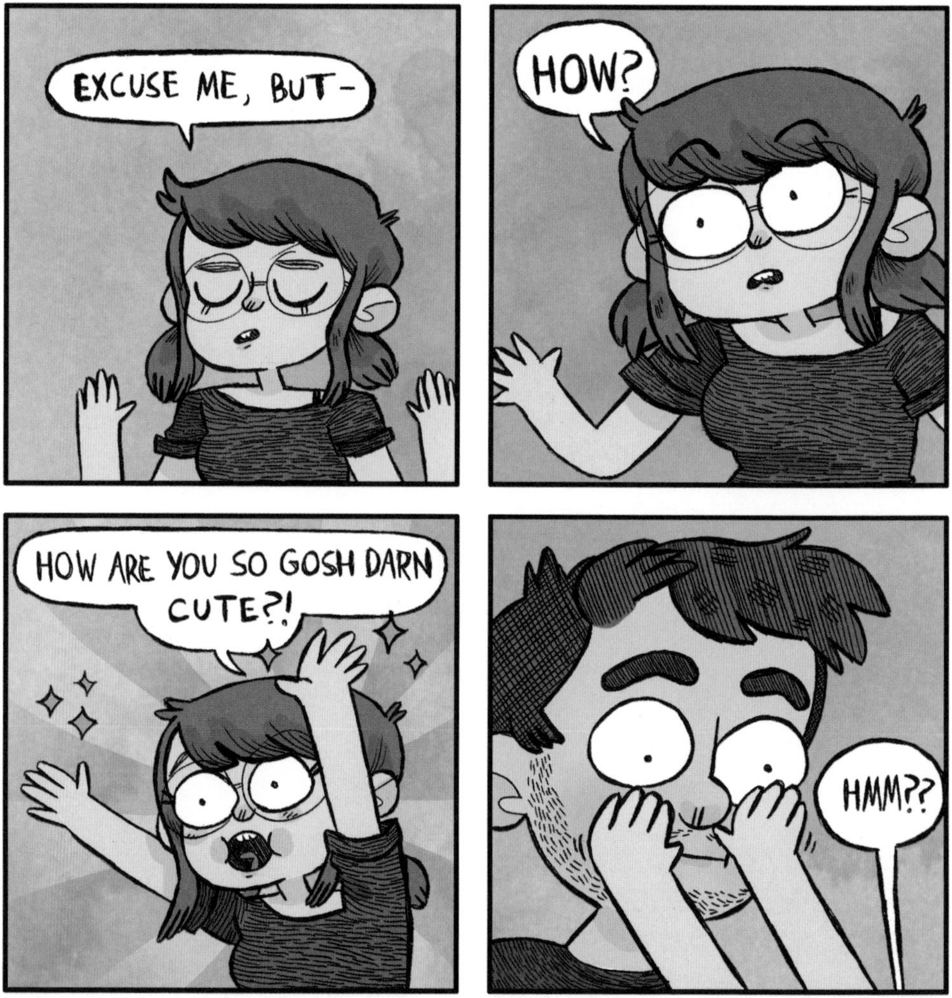
EXCUSE ME, BUT-
HOW?
HOW ARE YOU SO GOSH DARN CUTE?!
HMM??

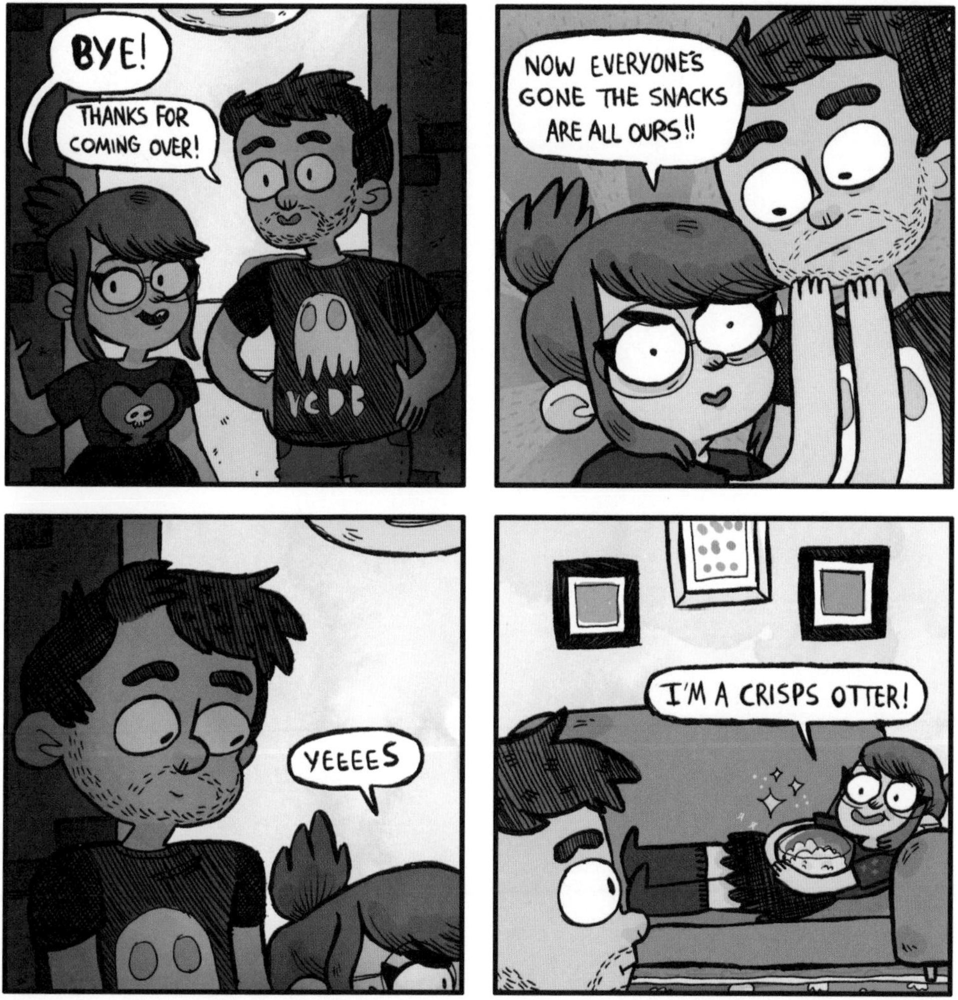
BYE!
THANKS FOR COMING OVER!
NOW EVERYONE'S GONE THE SNACKS ARE ALL OURS!!
YEEEES
I'M A CRISPS OTTER!

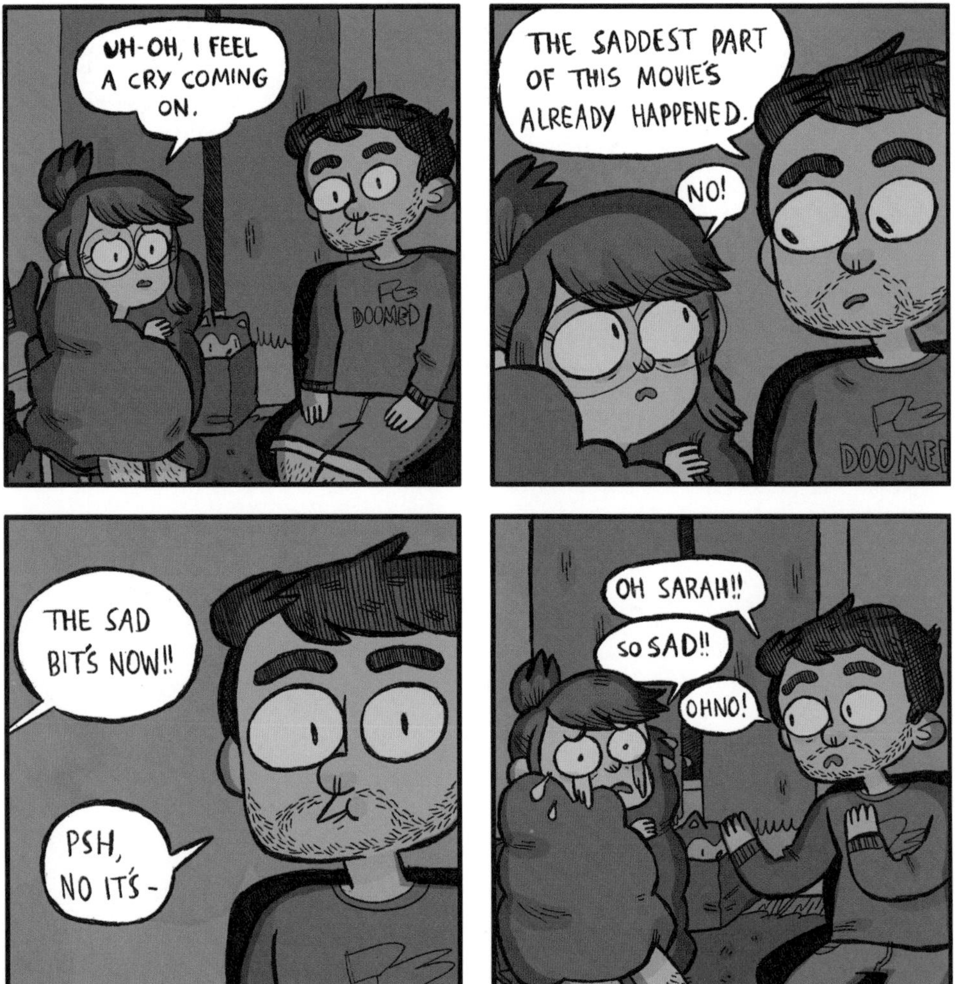
UH-OH, I FEEL A CRY COMING ON.
DOOMED
THE SADDEST PART OF THIS MOVIE'S ALREADY HAPPENED.
NO!
DOOMED
THE SAD BIT'S NOW!!
PSH, NO IT'S -
OH SARAH!!
SO SAD!!
OHNO!

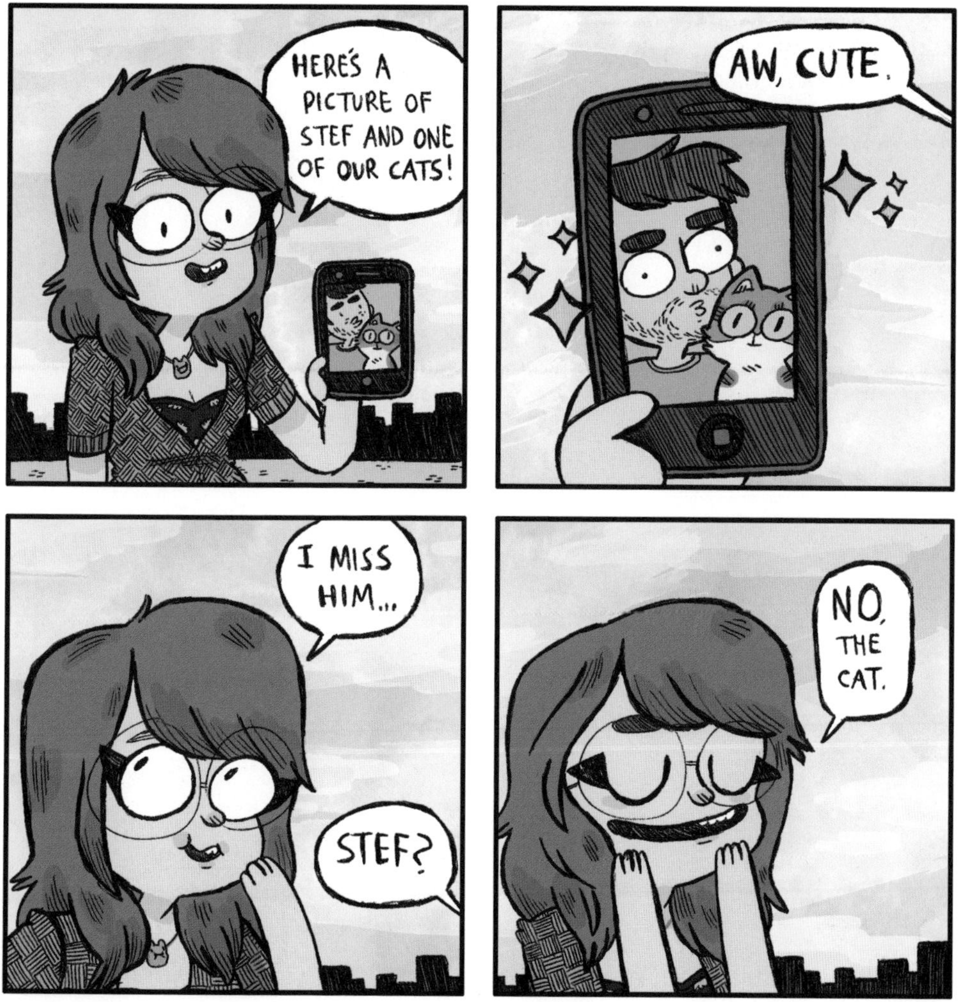
HERE'S A PICTURE OF STEF AND ONE OF OUR CATS!
AW, CUTE.
I MISS HIM...
STEF?
NO, THE CAT.

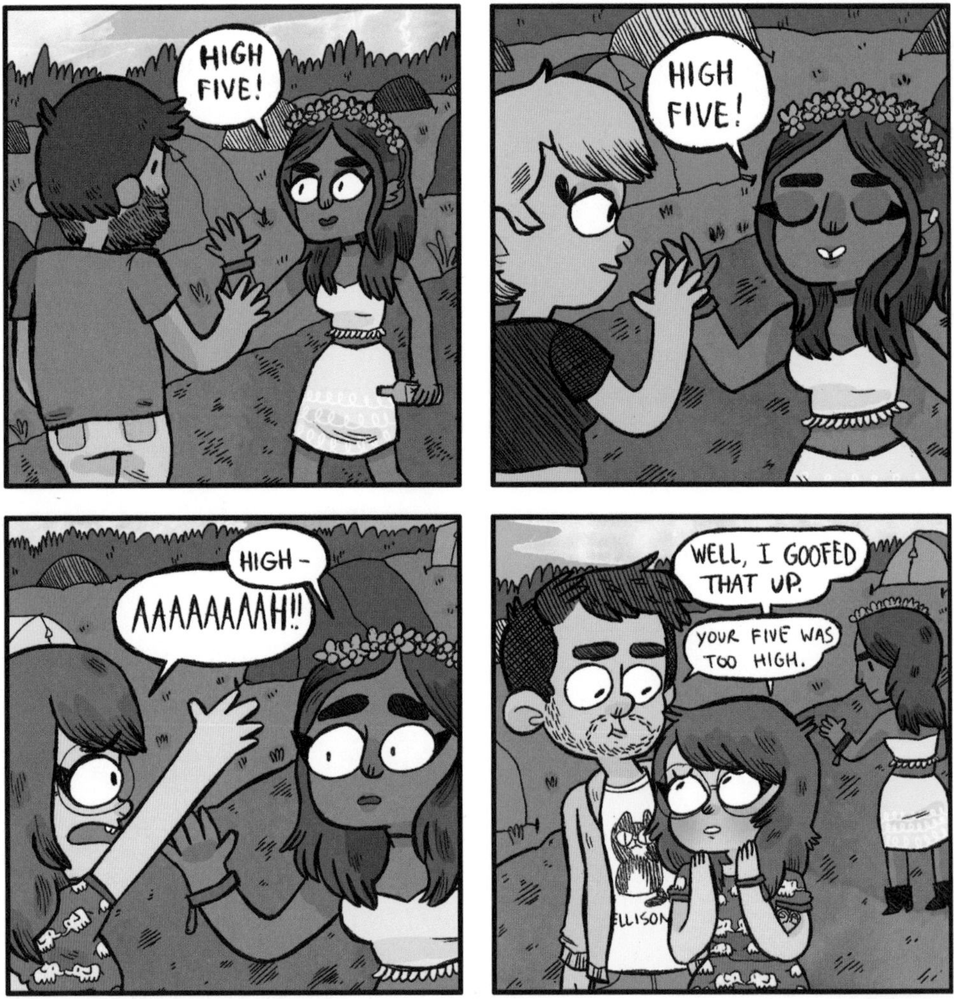
HIGH FIVE!
HIGH FIVE!
HIGH-
AAAAAAAAH!!
WELL, I GOOFED THAT UP.
YOUR FIVE WAS TOO HIGH.

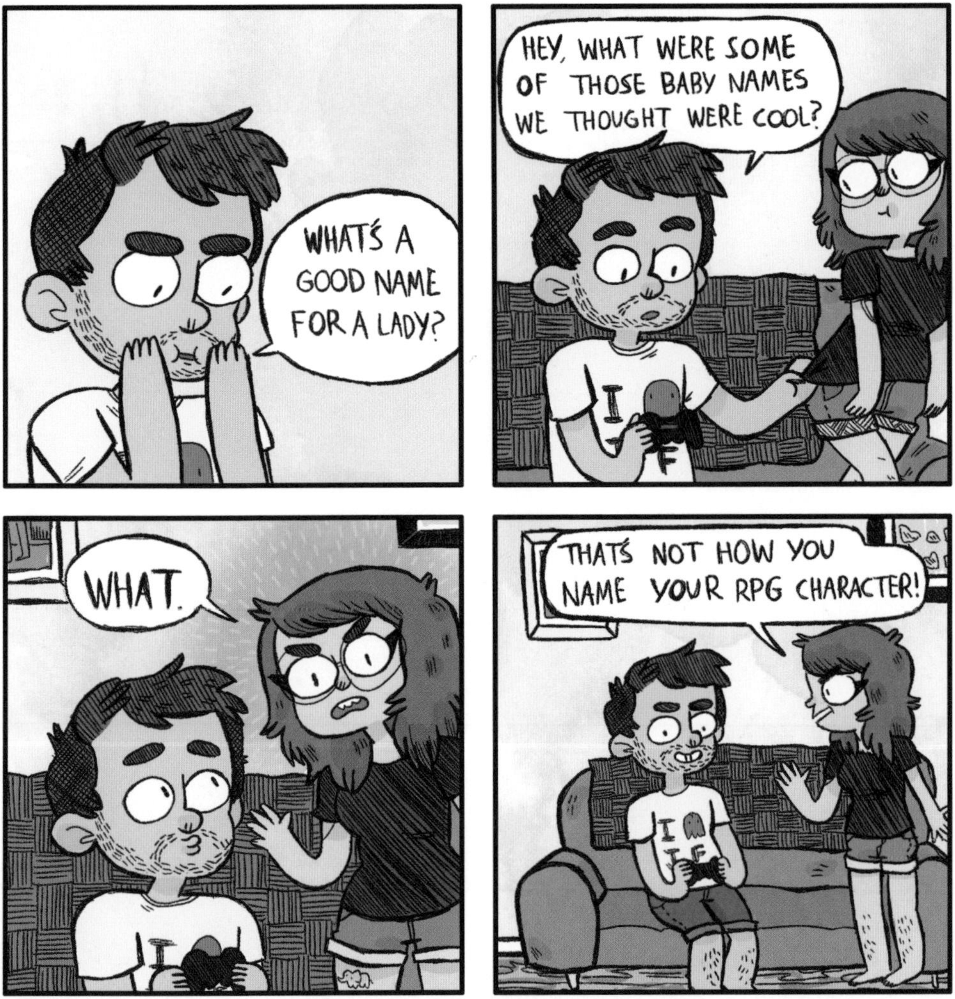
WHAT'S A GOOD NAME FOR A LADY?
HEY, WHAT WERE SOME OF THOSE BABY NAMES WE THOUGHT WERE COOL?
WHAT.
THAT'S NOT HOW YOU NAME YOUR RPG CHARACTER!

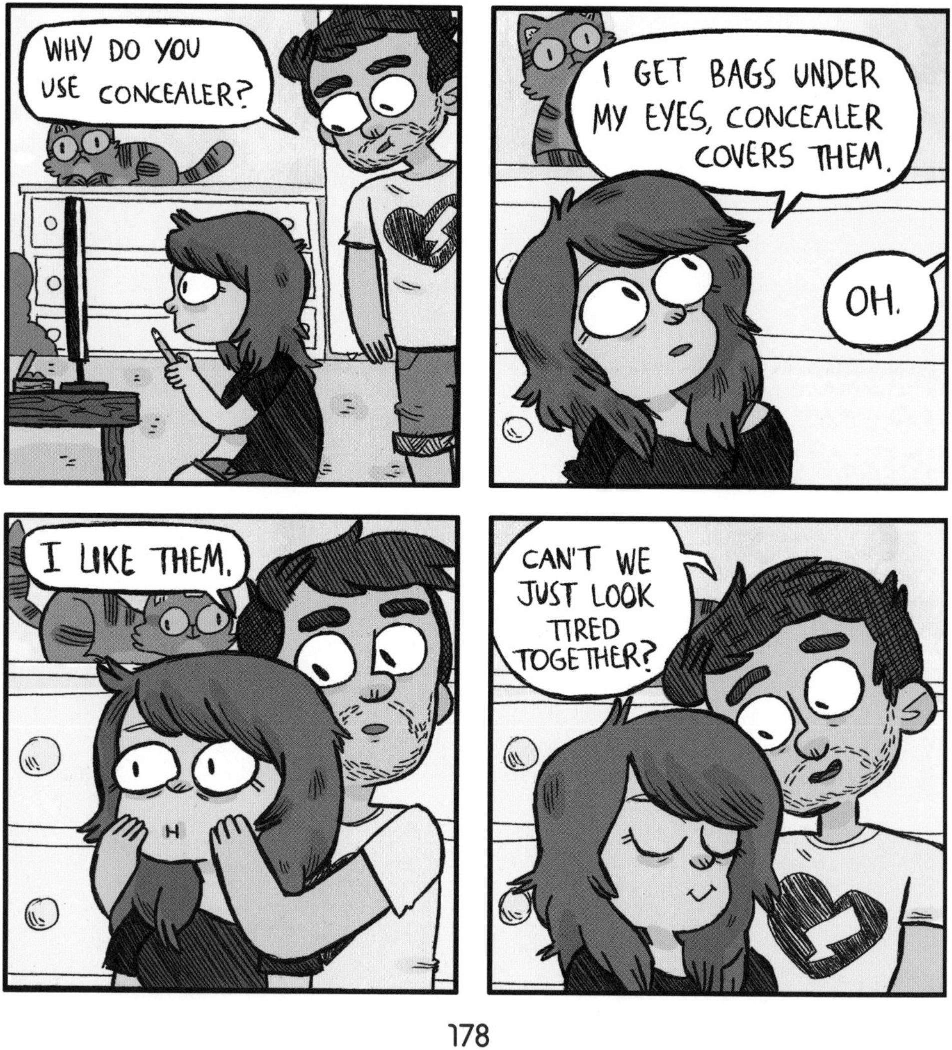
WHY DO YOU USE CONCEALER?
I GET BAGS UNDER MY EYES, CONCEALER COVERS THEM.
OH.
I LIKE THEM.
CAN'T WE JUST LOOK TIRED TOGETHER?

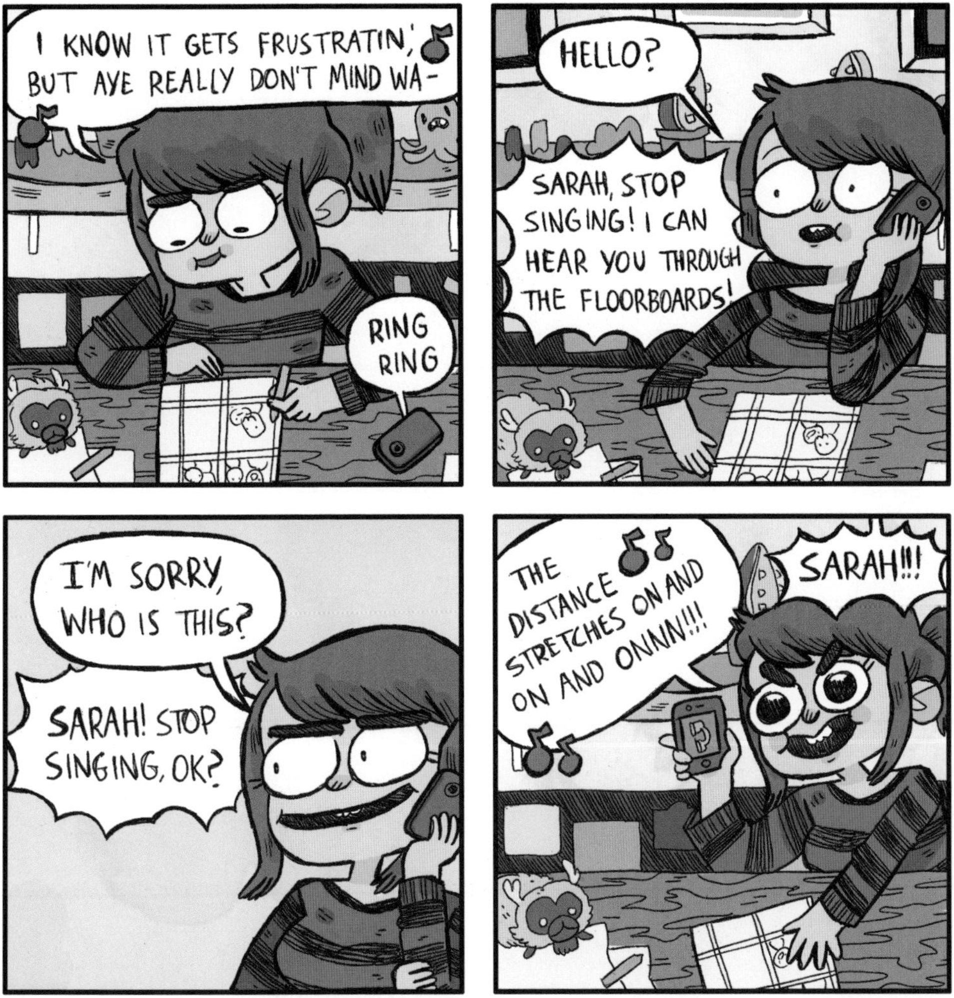
I KNOW IT GETS FRUSTRATIN', BUT AYE REALLY DON'T MIND WA-
RING RING
HELLO?
SARAH, STOP SINGING! I CAN HEAR YOU THROUGH THE FLOORBOARDS!
I'M SORRY, WHO IS THIS?
SARAH! STOP SINGING, OK?
THE DISTANCE STRETCHES ON AND ON AND ONNN!!!
SARAH!!!

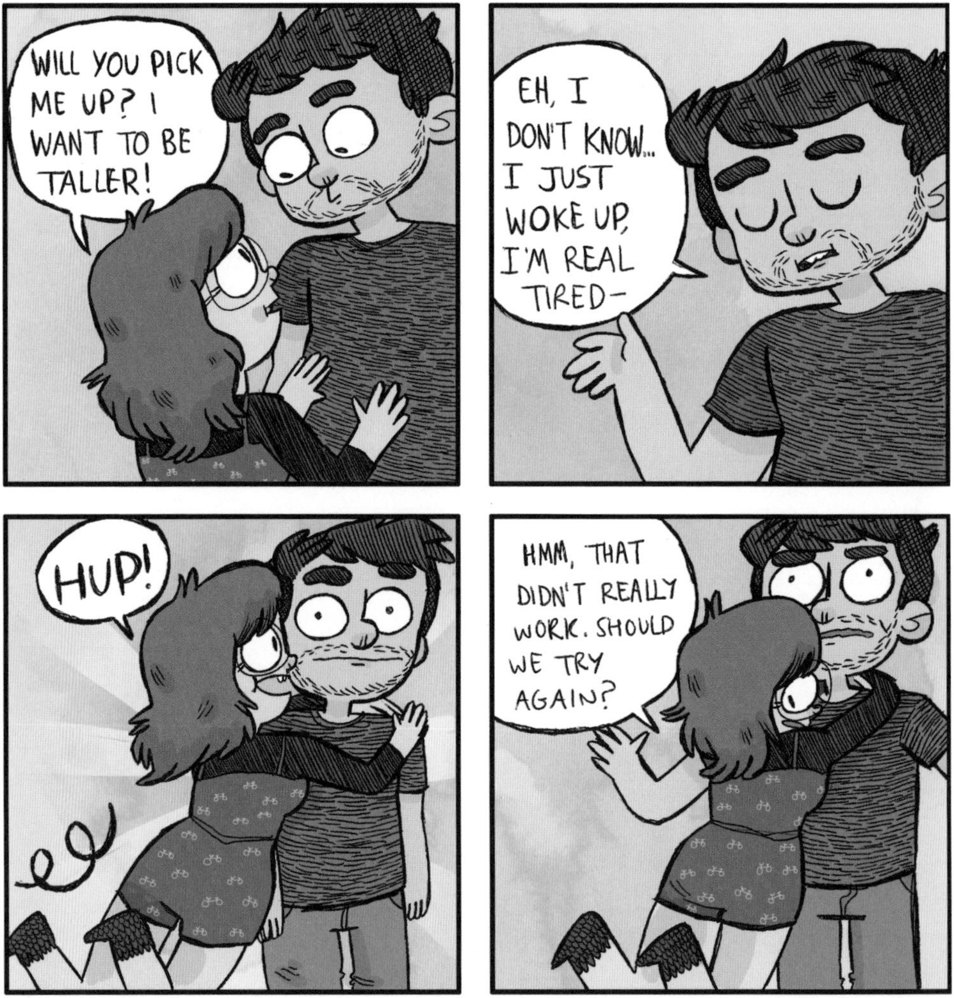
WILL YOU PICK ME UP? I WANT TO BE TALLER!
EH, I DON'T KNOW... I JUST WOKE UP, I'M REAL TIRED-
HUP!
HMM, THAT DIDN'T REALLY WORK. SHOULD WE TRY AGAIN?

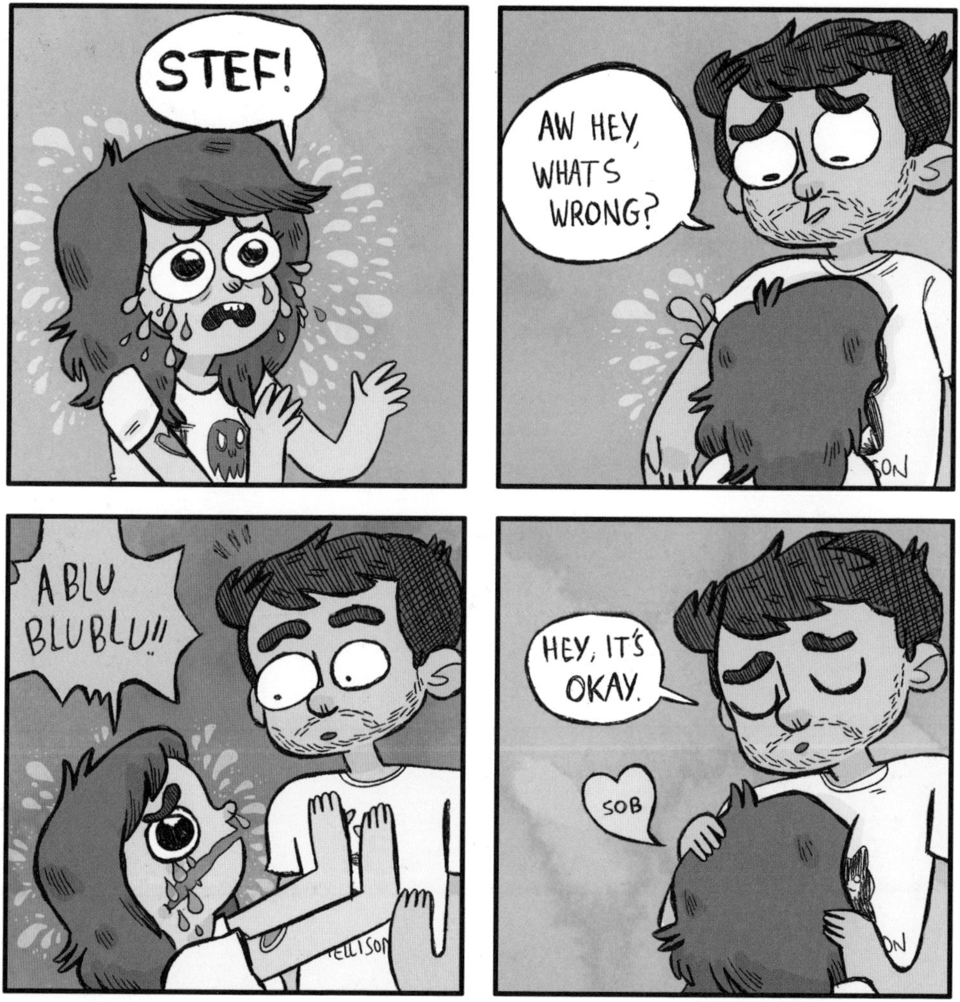
STEF!
AW HEY, WHAT'S WRONG?
ABLU BLUBLU!!
HEY, IT'S OKAY.
SOB

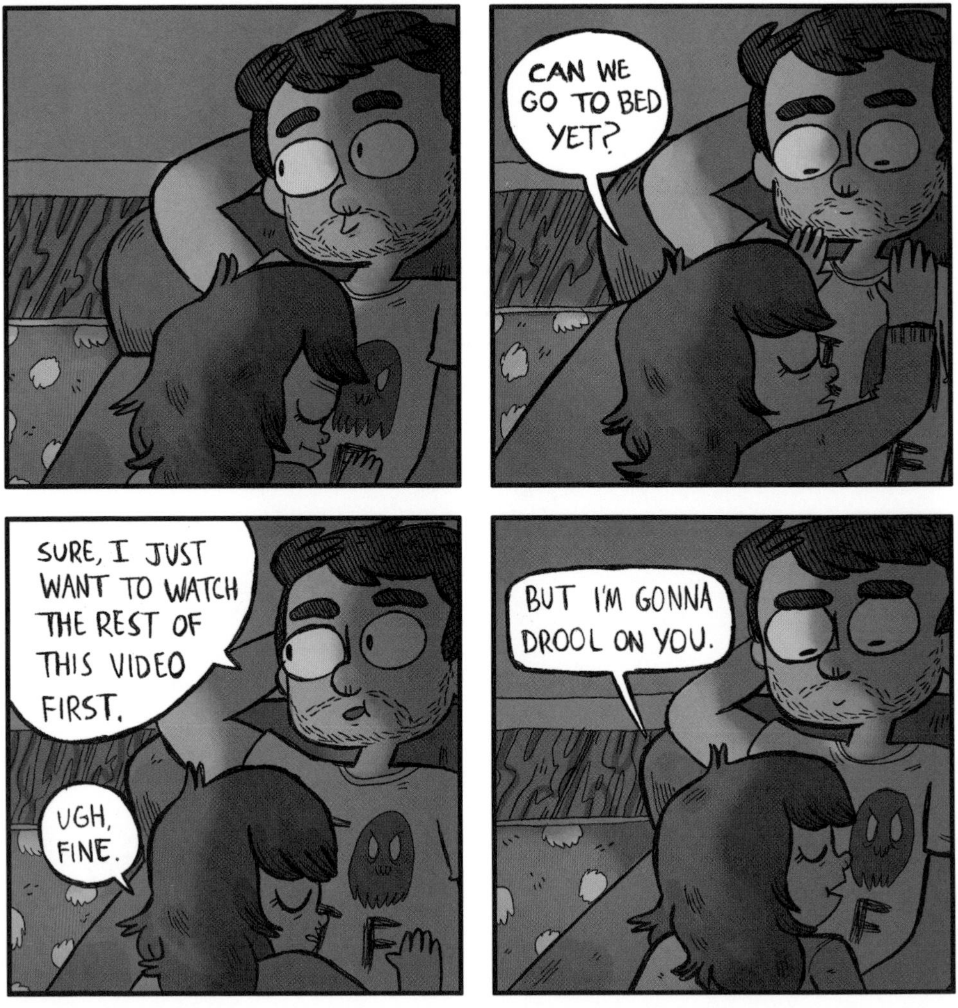
CAN WE GO TO BED YET?
SURE, I JUST WANT TO WATCH THE REST OF THIS VIDEO FIRST.
UGH, FINE.
BUT I'M GONNA DROOL ON YOU.

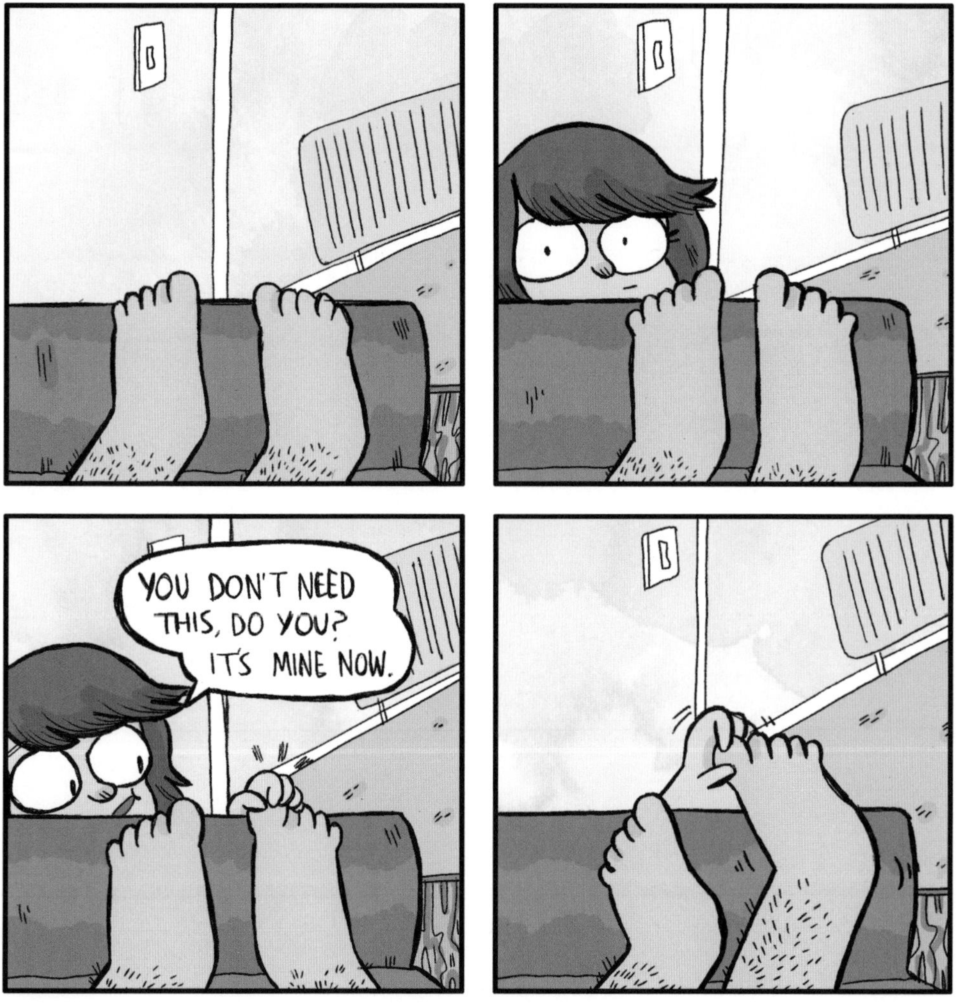
YOU DON'T NEED THIS, DO YOU?
IT'S MINE NOW.

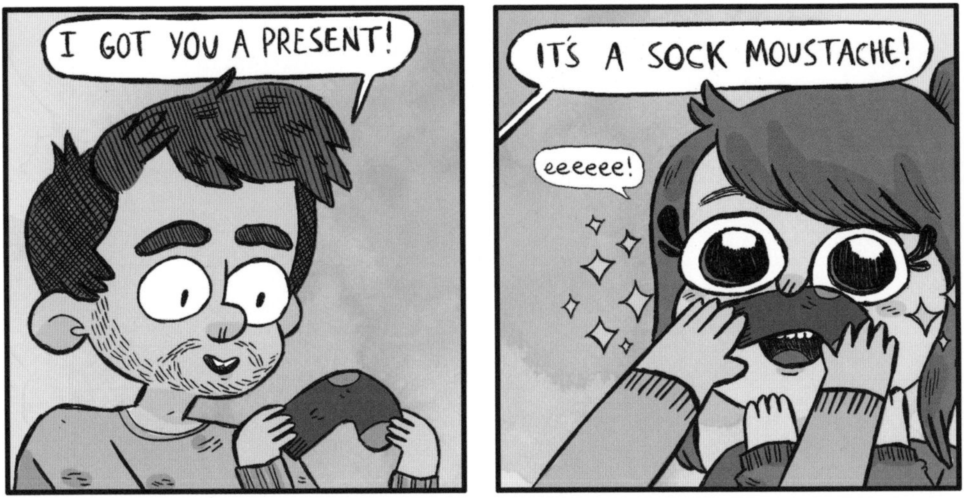
I GOT YOU A PRESENT!
IT'S A SOCK MOUSTACHE!
eeeeee!

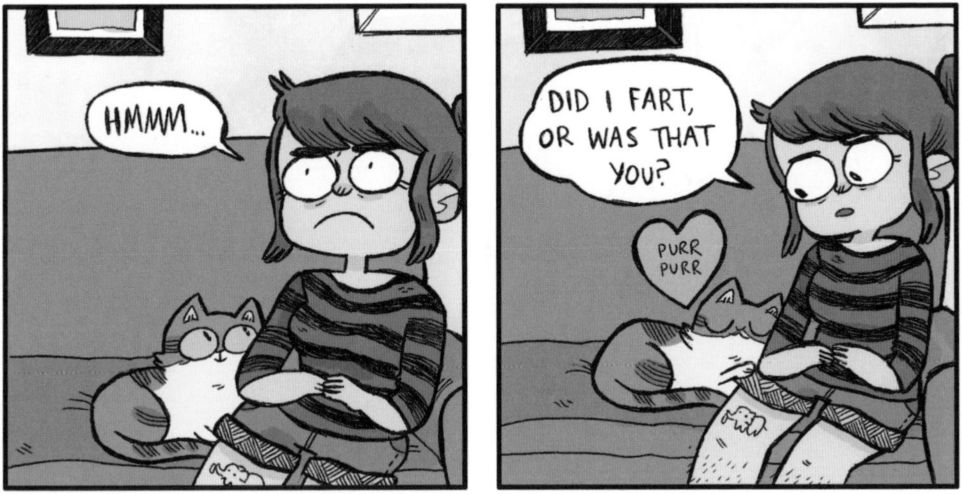
HMMM...
DID I FART, OR WAS THAT YOU?
PURR PURR

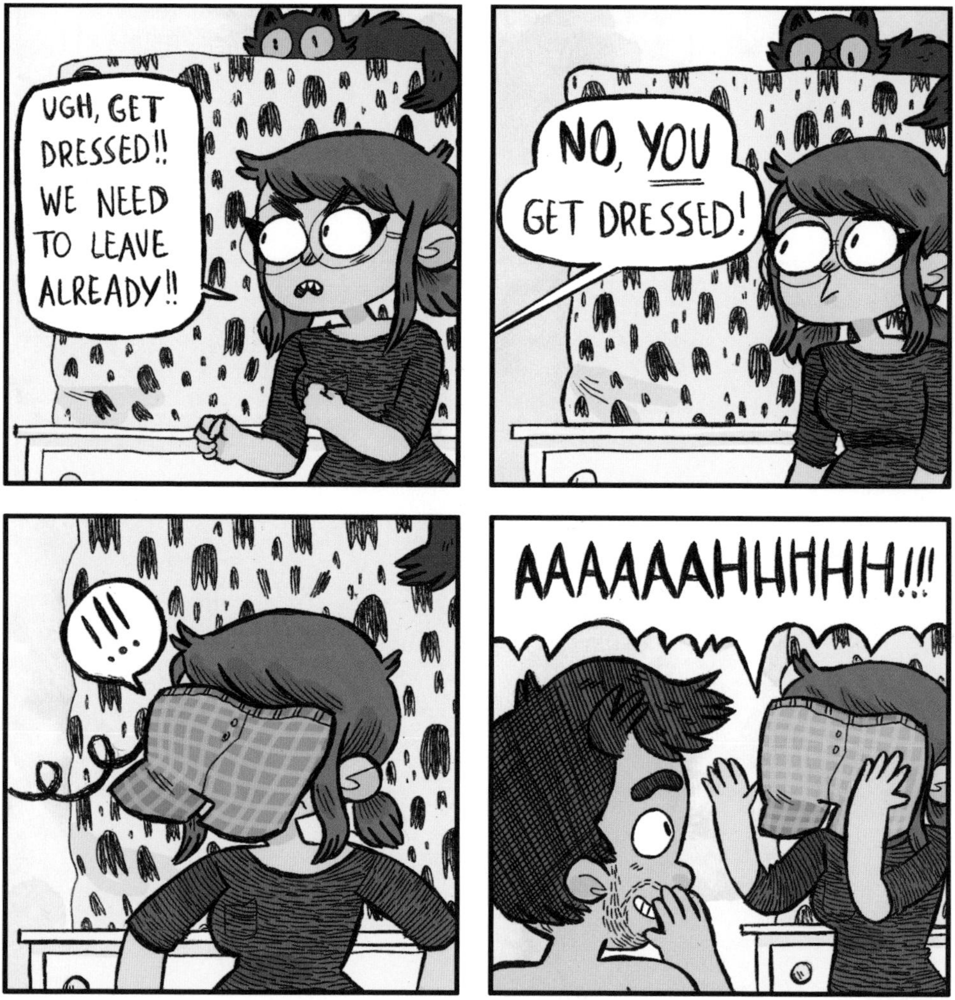
UGH, GET DRESSED!! WE NEED TO LEAVE ALREADY!!
NO, YOU GET DRESSED!
!!!
AAAAAAHHHHH!!!

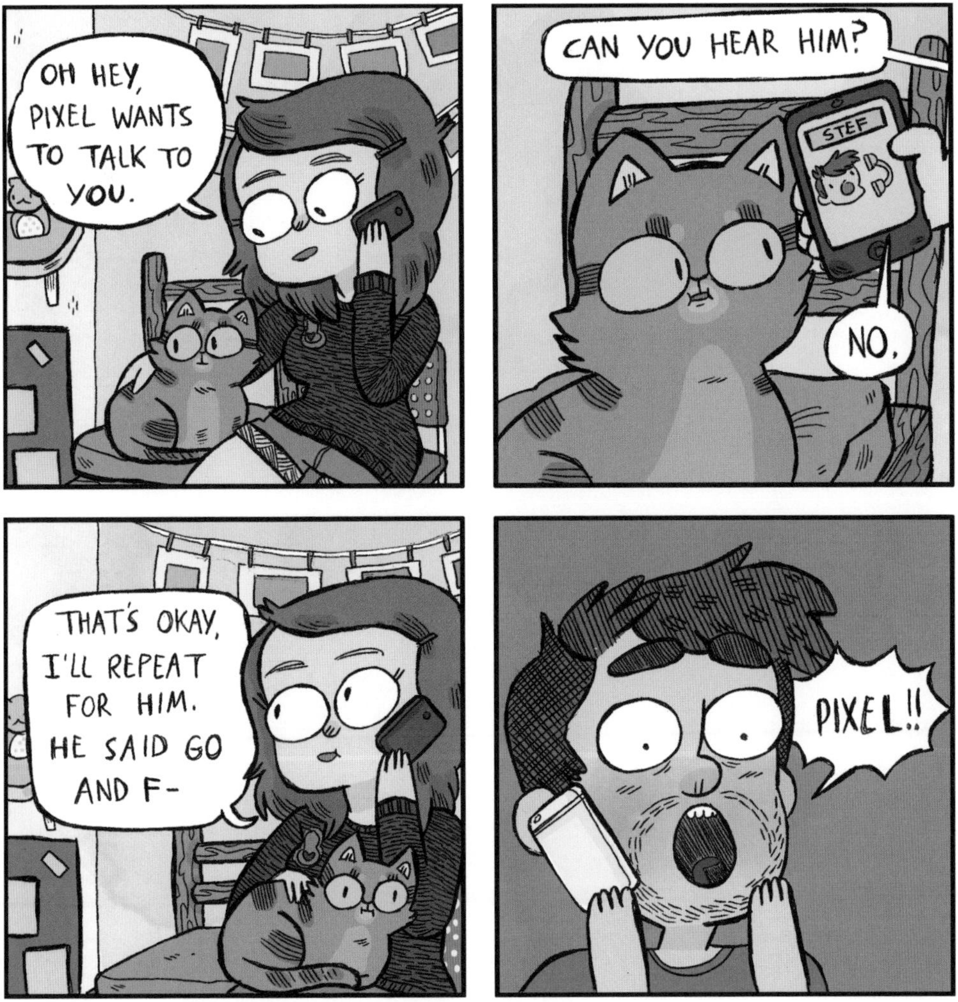
OH HEY, PIXEL WANTS TO TALK TO YOU.
CAN YOU HEAR HIM?
STEF
NO.
THAT'S OKAY, I'LL REPEAT FOR HIM. HE SAID GO AND F-
PIXEL!!

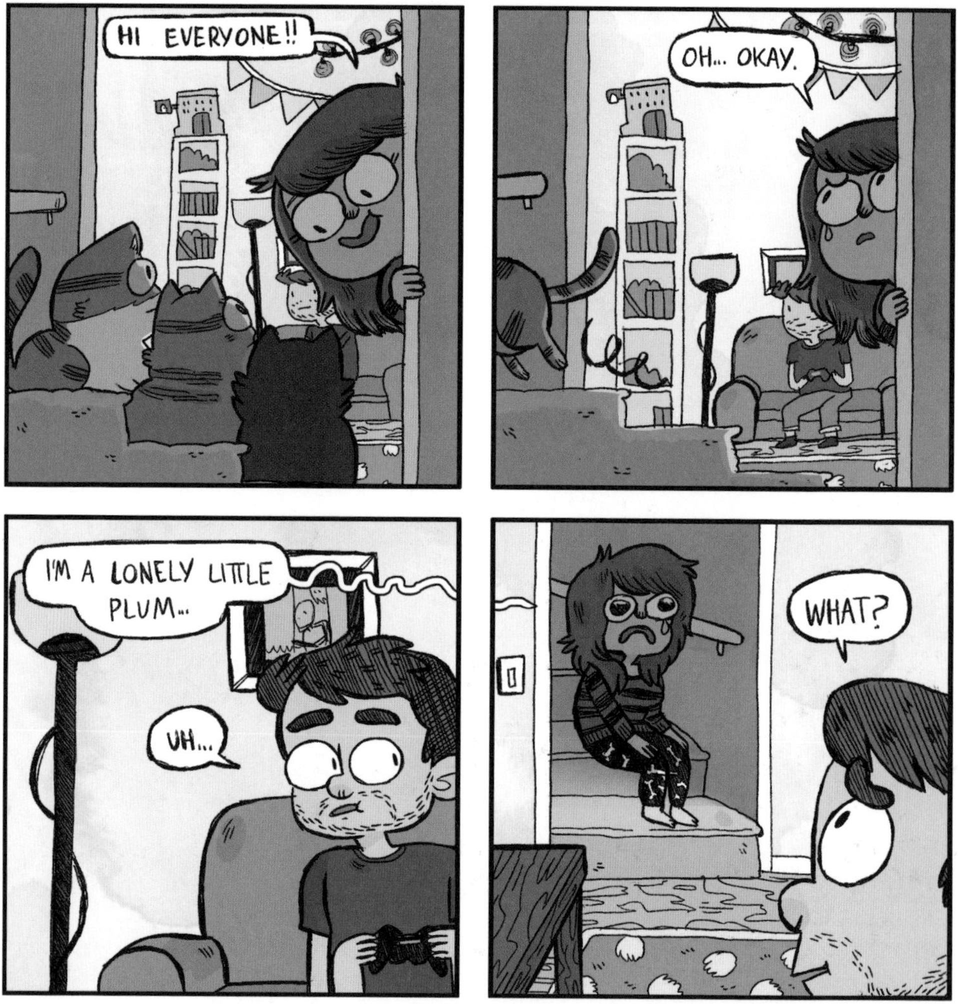
HI EVERYONE!!
OH... OKAY.
I'M A LONELY LITTLE PLUM...
UH...
WHAT?

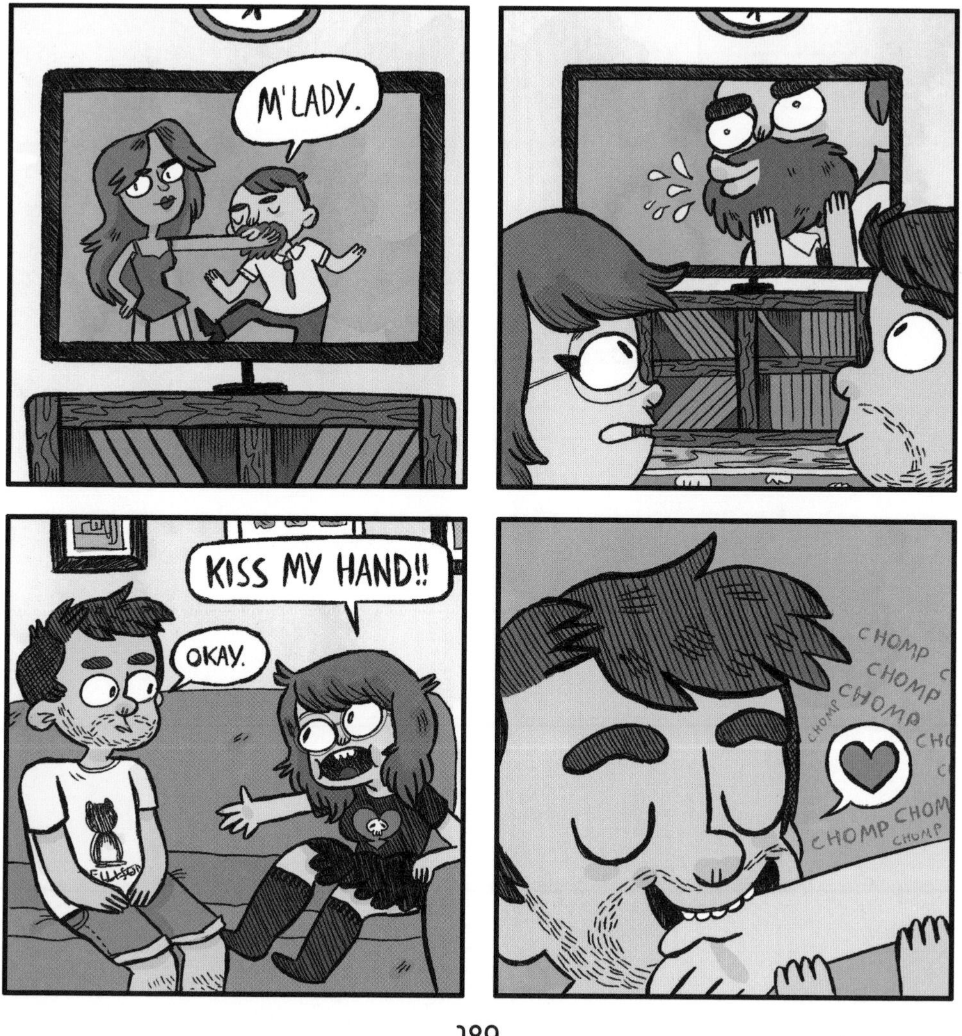
M'LADY.
KISS MY HAND!!
OKAY.
CHOMP
CHOMP
CHOMP
CHOMP
CHOMP CHOMP
CHOMP

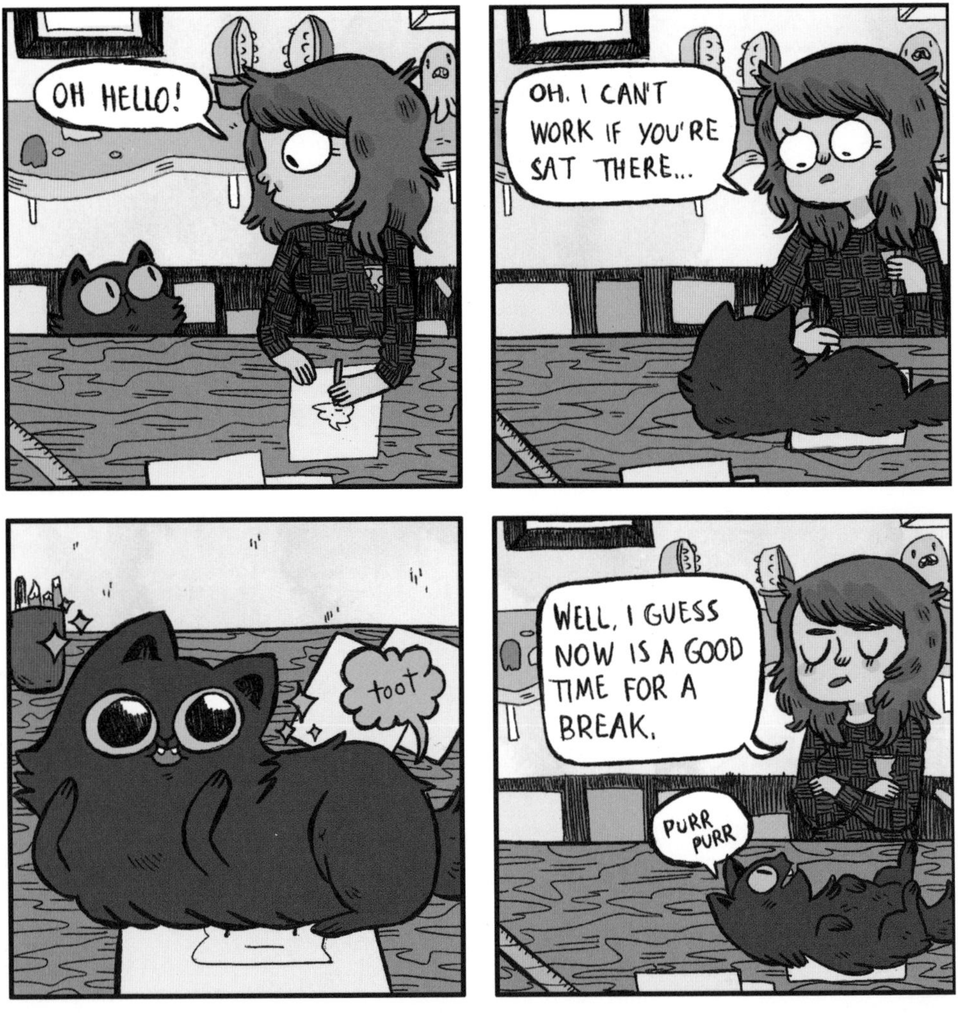
OH HELLO!
OH. I CAN'T WORK IF YOU'RE SAT THERE...
toot
WELL, I GUESS NOW IS A GOOD TIME FOR A BREAK.
PURR PURR

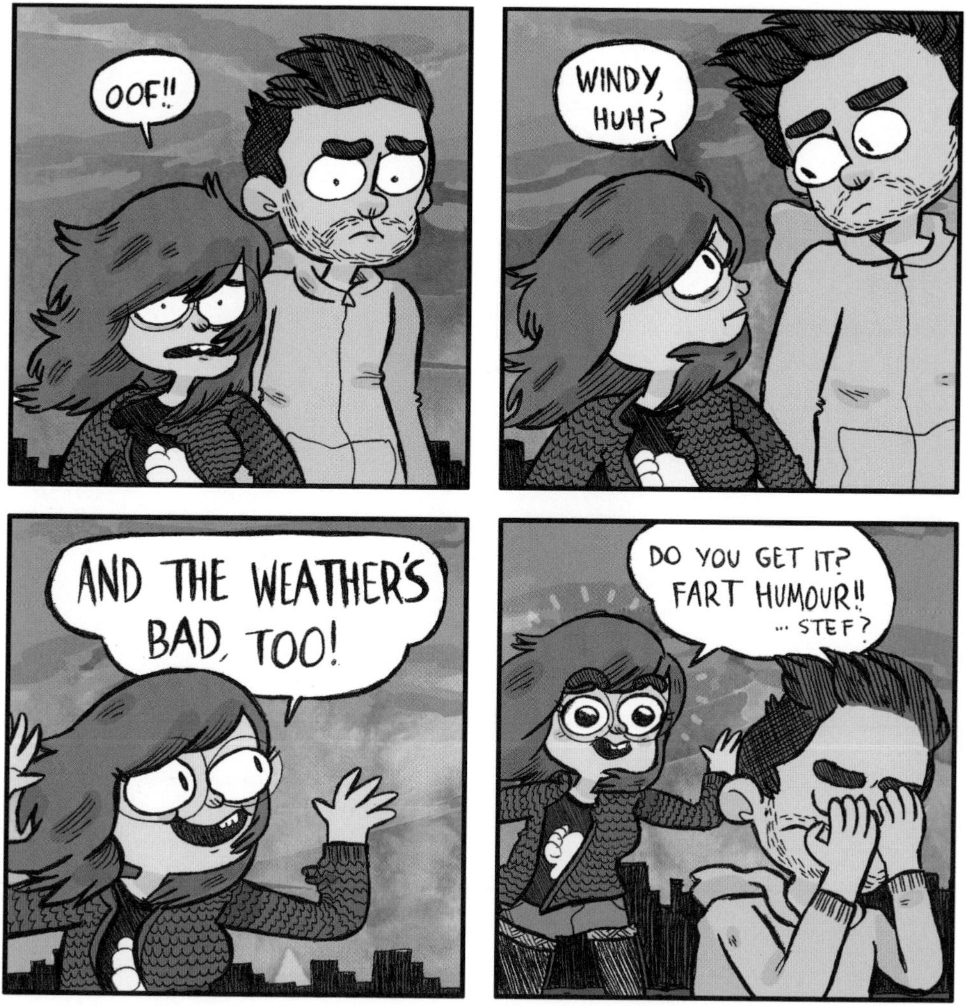
OOF!!
WINDY, HUH?
AND THE WEATHER'S BAD, TOO!
DO YOU GET IT? FART HUMOUR!!
... STEF?

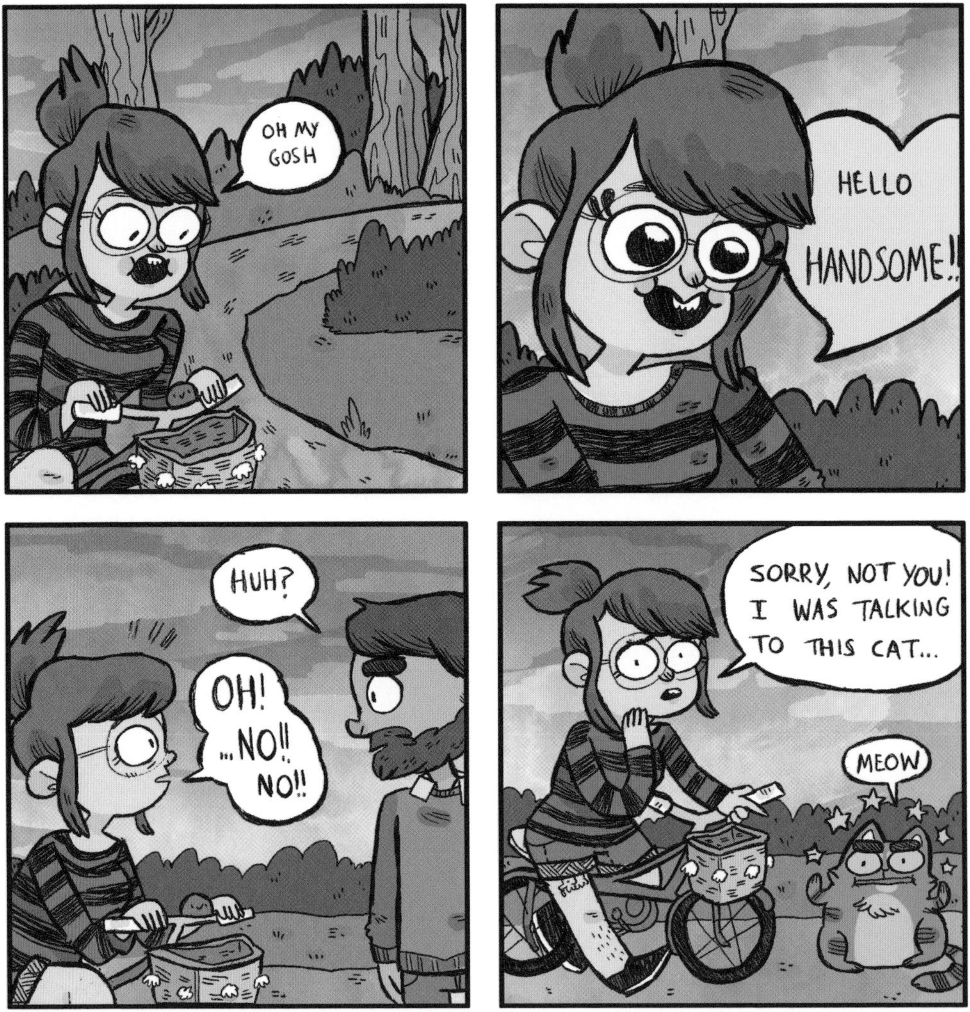
OH MY GOSH
HELLO HANDSOME!!
HUH?
OH! ...NO!!.. NO!!
SORRY, NOT YOU! I WAS TALKING TO THIS CAT...
MEOW

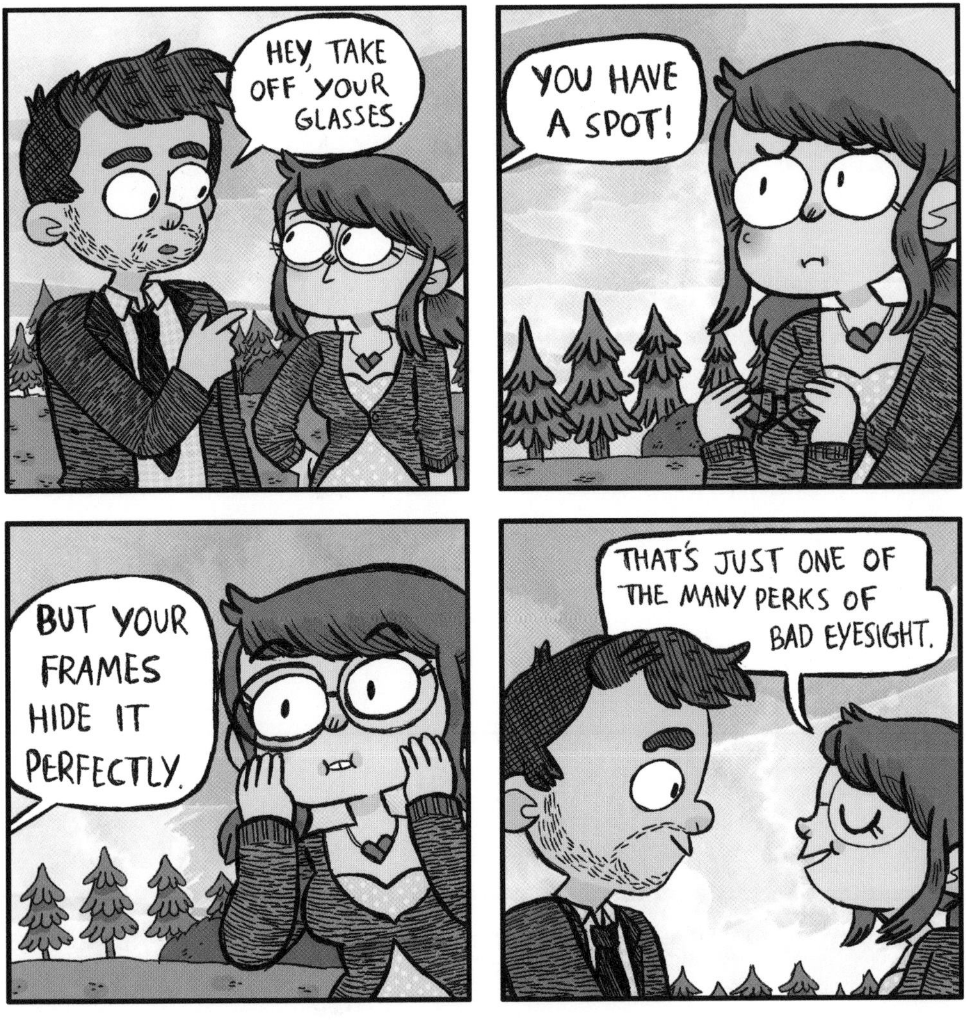
HEY, TAKE OFF YOUR GLASSES.
YOU HAVE A SPOT!
BUT YOUR FRAMES HIDE IT PERFECTLY.
THAT'S JUST ONE OF THE MANY PERKS OF BAD EYESIGHT.

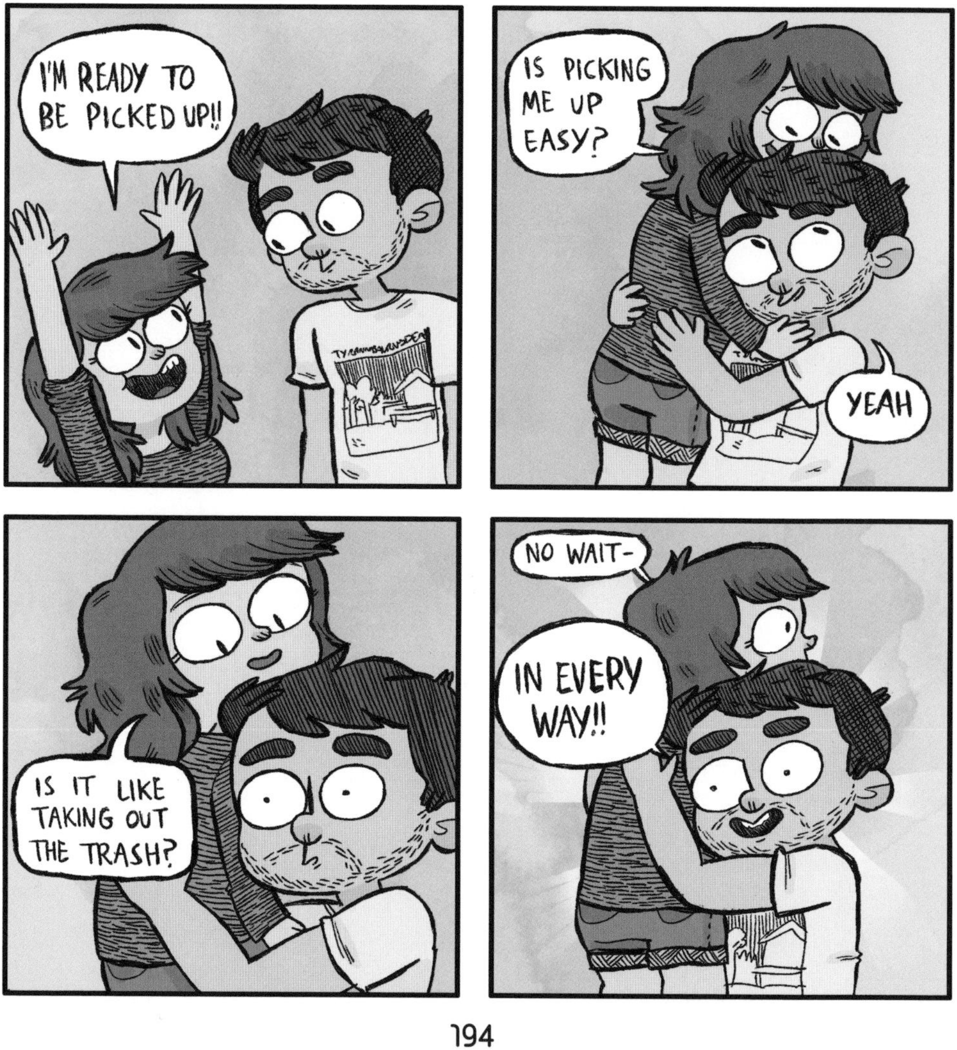
I'M READY TO BE PICKED UP!!
IS PICKING ME UP EASY?
YEAH
IS IT LIKE TAKING OUT THE TRASH?
NO WAIT-
IN EVERY WAY!!

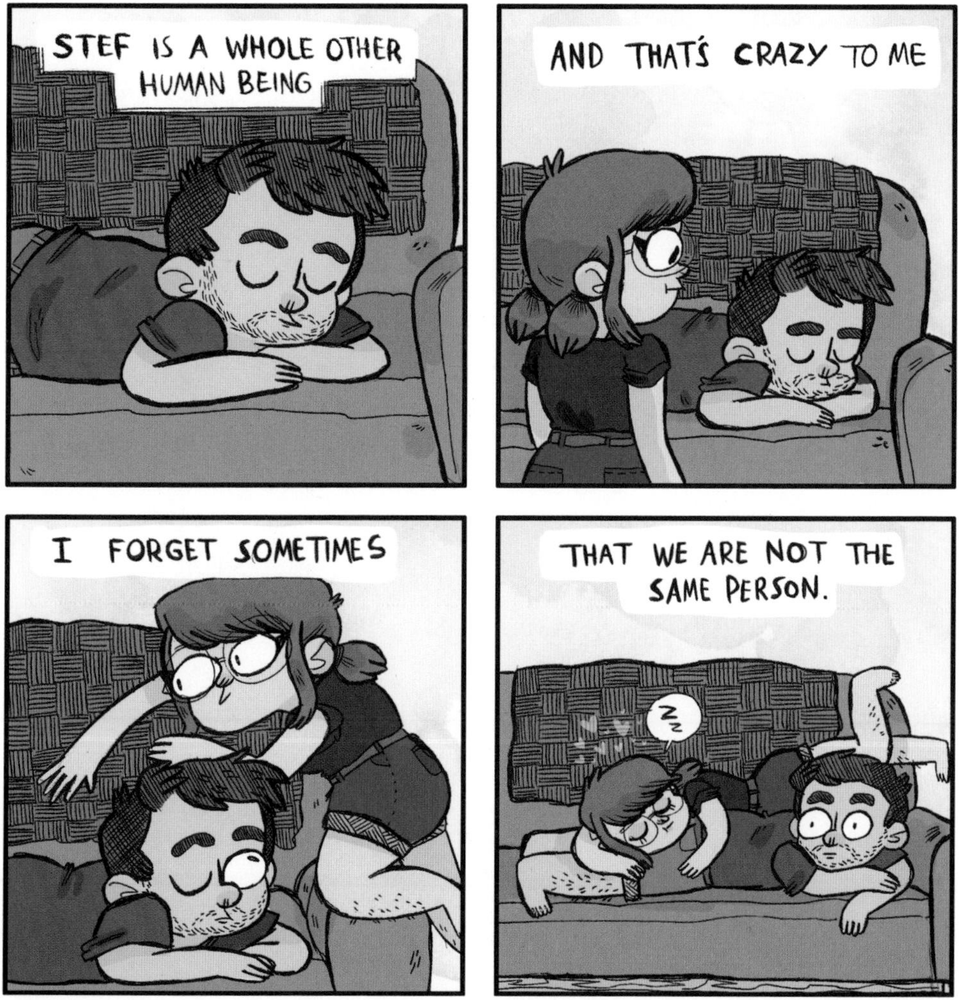
STEF IS A WHOLE OTHER HUMAN BEING
AND THAT'S CRAZY TO ME
I FORGET SOMETIMES
THAT WE ARE NOT THE SAME PERSON.
ZZ

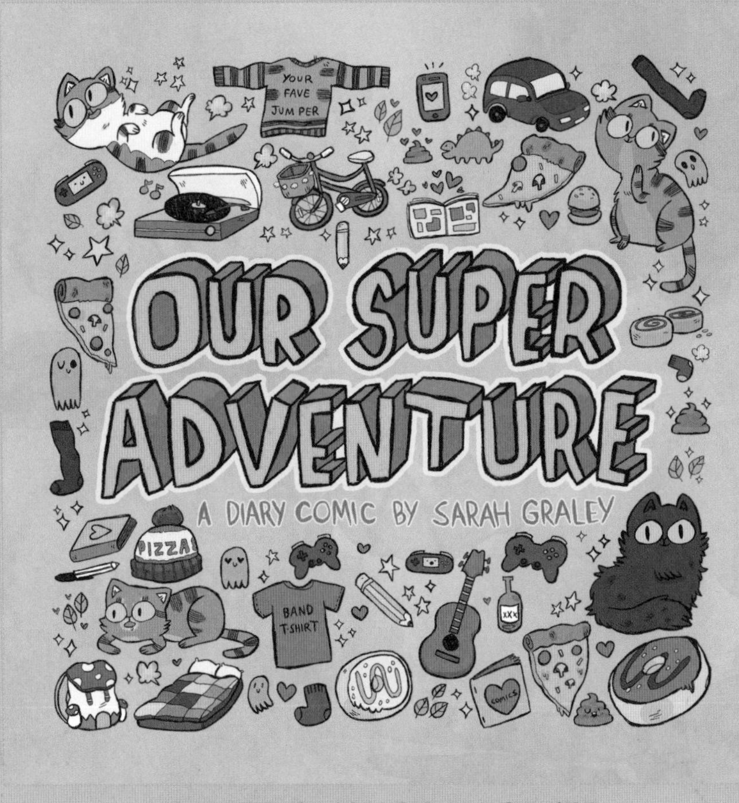
YOUR
FAVE
JUMPER
OUR SUPER
ADVENTURE
A DIARY COMIC BY SARAH GRALEY
PIZZA!
BAND
T-SHIRT
XXX
COMICS

THE ORIGINAL BOOK COVER

THIS WAS THE FRONT COVER OF ***OUR SUPER ADVENTURE*** BETWEEN 2015 AND 2019! WHEN ONI PRESS ASKED ABOUT CO-PUBLISHING THE ***OUR SUPER ADVENTURE*** BOOK SERIES, I THOUGHT IT MIGHT BE NICE TO RETIRE THIS COVER AND DESIGN A NEW ONE FOR THE NEW EDITION OF THE BOOK!

REDRAWN COMICS

WHEN MY *OUR SUPER ADVENTURE* BOOK KICKSTARTER CAMPAIGN REACHED ITS ORIGINAL FUNDING TARGET, I HAD THE OPPORTUNITY TO THINK OF SOME INTERESTING STRETCH GOALS TO REACH DURING THE REST OF THE CAMPAIGN!

ONE OF THESE STRETCH GOALS WAS TO TAKE TEN OF THE OLDER BLACK-AND-WHITE *OUR SUPER ADVENTURE COMICS* AND REDRAW THEM IN MY NEWER STYLE IN FULL COLOUR!

AS YOU CAN PROBABLY GUESS AT THIS POINT - WE WERE TOTALLY SUCCESSFUL IN REACHING THAT STRETCH GOAL! HUGE THANKS TO EVERYONE WHO BACKED THAT KICKSTARTER - THIS SECTION ESPECIALLY WOULDN'T HAVE HAPPENED WITHOUT YOU!

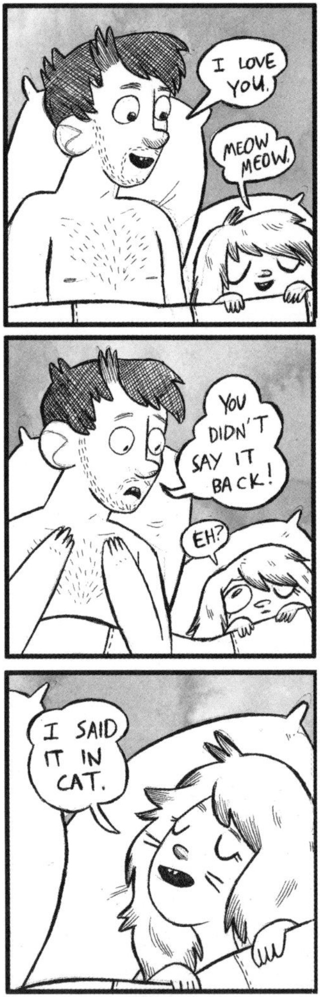
I LOVE YOU.
MEOW MEOW.
YOU DIDN'T SAY IT BACK!
EH?
I SAID IT IN CAT.

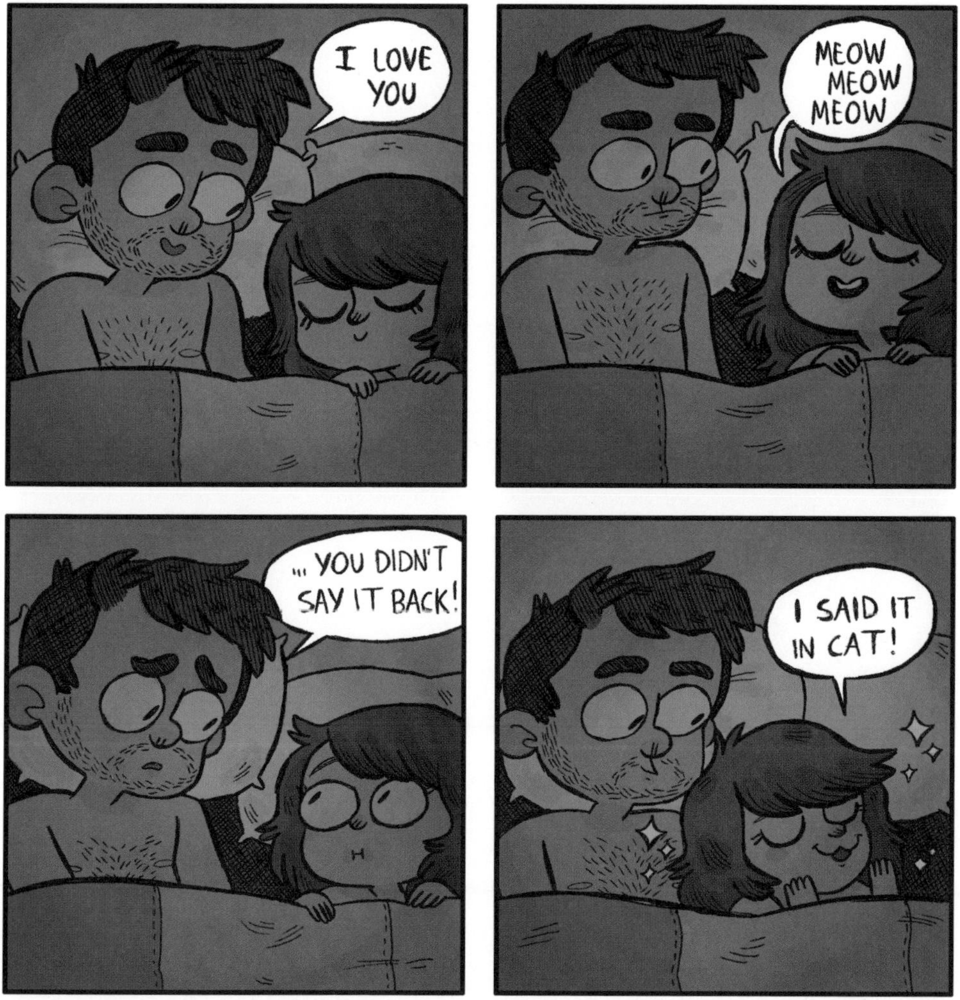
I LOVE YOU
MEOW MEOW MEOW
... YOU DIDN'T SAY IT BACK!
I SAID IT IN CAT!

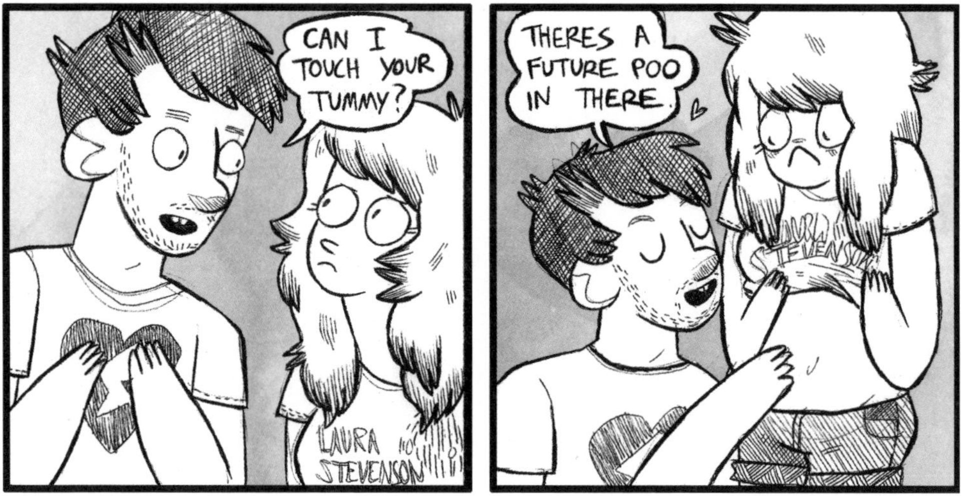
CAN I TOUCH YOUR TUMMY?
LAURA STEVENSON
THERES A FUTURE POO IN THERE.

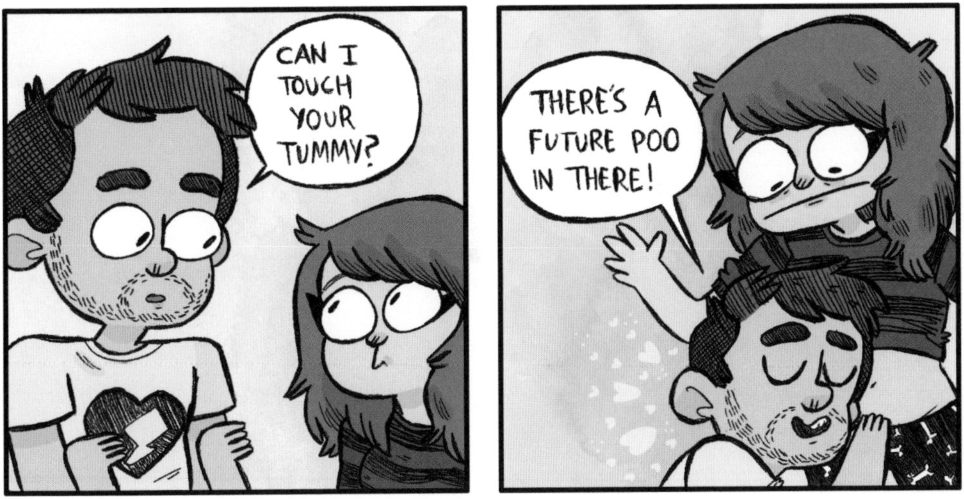
CAN I TOUCH YOUR TUMMY?
THERE'S A FUTURE POO IN THERE!

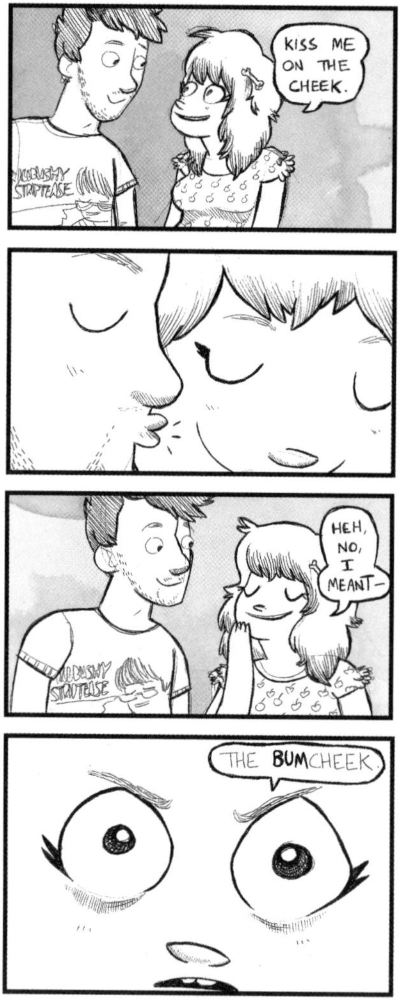
KISS ME ON THE CHEEK.
HEH, NO, I MEANT–
THE **BUM**CHEEK.

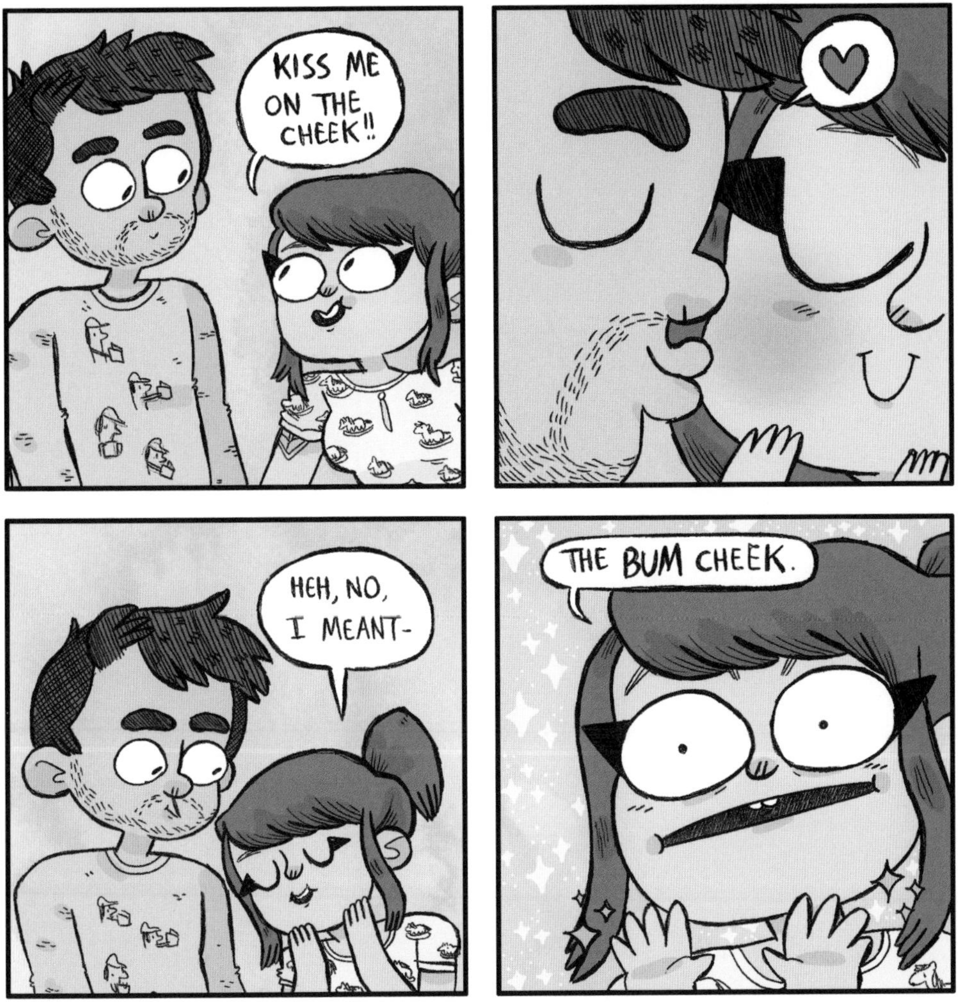
KISS ME ON THE CHEEK!!
HEH, NO, I MEANT-
THE BUM CHEEK.

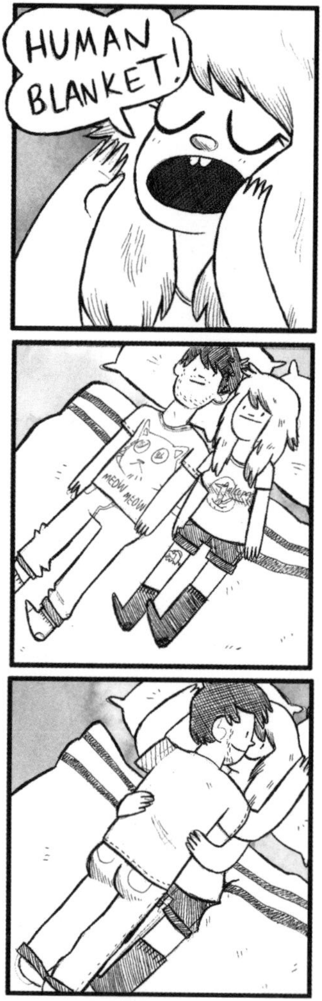
HUMAN BLANKET!
MEOW MEOW

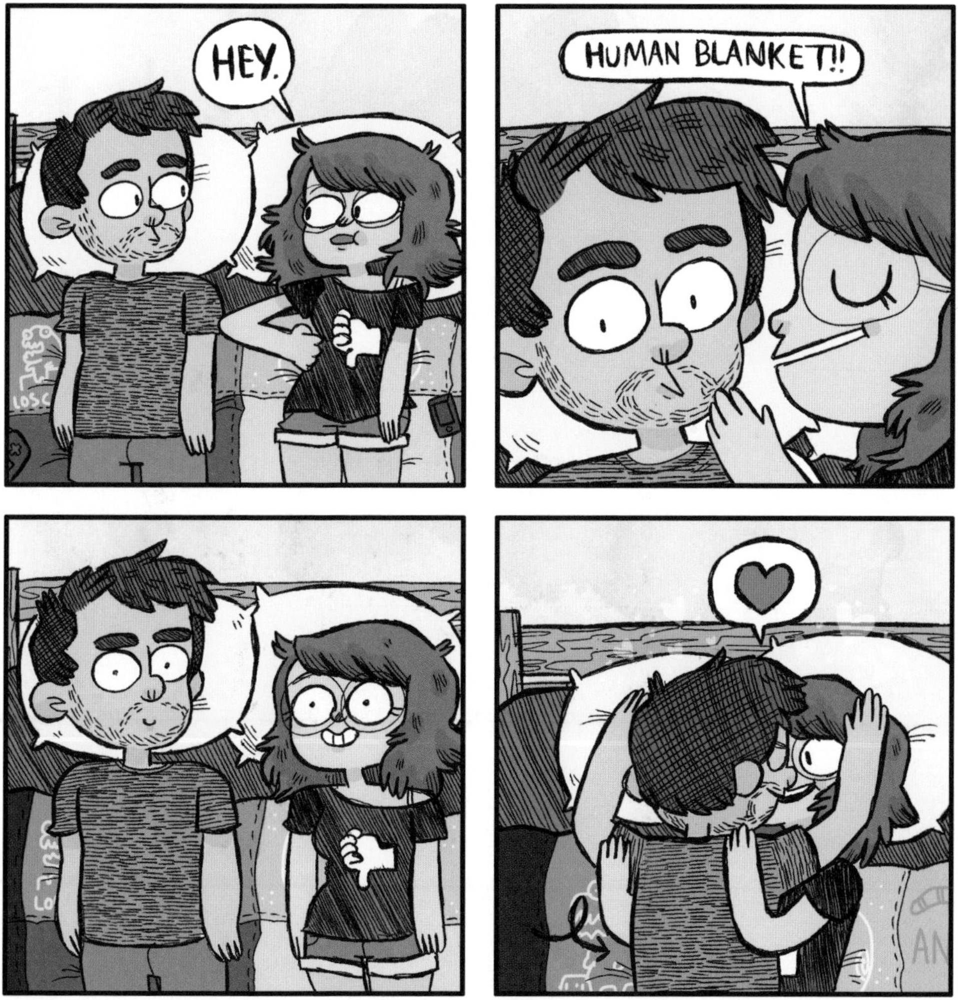
HEY.
HUMAN BLANKET!!

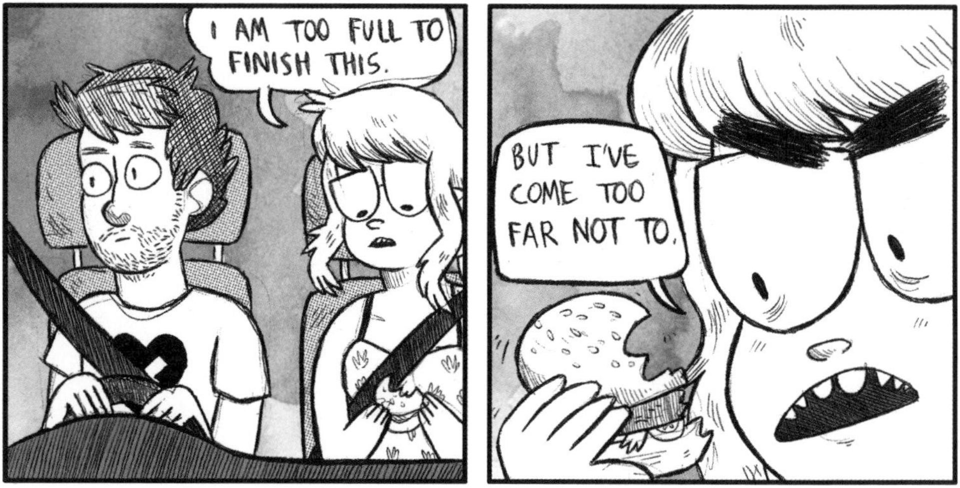
I AM TOO FULL TO FINISH THIS.
BUT I'VE COME TOO FAR NOT TO.

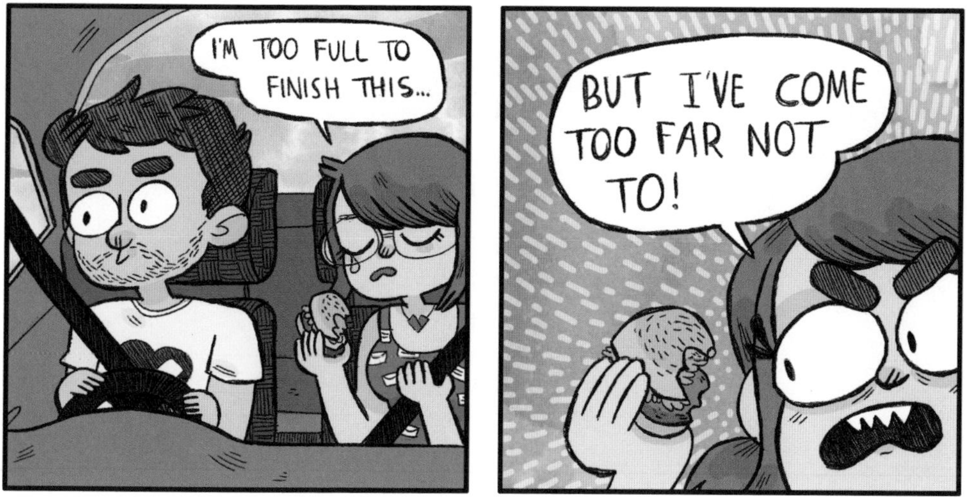
I'M TOO FULL TO FINISH THIS...
BUT I'VE COME TOO FAR NOT TO!

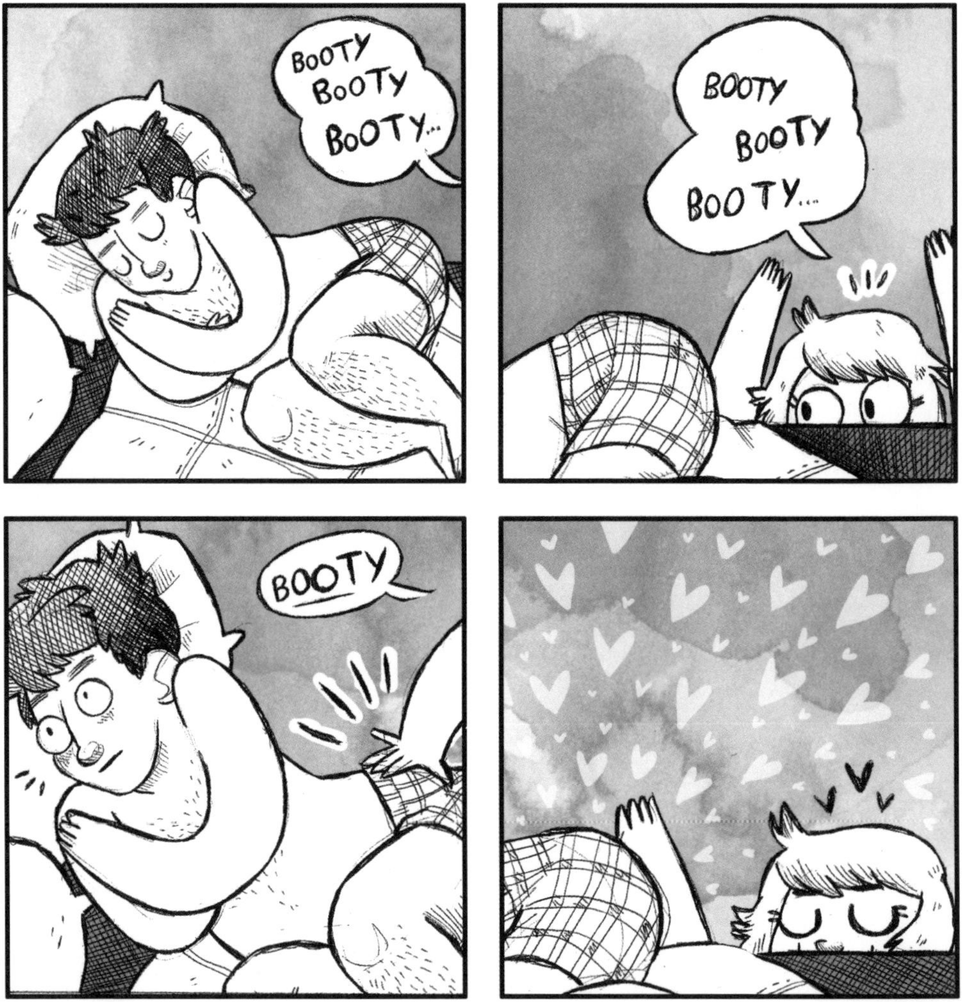
BOOTY BOOTY BOOTY...
BOOTY BOOTY BOOTY...
BOOTY

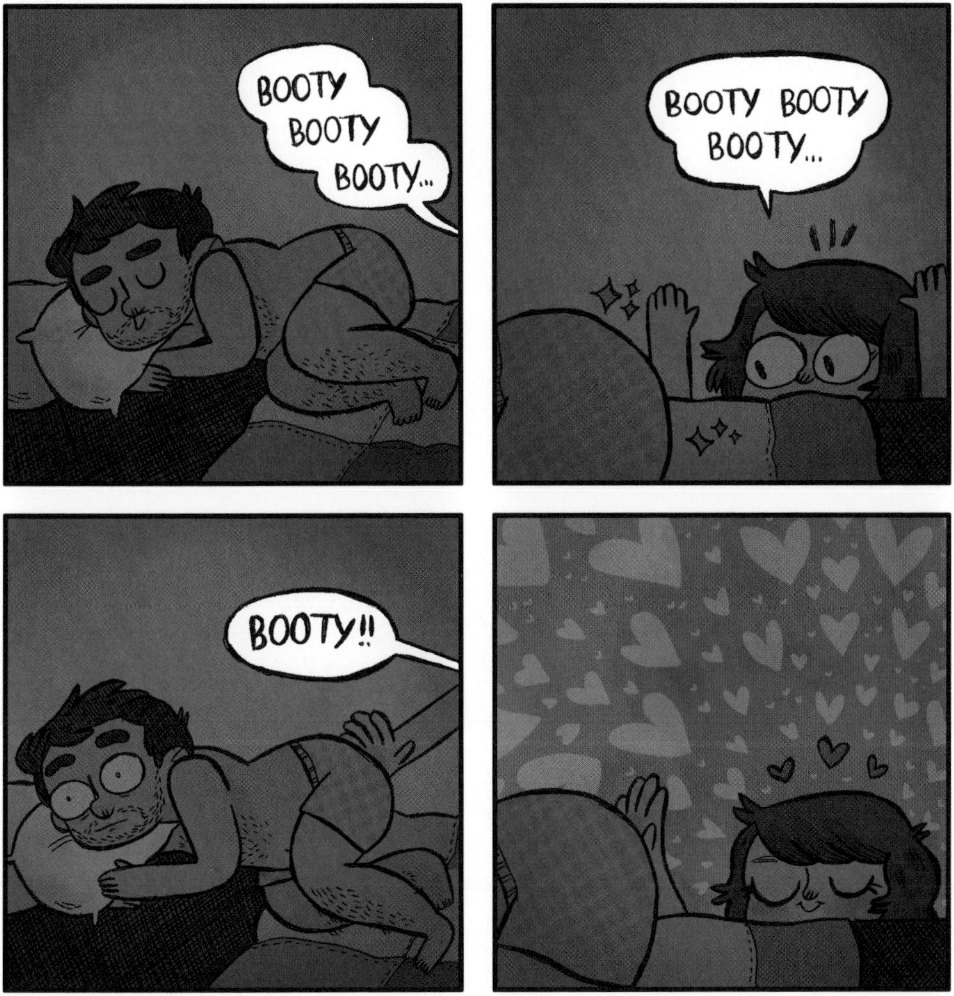
BOOTY BOOTY BOOTY...
BOOTY BOOTY BOOTY...
BOOTY!!

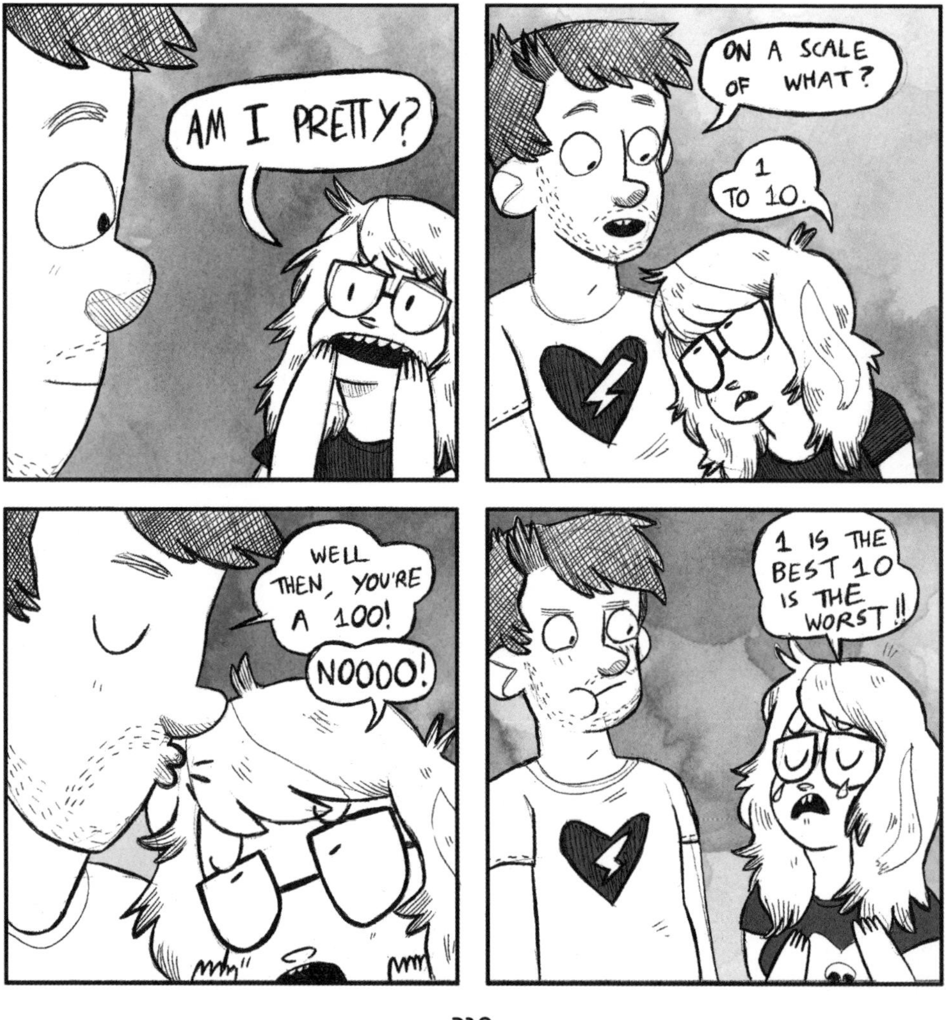
AM I PRETTY?
ON A SCALE OF WHAT?
1 TO 10.
WELL THEN, YOU'RE A 100!
NOOOO!
1 IS THE BEST 10 IS THE WORST!!

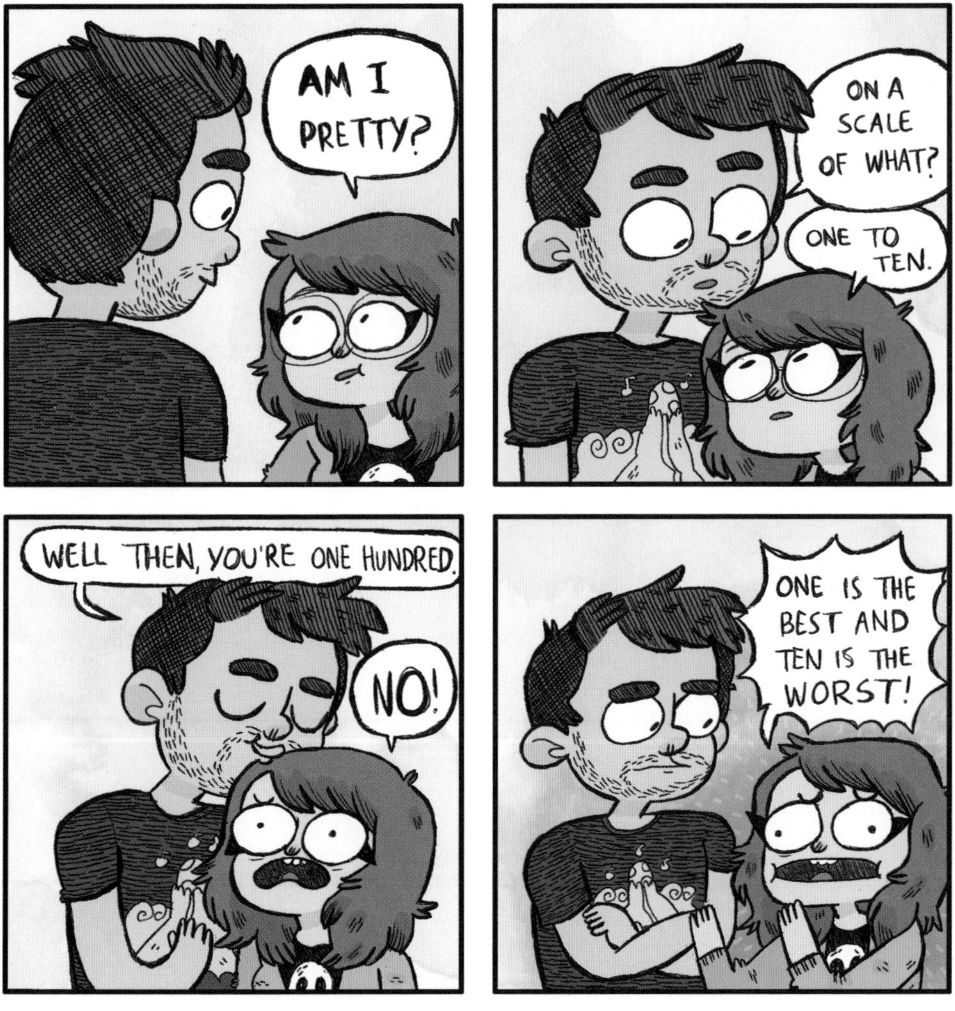
AM I PRETTY?
ON A SCALE OF WHAT?
ONE TO TEN.
WELL THEN, YOU'RE ONE HUNDRED.
NO!
ONE IS THE BEST AND TEN IS THE WORST!

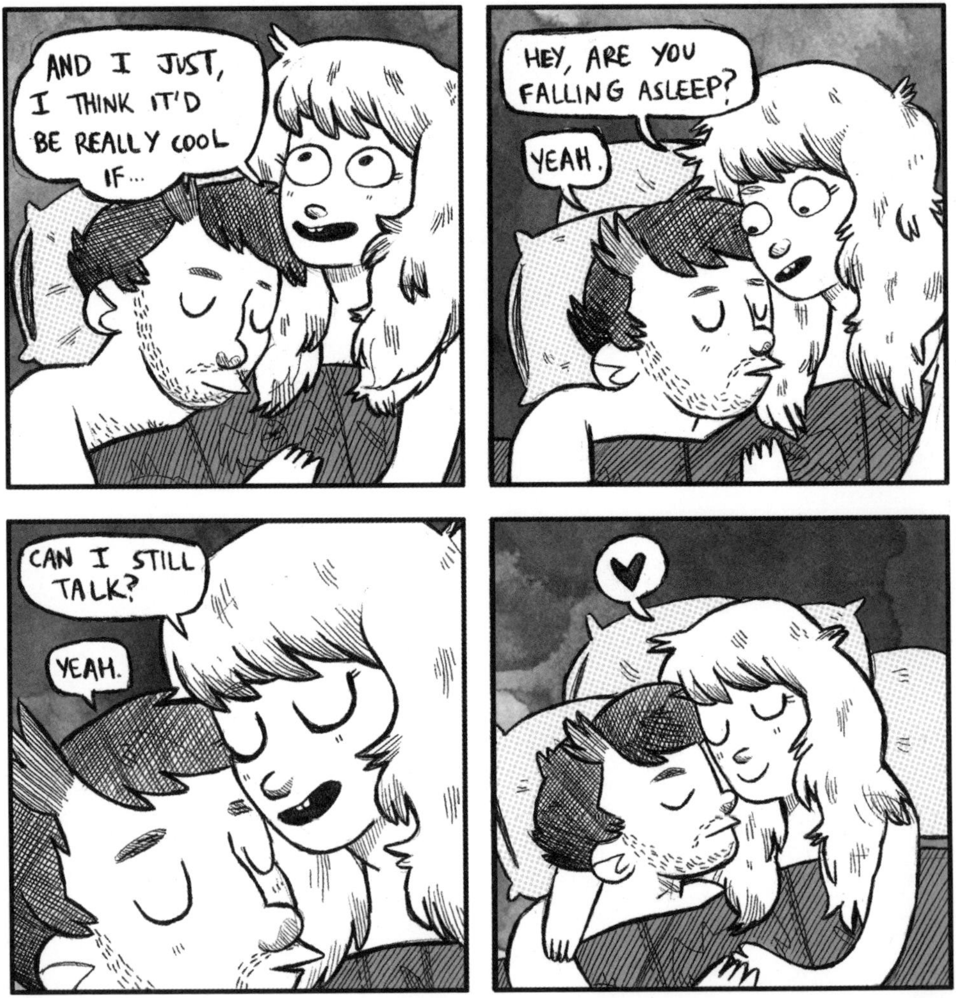
AND I JUST, I THINK IT'D BE REALLY COOL IF...
HEY, ARE YOU FALLING ASLEEP?
YEAH.
CAN I STILL TALK?
YEAH.

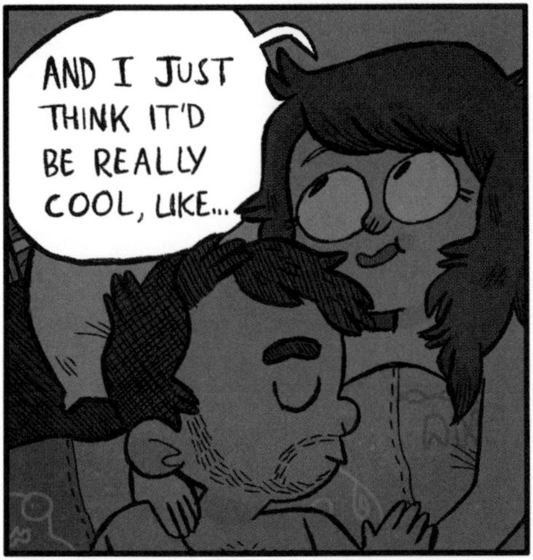
AND I JUST THINK IT'D BE REALLY COOL, LIKE...

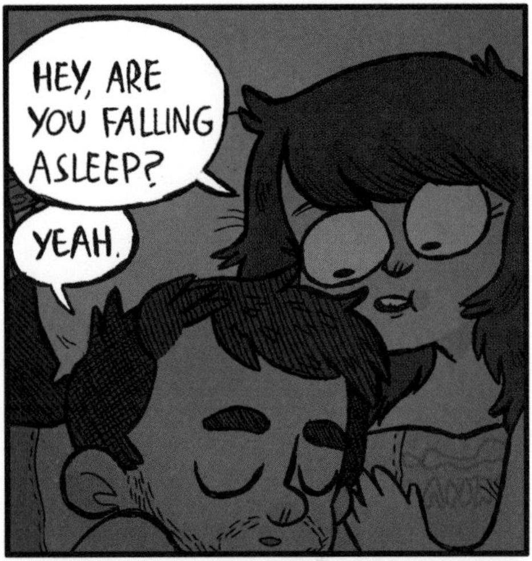
HEY, ARE YOU FALLING ASLEEP?
YEAH.

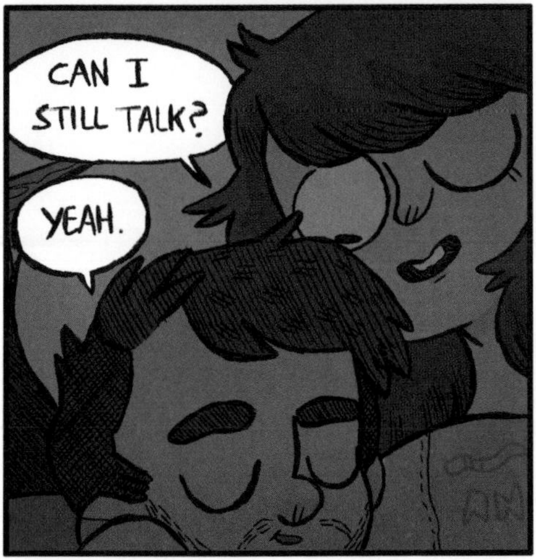
CAN I STILL TALK?
YEAH.

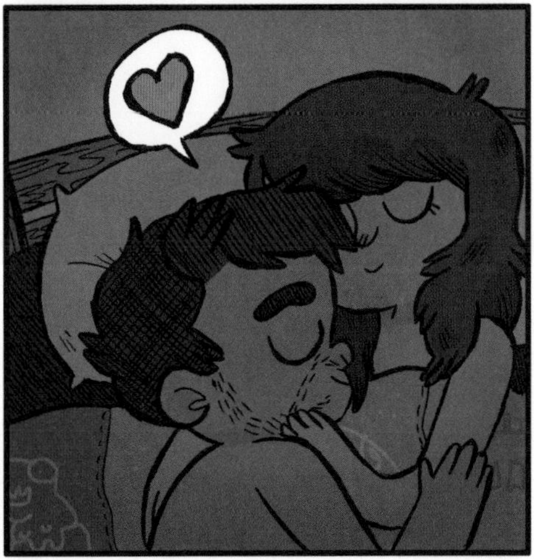

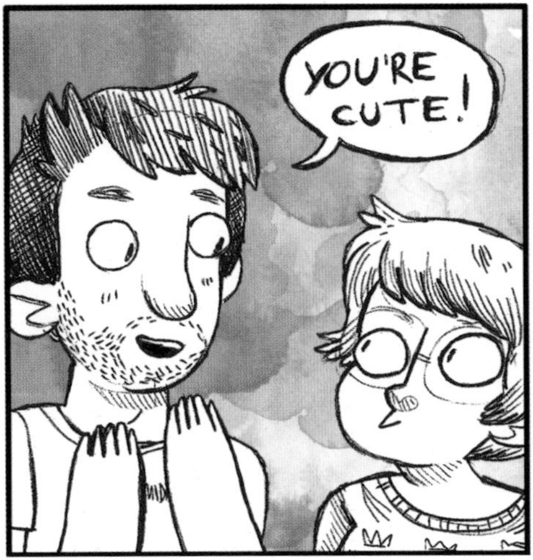
YOU'RE CUTE!

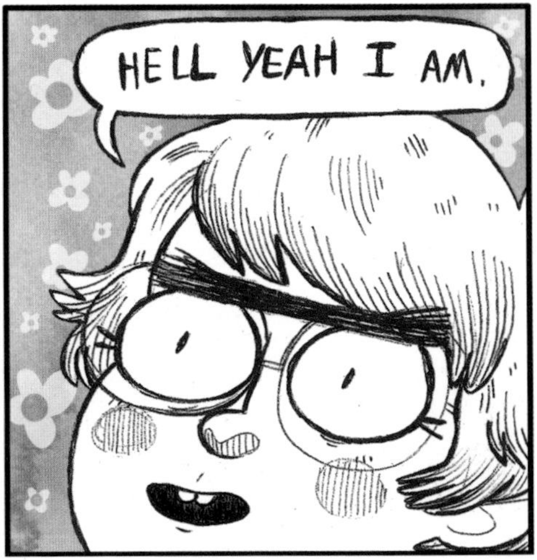
HELL YEAH I AM.

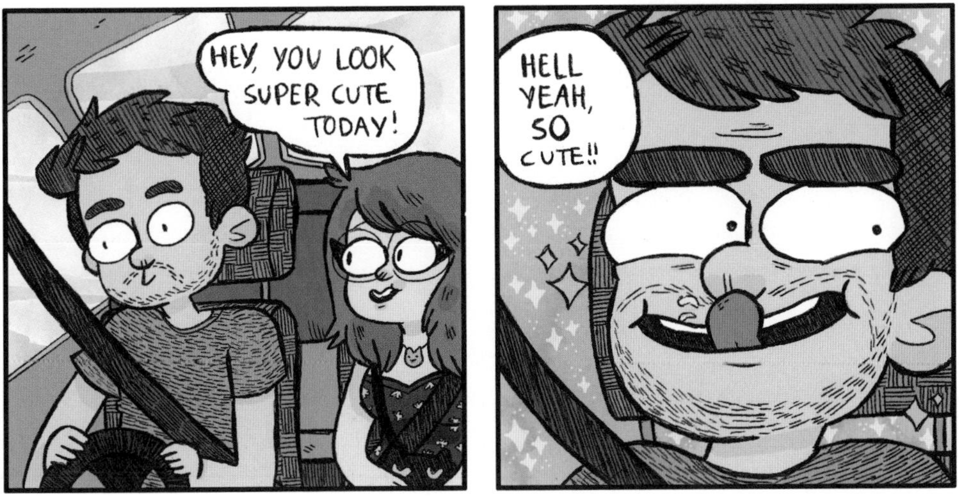
HEY, YOU LOOK SUPER CUTE TODAY!
HELL YEAH, SO CUTE!!

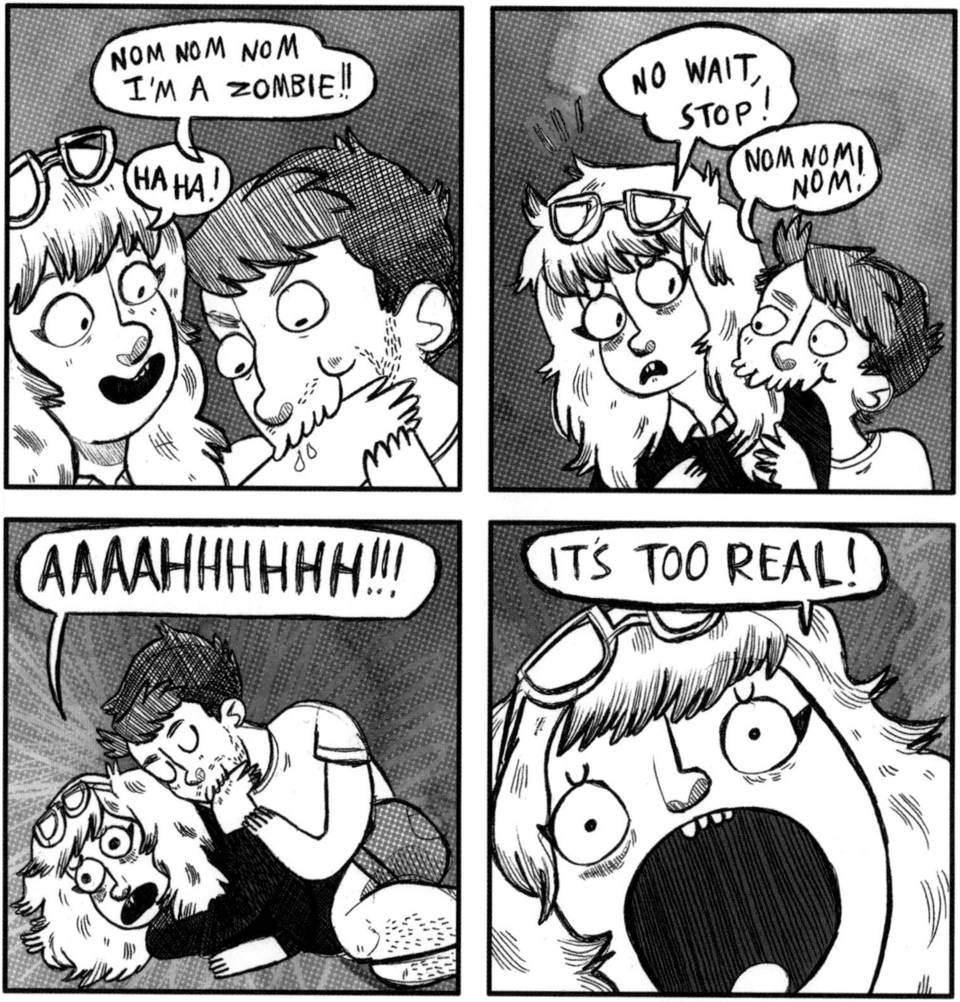
NOM NOM NOM I'M A ZOMBIE!!
HA HA!
NO WAIT, STOP!
NOM NOM NOM!
AAAAHHHHHHH!!!
IT'S TOO REAL!

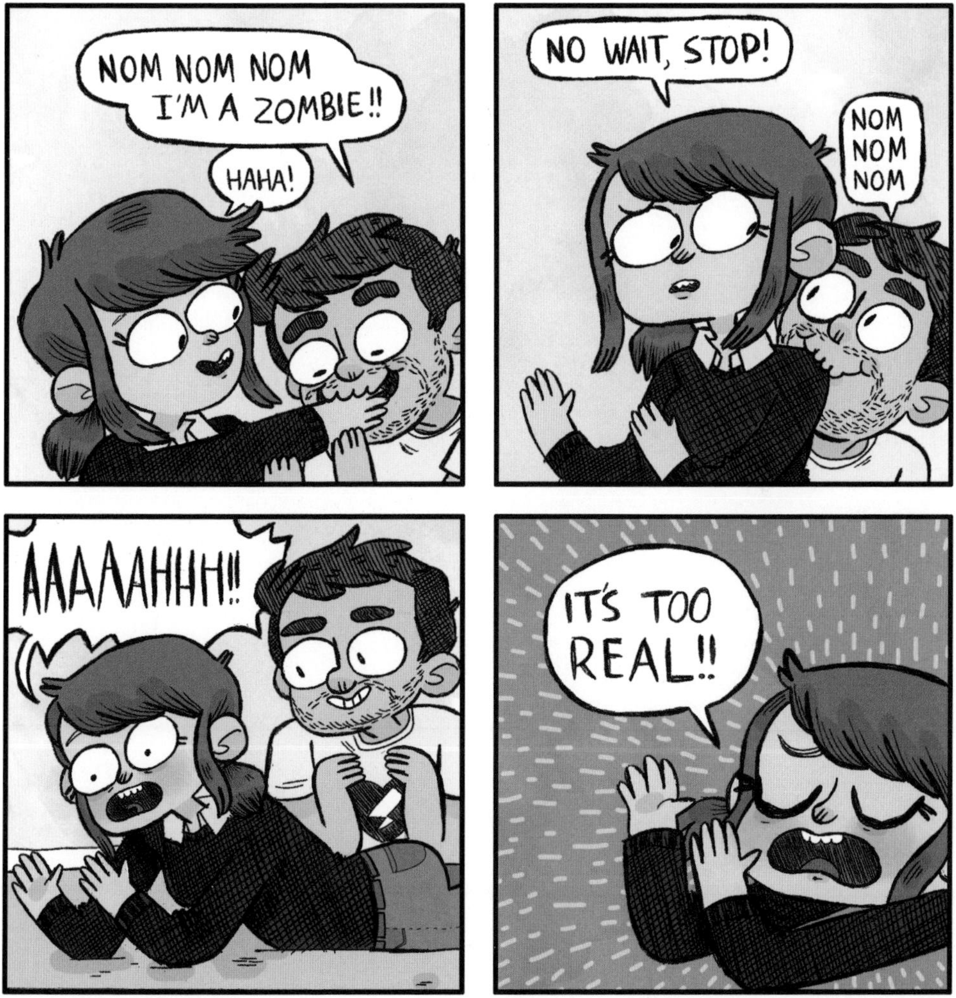
NOM NOM NOM
I'M A ZOMBIE!!
HAHA!
NO WAIT, STOP!
NOM
NOM
NOM
AAAAAHHH!!
IT'S TOO
REAL!!

THE SUPER ADVENTURERS

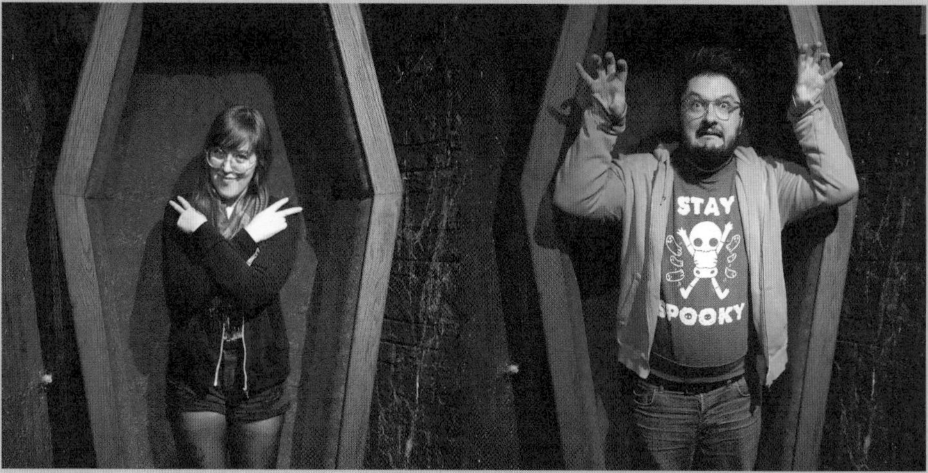
STAY
SPOOKY

SARAH GRALEY IS A COMIC WRITER AND ARTIST WHO LIVES IN BIRMINGHAM, UK, WITH FOUR CATS AND A CAT-LIKE BOY. SHE HAS BEEN DRAWING ***OUR SUPER ADVENTURE*** SINCE 2012, ALONGSIDE OTHER COMICS SUCH AS ***KIM REAPER (ONI PRESS), RICK AND MORTY: LIL' POOPY SUPERSTAR (ONI PRESS)*** AND ***GLITCH (SCHOLASTIC GRAPHIX).***

YOU CAN FIND OUT MORE ABOUT HER AT ***SARAHGRALEY.COM!***

STEF PURENINS IS A CAT-LIKE BOY WHO HELPS SARAH OUT WITH LETTERING AND DESIGN STUFF.

HE MAKES VIDEO GAME MUSIC OVER AT ***TINYSPELLS.BANDCAMP.COM.***

ABOUT OUR CATS

(THE ***REAL*** STARS OF THE BOOK!)

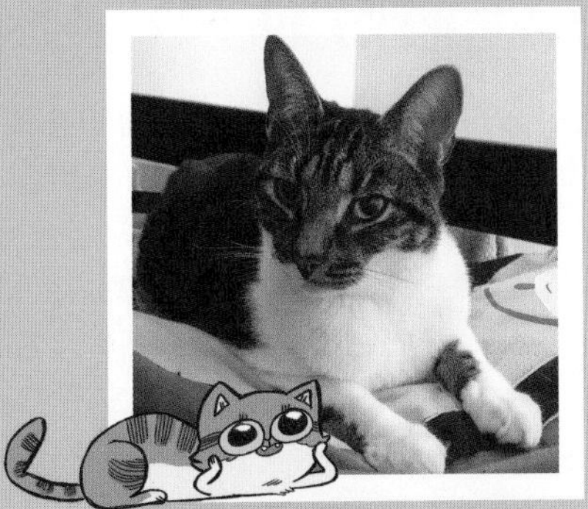

WILSON AKA "WILLY"
- MISCHIEVOUS
- PURRS ALL THE TIME

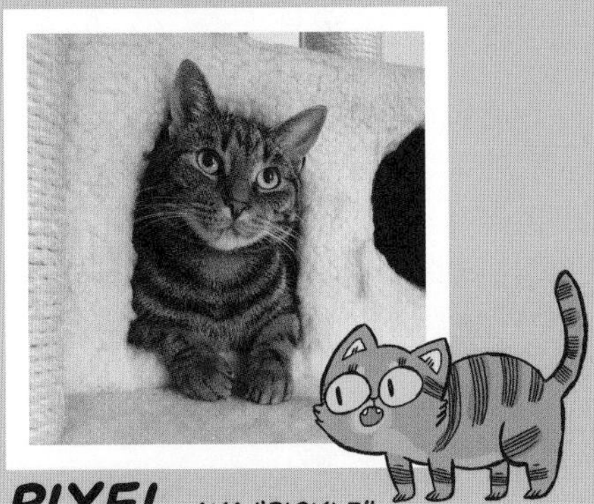

PIXEL AKA "PICKLE"
- ADORABLE
- IS LIKE A LITTLE SANDBAG

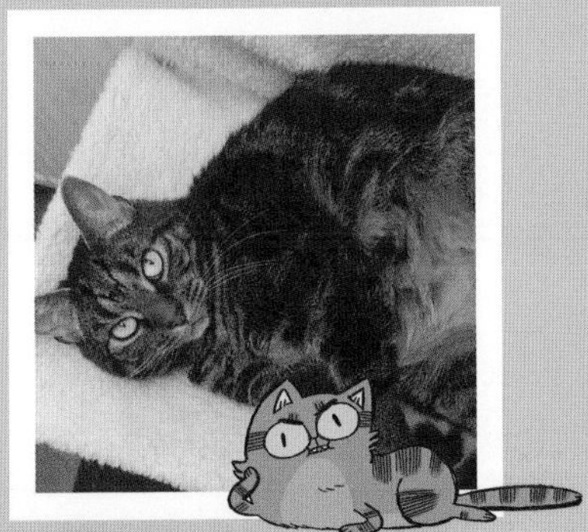

PESTO AKA "PESTOLI"
- ANGRY, YET VERY SWEET
- SLEEPS IN SARAH'S ARMPIT

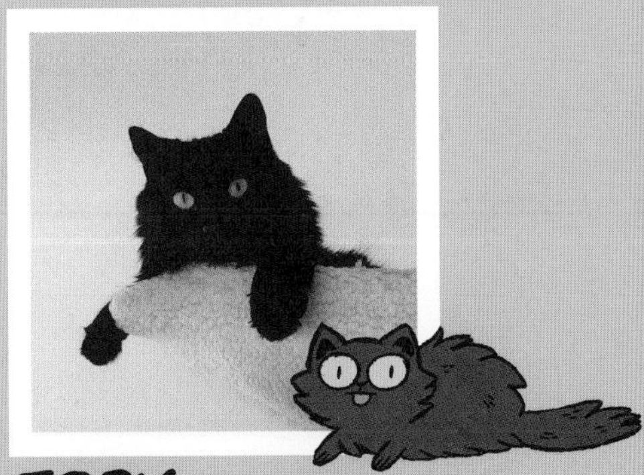

TOBY AKA "TOBES"
- FLUFFY BLACK CLOUD
- LOVES STEF A LOT

THANKS & ACKNOWLEDGEMENTS

SPECIAL THANKS TO MY PARENTS, WHO HAVE ALWAYS SUPPORTED AND ENCOURAGED MY ART.

THANKS TO STEF, FOR NOT ONLY IS HE THE CUTEST HUMAN THAT LETS ME DRAW COMICS ABOUT HIM, BUT HE ALSO HELPED ME PUT TOGETHER THIS BOOK AND FLATTED A LOT OF THESE COMICS.

HUGE THANKS TO MY EDITOR ARI AND THE REST OF THE ONI PRESS TEAM!

THANK YOU TO ALL OF THE PEOPLE MAKING COMICS THAT I LOVE!

THANK YOU TO EVERYONE WHO READS MY COMICS, AND A HUGE THANK YOU TO EVERYONE WHO SUPPORTED THE KICKSTARTER CAMPAIGN FOR THE INITIAL PRINT RUN - YOU HELPED MAKE THIS BOOK A REALITY!

FIND ME ONLINE

SARAHGRALEY.COM

OURSUPERADVENTURE.COM

@SARAHGRALEYART

FACEBOOK.COM/SARAHGRALEYART

INSTAGRAM.COM/SARAHGRALEY

SONICTHECOMIC.BANDCAMP.COM

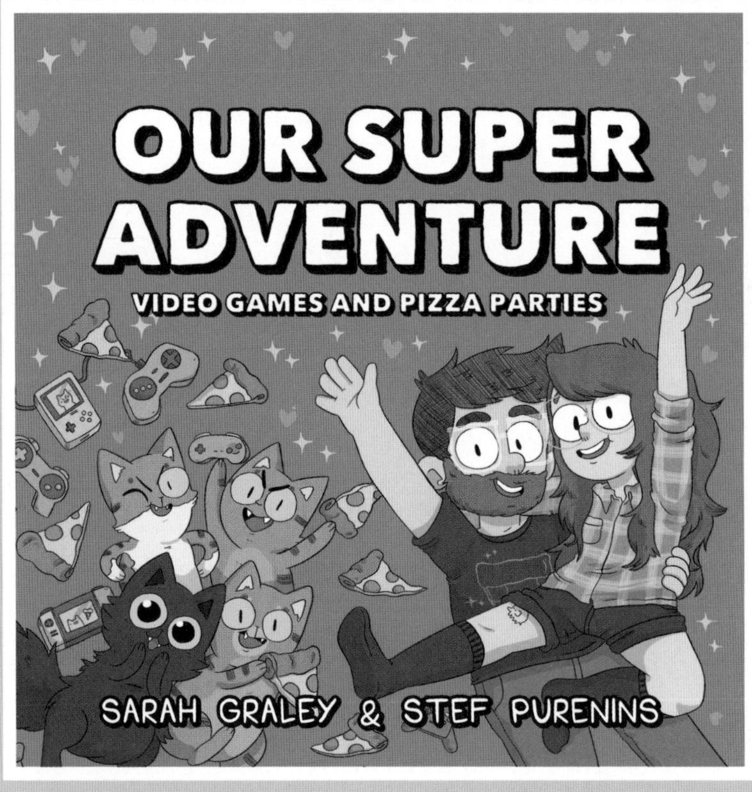
OUR SUPER ADVENTURE
VIDEO GAMES AND PIZZA PARTIES
SARAH GRALEY & STEF PURENINS

CHECK OUT THE NEXT ADVENTURE

JULY 2019!

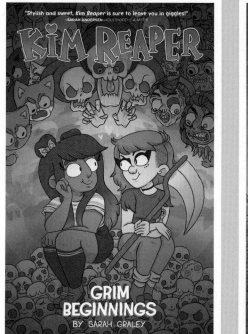

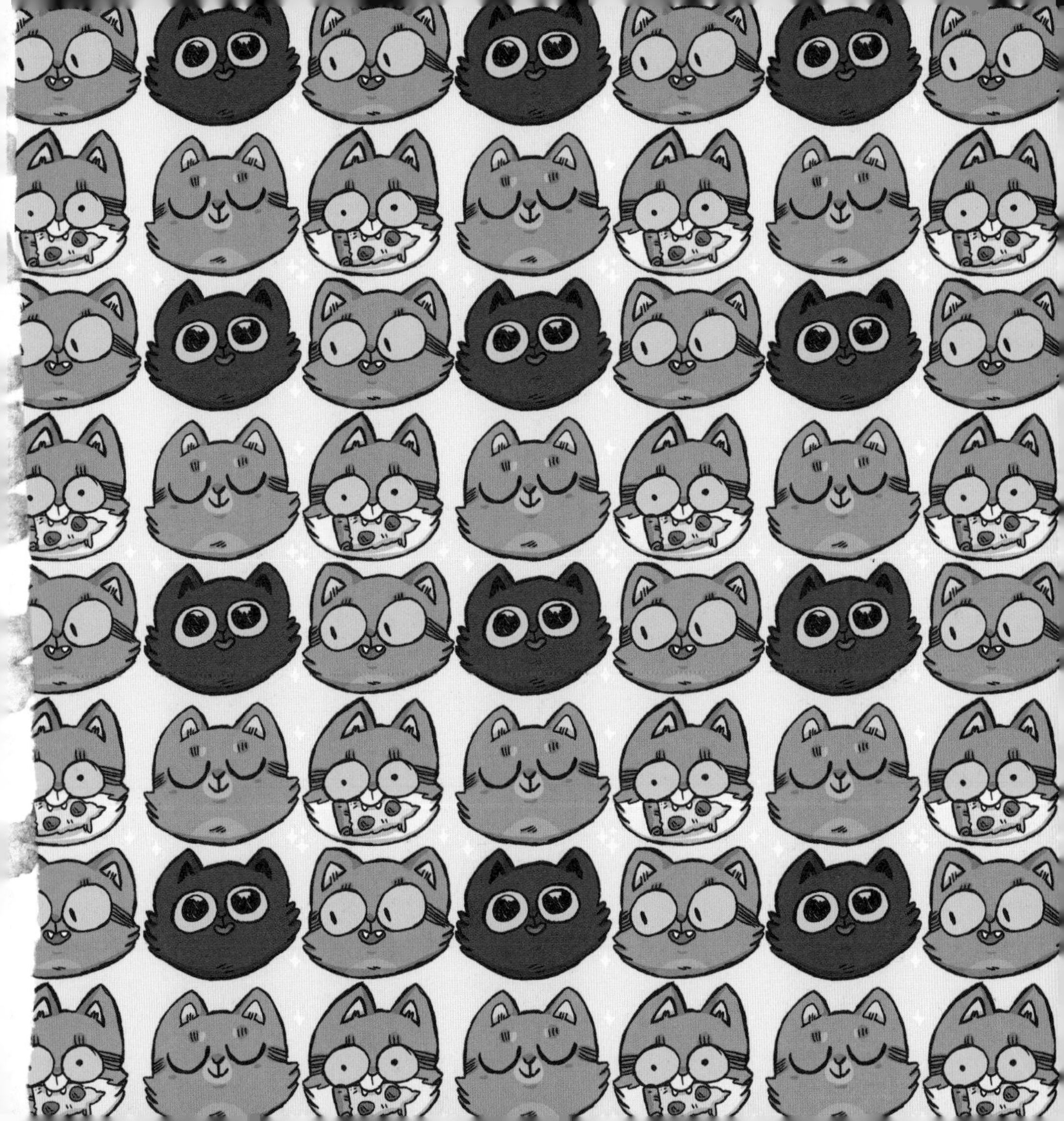

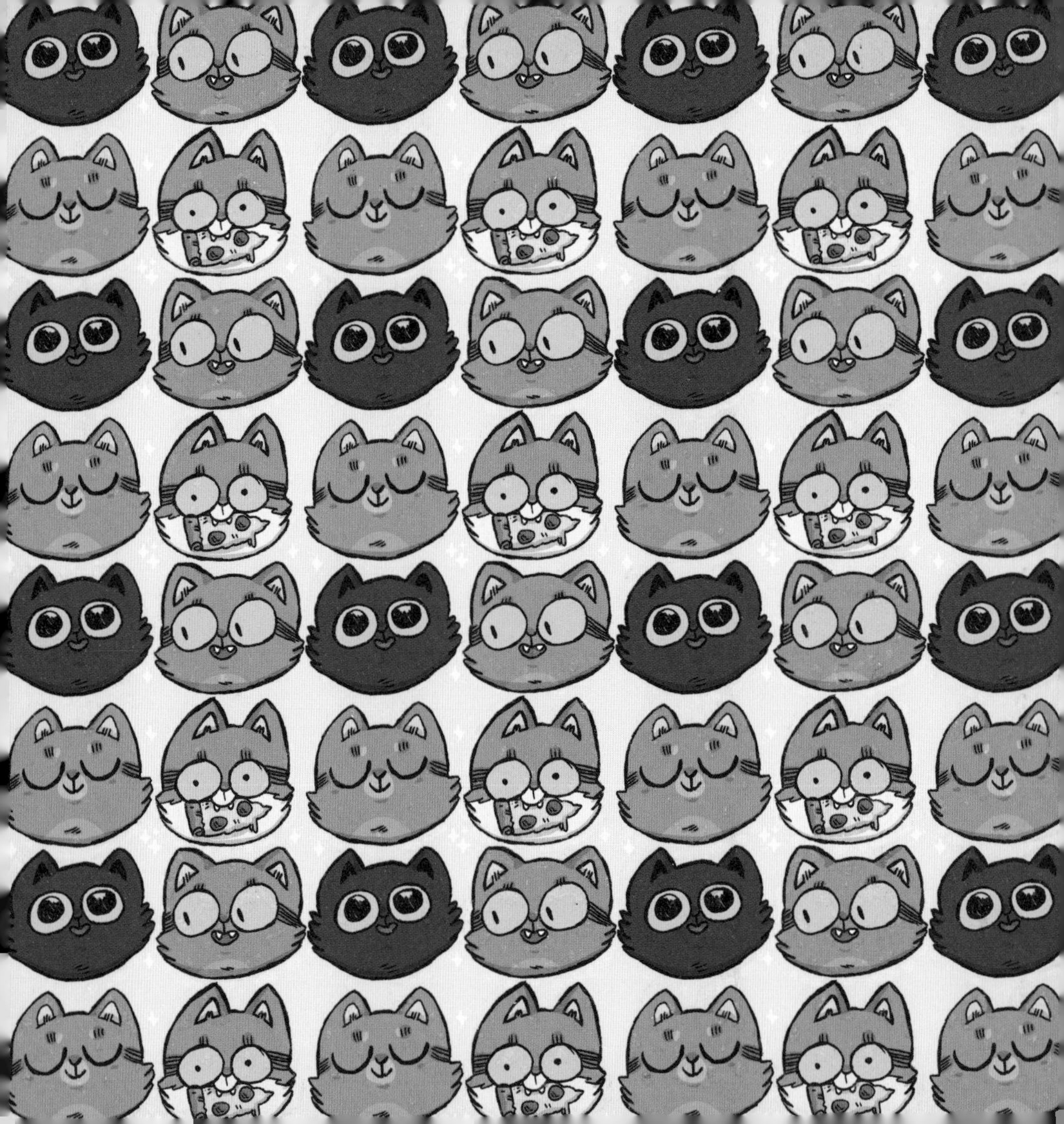